DEVELOPING MATHEMATICALLY PROMISING STUDENTS

DEVELOPING MATHEMATICALLY PROMISING STUDENTS

Edited by

Linda Jensen Sheffield
Northern Kentucky University
Highland Heights, Kentucky

National Council of Teachers of Mathematics
Reston, Virginia

Library of Congress Cataloging-in-Publication Data:

Developing mathematically promising students / edited by
   Linda Jensen Sheffield
         p.   cm.
   Includes bibliographical references.
   ISBN 0-87353-470-0
   1. Mathematics—Study and teaching—United States. 2. Gifted
children—Education. I. Sheffield, Linda Jensen, Date.
QA13.D49   1999
372.7—dc21   99-26177
                                                      CIP

Printed in the United States of America

CONTENTS

Part III—Creating a Culture of Opportunity

Part IV—Promises Fulfilled

PREFACE

In 1994, the NCTM Board of Directors appointed a Task Force on Mathematically Promising Students and asked its members to investigate issues involving the development of promising mathematics students and to make recommendations concerning topics such as the definition of promising students; the identification of such students; appropriate curriculum, instruction, and assessment; cultural influences; teacher preparation and enhancement; and appropriate next steps. One of the major recommendations of the task force was to define promising students as those who have the potential to become the leaders and problem solvers of the future. Mathematical promise was seen as a function of ability, motivation, belief, and experience or opportunity. The variables in the function were viewed as characteristics to be maximized in each individual child. One hope of the task force was that this definition of mathematically promising would include students who have been traditionally identified as gifted, talented, and precocious but would also include students who have previously been excluded from rich mathematical opportunities.

Members of the task force (Jennie Bennett, Manuel Berriozábal, Margaret DeArmond, Richard Wertheimer, and Linda Sheffield, chair) were educators who represented a number of different constituencies including public schools, programs for promising students, parents, university mathematicians and mathematics educators, and researchers. The Report of the Task Force was accepted by the NCTM Board of Directors and published in the December 1995 issue of the *NCTM News Bulletin.* This report appears in the appendix to this book and is referred to in several of the chapters. One of the recommendations of the task force was that the NCTM Educational Materials Committee should produce a number of materials that could be used for the advocacy and support of mathematically promising students, and this book is an outgrowth of that recommendation. Several of the other recommendations are currently being considered or implemented by the NCTM Instructional Issues Advisory Committee. For example, the recommendation that the NCTM join with other professional organizations to produce and publicize a joint position statement concerning the development of promising students was acted on in 1997–98. At that time, representatives from NCTM joined with representatives from more than twenty professional education organizations, including the National Education Association, the National Association for Gifted Children, the Association for the Gifted of the Council of Exceptional Children, and the Office of Educational Research and Improvement of the United States Department of Education, to develop position papers for consideration by each of the organizations and discuss an agenda for joint and individual organization efforts in "Educating America's Gifted and Talented Children."

Since the beginning of the work of both the Task Force on Mathematically Promising Students and the Editorial Panel for this book, the results of the Third International Mathematics and Science Study have been released, underlining once again the importance of paying attention to the development of our most promising students. This need to maximize both the numbers of promising students and their levels of mathematical development and achievement is not confined to the United States, as evidenced by the large number of manuscripts that were received from around the world for possible inclusion in this book. We were able to accept only about half of the manuscripts that were submitted, but we are very pleased that we were able to use the thirty-four chapters that you see in this book. These represent the efforts over a three-year period of nearly sixty dedicated authors representing teachers, researchers, mathematicians, mathematics educators, parents, and communities in ten countries from around the world. To all these authors, who labored through several revisions to produce what we believe should be a benchmark in the ways we view and serve promising mathematics students, the Editorial Panel and I are deeply grateful. As you read the different chapters in this book, you will notice that not all authors have exactly the same recommendations, but we hope that the various viewpoints will serve as the beginning for discussions and action plans to maximize the mathematical achievement of greatly increased numbers of our students from primary through university levels.

The Editorial Panel for this book consisted of outstanding professionals representing both mathematics and mathematics education from public schools and universities across the United States, and I am deeply indebted to them for the long hours they spent to help make this book a reality. The panel not only developed the guidelines for the book and reviewed all the submitted papers, they were invaluable in suggesting revisions and in ensuring that we had authors from around the world who represented some of the best thinking and most current research in the area of mathematically promising students. After spending several years working with this talented, generous, and forward-looking group, I have the utmost respect for them and I am grateful for the opportunity to work with them all:

Jennie Bennett	Houston Independent School District
Peggy House	Northern Michigan University
Harvey Keynes	University of Minnesota
Richard Wertheimer	Pittsburgh Public Schools

We would also like to thank Fran Curcio, who served as editor of the international chapter and was able to obtain and edit chapters from around the world, giving a unique flavor to this section of the book. In addition, we are grateful to the very professional editorial and production staff at the NCTM Headquarters Office for all their work with us throughout the development of this book.

I hope you will all be as excited reading the ideas in this book as I was and will endeavor to use some of the ideas to better serve our promising mathematics students. In the past, we have not always fulfilled our promises to these students, and I hope that this book will mark a turning point in the mathematics education of students around the world.

Linda Jensen Sheffield
Editor

Chapter 1

PROMISES, PROMISES, PROMISES

Peggy A. House

Few aspects of the U.S. educational system have been met with more ambivalence than the question of how to provide for gifted or talented students. Over the years we have witnessed a prevailing tension between, on the one hand, public claims that gifted children are a most valuable resource and, on the other hand, a reluctance to provide adequately for the special needs of those children on the grounds that such provisions are elitist and contrary to democratic principles of equal treatment for all. In general, programs designed to serve gifted students have been outside the mainstream of schooling, often supported by special appropriations or outside funding that is temporary or sporadic, and subject to cuts at the first signs of economic stress.

The situation of the mathematically gifted reflects the same tensions and trends. A quarter century ago the pendulum had swung to a major focus on "minimum essentials" and "back-to-the-basics," which translated into a heavy emphasis on computational arithmetic and instructional materials for the least successful students. Aside from a few lingering debates over whether to offer eighth-grade algebra for some students, little attention was directed toward special provisions for students on the high end of the achievement spectrum. Then, in 1980, the National Council of Teachers of Mathematics (NCTM), in its *An Agenda for Action,* acknowledged the peril in this situation with this warning (p. 18):

> The student most neglected, in terms of realizing full potential, is the gifted student of mathematics. Outstanding mathematical ability is a precious societal resource, sorely needed to maintain leadership in a technological world.

A subsequent publication of NCTM, titled *Providing Opportunities for the Mathematically Gifted K–12* (NCTM 1987), outlined options for meeting the needs of the mathematically talented. Two years later the *Curriculum and Evaluation Standards for School Mathematics* (NCTM 1989) elevated the discussion of mathematical goals for all students, especially those who have been traditionally underrepresented in fields heavily dependent on mathematics, science, and technology. Since that time, NCTM has repeatedly reiterated its commitment to a program of rich mathematics for every child. But again concerns were expressed that the every-child emphasis was skewed toward inclusion of those students who had, in the past, avoided mathematics or performed poorly in it, that with this emphasis, we did not adequately address educating the mathematically promising.

1

In response to those ongoing concerns, the NCTM Board of Directors appointed a Task Force on the Mathematically Promising. It was charged with the challenge of delineating the issues and making recommendations about the mathematically promising and gifted. This volume is one outcome of the task force report, the full text of which can be found at the end of this book. Since the publication of the task force report, the Third International Mathematics and Science Study (TIMSS) has released data showing that students in the United States performed at unacceptably low levels on mathematics assessments and that achievement declined precipitously between fourth grade and twelfth. Even our best students, those taking advanced mathematics in high school, ranked at the bottom of the international scale. (See Geiger and Kilpatrick, chapter 3.) These reports have again aroused public concern and raised questions about how well we are serving the academic needs of all our students.

PROMISING STUDENTS: WHO AND WHY

In the literature on gifted education, the two most discussed issues are the definition of giftedness and the identification of the gifted. In practice, the former drives the latter, and the more clearly and precisely educators define their target population of gifted students, the more effective they can be in identifying them.

The earliest systematic studies of giftedness, which date to the work of Lewis Terman in the 1920s, defined giftedness in terms of superior intelligence as measured by IQ tests. That conception predominated until well into the second half of the twentieth century, when other considerations, such as academic aptitude or potential, demonstrated achievement, creative production, precocity, and talent, began to emerge. In a 1972 report to Congress, the U.S. Office of Education described gifted and talented children as "those ... who by virtue of outstanding abilities are capable of high performance" (Marland 1972, p. 2).

The report further indicated that such high performance included

> demonstrated achievement or potential ability in any of the following areas, singly or in combination: (1) general intellectual ability, (2) specific academic aptitude, (3) creative or productive thinking, (4) leadership ability, (5) visual or performing arts, or (6) psychomotor ability.

(The last of these, psychomotor ability, was deleted from the list in 1978.) That 1972 definition of giftedness succeeded in supplanting previous conceptions based only on intelligence, and it predominated for the next two decades, although Renzulli (1978) criticized it for its failure to include motivational factors, for the nonparallel nature of its categories, and for its tendency to be misinterpreted and misused by practitioners. He proposed instead a Venn-diagram model that located giftedness in the intersection of three overlapping sets of traits: above-average general ability, task commitment, and creativity, and he explicitly stated that all three of these were required for giftedness.

Others have proposed different operational definitions of giftedness, including those that define the gifted in terms of some specified percentage of the population, such as the top 1 or 3 or 5 percent as measured on some test of achievement or ability. Even the U.S. Office of Education definition cited above was predicted to encompass a minimum of 3 to 5 percent of the school population. In general, the various definitions can be viewed as being located on a continuum from restrictive definitions, which may lead to tighter identification procedures but which may also exclude some qualified students, to inclusive definitions, which usually rely on less precise measures of identification and more subjective judgments but which are likely to produce more diverse groups of participants (NCTM 1987, pp. 6–7). Recognizing this, the Task Force on the Mathematically Promising opted for a more inclusive stance inspired by a broadened definition adopted by the federal government in the 1990s, a definition that recognized that "Outstanding talents are present in children and youth from all cultural groups, across all economic strata, and in all areas of human endeavor" (see the task force report in the appendix).

The task force also preferred the description *promising* rather than *gifted* or *talented* in an attempt to emphasize the goal of including students who have traditionally been excluded by previous definitions of giftedness. Thus, the task force defined mathematically promising students to be "those who have the potential to become leaders and problem solvers of the future." The task force report went on to say,

> We see mathematical promise as a function of—
>
> - ability,
> - motivation,
> - belief, and
> - experience or opportunity.
>
> These variables are not fixed and need to be developed so that success for these promising students can be maximized. This definition includes the students who have been traditionally identified as gifted, talented, precocious, and so on, and it adds students who have been traditionally excluded from previous definitions of gifted and talented and therefore excluded from rich mathematical opportunities. This definition acknowledges that students who are mathematically promising have a large range of abilities and a continuum of needs that should be met.

Whatever definition we ultimately espouse, we cannot be content merely to identify the promising students. We must focus on how to nurture, develop, and expand their gifts and actualize their promise.

THE PROMISE WITHIN

Promising students can be as different from one another as they are from their less-able peers. This makes characterization of the promising an elusive, albeit challenging, endeavor.

Over the years, attempts to characterize the gifted or promising have focused on differing traits. As noted above, early studies on the gifted characterized them solely in terms of IQ scores and scholastic achievement. Popular stereotypes, all of which have been discredited by later studies, caricatured gifted students as superior in intellectual abilities but deficient in physical, social, and emotional attributes.

After the middle of the twentieth century, owing in large measure to the work of E. Paul Torrance on creativity and of J. P. Guilford on divergent thinking, intelligence came to be viewed as multidimensional, and giftedness was characterized as including such components as superior ability or potential, motivation, and creativity. Another idea to gain acceptance was the notion of multiple talents that acknowledged that an individual may be labeled as gifted in some areas of performance but not in others. Thus, a student who is classified as *mathematically promising* may not be similarly classified with regard to other fields of study or performance.

Various attempts to develop characterizations of mathematically promising students have failed to yield a reliable list of defining characteristics, but certain generalizations can be drawn from the literature. One is that the mathematically gifted are not necessarily generally gifted, although frequently the two are positively correlated. Another observation is that mathematically promising individuals exhibit the same range of personal (physical, social, emotional, etc.) characteristics as are found in the general population. Moreover, mathematical promise cannot be equated either with school achievement or with performance on computational algorithms.

Mathematically promising individuals usually exhibit many of the traits associated with giftedness in general, such as superior verbal skills, keen powers of observation and perception, deep curiosity, active imagination, original thinking, quick mastery of new learning, good memory, analytical thinking, and the ability to concentrate and work independently. In addition, mathematically gifted individuals manifest certain characteristics directly related to mathematical performance.

Much of what is found in the literature concerning the particular characteristics of the mathematically gifted can be attributed to the observational studies reported by the Soviet researcher V. A. Krutetskii, whose work was translated into English and published in 1976. According to Krutetskii, mathematically gifted persons possess a unique neurological organization that gives rise to what he called a "mathematical cast of mind," a trait that typically emerges in children by the age of seven or eight. This mathematical cast of mind expresses itself in a continual effort to see the world mathematically by paying attention to the mathematical aspects of phenomena and by observing the spatial and quantitative relationships all around.

From his observations of mathematically gifted school children, Krutetskii identified the following special characteristics:

- A formalized perception of mathematical material and grasp of the formal structure of problems

- Logical thought about quantitative and spatial relationships and the ability to think in mathematical symbols
- Rapid and broad generalization of mathematical relations and operations
- Curtailment of mathematical reasoning and the ability to think in curtailed structures
- Flexibility of mental processes
- Striving for clarity, simplicity, economy, and rationality of solutions
- Rapid and free reconstruction of a mental process as well as reversibility of mathematical reasoning
- Generalized memory for mathematical relationships, characteristics, arguments, proofs, methods of solution, and principles of problem solving
- Energy and persistence in solving problems

Krutetskii concluded that talent is a qualitative combination of varied abilities that is unique in each person. Thus, mathematically promising students have different profiles of mathematical abilities, and identifying and working with them is not a one-dimensional challenge. Nor can the issues surrounding the education of promising students be viewed as dichotomous, yes-or-no situations. Rather, options will be found at many places along a continuum of alternatives, each with various pros and cons. No one response will fit all students. Hence, in assembling the papers in this volume the Editorial Panel sought to solicit authors who represent diverse points of view about the education of promising mathematics students.

PROMISES MADE, PROMISES KEPT?

As a society, we profess belief in the importance of individuals and in the right of all individuals to develop to their full potential, yet we seem to be ever pulled in opposing directions. As a consequence, we have often failed to properly challenge, encourage, and support promising students. Instead of fulfillment, we have left a legacy of broken promises. Some of the ways in which such broken promises manifest themselves are the following:

- We want to encourage and reward excellence, but we also want to espouse democratic principles of equality and egalitarianism. Thus we frequently are confronted with the argument that all students should be treated the same, and attempts to offer special provisions for the promising may be met with strong opposition and criticism.
- Despite professions of commitment to all students, programs for the promising almost always have to fight for funding, and they always seem to be among the most vulnerable to cutbacks or elimination. It is difficult to sustain programs without some measure of stability over the years.
- Educational alternatives are too often cast as dichotomous choices or either-or alternatives, such as "acceleration versus enrichment" or "tracking versus mainstreaming." Neither extreme proves satisfactory, and there are no clear-cut formulas for shaping the optimal middle-ground program.

- Even when there is agreement that promising students deserve special treatment, there is little agreement about just what mathematics they should study or what instructional methods are most appropriate.

- Few teachers participate in educational programs aimed at developing their expertise in working with promising students. They are not equipped to modify the curriculum effectively, to challenge promising students in appropriate ways, or to communicate effectively with them.

- Ours is a society that tolerates, indeed even takes pride in, individuals' mathematical inability. Adults boast of their mathematical inadequacies; parents accept as inevitable the poor performance of their children. Children take their cues from what they hear and set low expectations for themselves. There is little insistence that individuals excel in mathematics, despite widespread recognition that mathematics is and will continue to be important for functioning in a technological world.

- The track record for working with promising mathematical students shows that many segments of the population, including females and many ethnic groups, have been seriously underrepresented in the past.

- The disappointing performance of our students on international assessments occurs at all levels of student achievement. TIMSS found, for example, that if one were to assemble an international talent pool consisting of the top 10 percent of students worldwide, on the TIMSS 13-year-old (eighth grade) assessment, only 5 percent of U.S. students would make the cut. (NCES 1998)

These and other instances of broken promises are examined in the papers found in the first section of this volume, where the authors examine issues that surround the education of mathematically promising students and assess factors that can contribute to or detract from the development of the promising.

CREATING CULTURES OF MATHEMATICS AND OF OPPORTUNITY

If mathematics educators are serious about fulfilling their responsibilities to promising students, they must help to create an educational culture in which mathematics is valued, promoted, and incorporated as a lens through which we view the world. Papers in the second section of this book explore the question of how such a culture of mathematics can be developed and fostered both within and outside of formal schooling. Among the themes that emerge from this set of papers are recognition of the critical role of the individual teacher in actualizing the promise within students; emphasis on the imperative of accepting, developing, and accommodating the individual learning styles of all students; and insistence that promising students be regularly challenged by and engaged in rich mathematical content.

The third section of the book explores the equally important need to create cultures of opportunity: educational environments in which teachers of the mathematically promising are empowered and supported throughout their professional development; in which promising students of both genders from all social and economic strata are identified, supported, and encouraged; in which both in-school and extracurricular opportunities are maximized; in which promising students are connected to the resources available in the community; and in which parents are important partners in the educational enterprise—in short, educational milieus designed to actualize the promise inherent in students.

In the final section of this book, "Promises Fulfilled," writers share examples of successful programs and activities that have furthered the development of promising mathematics students, as well as candid discussions of lessons learned and pitfalls to be avoided. It is hoped that others will find in these papers replicable features and kernels of ideas that can be developed and tailored to their own situations.

Collectively, the papers in this book contribute to conceptualizing the issues inherent in fulfilling our promise to help students realize their own mathematical promise. These articles give an overview of a variety of theories, models, and programs to consider and articulate the pros and cons and trade-offs associated with various alternatives. They make no attempt to prescribe a unilateral solution for all students, for one single approach will never be valid in a world of diversity. But the writers have initiated an important dialogue that can significantly further our understanding of, and commitment to, this still-neglected group of students.

To paraphrase the poet Robert Frost, we have promises to keep and miles to go before we sleep.

REFERENCES

Krutetskii, V. A. *The Psychology of Mathematical Abilities in Schoolchildren.* Translated from the Russian by Joan Teller, edited by Jeremy Kilpatrick and Izaak Wirszup. Chicago: University of Chicago Press, 1976. (Original work published 1968.)

Marland, Sidney P. *Education of the Gifted and Talented: Report to the Congress of the United States by the U.S. Commissioner of Education.* Vol. 1. Washington, D.C.: U.S. Government Printing Office, 1972.

National Center for Education Statistics. Third International Mathematics and Science Study. <http://www.ed.gov/NCES/timss> (March 1998).

National Council of Teachers of Mathematics. *An Agenda for Action.* Reston, Va.: National Council of Teachers of Mathematics, 1980.

———. *Curriculum and Evaluation Standards for School Mathematics.* Reston, Va.: National Council of Teachers of Mathematics, 1989.

———. *Providing Opportunities for the Mathematically Gifted K–12,* edited by Peggy A. House. Reston, Va.: National Council of Teachers of Mathematics, 1987.

Renzulli, Joseph S. "What Makes Giftedness: Reexamining a Definition." *Phi Delta Kappan* 60 (November 1978): 180–84, 261.

Chapter 2

DEFINITION AND IDENTIFICATION OF MATHEMATICAL PROMISE

Richard Wertheimer

In 1994, the Board of Directors of the National Council of Teachers of Mathematics (NCTM) formed a task force to explore the topic of mathematically promising students. Because this term was a departure from traditional language used in discussions of ability (i.e., gifted or talented), the first job of the Task Force on the Mathematically Promising was to consider what was meant by the term *mathematical promise.* The task force report defined it in the following way:

> Students with mathematical promise are those who have the potential to become the leaders and problem solvers of the future. We see mathematical promise as a function of—
>
> • ability,
>
> • motivation,
>
> • belief, and
>
> • experience or opportunity.
>
> These variables are not fixed and need to be developed so that success for these promising students can be maximized. This definition includes the students who have been traditionally identified as gifted, talented, precocious, and so on, and it adds students who have been traditionally excluded from previous definitions of gifted and talented and therefore excluded from rich mathematical opportunities. This definition acknowledges that students who are mathematically promising have a large range of abilities and a continuum of needs that should be met. (NCTM 1995)

Exploring the topic of mathematical promise raises difficult questions for both educators and the general public. What is mathematical promise? Where does mathematical promise come from? How does one identify mathematical promise? What experiences are necessary for individuals to realize their promise? These questions create tension that often surfaces during discussions of ability: Must the identification of someone as "having special promise" suggest that the rest of the population is lacking in that promise to some degree?

The choice of terms, definitions, and identification procedures pertaining to mathematical promise reflects beliefs about intellectual and social hierarchy. Inherent in a definition that describes mathematical promise as *inborn* or *fixed* is a rationalization of identification procedures that dictate hierarchical comparisons of students. If, however, one defines mathematical promise as a cultural product dependent on ability, motivation, belief, and experience, then fulfillment of mathematical promise would not be predetermined and programs of identification would start from a radically different premise.

BACKGROUND

In U.S. culture, the concept of varying intellectual ability creates conflict between our country's professed goal of equal opportunity and its laissez faire, competitive nature. At best, this conflict can be perceived as cultural restraint toward issues of intellect. At worst, it appears as resentment toward those identified as showing promise (Resnick and Goodman 1994; Hofstadter 1970).

> Again and again … it has been noticed that intellect in America is resented as a kind of excellence, as a claim to distinction, as a challenge to egalitarianism, as a quality that almost certainly deprives a man or woman of the common touch. (Hofstadter 1970, p. 51)

Identification procedures that limit access also generate resentment from underrepresented populations. Critics suggest that identification procedures are often culturally biased, exclusionary, and intended to restrict educational opportunity (Ford 1995; Harris and Ford 1991; Ogbu 1995; Patton 1992; Hilliard 1976).

> Abundant data suggest that gifted programs are the most segregated educational programs in the nation and that concerted efforts must be made to ensure that minority students, economically disadvantaged students, underachievers, and other nontraditional students receive the education to which they are entitled. (Ford 1995, p. 52)

Others suggest a lack of purpose or ideology that guides the identification and development of gifted students.

> Giftedness in American schools, at least since the 1920s, has been seen as both a troublesome expression of deviance and a valuable human resource, playing out the ambivalent feelings about distinction that were clearly visible in the preceding century. The schools reflect the tensions within our culture surrounding both equality and intellect without offering a way to resolve them. Schools have devoted significant effort to identifying young people who are talented but have not found ways to respond to their needs. (Resnick and Goodman 1994, p. 110)

The ambivalence between equality and intellect as described by Resnick and Goodman is reflected in recommendations made by the U.S. government. Recent reports articulate the need to develop the nation's best and brightest students while simultaneously attempting to address the issue of underrepresentation of minorities (U.S. Department of Health, Education, and Welfare 1971; U.S. Department of Education [USDE] 1993).

That so many of our students work below their potential has grave implications for the nation. The scholarship, inventiveness, and expertise that created the foundation for America's high standard of living and quality of life are eroding. Most top students in the United States are offered a less rigorous curriculum, read fewer demanding books, complete less homework, and enter the workforce or postsecondary education less well prepared than top students in many other industrialized countries. These deficiencies are particularly apparent in the areas of mathematics and science.

The talents of disadvantaged and minority children have been especially neglected. Almost one in four American children lives in poverty, representing an enormous pool of untapped talent. Yet, most programs for these children focus on solving the problems they bring to school, rather than on challenging them to develop their strengths. It is sometimes assumed that children from unpromising backgrounds are not capable of outstanding accomplishment. Yet, stories abound of disadvantaged children who achieve at high levels when nurtured sufficiently.

Ultimately, the drive to strengthen the education of students with outstanding talents is a drive toward excellence for all students. (USDE 1993, pp. 5–6)

In theory, these reports suggest attacking the ability and equity issue at the same time. In practice, lack of funding, cultural bias, and ideological differences complicate the issues raised by definition and identification.

The tension between intellect and equity can be found in other cultures. A graphic example of this occurred in the Soviet Union. Because the Soviet economy was based on socialist principles of equal opportunity and achievement, the entire concept of identification and special programming for selected children appeared to be counter to that country's ideology.

It is well known that persons who show ability in a certain science make a basic contribution to the development of that field. All of this confronts the Soviet schools with the task of developing to the maximum pupils' mathematical abilities, inclinations, and interests, with the goal of raising the level of mathematical culture—the level of the pupils' mathematical development. At the same time, our schools should pay particular attention to pupils who show high abilities in mathematics and should promote the mathematical development of pupils who show a special inclination for the study of mathematics. Mathematical talent should be sought out in the schools, among schoolchildren, since "the golden age for a research mathematician," as the academician S. L. Lobolev claims, sets in between the ages of 22 and 24.

Some believe that instead of selecting mathematically able pupils we should undertake an investigation of the possibilities for the maximal mathematical development of all pupils. But the one will always complement the other, since even with perfect teaching methods individual differences in mathematical abilities will occur—some will be more able, others less. Equality will never be achieved in this respect. Consequently, mathematics teachers should work systematically at developing the mathematical abilities of all pupils, at cultivating their interests in and inclinations for mathematics, and at the same time should give special attention to pupils who show above-average abilities in mathematics by organizing special work with them to develop these abilities further. (Krutetskii 1976, pp. 6–7)

This rationale, from the opening chapter of V. A. Krutetskii's book, *The Psychology of Mathematical Abilities in Schoolchildren* (1976), presents a theme similar to that of the U.S. Department of Education, each arguing simultaneously from both the ability and equity perspectives. The concept of identifying promising students in general and mathematically promising students in particular becomes mired in issues of definition, process, equity, and purpose:

> Societies traditionally place a high value on excellence, whether expressed through intellectual or artistic production, athletic prowess, technological or industrial leadership, wealth, military superiority, or some other societal value. Democratic societies, founded on the principles of equality and egalitarianism, at the same time profess strong belief in the values of individualism and personal freedom. Thus, educators are propelled by the twin goals of equity in educational opportunity for all and the simultaneous provision for the particular needs of individuals. Yet equality and excellence frequently pull in opposing directions, and to date this country has made more progress toward the former goal than toward the latter. (NCTM 1987, p. 3).

There is no easy resolution to the ability-equity dilemma.

The Task Force on the Mathematically Promising suggested, through its report to NCTM (NCTM 1995), that the definition of mathematical promise be broadened to focus on ability, belief, motivation, and opportunity. By taking into account psychological and social variables, the task force expanded our concept of mathematical promise and began to address the ability-equity dilemma. The report suggested that there may be no single best approach to identifying students. If that is the case, then a framework must be developed for comparing and contrasting different definitions and methods of identification.

A CONCEPTUAL FRAMEWORK BASED ON PURPOSE

Ernest and others (Ernest 1991; Apple 1990; Krutetskii 1976) suggested that mathematical ability and its actualization are more dynamic and less hierarchical than traditional theories would suggest. They believe that mathematical ability can be influenced by cultural and educational experiences. This is consistent with the NCTM Task Force Report on the Mathematically Promising (1995). Ernest stated that psychological development is closely linked with socially mediated experience. He pointed out that Krutetskii "acknowledges individual differences in mathematical attainment, but gives great weight to the developmental and formative experiences of the learner in realizing his or her mathematical potential" (Ernest 1991, p. 245). This suggests that educational opportunity has a high degree of influence on developing mathematical promise.

Ernest states that "ideologies have a powerful, almost determining impact on mathematical pedagogy" (p. 137). (For further information on educational ideologies and their effect on curriculum, instruction, and assessment, see Kliebard

[1995].) He described five educational ideologies (see fig. 2.1) with differing concepts of mathematical ability based on their perspective.

	Industrial Trainer	Technological Pragmatist	Old Humanist	Progressive Educator	Public Educator
Theory of Ability	Fixed and inherited, realized by effort	Inherited ability	Inherited cast of mind	Varies, but needs cherishing	Cultural product, not fixed
Theory of Society	Rigid hierarchy Marketplace	Meritocratic hierarchy	Elitist Class stratified	Soft hierarchy Welfare state	Inequitable hierarchy needing reform
View of Mathematics	Set of truths and rules	Unquestioned body of useful knowledge	Body of structured pure knowledge	Process of personalized mathematics	Social constructivism

Fig. 2.1. Educational ideologies with differing concepts of mathematical ability

The Progressive Educator ideology is *child-centered,* focusing on the individual. Its goal for defining and identifying mathematical promise is to help individual students reach their unique potential. This ideology is common among educators and psychologists. It tends to use a variety of tools for identification and then develops individual educational plans for promising students.

The Old Humanist ideology is based in the belief that the study of mathematics is *intrinsically valuable.* Old Humanists believe that mathematics is a pure science and only a small group of people is capable of truly understanding it. They speak from the mathematician's perspective. Their goal for defining and identifying mathematical promise would be to find a small group of very capable individuals and accelerate their study of mathematics. The focus in this ideology is not on the individual but on the mathematics itself.

The Industrial Trainer and Technological Pragmatist ideologies are *utilitarian approaches* to education. These ideologies are pragmatic in nature, attempting to meet the needs of the job market. This perspective is common among employers and policymakers. Their goal for defining and identifying mathematical promise would be to find the most able students to serve the needs of industry, trade, defense, commerce, and the professions. Although they appear to be neutral with regard to issues of equity, their policies often "reproduce the existing stratification of society" (Ernest 1991).

Finally, the Public Educator ideology reflects a *social activist* agenda. It is based in the belief that there are social inequities with respect to mathematical experience and opportunity. The Public Educator goal for defining and identifying mathematical promise would be to help students—especially those from underrepresented populations—to gain access to mathematical knowledge, opportunity, and careers. Public Educators would like to break down the rigid hierarchy they perceive in our society.

Each ideology has a different focus: the individual, the content area, the job market, and the society. Each ideology is driven by different beliefs and goals, and each has a different concept of ability, social hierarchy, mathematics, and educational purpose. Programs that identify mathematically promising students can be categorized according to their educational ideology.

(A caveat is in order. When one moves from ideology to real-world programming, there is a blurring of perspective. Seldom does a program fit cleanly into a single ideology. Pragmatic issues such as funding, political pressure, or dual purpose cause programs to try to meet a number of needs. That said, categorizing programs according to perspective, ideology, and purpose provides a framework for the discussion and comparison of programs. The goal of using this framework is to point out that the dissonance pertaining to the ability-equity dilemma is based in ideology.)

THE PROGRESSIVE EDUCATOR (EDUCATOR-PSYCHOLOGIST'S) PERSPECTIVE

Typically, discussions of ability from an educational perspective focus on the needs of students and teachers. The need to classify students according to ability began in the United States at the turn of the century. The use of tests of ability coincided with the influx of immigrants, farmers, and underprivileged students into public schools. The increase in school population during the Industrial Revolution placed demands on educators to address a growing diversity in their classrooms. The development of a tool to measure intelligence gave these educators a tool that at best would identify and nurture the needs of all students and at worst would categorize students and maintain the social and economic hierarchy.

Throughout this century, the standard measure of ability was IQ (intelligence quotient). IQ is a measure of mental age normed to the overall population.

$$IQ = \frac{\text{mental age}}{\text{developmental age}} \times 100$$

Statistically IQ is a measure of how an individual ranks in the total population on a given set of skills and abilities. IQ tests quantify differences among people and use this information to strengthen educational practice. Terman, who pioneered IQ testing in the United States, defined giftedness as the top 1 percent level in general intellectual ability, as measured by the Stanford-Binet Intelligence Scale (Terman 1925, 1926). Intelligence tests, such as the Stanford-Binet, continue to be used.

However, two particular studies made educators and psychologists rethink their use of IQ tests. The first one found certain aspects of creative thinking in mathematics, particularly in the area of problem posing, that did not correlate highly with intelligence as measured by IQ tests (Getzels and Jackson 1962). The second, more-controversial study attributed differences on IQ scores between the races to genetic factors (Jensen 1969, 1973). These and other studies forced the educational community to confront the ramifications of using IQ as a basis for educational placement and programming. There are a number of reservations about using statistically normed tests such as IQ for identification purposes:

- General IQ scores do not take into account domain-specific talent in areas such as mathematics. (Gardner 1983, 1984)

- Psychometric techniques that rely on factor analysis, standard deviation based on normally distributed populations, and timed competitive tests tell little about a student's mathematical ability and thought processes. (Krutetskii 1976)

- Creativity may not be completely correlated with intelligence and therefore should be factored into any identification procedure. (Getzels and Jackson 1962; Torrance 1975; Wallach 1985; Guilford 1967)

- IQ and standardized tests of achievement and ability are believed to contain biases against minority populations, (Harris and Ford 1991)

- Nonintellective factors such as motivation and task commitment influence learning outcomes and should be assessed. (Ridge and Renzulli 1981)

As educators grappled with these issues, psychologists began to broaden their conception of intelligence (Gardner 1983; Guilford, 1967; Sternberg 1985). During the last thirty years of the twentieth century, a number of identification programs were created based on psychological models (see fig. 2.2).

Perspective	Program	Definition	Identification Procedure
General Intelligence	School-based student profiling	Two standard deviations above the norm	Greater than 130 IQ
Content-specific Psychometrics	Study of Mathematically Precocious Youth (SMPY) (Julian Stanley)	Youths who reason exceptionally well as measured by a standardized test of aptitude	A high score at an early age on the mathematics section of the SAT-M
Content-specific Cognitive abilities	Structure of Mathematical Abilities (V. A. Krutetskii)	"Mathematical giftedness is the name we shall give to a unique aggregate of mathematical abilities that opens up the possibility of successful performance in mathematical activity" (Krutetskii 1976, p. 77)	Tasks used to identify mathematical structure, clarity, logical thought, reverse reasoning, generalization, mathematical memory, curtailment, mathematical cast of mind, and flexibility
Ability Creativity Motivation	Revolving Door Identification Model (RDIM) (Joseph Renzulli)	Above-average general abilities, high levels of task commitment, and high levels of creativity	Identify students with above-average ability (top 15 to 20 percent), then provide rich and challenging learning experiences. Allow students to self-select into the program.

Fig. 2.2. Identification programs based on psychological models

Definition and Identification of Mathematical Promise   15

Julian Stanley was one of the first to move beyond general intelligence as measured by IQ to focus specifically on mathematically gifted students. He thus foreshadowed the work of Howard Gardner (1983), who suggested that there were at least seven separate intelligences, one of which was logical-mathematical intelligence. Stanley developed the Study of Mathematically Precocious Youth (SMPY) at Johns Hopkins University (Stanley, Keating, and Fox 1974; Keating 1976; Stanley 1984; Stanley and Benbow 1986). SMPY expanded on traditional definitions of ability by focusing on mathematical aptitude. It pioneered the use of out-of-grade-level tests for identification purposes using the mathematics portion of the SAT Program tests (SAT-M, published by the Educational Testing Service) with seventh and eighth graders.

By using the SAT-M (a predictive instrument for determining success in college) for identification purposes, Stanley defined mathematically talented students as those children who would excel within the existing system of school and university mathematics. Although Stanley's talent-search model has been expanded to include many universities around the country (Van Tassel-Baska 1984), it is still subject to the criticisms that are common to IQ tests. As a psychometric model—and one that identifies a disproportionate number of white or Asian males—the Stanley talent-search model is criticized for not addressing issues of equity, creativity, motivation, and specific talents within mathematics that are not necessarily measured through school performance or performance on an achievement test.

At the same time that Stanley began to develop the SMPY model, Krutetskii's study of mathematical ability was translated from the Russian by researchers at the University of Chicago (Krutetskii 1976). Krutetskii was critical of definitions of mathematical ability that relied on either general intelligence measures or psychometric models based in factor analysis. Through his exhaustive study of Soviet youth, he delineated a number of cognitive abilities within the general term *mathematical abilities*. Krutetskii argued that the way to identify mathematically gifted students was by observing them as they did experimental problem sets of increasing difficulty that were designed to elicit the abilities that he identified (see fig. 2.3). Although numerous dissertation studies confirmed the existence of the abilities identified by Krutetskii, his work has barely reached the K–12 community. No one has found a way to organize Krutetskii's work so that it can be used as an identification tool in schools in the United States. Possibly, it is too time-consuming. Certainly, it places great demands on the test administrator from both the content and process perspectives.

A third psychology-based model for defining and identifying gifted students emerged at approximately the same time as Stanley's model. Joseph Renzulli developed the Revolving Door Identification Model (RDIM), which lessened emphasis on the aptitude and cognitive domain in favor of creativity and task commitment (Renzulli and Smith 1977; Renzulli 1977, 1986). RDIM was predicated on the idea that students with above-average intelligence could achieve great things if they were motivated and creative in their learning. Renzulli defines *gifted children* as those capable of developing the composite set of traits—above average abilities, high levels of task commitment, high levels of creativity—and applying them to any

1. Obtaining mathematical information
   a. The ability for formalized perception of mathematical material, for grasping the formal structure of a problem
2. Processing mathematical information
   a. The ability for logical thought in the sphere of quantitative and spatial relationships, number and letter symbols; the ability to think in mathematical symbols
   b. The ability for rapid and broad generalization of mathematical objects, relations, and operations
   c. The ability to curtail the process of mathematical reasoning and the system of corresponding operations; the ability to think in curtailed structures
   d. Flexibility of mental processes in mathematical activity
   e. Striving for clarity, simplicity, economy, and rationality of solutions
   f. The ability for rapid and free reconstruction of the direction of a mental process, switching from a direct to a reverse train of thought
3. Retaining mathematical information
   a. Mathematical memory (generalized memory for mathematical relationships, type characteristics, schemes of arguments and proofs, methods of problem-solving, and principles of approach)
4. General synthetic component
   a. Mathematical cast of mind

Fig. 2.3. Krutetskii model for identifying mathematically gifted students (Krutetskii 1976, p. 350)

area of human performance. It is in the interaction of these traits that so-called "giftedness" is exhibited. The Revolving Door Identification Model (RDIM) for identifying giftedness follows:

1. Identify the top 15–20 percent of the students by traditional means.
2. Provide experiences for students that offer more advanced levels of involvement in areas of interest (Type I activities).
3. Provide general enrichment designed to promote higher-order reasoning, research and reference skills, and processes related to personal and social development (Type II activities).
4. Provide enrichment that includes individual or small-group investigations into real problems (Type III activities).
5. Through observations, anecdotal information, and self-selection, students will revolve into Type III activities if so inclined. This then represents a second level of selection.

(Ridge and Renzulli 1981; Renzulli 1986)

Renzulli's RDIM to identify mathematically promising students found support in the mathematics education community because it is more tolerant of individual differences, allows for a higher degree of self-selection, and addresses the creativity issue (Ridge and Renzulli 1981; NCTM 1987). The Type I, II, and III activities can include classroom activities, competitions, problem solving, mathematical applications, and long-term projects. This open-ended model of identification is the most forgiving of those described, yet it has not found widespread acceptance. That may be due to changes—attitudinal, curricular, and pedagogical—that would have to occur in the classroom, the school, and the community.

All the models presented from the Progressive Educator's perspective take a psychological approach to identification. Some deal specifically in measuring general intelligence; others use norm-referenced mathematical aptitude tests; others look at cognitive abilities within mathematical activity; and still others focus on developmental and social-psychological issues such as motivation, context, and creativity.

A final point pertains to the practicality of identification procedures in a school setting. Norm-referenced tests, such as group IQ tests, SAT tests, and mathematics achievement tests, are all easily scored, appear to be impartial, and are efficient from a time perspective. They are also highly correlated with success in traditional school settings. Hence, although Krutetskii and Renzulli have made important contributions to the literature on definition and identification of mathematical ability, neither has made significant inroads into the procedures used by school districts as they attempt to identify students with mathematical ability.

THE OLD HUMANIST (MATHEMATICIAN'S) PERSPECTIVE

From a mathematician's perspective, identifying children who are gifted in mathematics is a matter of predicting who can or will become a mathematician. Mathematicians tend not to define mathematical ability in specific terms, but they talk about it in rarefied tones, suggesting that it is artistic in nature and that few, if any, in the general population have it. In essence, they see mathematical ability as a form of genius. In addition, mathematicians place their emphasis not on the individual but on the mathematics (Davis and Hersh 1981, pp. 85–86). Identification procedures from the mathematician's perspective consist of doing challenging mathematics, often in competitive settings (see fig. 2.4).

One method of identifying promising students is to allow placement or self-selection into an acceleration program. The acceleration model suggests that promising students should be allowed to move as quickly as possible through the traditional sequence of the mathematics curriculum—algebra, geometry, analysis, and calculus. In most schools, a small group of students are chosen for acceleration starting in middle school (sixth to eighth grade). Identification procedures are locally determined and are often based on IQ scores, scores on mathematics achievement tests, or teacher recommendation. Students in the advanced track ultimately take calculus in high school. Often those students who remain in the accelerated classes take the College Board Advanced Placement examination and, if they score high enough, are given advanced credit when entering a university. The acceleration model is similar to the talent-search model developed by Julian Stanley. Longitudinal studies indicate that highly advanced students who are accelerated in their mathematical learning suffer no negative consequences as a result of the experience and, in fact, often follow careers into mathematics or science (Swiatek and Benbow 1991).

Perspective	Program	Definition	Identification Procedure
Acceleration	Advanced-placement classes	Students who desire more challenging mathematics classes in high school	School district selection via aptitude tests, achievement tests, and teacher recommendation
Competitions	American Mathematics Competition	Students with exceptional mathematics talent	Teacher selection, Competitive selection
	USA Mathematics Talent Search	Development of talents through year-round, creative problem solving	Invitation or self-selection
	MATHCOUNTS	Middle school students with an interest in mathematics	Self-selection or teacher selection
Apprenticeships	Ohio State University Young Scholars Program	Students with a strong desire to pursue careers in mathematics, science, or technology	Self-selection, essay, transcript, teacher recommendation, problem solving
	Gelfand Outreach Program in Mathematics	Useful for all students, not only for future mathematicians	Self-selection, problem solving through the mail

Fig. 2.4. Identification procedures from a mathematician's perspective

A second form of identification occurs through competitions. The mathematics community sponsors numerous competitions that attempt to inspire and identify students by offering increasingly challenging levels of competition, mathematical rigor, and problem solving. A well-known competition is the American High School Mathematics Examination (AHSME), which is open to all students (Mauer and Mientka 1982). (The AHSME is open to all students with the caveat that it is not offered at all U.S. high schools and the teachers often select who may take the examination.) Students take a 90-minute multiple-choice examination. Students who perform far above the norm (approximately 1 percent of those who take the examination) advance to the American Invitational Mathematics Examination (AIME). Approximately fifty of the top students on the AIME move on to the United States Mathematics Olympiad (USAMO). From this group, a small team is selected to represent the United States at the International Mathematics Olympiad. Competitive models use increasingly difficult problems to identify a small group of students who exhibit extraordinary ability.

Even competitions that specifically attempt to motivate more diverse groups of students, such as MATHCOUNTS and the USA Mathematical Talent Search, ultimately filter the population and identify a small group of extremely talented students. Competitions are part of the culture of the mathematics community. Not surprisingly, they come under criticism from those outside it. Due to their frequently timed and intensely competitive nature, the competitions are often accused of measuring certain test-taking skills rather than mathematical abilities. Although this limits the population identified, most would agree that competitions successfully identify a very talented group of mathematically gifted students.

Mathematical apprenticeships that give students an opportunity to work with practicing mathematicians are another way of identifying and nurturing mathematically promising students. Summer programs such as the National Science Foundation's Young Scholars Program give students opportunities to work with mathematicians. These programs can be highly selective and are based on openings and demand. Other programs enable students to work with mathematicians through the mail (Gelfand Outreach Program in Mathematics [GOPM]) or even through e-mail (Ask Dr. Math at forum.swarthmore.edu).

An important element in apprenticeship programs is the student's motivation. Whether they attend a summer program, work on the Internet, or do problem solving through the mail, the students must have a personal desire to pursue mathematics outside the school setting. The one constant in programs of identification in the mathematics community is that they identify mathematical talent by the means they know best—doing mathematics through ever-more-challenging problems.

THE UTILITARIAN (POLICYMAKER'S) PERSPECTIVE

The policymaker's perspective has little to do with psychological models or mathematical problem solving. It vacillates between a nation's need for workers, scientists, and leaders and a nation's desire for equal opportunity for all its citizens. Policymakers furnish federal guidelines, state laws, and local funding to meet the nation's needs. There have been two influential federal initiatives since 1970 attempting to define giftedness (see fig. 2.5).

The first initiative was the Marland Report to Congress (Marland 1972), which expanded the concept of giftedness to include domain-specific ability, creativity, leadership ability, ability in the visual and performing arts, and psychomotor ability. Although the report did not suggest specific identification procedures, it did expand the definition of giftedness beyond IQ. The second was the Jacob Javits Gifted and Talented Education Act of 1988 that, like the Marland report, attempted to expand the definition of gifted and talented. The Javits act provided funds for research into new identification procedures and other areas of concern pertaining to the education of gifted and talented students.

Individual states address the issue of giftedness in their own way. Although they must follow federal guidelines regarding special education, there is a great deal of latitude as to how the states support the identification and nurturing of students with promise in particular content areas. Some states have no provisions; others provide funds for gifted services to local schools on the basis of a formula they devise; and others still offer resources on a state level, such as special summer programs or schools for the mathematically promising.

Locally, each school attempts to follow the statutes of both the federal and state governments and offer programming as appropriate, but there is little consistency across the country as to how school districts address the needs of gifted students,

Perspective	Program	Definition	Identification Procedure
Federal	Marland Report Public Law 91–230 (1972)	Gifted and talented children are those identified by professionally qualified persons, who by virtue of outstanding abilities are capable of high performance. These are children who require differentiated educational programs or services beyond those normally provided by the regular school program in order to realize their contribution to self and society.	Children capable of high performance include those with demonstrated achievement or potential ability in any of the following areas, singly or in combination: general intellectual, specific academic ability, creative or productive thinking, leadership ability, visual and performing arts, psychomotor ability. It can be assumed that utilization of these criteria for identification of the gifted and talented will encompass a minimum of 3 to 5 percent of the school population.
	Javits Gifted and Talented Education Act (1988)	Children and youth with outstanding talent perform or show the potential for performing at remarkably high levels of accomplishment when compared with other of their age, experience, or environment	These children and youth exhibit high performance capability in intellectual, creative, or artistic areas, possess an unusual leadership capacity, or excel in specific academic fields. They require services or activities not ordinarily provided by the schools. Outstanding talents are present in children and youth from all cultural groups, across all economic strata, and in all areas of human endeavor.
State	North Carolina School for Science and Mathematics	Eleventh and twelfth grade students who show promise of exceptional development, as well as special interest, in science and mathematics and who reflect the demographics of North Carolina	SAT scores, an essay, an abstract reasoning test and a mathematics diagnostic test, intellectual curiosity, analytical thinking, and imagination
Local	Bronx High School of Science		Comprehensive examination with both mathematics and verbal sections

Fig. 2.5. Identification procedures from a policymaker's perspective

much less students who are mathematically promising. Some districts offer in-class support, others choose pullout programs, and others create schools of special emphasis, such as the Bronx High School for Science. Although policymakers have attempted to broaden the definition of giftedness, little has changed in the procedures used by most local school districts (USDE 1993, p. 16).

From the policymaker's perspective, one example that ties federal reform efforts to state funding and addresses the concerns of both the mathematics and mathematics education community is the North Carolina School for Science and Mathematics (NCSSM). NCSSM is a statewide initiative to define, identify, and nurture mathematically promising students. The school is seen as a way to aid the economic well-being of the state by improving science and mathematics education for talented students and furnishing a source of new teaching methods, curriculum materials, and teacher training (Davis and Frothingham 1987). The North Carolina School of Science and Mathematics has defined mathematical promise as a combination of ability, performance, curiosity, motivation, and imagination. The identification procedures NCSSM uses are consistent with this definition, and because the program is state funded, participants are demographically and geographically balanced. Two drawbacks of the program are that it is residential—meaning students must live away from home—and that the program is only open to eleventh and twelfth graders.

THE PUBLIC EDUCATOR (SOCIAL ACTIVIST'S) PERSPECTIVE

Ernest stated that the Public Educator ideology suggests that ability is a cultural product and that at birth all students have mathematical promise. Programs consistent with this ideology purport that all students can achieve. Programs that address the issue of mathematical promise from a social activist perspective often work with underrepresented populations, typically are led by charismatic individuals, and are small or local in nature (see fig. 2.6).

Perspective	Program	Definition	Identification Procedure
Curriculum	The Algebra Project (Robert Moses)	All children can do algebra	Urban middle school students
Creating Culture	The Math Workshop Program (Uri Treisman)	University under-graduates taking freshman mathematics	Student interest in career involving mathematics
Role Model	The Escalante Mathematics Program (Jaime Escalante)	If motivated properly, any student can learn mathematics. Promising students are those with *ganas* (the will to succeed).	Ninth graders with the desire to succeed

Fig. 2.6. Identification procedures from a public educator's viewpoint

The Algebra Project, directed by Robert Moses, is based on the belief that all children have mathematical promise (Silva and Moses 1990). The program suggests that, with appropriate curriculum and support in middle school, all children can succeed at algebra and advance to college preparatory mathematics. The ideology of the Algebra Project finds its roots in the Civil Rights movement.

> Moses approached the challenge of preparing middle school students for college preparatory mathematics in a manner similar to that which he and others had used in organizing the African American community of Mississippi to seek political power through the vote in the early 1960s. (Silva and Moses 1990, p. 378)

The program has no specific identification procedure, given that it works with all students. The program is based on the following components:

- The curriculum must address the conceptual leaps from arithmetic to algebra.
- The curriculum must be experiential, linking familiar physical experiences to abstract mathematics.
- Students, teachers, parents, and administrators must expect all students to achieve.
- Staff must receive adequate training and support.

The majority of the Algebra Project's students are Hispanic or African American. To expand its reach, the project is attempting to disseminate its curriculum and professional-development model to other school districts.

The Escalante Mathematics Program shares the belief of the Algebra Project that all students are mathematically promising (Escalante and Dirmann 1990). The fundamental principles of his program are based on accountability, hard work, demand, love, parental involvement, respect, values, nutrition, and prevention of drug abuse. Its origin was in Jaime Escalante's calculus class in the East Los Angeles public schools. Escalante, who is Bolivian and worked with Hispanic students, gained national notoriety when he demonstrated that his students were capable of performing at superior levels on the College Board's AP Calculus examination. He believes that if they start early enough, all students have mathematical promise that can be fulfilled. He created a comprehensive program that reaches down into the middle schools and prepares students for college preparatory mathematics. His only identification procedure is to determine that the student must have *ganas,* the desire to succeed. What differentiates his program from the Algebra Project is that he focuses on psychological, social, and cultural issues rather than on the curriculum.

The Mathematics Workshop Program (MWP), developed by Uri Treisman at the University of California at Berkeley, works with mathematically promising students at the university level (Fullilove and Treisman 1990). The premise is that all students that come to the university have mathematical promise, but their promise must be nurtured by developing appropriate learning and collaborative strategies. The program grew out of research Treisman conducted into the study habits of freshman students at the university. In comparing the study habits of Chinese American students with African American students, Treisman found two important differences. First, the Chinese American students studied twice as long as their professors recommended, and second, they worked collaboratively in study groups. He found that many African American students believed that collaboration was inappropriate and therefore did not reach out to their peers for assistance.

The MWP built on this research by creating an honors study program for African American students. Treisman found that African American students who joined the program, worked collaboratively, and studied extensively scored the same as Chinese American students. The MWP pointed out cultural attributes that contribute to success in a university environment.

These three programs are representative of the Public Educator perspective: that everyone has mathematical promise and that belief, motivation, and opportunity can help to fulfill that promise. They address difficult cultural issues and align their identification procedures and programming accordingly.

FINAL THOUGHTS

It seems straightforward. If you want to identify individuals with mathematical promise, you give a group of people mathematics problems and see how they do. Those who have promise will do well on the problems, obtaining correct answers. They are labeled as mathematically gifted, are grouped into classes, accelerated through the curriculum, and ultimately go on to careers in mathematics. Unfortunately, this approach to identification leads to traditional arguments about ability and equity, about haves and have-nots. And, more important, it does not identify many students who show promise and who would like to pursue mathematics in one form or another.

The NCTM task force's definition of mathematical promise states that ability, belief, motivation, and opportunity are important variables that must be taken into account. Consideration of these variables forces various ideologies to surface. Who is mathematically promising from an employment perspective? How is mathematical promise realized in underrepresented populations? Can or should all mathematically promising students become mathematicians? How can the needs of each individual student be addressed in our present educational system?

By changing the language from "gifted and talented" to "mathematically promising," the task force has opened up the dialogue: It is offering mathematics educators the opportunity to expand the perspective, gain insight into alternative approaches, and move beyond traditional rhetoric. As the task force report states, "Identification should be inclusive, rather than exclusive."

REFERENCES

Apple, Michael W. *Ideology and Curriculum.* 2nd ed. New York: Routledge, Chapman, and Hall, 1990.

Davis, Philip J., and Reuben Hersh. *The Mathematical Experience.* Boston: Houghton Mifflin Publishing Co., 1981.

Davis, Steve, and Phyllis Frotheringham. "A Special School in North Carolina." In *The Secondary School Mathematics Curriculum,* edited by Christian R. Hirsch, pp. 184–88. Reston, Va.: National Council of Teachers of Mathematics, 1985.

Ernest, Paul. *The Philosophy of Mathematics Education.* London: Falmer Press, 1991.

Escalante, Jaime, and Jack Dirmann, "The Jaime Escalante Math Program." *The Journal of Negro Education* 59 (Summer 1990): 407–23.

Ford, Donna Y. "Desegregating Gifted Education: A Need Unmet." *The Journal of Negro Education* 64 (Winter 1995): 52–62.

Fullilove, Robert E., and Philip Uri Treisman. "Mathematics Achievement among African American Undergraduates at the University of California, Berkeley: An Evaluation of the Mathematics Workshop Program." *The Journal of Negro Education* 59 (Summer, 1990): 463–78.

Gardner, Howard (1984). "Assessing Intelligences: A Comment on Testing Intelligences without IQ Tests." *Phi Delta Kappan* 65, no. 10 (1994): 699–700.

Gardner, Howard. *Frames of Mind: The Theory of Multiple Intelligences.* New York: Basic Books, 1983.

Getzels, Jacob W., and Phillip Jackson. *Creativity and Intelligence: Explorations and Gifted Students.* New York: Wiley, 1962.

Guilford, Joy P. *The Nature of Human Intelligence.* New York: McGraw-Hill Book Company, 1967.

Harris, Joseph, and Donna Y. Ford. "Identifying and Nurturing the Promise of Gifted Black American Children." *The Journal of Negro Education* 60, no. 1 (1991), 3–18.

Hilliard, Asa G., III. *Alternative IQ Testing: An Approach to the Identification of Gifted 'Minority' Children.* (Report No. 75175). San Francisco, Calif.: San Francisco State University, 1976. (ERIC Document Reproduction Service No. ED 147 009).

Hofstadter, Richard. *Anti-Intellectualism in American Life.* New York: Alfred A. Knopf, 1970.

Jensen, Arthur R. "How Much Can We Boost IQ and Scholastic Achievement?" *Harvard Educational Review* 39, no. 1 (1969): 1–123.

———. *Educability and Group Differences.* New York: Harper and Row, 1973.

Keating, Daniel P., ed. *Intellectual Talent: Research and Development.* Baltimore, Md.: Johns Hopkins University Press, 1976.

Kliebard, Herbert M. *The Struggle for the American Curriculum.* New York: Routledge, 1995.

Krutetskii, V. A. *The Psychology of Mathematical Abilities in Schoolchildren.* Translated from the Russian by Joan Teller, edited by J. Kilpatrick and I. Wirszup. Chicago: University of Chicago Press, 1976. (Original work published 1968).

Marland, Sidney P. *Education of the Gifted and Talented: Report to the Congress of the United States by the U.S. Commissioner of Education.* Vol. 1. Washington, D.C.: U.S. Government Printing Office, 1972.

Mauer, Stephen B., and Walter E. Mientka. "AHSME, AIME, USAMO: The Examinations of the Committee on High School Contests." *Mathematics Teacher* 75 (October 1982): 548–57.

National Council of Teachers of Mathematics. *Providing Opportunities for the Mathematically Gifted K–12,* edited by Peggy A. House. Reston, Va.: National Council of Teachers of Mathematics, 1987.

———. "Report of the NCTM Task Force on the Mathematically Promising." *NCTM News Bulletin* 32 (December 1995): Special insert.

Ogbu, Jonathan. U. "IQ and Racial Stratification." Paper presented at the Annual Conference of the American Educational Research Association, San Francisco, 1995.

Patton, James M. "Assessment and Identification of African American Learners with Gifts and Talents." *Exceptional Children* 59, no. 2 (1992).

Renzulli, Joseph. *The Enrichment Triad Model: A Guide for Developing Defensible Programs for the Gifted and Talented.* Wethersfield, Conn.: Creative Learning Press, 1977.

———. "The Three-Ring Conception of Giftedness: A Developmental Model for Creative Productivity." In *Conceptions of Giftedness,* edited by R.J. Sternberg and J.E. Davidson, pp. 53–92. New York: Cambridge University Press, 1986.

Resnick, Daniel P., and Madeline Goodman. "American Culture and the Gifted." In *National Excellence: A Case for Developing America's Talent,* edited by Patricia O'Connell Ross, pp. 109–21. Washington, D.C.: U.S. Department of Education, 1994.

Ridge, H. Laurence, and Joseph Renzulli. "Teaching Mathematics to the Talented and Gifted." In *The Mathematical Education of Exceptional Children and Youth,* edited by Vincent J. Glennon, pp. 191–266. Reston, Va.: National Council of Teachers of Mathematics, 1981.

Silva, Cynthia M., and Robert P. Moses. "The Algebra Project: Making Middle School Mathematics Count." *The Journal of Negro Education* 59 (Summer 1990): 375–91.

Stanley, Julian C., and Camilla P. Benbow. "Youths Who Reason Exceptionally Well Mathematically." In *Conceptions of Giftedness,* edited by Robert J. Sternberg and Janet E. Davidson, pp. 362–87. New York: Cambridge University Press, 1986.

Stanley, Julian C. "Use of General and Specific Aptitude Measures in Identification: Some Principles and Certain Cautions." *Gifted Child Quarterly* 28, no. 4 (1984): 177–80.

Stanley, Julian C., Daniel P. Keating, and Lynn H. Fox, eds. *Mathematical Talent: Discovery, Description, and Development,* Baltimore, Md.: Johns Hopkins University Press, 1974.

Sternberg, Robert J. *Beyond IQ: A Triarchic Theory of Human Intelligence.* New York: Cambridge University Press, 1985.

Swiatek, M. A., and Camilla Benbow. "A Ten-Year Longitudinal Follow-Up of Participants in a Fast-Paced Mathematics Course." *Journal for Research in Mathematics Education* 22 (1991): 138–50.

Terman, Lewis M. "Mental and Physical Traits of a Thousand Gifted Children." In *Genetic Studies of Genius,* Vol. 1, edited by Lewis M. Terman. Stanford, Calif.: Stanford University Press, 1925.

———. *Genetic Studies of Genius.* Vol. 2. Stanford, Calif.: Stanford University Press, 1926.

Torrance, E. Paul. "Creativity Research in Education: Still Alive." In *Perspectives in Creativity,* edited by Irving A. Taylor and Jacob W. Getzels, pp. 278–96. Chicago: Aldine, 1975.

United States Department of Health, Education, and Welfare. *Education of the Gifted and Talented.* Washington, D.C.: Government Printing Office, 1971.

United States Department of Education (USDE). *National Excellence: A Case for Developing America's Talent.* Washington, D.C.: U.S. Government Printing Office, 1993.

Van Tassel-Baska, Joyce. "The Talent Search as an Identification Model." *Gifted Child Quarterly* 28, no. 4 (1984): 172–76.

Wallach, Michael A. "Creativity Testing and Giftedness." In *The Gifted and Talented: Developmental Perspectives,* edited by F. D. Horowitz and M. O'Brien, pp. 99–123. Washington, D.C.: American Psychological Association, 1985.

Chapter 3

MATHEMATICALLY PROMISING STUDENTS: NATIONAL TRENDS AND INTERNATIONAL COMPARISONS

Judith Lynn Gieger
Jeremy Kilpatrick

The health of the U.S. educational system is a subject of ongoing debate among educators and commentators (Bracey 1991, 1992, 1993; Celis 1993; McKnight et al. 1987; Raspberry 1991, 1993; Stedman 1994, 1995). Special concern has recently been expressed about the future of our brightest and most capable students (Callahan 1994; Ross 1996). Our promising mathematics students, in particular, are seen as crucial to the well-being of our country (Sheffield 1994). It is important, therefore, for U.S. educators to determine whether we are doing all we should to promote and develop these precious resources. Evidence for that determination can be found in essentially two ways: by looking at the progress of talented U.S. mathematics students over time and by comparing these students with their intellectual peers around the world. In this paper, we review recent research in these two directions, attempting to synthesize a variety of arguments and perspectives.

NATIONAL TRENDS

How have promising mathematics students in the United States been progressing over the last twenty years? This question is more complex than it might appear and has no simple answer. First, *progress* may refer to any of several different qualities. The literature reports studies of ability, achievement, and interest in mathematics. Second, even if the question covers all these qualities, the results may not be definitive. One should expect a mixed and qualified answer at best.

Upward Trends

There is considerable evidence to support the claim that high-ability students in the U.S. have been performing better in recent years. Some of the evidence comes from measures of developed ability. The SAT Program, constructed and administered by the Educational Testing Service (ETS) for the College Board, is one of the best known indicators of readiness for college. Trends in the mathematics portion (SAT-M) over the last twenty years have shown that an increasing number of students are reaching high levels of test performance. Figure 3.1 shows the number of students in each of the twenty-one years from 1976 to 1996 earning a score above 750 on a scale on which 500 is the mean and 800 the maximum. As the graph (fig. 3.1) shows, after a drop in the late 1970s and early 1980s, the number of high SAT-M scores has been steadily rising. The pattern for scores above 700 is much the same.

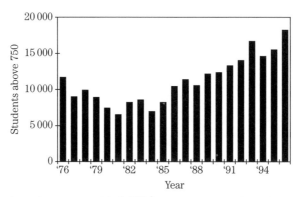

Fig. 3.1. Number of students with SAT-M scores above 750 (ETS 1976–1986, 1987–1994, 1995, 1996)

Another standardized measure of developed mathematical ability is the quantitative portion of the Graduate Record Examination (GRE-Q), also constructed and administered by ETS. This examination is required by many colleges and universities offering graduate programs, and all students who take the examination take the quantitative portion. Figure 3.2 shows that the trend in the number of students scoring above 700 on the quantitative portion of the GRE is similar to the trend shown in the SAT-M case.

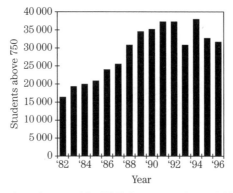

Fig. 3.2. Number of students with GRE-Q scores above 700, U.S. citizens only (Grandy forthcoming)

The SAT and the GRE are not linked to mathematics course content and therefore do not reveal much about what students are learning in mathematics courses. Some measures of mathematical achievement, however, have also shown an upward trend for high-ability mathematics students. For example, students who take the achievement tests offered by the College Board tend to apply to selective colleges and universities, so the trend in achievement test scores can provide some useful information about promising students. The achievement tests for mathematics are generally divided into two examinations, Math Level I and Math Level II, with alternate forms available in recent years for students who want to use calculators on the examinations. The number of students electing to take the Math Level I exam has remained relatively constant over the last twenty years, but the number of students electing to take the more difficult Math Level II exam has more than doubled. Even with this dramatic increase in test takers, the percentage of scores above 700 on this test has not declined. On average, 40 percent of those students who elect to take the Math Level II exam score above the 700 level (Educational Testing Service 1976–1986, 1987–1994, 1995, 1996).

Another indicator of positive achievement among high-ability mathematics students is the Graduate Record Examination Subject Test in Mathematics, taken by most students who plan to do graduate work in mathematics. Over the last decade, the number of students electing to take this portion of the GRE has gradually increased, with a 35 percent increase in the number of test takers from 1981 to 1990 (ETS 1991). As might have been expected, there have been slight drops in mean scores on the test for years with particularly high participation rates. For example, the highest mean score of 684 occurred in the year with the lowest participation rate (1549 test takers in 1982), and the lowest mean score of 668 occurred in the year with the highest participation rate (2191 test takers in 1986). These decreases in mean scores have been slight, however, and have been offset by increases in other years so that no downward trend is visible.

Some indicators suggest that interest in mathematics may also be increasing among high-ability students. One indication comes from the dramatic increase in the number of students participating in the Advanced Placement calculus program. The number of students taking the AP Calculus exam has increased from 32 000 test takers in 1982 to 123 000 test takers in 1996 (Kenelly et al. 1985; College Board 1996). The average scores of these students yields little information because the test varies from year to year and the average score is always set at approximately 3. The increase in participation in AP mathematics courses, however, indicates that more students are interested in taking advantage of challenging opportunities in mathematics. Moreover, the increase in the number of courses taken in mathematics goes beyond just AP courses. By 1996, 68 percent of college-bound seniors taking the SAT had taken four years or more of mathematics (ETS 1996), an increase from only 50 percent in 1976 (ETS 1976–1986). Also, the percentage of college-bound seniors participating in honors courses in mathematics has been on a steady rise for the last decade, from 22 percent in 1986 to 29 percent in 1996 (ETS 1987–1994, 1995, 1996). This increase in mathematics course taking has been suggested as contributing to the rise in SAT-M and Mathematics Achievement Test scores (Callahan 1994).

The simple fact that students are taking more mathematics courses in high school may not reveal much about the potential of high-ability students, but there is evidence to suggest that participation in challenging courses does have some effect on future achievement in mathematics. Brody and Benbow (1990) compared two groups of gifted students who had been identified at age thirteen through the SAT-M. One group chose to participate in challenging mathematics courses and extracurricular activities (such as summer programs and after-school teams or clubs), while the other group did not. The group that elected to take the challenging opportunities showed significantly higher rates of participation in advanced mathematical studies and related fields.

Downward Trends

Some indicators of interest in mathematics have shown an upward trend but others have not. Although course taking among college-bound seniors has increased, the number of students who express an interest in majoring in mathematics in college has been steadily declining. For example, of the 1 160 000 SAT test takers in 1987, 7 100 planned a major in mathematics (ETS 1987); whereas, of the 1 153 000 test takers in 1996, the number of prospective mathematics majors had fallen to 5 300 (ETS 1996). Of course, these numbers refer to the students who took the SAT and not just those who exhibited mathematical promise. It is therefore important to consider the preferences among high-scoring students only. The graph in figure 3.3 gives data for students scoring higher than the 90th percentile on the SAT-M. It shows a clear downward trend in the number of high scoring SAT-M test takers who are planning to major in mathematics as undergraduates. Since 1991, a similar downward trend is evident in the number of undergraduates who score above 700 on the GRE-Q who plan graduate work in mathematics (see fig. 3.4). Although the GRE-Q data indicate that some increase occurred in the 1980s, there has been a sharp drop in the 1990s. Even when the group of high-scoring GRE-Q test takers is limited to those who had undergraduate degrees in mathematics, a similar downward trend in the 1990s (though not as severe) is visible in the number who are planning on continuing in graduate study in mathematics (see fig. 3.5).

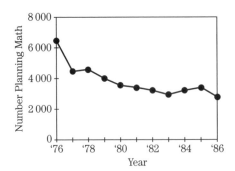

Fig. 3.3. Number of students with SAT-M scores in the 90th percentile planning undergraduate major in mathematics (Grandy 1987)

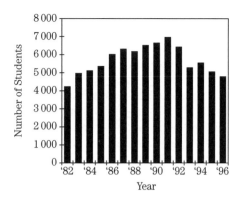

Fig. 3.4. Number of students with GRE-Q scores above 700 who plan graduate work in mathematics, U.S. citizens only (Grandy forthcoming)

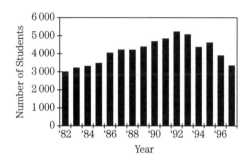

Fig. 3.5. Number of students with undergraduate major in mathematics and GRE-Q scores above 700 planning graduate work in mathematics, U.S. citizens only (Grandy forthcoming)

Unfortunately, information about college plans among high scorers on the SAT-M was not collected after 1986. The stable number of SAT test takers and the decline in the percentage who intend to major in mathematics, however, suggest that the trend may have continued (ETS 1987–1994, 1995, 1996). Therefore, whereas the percentage of all undergraduate and graduate degrees awarded in mathematics has remained relatively stable since 1986 (National Center for Education Statistics [NCES] 1995), fewer U.S. students who have shown promise in mathematics (according to standardized tests) are choosing to major in it.

Steady Trends

One indicator of mathematical achievement, the National Assessment of Educational Progress (NAEP), has shown very little change in average scores over the last twenty years. Performance on the NAEP tests is defined by various levels of proficiency, on a scale ranging from 0 to 500, with the highest achievement level termed *advanced*. An advanced achievement level requires a score of 333 for eighth graders and 367 for twelfth graders (NCES 1997). There was a significant change from 1990 to 1996 in the percentage of eighth graders who scored at the advanced level (from 2 percent to 4 percent), but there was no significant change in the percentage of twelfth grade students who demonstrated proficiency at the advanced level during these years (NCES 1997). The percentage of twelfth graders at the advanced proficiency level remained steady, hovering around 2 percent. Although the NAEP study is not intended to be used as a performance indicator for the gifted, this low performance is surprising and difficult to explain. (The 1996 NAEP did include a special study assessing the performance of students taking advanced courses in mathematics [algebra or above for eighth graders and advanced algebra or above for twefth graders], but no trend data are available from this study.) For example, none of the items for twelfth graders at the advanced level involves mathematics at or above the level of calculus, and yet 23 percent of the college-bound seniors taking the SAT in 1996 indicated that they were taking calculus in high school (ETS 1996). Part of the explanation may lie in the difference in populations: The NAEP tests are given to all twelfth-grade students, but only a fraction of them take the SAT. For example, in 1995, only 41 percent of all graduating seniors took the SAT (NCES 1996b). The NAEP studies sample all twelfth graders, including some who may not have graduated.

One indicator of the level of student participation and interest in studying mathematics has remained steady over the years. Although interest in majoring in mathematics has declined, the percentage of total graduate degrees in mathematics has remained relatively steady. Since 1980, approximately 1 percent of all master's degrees and 2.5 percent of all doctoral degrees in the U.S. have been awarded in mathematics (Madison and Hart 1990; NCES 1995). Therefore, while the number of high-scoring students from the United States who are choosing to study mathematics at the graduate level has dropped slightly, this drop has not affected the proportional size of the graduate population in mathematics. The lack of an overall change may be explained by the number of foreign-born students who are entering graduate programs in the United States. Although their performance in U.S. graduate programs certainly benefits the U.S. mathematics community, their presence raises questions about the quality of preparation that U.S. students are receiving in comparison to their foreign-born peers. This leads to the next question: How do the most talented U.S. mathematics students compare with their intellectual peers from other countries?

INTERNATIONAL COMPARISONS

The performance of top mathematics students in the United States can be analyzed and understood by comparing them not only with each other but also with top students in other countries. A difficult issue is how that comparison will be made, particularly when attention is limited to the students in the top 1 to 5 percent in each country. Existing international comparisons of quite different educational systems do not permit firm conclusions concerning the status of top U.S. students. There are problems everywhere—in sampling, devising comparable measures, applying statistical techniques, and making interpretations (Bracey 1996; Rotberg 1990).

Despite the general view that U.S. students perform poorly in international comparisons (Baker 1993; McKnight et al. 1987; Stevenson 1986, 1993), our top students have tended to excel in international competitions such as the International Mathematics Olympiad (IMO). Since 1975, when the United States first participated in the IMO, the U.S. team score has been among the top five of all countries participating (Turner 1985), with the exception of 1988, when the team placed sixth (Stanley 1989). The 1994 team earned first-place honors (Pratt 1994), and the 1996 team scored second among a record number of seventy-five participating countries (MAA 1996). One member of the 1997 IMO team, Carl Bosley, was one of only four students out of the 460 participants to make a perfect score (MAA 1997).

Participation in the U.S. IMO team is limited to "American citizens or permanent residents; in other words, those seeking citizenship and currently possessing a U.S.A. Immigration 'green card'" (MAA 1997), which means that some members of the team may be foreign-born. However, of sixty-six team members in the years from 1987 to 1997, only seven were born outside of the United States, and only one team member received his secondary schooling outside of the United States. (Special thanks to Walter Mientka for information on the composition of the U.S. Mathematics Olympiad teams.) Of course, it is impossible to draw any conclusions about the comparative capabilities of all top U.S. students from the performance of the small number of IMO team members (six members per year), but these results indicate that at least some of our most promising mathematics students do excel in an international setting.

The results are not as positive for international comparisons using larger samples. The first—and for many years the only—organization conducting large-scale international comparisons in education was the International Association for the Evaluation of Educational Achievement (IEA). Two IEA studies dealt exclusively with mathematics: the First International Mathematics Study (FIMS) in 1964 and the Second International Mathematics Study (SIMS) in 1980–1982. The SIMS yielded some particularly interesting (and disappointing) information concerning the progress of top U.S. mathematics students in comparison with top students from the other twelve countries studied. The study included two sample groups, population A and population B. The population A students were in the eighth grade. The population B students were in the last year of secondary school and were studying mathematics as a substantial part of their curriculum; these students were considered the elite of the mathematics students in each country (McKnight et al. 1987).

The IEA researchers attempted to control for selectivity among countries by studying the top 1 and 5 percent in each country. On the algebra items, the top 1 percent of U.S. students in population B scored lower on average than those in any other country studied, and the top 5 percent scored only slightly higher than their counterparts in Israel. The results were similar in geometry, with the top 1 and 5 percent of U.S. twelfth graders scoring the second lowest, with again only the Israeli students scoring lower. In calculus, the top 5 percent of U.S. students had the lowest mean score, and the top 1 percent exceeded only British Columbia (Robitaille and Garden 1988). However, calculus is not part of the British Columbia mathematics curriculum (McKnight et al. 1987). Finally, in each of the subject areas listed above, the average score of all population B students from Japan was higher than the average of the top 5 percent of U.S. students (McKnight et al. 1987; Robitaille and Garden 1988).

Another major international comparison is provided by the International Assessments of Educational Progress, conducted by the Educational Testing Service. The first IAEP, conducted in 1988, yielded little information concerning the progress of the top students in the participating countries. There was limited information overall from this study, given that only six countries participated (Robitaille and Travers 1992). The second IAEP, conducted in 1991, had twenty participating countries. A study of the thirteen-year-old participants in the IAEP-2 yielded some differences in achievement among the top-scoring students across countries. For example, the score required for the 95th percentile among U.S. participants was 90.7 (out of 100), while the highest 95th-percentile score, in Taiwan, was 98.7. The differences were less pronounced at the 99th percentile. The 99th-percentile score among U.S. eighth graders was 97.3. Only Taiwan, China, and Korea, which had 99th-percentile scores at 100, had a higher score (Lapointe et al. 1992).

The latest, and largest, international mathematics comparison, the Third International Mathematics and Science Study (TIMSS), was recently completed by the IEA. At the fourth-grade and eighth-grade levels, the study did not focus on the performance of top students in mathematics, but one question was asked that dealt with this exceptional group of students. If an international talent search (using the TIMSS mathematics test) were to select the top 10 percent of all students in the forty-one TIMSS countries combined, what percentage of U.S. students would be included? A preliminary analysis of the data indicates that 5 percent of U.S. eighth graders would be a part of this select group, compared with 45 percent in Singapore and 32 percent in Japan. At the fourth-grade level, the results were slightly more encouraging, with 9 percent of U.S. students being selected. This number still falls short of the 39 percent that would be selected from Singapore and the 26 percent that would be selected from Korea (NCES 1998).

The TIMSS results at the twelfth grade give us more information about advanced mathematics students. In addition to a study on general mathematics and science knowledge at this age level, a separate study looked at the performance of students who were studying advanced mathematics. According to the report from TIMSS (NCES 1998):

> It is useful to look beyond the general levels of science and mathematics general knowledge and focus on the advanced levels of knowledge of those who are likely to become our next generation of professionals in fields related to mathematics and science.

The sample for this special study included all U.S. students who were taking precalculus, calculus, AP calculus, or calculus and analytical geometry. This group represented approximately 15 percent of the age cohort in the United States.

The performance of this entire group in comparison with the other sixteen participating countries was quite poor—eleven nations had scores that were significantly higher than the United States, and no nation had a score that was significantly lower. However, when the sample for the United States was limited to students taking calculus or AP calculus (which represents about 7 percent of the age cohort), the comparisons showed a much more favorable U.S. performance. There were only six countries that scored significantly higher than the U.S. calculus students, and two scored significantly lower. However, in both of these samples, the United States still scored below the international average.

One more sampling limitation was made, using only U.S. students who were studying AP calculus (approximately 5 percent of the age cohort), and this group did score above the international average. Only one country had a score that was significantly higher than this U.S. group, and five countries had scores that were significantly lower (NCES 1998).

Almost all the available evidence seems to indicate that the United States is far from its goal of being first in the world in mathematics, even when that goal is restricted to the top students from around the world. Before rushing to imitate the educational systems of countries having high-scoring students, however, educators should note the problems inherent in any type of international comparison. First, one must consider the sample. For example, in the IAEP-2, many participating countries submitted a limited population for the study, and the decisions about whom to include were usually based on language (Lapointe et al. 1992). There was also potential sampling bias in the SIMS. The choice of whom to include in the target population for population B could be interpreted differently by different countries, and this led to wide variances in participation rates. For example, in Japan, population B represented only 12 percent of the age cohort, while population B in Hungary represented 50 percent of the age cohort (Robitaille and Garden 1988). Similar sampling difficulties occurred in the TIMSS study: Of the sixteen countries that participated in the advanced mathematics study at the twelfth-grade level, six countries, including several that did not follow the sampling procedures, failed to meet the participation criterion. However, the scores for all countries, regardless of their eligibility status, were reported. The National Council of Teachers of Mathematics issued the following warning with its report of the TIMSS results (NCTM 1998, p. 2):

> Unlike the situation at grades 4 and 8, however, where eligibility and sampling problems affected only a small fraction of the participating countries, the problems in obtaining representative data for the end of secondary school appear to have been serious enough across the sample of countries to warrant extreme caution in interpreting the results, and particularly those results in which countries were rank ordered by level of achievement.

Another problem inherent in international comparisons is the issue of comparing curriculums. For example, in most of the countries in the TIMSS advanced mathematics assessment, the students assessed had studied at least a year of calculus, and in some (such as Sweden), they had studied topics as advanced as second-degree differential equations (NCTM 1998). To get a fraction of the population that would be comparable to the fraction in other countries, U.S. twelfth graders were given the advanced assessment if they were taking a precalculus course (which is not an advanced course at twelfth grade). These students, more than half the group sampled, had not studied many of the topics included on the advanced assessment. It is no surprise that the smaller group of students who were taking AP calculus fared much better on the comparisons made in TIMSS. Of course, the lack of exposure to advanced topics says something about curriculum, expectations, and opportunity in the United States, but it is problematic to extend that reasoning to discussions of academic potential.

These comments are not intended to convince the reader to ignore large international comparisons; rather, they are intended to make the reader more aware of the underlying issues. Unfortunately, such information is rarely examined in the public press. For example, although the ETS cautioned against using the results from the IAEP-2 to rank nations (Lapointe et al. 1992, pp. 4–11), that is exactly what they did in their reporting (p. 17). It is no surprise, then, that the press has also focused on rankings from these studies. Also, information in the press has tended to describe U.S. schools in comparison with other countries as being "pretty good" or "pretty bad," with very little in between (Baker 1993; Bracey 1991, 1992, 1993, 1995; Celis 1993; Raspberry 1991, 1993). It is no wonder that the public has such a difficult time making sense of these large international comparisons.

A quite different study, conducted by the National Center for Improving Science Education (Britton and Raizen 1996), compared college entrance examinations already in use instead of trying to create a uniform examination for all countries. This study looked at twelve major countries that were participants in the TIMSS and compared their college entrance examinations on the basis of item type (use of graphs and diagrams, multiple-choice questions, etc.) and examination topics. Of all of the examinations considered, the AP Calculus AB examination from the United States was judged to be the easiest, and the Japanese examination was judged to be the most difficult. A similar comparison of U.S. and Japanese examinations by the MAA found comparable results (Cipra 1993). The inclusion of the AP Calculus exam in the Britton and Raizen study rather than the SAT (as in the Cipra study) is somewhat problematic, given that the AP Calculus exam is not a college entrance examination. In fact, it was the only exam included in the study that was not a requirement for entering college. The Japanese examination, on the other hand, plays a decisive role in determining college entrance qualifications for that graduating class.

It is important to notice whether the exams being compared are being used to measure proficiency or potential. However, the Britton and Raizen study used the AP Calculus exam because there were no subject specific examinations that were a required part of admission to U.S. colleges and universities, unlike all the other countries studied. Also, despite the conclusion about the relative difficulty level of the AP Calculus exam in comparison with exams in other countries, the exam was chosen because the content level was considerably more difficult than the SAT (Britton and Raizen 1996).

All the above studies have compared ability and achievement. The picture of international comparisons looks different when one considers the interest and productivity of U.S. mathematicians in comparison with their international colleagues. Mathematics education and research at the graduate level and beyond in the United States is generally considered to be the strongest in the world. The most prestigious award for research in mathematics, the Fields Medal, has often been awarded to mathematicians from the United States, and close to 40 percent of the world's publications in mathematics have come from U.S. researchers (Madison and Hart 1990). Students from around the world see the United States as the place to come to study mathematics (Servan-Schreiber and Simon 1987; Kolata 1985), which leads to another interesting dilemma. The percentage of U.S. students in U.S. graduate mathematics departments has been dropping steadily over the past two decades, with an accompanying drop in the percentage of doctoral degrees in mathematics awarded to U.S. citizens (see fig. 3.6). It is particularly worth noting the large percentage of international students in the top graduate mathematics programs in the United States. Table 3.1 gives a list of fourteen graduate programs commonly ranked among the top mathematics programs in the United States (Gourman 1996; Hattendorf 1997; U.S. News and World Report 1997), along with the percentage of international students enrolled in that program (Peterson's 1997).

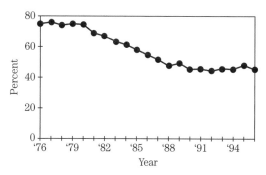

Fig. 3.6. Percentage of U.S. citizen doctoral recipients from U.S. institutions (Fulton 1996)

Whereas U.S. graduate mathematics programs continue to produce internationally competitive mathematicians, fewer students entering these programs are U.S. citizens. Of course, it is difficult to attract top U.S. students to mathematics programs when they do not see the pursuit of a graduate degree as a profitable venture. For example, in 1995, the average salary for a recent graduate with a bachelor's degree in mathematics was $30,200 (U.S. Bureau of the Census 1996). In contrast, the average salary for a 1995 graduate with a doctoral degree in mathematics who went into a faculty position was only $35,900 (Fulton 1996). Also, the unemployment rate for new doctoral recipients in 1995 was a record high 10.7 percent (Davis 1997). Thus, many U.S. students may not see the benefits of entering a mathematics program.

Table 3.1

Selected U.S. Doctoral Programs, Listed in Descending Order by Percentage of International Students Enrolled in That Program

University	Percent International Students
California Institute of Technology	81
University of Minnesota	61
Columbia University	60
Stanford University	59
Yale University	59
Massachusetts Institute of Technology	56
Princeton University	55
New York University	46
University of Chicago	42
Cornell University	42
Harvard University	34
University of Michigan, Ann Arbor	28
University of California, Los Angeles	28
University of California, Berkeley	17

CONCLUSION

We have noted several times the difficulty of drawing firm conclusions about the success of U.S. education for the mathematically promising. Most of our data come from tests, and the majority of these tests were given to a cross section of students, not simply students of high mathematical ability. Is the solution to give an even more difficult test? Unfortunately, even the most difficult exam may not provide the kind of information that we are looking for. Consider, for example, the Hungarian Eötvös competitions for high school students. Students are given four hours to complete this examination, which consists of three nonroutine problems requiring only high school level mathematics. It is considered similar in nature to the IMO questions and to those on the Putnam examination, which is aimed mainly at U.S. undergraduates.

Although some winners of the Hungarian Eötvös competition later became famous mathematicians, other well-known and extremely successful mathematicians were not successful on it. Similar conclusions about such examinations exist among U.S. mathematicians: "[The examinations] do not measure all the abilities important in mathematical research and are not considered important predictors of future success in mathematics" (Kessel and Linn 1996, p. 16). The difficulty level of the examinations, therefore, does not necessarily imply that more talented mathematicians will be identified. If the object of these trend data and these international comparisons is to determine whether the United States is capable of producing talented mathematicians from our most able mathematics students, perhaps we need to look beyond tests. We need to look deeper into how our promising students, as well as our most talented mathematicians, are thinking about and doing mathematics.

REFERENCES

Baker, David P. "Compared to Japan, the U.S. Is a Low Achiever ... Really." *Educational Researcher* 22, no. 3 (1993): 18–20.

Bracey, Gerald W. "Why Can't They Be Like We Were?" *Phi Delta Kappan* 73 (October 1991): 104–17.

——. "The Second Bracey Report on the Condition of Public Education." *Phi Delta Kappan* 74 (October 1992): 104–17.

——. "The Third Bracey Report on the Condition of Public Education." *Phi Delta Kappan* 75 (October 1993): 104–17.

——. "Stedman's Myths Miss the Mark." *Educational Leadership* (March 1995): 75–80.

——. "International Comparisons and the Condition of American Education." *Educational Researcher* 25, no. 1 (1996): 5–11.

Britton, Edward D., and Senta A. Raizen, eds. *Examining the Examinations: An International Comparison of Science and Mathematics Examinations for College-Bound Students.* Norwell, Mass.: Kluwer Academic Publishers, 1996.

Brody, Linda E., and Camilla P. Benbow. "Effects of High School Coursework and Time on SAT Scores." *Journal of Educational Psychology* 82 (1990): 866–75.

Callahan, Carolyn M. *The Performance of High Ability Students in the United States on National and International Tests.* Washington, D.C.: U.S. Department of Education, 1994. (ERIC, ED 372581.)

Celis, William. "International Report Card Shows That U.S. Schools Work." *The New York Times,* (9 December 1993).

Cipra, Barry. "An Awesome Look at Japan's Math SAT." *Science* 259 (1993): 22.

College Board. *Almost One-Fifth of Students Entering Four-Year Colleges Are Eligible for Credit Through Advanced Placement* <http://www.collegeboard.org/index_this/press/html/960822c.html> (December 1996).

Davis, Paul W. "1996 AMS-IMS-MAA Annual Survey (Second Report)." *Notices of the AMS* 44, no. 8 (1997): 911–21.

Educational Testing Service. *College-Bound Seniors* [Yearly publication]. Princeton, N.J.: Educational Testing Service, 1976–86.

——. *Profile of SAT and Achievement Test Takers* [Yearly publication]. Princeton, N.J.: Educational Testing Service, 1987–94.

——. *Performance at the Top: From Elementary through Graduate School.* Princeton, N.J.: Educational Testing Service, 1991.

——. *Profile of SAT Program Test Takers.* Princeton, N.J.: Educational Testing Service, 1995.

——. *1996 College-Bound Seniors.* Princeton, N.J.: Educational Testing Service, 1996.

Fulton, John D. "1996 AMS-IMS-MAA Annual Survey: Report on the 1996 Survey of New Doctoral Recipients." *Notices of the AMS* 43, no. 12 (1996): 1493–508.

Gourman, Jack. *The Gourman Report: A Rating of Graduate and Professional Programs in American and International Universities.* 7th ed. Los Angeles, Calif.: National Educational Standards, 1996.

Grandy, Jerilee. *Trends in the Selection of Science, Mathematics, or Engineering as Major Fields of Study among Top Scoring SAT Takers.* Princeton, N.J.: Educational Testing Service, 1987.

——. *Trends and Profiles: Statistics About GRE General Test Examinees by Sex, Age and Ethnicity* (ETS Research Report RR-96-07 and RR-96-07a). Princeton, N.J.: Educational Testing Service, forthcoming.

Hattendorf, Lynn C., ed. *Educational Rankings Annual,* 1997. Detroit, Mich.: Gale Research, 1997.

Kenelly, John, Patricia Henry, and Chancy O. Jones. "The Advanced Placement Program in Calculus." In *The Secondary School Mathematics Curriculum: 1985 Yearbook of the National Council of Teachers of Mathematics,* edited by Christian R. Hirsch: pp. 166–76. Reston, Va.: The National Council of Teachers of Mathematics, 1985.

Kessel, Cathy, and Marcia C. Linn. "Grades or Scores: Predicting Future College Mathematics Performance." *Educational Measurement: Issues and Practice* 15 (Winter 1996): 10–14, 38.

Kolota, Gina. "Americans Score in Math Grad Schools." *Science* 230 (4727): 787.

Lapointe, Archie E., Nancy A. Mead, and Janice M. Askew. *Learning Mathematics.* Princeton, N.J.: Educational Testing Service, 1992.

Madison, Bernard L., and Therese A. Hart. *A Challenge of Numbers: People in the Mathematical Sciences.* Washington, D.C.: National Academy of Sciences—National Research Council, 1990. (ERIC, ED 328409.)

Mathematical Association of America. *U.S.A. Team Excels in International Mathematical Olympiad.* <http://www.maa.org/past/imo.html> (December 1996).

———. *U.S.A. Team Excels Again at the International Mathematical Olympiad.* <http://www.unl.edu/amc> (March 1997).

McKnight, Curtis C., F. Joe Crosswhite, John A. Dossey, Edward Kifer, Jane O. Swafford, Kenneth J. Travers, and Thomas J. Cooney. *The Underachieving Curriculum: Assessing U.S. School Mathematics from an International Perspective.* Champaign, Ill.: Stipes, 1987.

National Center for Education Statistics. *Digest of Educational Statistics 1995.* Washington, D,C.: U.S. Department of Education, 1995.

———. *1994 Trends in Academic Progress: Achievement of U.S. Students in Science, 1969 to 1994; Mathematics, 1973 to 1994; Reading, 1971-1994; and Writing, 1984 to 1994.* Washington, D.C.: U.S. Department of Education, 1996a.

———. *Digest of Educational Statistics 1996.* Washington, D.C.: U.S. Department of Education, 1996b.

———. *NAEP 1996 Mathematics: Report Card for the Nation and the States.* Washington, D.C.: U.S. Department of Education, 1997.

———. *Third International Mathematics and Science Study* <http://www.ed.gov/NCES/timss> (March 1998).

National Council of Teachers of Mathematics. *U.S. Mathematics Teachers Respond to the Third International Mathematics and Science Study: Grade 12 Results.* <http://www.nctm.org/publications/releases/1998/02/timss.12.reaction/index.html> (March 1998).

Pratt, Chastity. "U.S. Math Team: Perfect." *The Washington Post* (20 July 1994).

Peterson's Graduate Programs in the Physical Sciences, Mathematics & Agricultural Sciences, 1997. Princeton, N.J.: Peterson's, 1997.

Raspberry, William. "U.S. Schools: Better Than We Think." *The Washington Post* (28 October 1991).

———. "The Brighter Side of American Schools." *The Washington Post* (8 October 1993).

Robertson, Nancy J. *Documentation of GRE Talent Flow—1978 to 1987.* Princeton, N.J.: Educational Testing Service, 1993. (ERIC, ED 386489.)

Robitaille, David F., and Robert A. Garden, eds. *The IEA Study of Mathematics II: Contexts and Outcomes of School Mathematics.* Oxford, England: Pergamon, 1988.

Robitaille, David F., and Kenneth J. Travers. "International Studies of Achievement in Mathematics." In *Handbook of Research on Mathematics Teaching and Learning,* edited by Douglas A. Grouws, pp. 687–709. New York: Macmillan Publishing Co., 1992.

Ross, Patricia O'Connell. *National Excellence: A Case for Developing America's Talent.* Washington, D.C.: U.S. Department of Education, Javits Gifted and Talented Education Program, 1996.

Rotberg, Iris. "I Never Promised You First Place." *Phi Delta Kappan* 72 (December 1990): 296–303.

Servan Schreiber, Jean Jacques, and Herbert Simon. "America Must Remain the World's University." *The Washington Post* (15 November 1987).

Sheffield, Linda J. *The Development of Gifted and Talented Mathematics Students and the National Council of Teachers of Mathematics Standards.* Storrs, Conn.: National Research Center on the Gifted and Talented, 1994. (ERIC, ED 388011.)

Stanley, Julian. "How Greatly Do Chinese Students Eclipse Ours?" *Journal for the Education of the Gifted* 12 (1989): 306–09.

Stedman, Lawrence C. "The Sandia Report and U.S. Achievement: An Assessment." *Journal of Educational Research* 87 (1994): 133–46.

———. "The New Mythology About the Status of American Schools." *Educational Leadership* (February 1995): 80–85.

Stevenson, Harold W., Chuansheng Chen, and Shin-Ying Lee. "Mathematics Achievement of Chinese, Japanese, and American Children: Ten Years Later." *Science* 259 (1993): 53–58.

Stevenson, Harold W., Shin-Ying Lee, and James W. Stigler. "Mathematics Achievement of Chinese, Japanese, and American Children." *Science* 231 (1986): 693–99.

Turner, Nura D. "A Historical Sketch of Olympiads: U.S.A. and International." *College Mathematics Journal* 16 (1985): 330–35.

U.S. Bureau of the Census. *Statistical Abstract of the United States: 1996.* Washington, D.C.: U.S. Bureau of the Census, 1996.

U.S. News and World Report. "Graduate Liberal Arts Rankings, Mathematics." <http://www4.usnews.com/usnews/edu/beyond/gmath/htm> (March 1997).

Chapter 4

SERVING THE NEEDS OF THE MATHEMATICALLY PROMISING

Linda Jensen Sheffield

At times, it seems that we spend so much time and energy arguing about who are the promising, gifted, or talented students and how we identify them that we lose sight of more important issues. These issues include why we should recognize and promote promising students, how we can best meet their needs and desires, and how we can find the best ways to serve the needs and wants of our society.

THE NEED FOR SERVICES FOR THE MATHEMATICALLY PROMISING

If we believe that all students can learn at high levels and that mathematical promise is a function of ability, motivation, beliefs, and opportunity or experience, then we must believe that there is a great deal that teachers and parents can do to help students develop their abilities to a far greater extent. We need to help all our students move along the following continuum:

| Innumerators | Doers | Computers | Consumers | Problem solvers | Problem posers | Creators |

At one end of the continuum, there are students who have almost no mathematical skills or knowledge. Next come students who can do some mathematics—and may even be good at computation—but who are unable to apply their knowledge to everyday consumer problems. Once, we were satisfied if our students were intelligent consumers and good problem solvers. Now, we realize that is not enough. Students must be able to pose new problems and to create original solutions to them. This is especially true of our most promising students.

As we plan programs for these top students, we should first examine the purposes behind our programs. There are many reasons that we might want to help students develop their mathematical abilities. These include:

1. *Helping students become deep mathematical thinkers.* The ability to analyze a problem and to think deeply about its solution is necessary in all walks of life. Students—especially those who demonstrate the most mathematical

promise—must have the opportunity to learn to think like a mathematician rather than just learning to memorize facts and algorithms from textbooks.

2. *Developing an informed citizenry.* Everyone must be able to understand the issues of our complex society and decide on the best course of action. It is important that all citizens be able to understand the charts, graphs, and figures that we see every day and to use that information when voting on issues, making consumer decisions, or speaking out to influence public policy. This competence is needed regardless of the occupation of the individual; our best students must become intelligent, well-informed leaders in whatever their chosen fields.

3. *Allowing students to experience the joy and the beauty of mathematics.* Through the ages, mathematics has been used for pure enjoyment and to build monuments of lasting beauty for future generations. Students should be given the time it takes to explore and fully develop mathematical ideas. This activity is intrinsically much more interesting and satisfying to them than being quizzed on how rapidly they can complete a number of mathematical memory exercises.

4. *Enabling students to be competitive at the university level and beyond.* In many of our schools, the low expectations we have for our most promising students allow them to perform far below both their own capabilities and those of top students from other countries who are competing for the same spots in our most prestigious colleges and universities. These students are often at a disadvantage compared to their foreign counterparts when they enter mathematics-intensive graduate or undergraduate programs.

5. *Developing world leaders in our increasingly technological world.* It is apparent that students in the United States do not lead the world in mathematics and science, as was stated in the goals in *America 2000* (Alexander 1991). If today's students are to become adults who can continue to lead the world in technological advances, we must give them the skills and abilities needed to be leaders. We do our top students a great disservice when they receive all A's on their report cards and score at the 99th percentiles on their standardized tests without being challenged to excel and stretch their abilities to the fullest. It is sad when a student who is at the 95th percentile in the United States on a standardized mathematics test finds that he or she would only be at the 50th percentile in Japan (Ross 1993, p. 9). These top students are frequently lulled into believing that they can coast by and still be number one, but this does not work on a global level. Students need to know that becoming a world-class mathematician is hard work and not just the luck of the draw from the genetic pool.

ENRICH, ACCELERATE, OR DEEPEN

To help students develop their mathematical abilities, we need to drop the old arguments of whether a program should enrich or accelerate. The model for a good mathematics program must take into consideration the depth of mathematics that is being learned. The Third International Mathematics and Science Study (TIMSS) has called the U.S. curriculum "a mile wide and an inch deep." (Schmidt et al. 1996).

That is, U.S. students often learn a little bit about everything (and repeat that little bit for years) but do not seem to explore the rich depths of mathematics. We need to look at a program that provides challenges along at least three dimensions of learning.

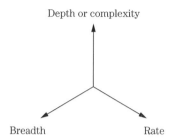

This multidimensional model is an attempt to illustrate that services for our most promising students should look not only at changing the rate or the number of the mathematical offerings but also at changing the depth or complexities of the mathematical investigations. Promising students should be encouraged to explore the complexities of patterns and problems and to investigate connections among mathematical concepts. However, in many school districts, bright students often have to choose between sitting in a regular mathematics class or moving into an enrichment mathematics program. In the second instance, either they study topics not normally encountered in a typical mathematics program or their mathematics program is accelerated so they cover the same curriculum at a faster rate. In many cases, both enrichment and acceleration programs have missed the mark; if the curriculum is "a mile wide and an inch deep," it does not help to widen the curriculum even further or to ask the students to run the mile faster.

Programs that simply accelerate students through a shallow look at mathematical topics (so that they may reach the pinnacle of calculus at an early age) frequently do not allow students the opportunity to enjoy the beauty of mathematics or to explore the mathematics deeply enough to become real mathematicians. Students may be good technicians who can follow rules and apply those rules to routine exercises, but they have difficulty analyzing nonroutine problems and digging beneath the surface of the problem to see the elegance of the mathematics below.

Many popular programs for gifted students at the middle and high school levels have been acceleration programs. The Talent Search for Mathematically Precocious Youth that originated with Julian Stanley at Johns Hopkins University asks students in the seventh grade to take the SAT Program tests or the American College Test (ACT), which are taken by high school juniors and seniors (Stanley, Keating, and Fox 1974). Seventh-grade students who score above a certain level on this test are then given the opportunity to take courses, frequently in the summer on a university campus, where they sometimes can finish the high school mathematics curriculum in a few weeks during a summer or two. On some campuses, the mathematics program that is chosen for these highly motivated and highly advanced mathematics students is a highly structured, algorithmic program where students spend hours every day memorizing the mathematics necessary to move through the books at a very accelerated pace. But they rarely get to explore, extend, and enjoy the mathematics they are learning.

Conversely, enrichment programs that are popular in many elementary schools often treat mathematics as the "puzzle of the week." Students sometimes say, "Oh, good, today is Tuesday, so today I am gifted. I get to play with tangrams." Enrichment books abound that have "fun" mathematics activities designed to expand students' mathematical horizons, but they seldom ask students to think deeply about mathematics, to connect the new topics to earlier knowledge, or to investigate new problems creatively. Of course, mathematics should be enjoyable, but this means a lot more that filling in puzzles with tangram pieces or playing the latest computer game. The enrichment activities that are used should be closely tied to the goals and objectives in the mathematics curriculum, with a mathematical purpose beyond fun.

DEVELOPING MATHEMATICAL CREATIVITY AND COMPLEX REASONING

A program that helps students develop their mathematical abilities to the fullest may allow them to move faster than others in the class to avoid deadly repetition of material that they have already mastered. Such a program may also introduce them to topics that others might not study but, most important, it introduces students to the joys and frustrations of thinking deeply about a wide range of original, open-ended, or complex problems that encourage them to respond creatively in ways that are original, fluent, flexible, and elegant.

One way to help students creatively develop their mathematical abilities is to follow an open-ended heuristic such as the following (Jenson 1980).

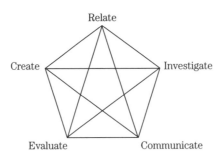

Using this model, either the teacher or the student suggests a problem to work on, and students begin at any point on the heuristic model; they do not need to follow the steps sequentially. For example, a student may first *relate* the problem to earlier mathematical ideas and develop a variety of strategies for attacking the problem. As the original problem is *investigated*, a new related problem might be *created* that the student finds interesting to explore. This new problem is investigated, and the student suggests several hypotheses that are *evaluated* and either verified or rejected. New findings are *communicated* to classmates, the teacher, or another audience, and then the student is off on a new investigation that has been suggested during the course of solving the earlier problems.

The original problem given to the students might be simple, but it should be interesting, open, and challenging. All too often, mathematical tasks are one-dimensional. For example, if a third- or fourth-grade mathematics class is reviewing addition of two-digit numbers with regrouping, often the teacher asks students to complete a page of exercises such as:

$$
\begin{array}{lll}
1.\quad 57 & 2.\quad 48 & 3.\quad 59 \\
\quad +45 & \quad +68 & \quad +37
\end{array}
$$

Some teachers decide that if the assignment for the class is to complete the odd-numbered exercises of a page of such problems, then the brighter and faster students should do all the exercises on the page. Alternatively, the teacher might decide that if the class is adding two 2-digit numbers, then the brighter students should add three or four 3- or 4-digit numbers with regrouping. These choices may be more difficult for a student because they are longer and more time-consuming, but they are not more complex or more mathematically interesting. Frequently choices such as these simply teach the faster children to hide their abilities from the teacher so they will not be asked to do more meaningless work.

A better multidimensional option would be to ask students to solve a problem similar to one suggested by Hashimoto and Becker (chapter 9) such as the following. While working on the problem, students should pose related questions and create new mathematical understandings.

Find three consecutive integers with a sum of 162.

Students would continue to get the practice of adding two-digit numbers with regrouping, but they also would have the opportunity to make interesting discoveries along the way. Students who are challenged to find the answer in as many ways as possible, to pose related questions, to investigate interesting patterns, to make and evaluate hypotheses about their observations, and to communicate their findings to their peers, teachers, and others will get plenty of practice adding two-digit numbers, but they will also have the chance to do some real mathematics.

The following are some examples of ways in which students might attack the problem and some of their observations along the way.

1. Ben solves this using the method of "guess and test." He guesses 60, 61, and 62 and adds these to note that the sum is 183. Seeing that this is too much by more than 20, Ben tries 50, 51, and 52, finding a sum of 153. He observes that by making the first number 10 less than the first guess the new sum is now 30 less than the original sum. Ben then hypothesizes that this might work for other numbers also. He tries it out and looks for an explanation. He

reasons that since $50 + 51 + 52 = 153$ and he is trying to get a sum of 162, which is nine more, then all three numbers should be increased by three. Trying $53 + 54 + 55$, Ben finds that this does indeed give a sum of 162. Similar reasoning could then be applied for finding other sums.

2. Kelly focuses on the ones place, looking for three consecutive numbers that add to 2. She reasons that since $0 + 1 + 2 = 3$, the three digits in the ones place must add to 12 and not 2. Through trial and error, Kelly finds that these numbers are $3 + 4 + 5$. Reasoning that since $3 + 4 + 5 = 12$, the numbers in the tens place must then add to 150 not 160. Kelly quickly finds that all three numbers must be in the 50s, given that $50 + 50 + 50 = 150$. Combining this with her reasoning about the numbers in the ones place, she finds the numbers 53, 54, and 55.

3. Dan notes that the sum is an even number and wonders whether he could do the same problem with an odd sum. Trying this for several combinations of three consecutive numbers ($59 + 60 + 61$; $47 + 48 + 49$; $35 + 36 + 37$), he hypothesizes that three consecutive numbers always have an even sum and looks for a way to verify this hypothesis. When Sasha points out that $60 + 61 + 62 = 183$, Dan realizes that he must rethink his hypothesis. He notes that in all his examples, the first number is odd, the second number is even, and the third number is odd. If the two odd numbers are added, the sum is even. Adding the middle even number to that gives an even sum. However, if the first of the three numbers is even, you are adding an even number plus an odd number plus another even number. The two even numbers added together will give an even sum. When that is added to the remaining odd number, the sum is also odd. Dan then decides to expand his search to the sums of four or five consecutive numbers. He discovers that whenever four consecutive numbers are added, the sum is even, and when five consecutive numbers are added, whether the sum is even or odd depends on whether the first number in the sequence is even or odd. He then proceeds to generalize this to any number of consecutive numbers.

4. Latisha has just learned about averages and she notices that there is a connection between averages and the middle number of the sequence. When she finds that 53, 54, and 55 have a sum of 162, she decides to find the average of 53, 54, and 55. She notes that the average is $162 \div 3$, or 54, the middle number in the sequence. She predicts that this will work for any three consecutive numbers, and she tries several others to see if she is correct. She then wonders what would happen if she tried four or five consecutive numbers, or if the numbers were consecutive odd or consecutive even numbers instead. She soon begins to explore those questions.

5. Josephina has been learning some algebraic notation at home from her older brother. When she attacks this problem, she decides to write the first number in the sequence as n. She reasons that the next number must be $n + 1$, and the third number must be $n + 2$. She then writes:

$$n + (n + 1) + (n + 2) = 162$$

She reasons that this must be the same as $3n + 3 = 162$. She realizes that if $3n + 3 = 162$, then $3n = 159$. If $3n = 159$, then $n = 159 \div 3$ or 53. She now writes the three numbers in the sequence as $53 + 54 + 55$ and checks to see that the answer is 162. She then decides to see what would happen if the problem were to find three consecutive numbers that add to 175. She again writes $n + (n + 1) + (n + 2) = 175$ and tries $3n + 3 = 175$. She realizes that $3n$ must equal 172, but when she divides 172 by 3 she gets 57.33333. This surprises her, and she begins to investigate which sums are possible for three consecutive numbers and which are not. She predicts that sums must be divisible by three, and she proceeds to verify her prediction.

These are only a few examples of what students can do with interesting, open-ended problems. Students in a class who have been taught to explore problems, patterns, and connections, posing new problems and creating their own solutions, approach mathematics very differently from students who have been taught that there is one right way to solve a problem, that the teachers and the textbooks know what it is, and that it is the students' job to listen and find out. Our most promising students are angered and frustrated by the "one right method" approach, especially when they are told that their answers to the questions on the worksheet will all be counted wrong unless they show their work—and that work had better include all the steps shown in the book or by the teacher. On the other hand, students flourish and blossom when they are asked to investigate problems in depth—creating a variety of approaches, looking for patterns, making and evaluating hypotheses and generalizations, relating new knowledge to earlier learning, and communicating their results.

As students work on open-ended problems, they should be encouraged to ask themselves a number of questions that will help them dig more deeply into the problems. The following is a list of phrases or questions that are good to use when investigating problems:

1. Why?
2. Why not?
3. What if …?
4. What if … not …?
5. What patterns do I notice?
6. What predictions or generalizations can I make?
7. How is this like …?
8. How is this different from …?
9. Will that always work?
10. Will that ever work?
11. Can I do that another way? How many ways might I?
12. What is the largest? The smallest?
13. Convince me. Prove it. Show me.
14. Explore the converse or the inverse of the problem.
15. What other related problems might I explore?

In the example given earlier about finding three consecutive numbers with a sum of 162, students might ask such questions as:

1. Why is the sum of three consecutive numbers a multiple of 3?

2. Why is the sum of three consecutive numbers not always an even number?

3. What if I want to find the sum of three consecutive even numbers? What if I find the sum of four or five consecutive numbers?

4. What if I do not use base-ten? Will I find the same patterns using base-five or base-two?

5. I notice that not all numbers are possible sums for three consecutive numbers. Is there a pattern to the numbers that are possible sums? Is this pattern the same for the sum of consecutive even or consecutive odd numbers?

6. If I call the first number of the three consecutive numbers n, what is the sum? What if I add four or five or m consecutive numbers?

7. How is finding the sum of consecutive numbers like finding averages?

8. How is finding the sum of consecutive odd numbers different from finding the sum of consecutive even integers?

9. Will the sum of three consecutive integers always be three times the middle number? Why?

10. Will the sum of four consecutive numbers ever be an odd number? Why or why not?

11. How many different ways can I find three consecutive numbers when given the sum?

12. What is the smallest possible sum of three consecutive integers? Of three consecutive even integers? Of three consecutive odd integers? Of x consecutive integers?

13. How might I prove that the sum of 5 consecutive integers will always be a multiple of 5?

14. What if I know the first of the consecutive integers but not the sum? How many different ways might I find the sum?

15. How does the problem change if I change the sum? If I change the number of consecutive numbers being added? If I change from consecutive to consecutive odd or consecutive even numbers? If I change to numbers in an arithmetic sequence that differ by 5, by 10, or by x? If I change to the sum of numbers in a geometric sequence?

Students who have learned to pose these types of questions can easily challenge themselves to think more deeply about any mathematical problem. In asking and exploring these questions, students not only develop their mathematical skills in computation, problem solving, and problem posing but they also develop the thinking skills and habits of mind needed to continue as lifelong learners and creators of mathematics. Most students find this type of exploration enjoyable and are eager to share their findings with others. They are also interested in seeing how other students have attacked the problem, and they can build on each others' solutions and questions.

Teachers who encourage this type of open problem solving and problem posing do not need to worry excessively about finding problems that are on the correct level for each student in the class. Frequently, the same problem can challenge students on a number of different levels. In the example given, students who are still unsure about how to add two-digit numbers with regrouping can explore a number of concepts related to that while other students can move on to the challenges of algebraic proofs. Students themselves often recognize which questions and solutions are the most elegant or represent the deepest thinking, and when they see high-level problem solving from their peers, they challenge themselves to find even better solutions, patterns, generalizations, or related explorations. In this way, students can work at their own developmental levels using learning styles that are comfortable for them. As they share insights and solutions with other students, they can begin to expand and develop their levels and their learning styles, becoming increasingly capable of doing and understanding significant mathematics.

BRAIN FUNCTIONING RESEARCH

Research on brain functioning shows that solving challenging, significant problems can promote growth in various parts of the brain, making the brain even more capable of solving problems. Clark (1997, p. 8) stated the following:

> No child is born gifted—only with the potential for giftedness. Although all children have amazing potential, only those who are fortunate enough to have opportunities to develop their uniqueness in an environment that responds to their particular patterns and needs will be able to actualize their abilities to high levels. Research in psychology, neuroscience, linguistics, and early learning can help parents create responsive environments that allow their children to develop their potential to the fullest—that is to create giftedness.

Jensen (1995, p. 174) cites studies by Denney that concur with Clark, indicating that problem solving

> creates a virtual explosion of activity (in the brain), causing synapses to form, neurotransmitters to activate, and blood flow to increase. Her studies indicate that your brain will stay younger, smarter, and more useful by working out with these mental weights. Especially good for the brain are challenging, novel, and complex tasks requiring multitasking and think time.

Research on rats by Marion Diamond (1988) of the University of California at Berkeley found that the brain could grow new connections with various stimulations. In more than thirty years of research, she has found that rats in enriched environments have brains that are larger and heavier, with more dendritic branching (making connections between brain cells); have more glial cells for support of the neurons; and have increases in the size of the synapses (the junctions between cells). Additionally, studies by neuroscientist Robert Jacobs and his colleagues have shown that research on brain enrichment translates to human brains (Jensen 1995). He found that brains of graduate students who were challenging themselves daily not only had more overall brain growth in the branching of dendrites than high school dropouts but also had more growth than underchallenged graduate students.

This research on brain functioning may have significant implications for mathematics teachers. If we want students to develop their mathematical potential, we must challenge them daily with new, engaging, complex problems and encourage them to continually challenge *themselves* to even higher levels of achievement. Our society cannot afford to allow students to convince themselves that they were born with nonmathematical minds and therefore lack the potential to learn significant mathematics. Research shows that any child born with an undamaged brain can develop it far beyond our current expectations.

MATHEMATICAL BELIEFS AND EXPECTATIONS

Frequently, the development of mathematical promise means that we must not only provide students with significant, challenging mathematics but also help them do two things: change their perceptions of themselves as mathematical learners and modify their attitudes toward the significance of learning mathematics. Parents who say that they themselves have no mathematical mind—or that they learned algebra in high school and never again had to use it—must also be encouraged to change their attitudes to help their children develop their mathematical capabilities.

Exceptionally Gifted and Talented Students

Changing attitudes toward learning mathematics and the methods of teaching mathematics will increase the numbers of mathematically promising students in all our classes, but it may not be enough to challenge all our students. Just as special education teachers distinguish among levels of intellectual difficulties by defining students of lower abilities as mildly, moderately, severely, or profoundly retarded, we can also look at different levels of mathematically promising children. Students whose mathematical performances are at or slightly above the level of their peers might show mathematical promise if given opportunities, encouragement, and sufficiently interesting open problems. These students might find all the opportunities they need between a regular classroom with a challenging mathematics teacher (and the collaboration of a teacher trained in the needs of the gifted) and a home with supportive parents. In a sense, their situation resembles that of mildly mentally retarded students who are mainstreamed into the regular classroom and given the support of a collaborating teacher.

Other students, however, such as those whose performance or abilities are three or more standard deviations above the mean, may need more support than can be given by the classroom teacher—even with the help of a collaborating teacher. It is not sufficient to give these students the book and ask them to accelerate through the work on their own or to send them to a teacher of students one, two, or more years older than this moderately gifted, talented, or promising student who is in need of more challenge. Too often, the textbook or the teacher of older children will continue to cover the mathematics in a shallow fashion. They may not ask the students to think deeply about a topic or investigate fully the patterns and complexities of the mathematics. These students need a teacher who not only is trained in mathematics but who also understands outstanding students and can challenge them fully. In fact, these students might need a full-time program, such as a magnet school for mathematics, where they can develop their potential. They are the counterparts of the moderately retarded students whose least restrictive environment might be a special school or classroom where they receive services from several teachers trained to work with their specific needs.

Then we have the severely and profoundly promising, gifted, talented, and motivated students who may come along only once in a teacher's career. These students may be performing more than four standard deviations above the mean on standardized tests. They may be ready for algebra or even calculus at age seven. They are so rare in the population that few school districts can justify a special class or a magnet school for them. They need far more individualized services from highly trained specialists who have a background both in higher level mathematics and in understanding exceptional students. As do the severely and profoundly mentally retarded students, the severely and profoundly mathematically promising students need a teacher who is working with only one or two highly exceptional students. They need a mentor who can understand and challenge them and help them fully develop their potential. For our part, we need to be more creative in finding ways to serve these students. This may mean making use of existing technologies for finding support online from similar students and adults, offering courses through interactive television, or finding mathematicians willing to mentor students even at a distance. In any case, bored underachieving, but profoundly promising students cannot be ignored or forced to repeat low-level mathematics they learned years earlier.

As we look to expand services for promising students as we have expanded them for other exceptional students, we also must look at the need to expand the funding for these services as we have for the other exceptionalities. It is foolish not to invest in developing these promising students, who are one of our greatest national resources.

ASSESSING MATHEMATICALLY PROMISING STUDENTS

If we want students to learn to think more deeply about the mathematics they are learning, we must also assess their learning in such a way that they can demonstrate this higher level reasoning. This means that we cannot use multiple-choice or fill-in-the-blank testing as the sole means of assessing student learning. We need a variety of means of assessment, and at least one of the measures should be a portfolio in which a student can display his or her best work. In developing a portfolio to best demonstrate his or her complex mathematical understanding, the student needs access to examples of best work from other students. Teachers should make copies of exemplary work on each topic available so students know what is expected and have something to strive for. Students generally live up to and exceed high expectations, and teachers are likely to get better examples of outstanding work each time they collect student projects. (Of course, teachers should get students' permission to keep samples of their work as examples for other students.)

In assessing work, students and teachers together should develop a scoring rubric that delineates what is important in the project. This rubric might include such factors as depth of understanding of core mathematics, patterns noted and generalized, predictions made and verified, interesting related problems posed and investigated, and the traditional measures of creativity—fluency (the number of different solutions), flexibility (the variety of solutions), originality (the uniqueness of solutions), and elegance (the clarity of expression). In revising work for portfolios, students should use the rubrics to comment on the work of their peers and to improve their own work; teachers might use the same rubric as the students in their evaluations.

Portfolios are not the only means of assessing student work, but other measures should encourage depth of understanding and demonstrate high standards of performance.

CONCLUDING REMARKS

It will not be enough for teachers to raise their expectations. In a national study of over 12 000 high school students a year over a four-year period, Steinberg (1996) found that parents and peers have the greatest influence over a student's classroom performance. He stressed making academic excellence a national priority based on his findings that parental and peer attitudes toward excelling in school had a far greater influence on a student's scholastic success than teachers or even the student's IQ score. For example, Asian students tend to perform much better in school than could be predicted by their IQ scores due to the expectations of their families and friends. Conversely, students from other minority populations perform below the level that would be predicted by their IQ scores for the same reason. If we aspire to have the best students in the world in mathematics and science, we must make a national commitment to that goal and let students know that excellence is expected and valued. Until we can make that change, school reform will continue to be a disappointment.

REFERENCES

Alexander, A. *America 2000: An Education Strategy.* Washington, D.C.: U.S. Department of Education, 1991.

Clark, Barbara. "No Child is Just Born Gifted: Creating and Developing Unlimited Potential," *Parenting for High Potential* (March 1997): 8–11.

Diamond, Marian. *Enriching Heredity: The Impact of the Environment on the Brain.* New York: Free Press, 1988.

Jensen, Eric. *Brain-Based Learning and Teaching.* Del Mar, Calif.: Turning Point Publishing, 1995.

Jensen, Linda R. *A Five-Point Program for Gifted Education.* Presentation made at the International Congress on Mathematics Education, Berkeley, Calif., August 1980.

Ross, Patricia O'Connell. *National Excellence: A Case for Developing America's Talent.* Washington, D.C.: Office of Educational Research and Improvement, 1993.

Schmidt, William H., Curtis C. McKnight, and A. Raizen. *Splintered Vision: An Investigation of U.S. Mathematics and Science Education.* Washington, D.C.: U.S. National Research Center, 1996.

Stanley, Julian C., Daniel P. Keating, and Lynn H. Fox, eds. *Mathematical Talent: Discovery, Description, and Development.* Baltimore, Md.: The John Hopkins University Press, 1974.

Steinberg, Laurence. *Beyond the Classroom: Why School Reform Has Failed and What Parents Need to Do.* New York: Simon & Schuster, 1996.

Chapter 5

THE MATHEMATICALLY PROMISING AND THE MATHEMATICALLY GIFTED

Zalman Usiskin

The popular notions of giftedness among mathematicians stem from just a few stories. Among the most famous is that of Gauss, who at the age of 10 added the numbers from 1 to 100 by thinking of the sum in reverse, seeing that corresponding numbers of the two sums added to 101, so the total of the two sums was 100×101, and the total of each sum was half that—all in his head (Eves 1983). At the age of twenty, Gauss provided the first proof of the Fundamental Theorem of Algebra (that every polynomial with complex coefficients and degree ≥ 1 has a complex zero). At the same age, he published a monumental work, *Disquisitiones Arithmeticae,* in which many new ideas were introduced, including modular arithmetic and a proof showing which regular polygons could be constructed by ruler and compass. For these reasons, by this age he was already famous as a prodigious talent, and he went on to maintain this level of greatness in his later work.

Legendary, too, is Euler, though his life story is not as well known. He was probably the most productive mathematician of all time, with an output that 200 years after his death has still not yet all been published. Like Gauss, he was extraordinary at mental computations, and during the last part of his life, while blind, he dictated articles to two secretaries to sustain his productivity.

In this century, perhaps the most famous and surely the most romantic story of giftedness concerns the Indian mathematician Srinivasa Ramanujan. Self-taught for the most part, at the age of twenty-three, Ramanujan wrote the British mathematician G. H. Hardy and included about 120 results involving infinite series and other ideas with his letter. Hardy's amazement at receiving these results—unlike any he had ever seen—led him to invite Ramanujan to Cambridge (Newman 1956). Thus began a fruitful collaboration that has been well-chronicled (Hardy 1940; Kanigel 1991).

Until the appearance in recent decades of biographies (e.g., Reid [1970]; Reid [1976]; Halmos [1985]; Ulam [1976]), and collections (Albers and Alexanderson 1985; Albers, Alexanderson, and Reid 1990) that give us more insight into the minds of many of this century's important mathematicians, the major source of information about the lives of mathematicians was E. T. Bell's *Men of Mathematics* (1937). Bell's work is now considered overromanticized, but his visions of the twenty-one-year-old Galois working feverishly the night before a duel that he knew he would lose and of the young Norwegian Abel working in obscurity remain vivid in the minds of many of us who read this work.

Taken as a group, these older sources promote mathematical giftedness as being a male sex-linked trait that appears early, if at all, that requires outstanding computation ability, and whose benefits are achieved by solitary work with few outside stimuli. There is also more than a hint of the notion that these people are so brilliant that they are not understood by their contemporaries. Exceptions to this rule, like the female mathematician Emmy Noether or the gregarious mathematician Paul Erdös, are considered just that: exceptions that do not disprove the rule. As for implications for teaching, if one follows this theory, there is little the teacher can do but get out of the way of these students and direct them towards more advanced materials and top-flight mathematicians who might be able to understand their work and guide them accordingly.

CHALLENGING THE POPULAR NOTION

In his book *The Psychology of Mathematical Abilities in Schoolchildren,* the Russian psychologist V. A. Krutetskii (1976) details a number of studies of what he calls "not capable," "capable," and "very capable" students of mathematics from ages six to sixteen. A goal of the studies was to characterize those abilities that distinguish capable from not-so-capable students in order to obtain a structure of abilities that constitutes the quality of mind known as mathematical giftedness. Following is Krutetskii's summary of the structure (pp. 350–51):

1. Obtaining mathematical information

   a. The ability for the formalized perception of mathematical material, for grasping the formal structure of a problem.

2. Processing mathematical information

   a. The ability for logical thought in the sphere of quantitative and spatial relationships, number and letter symbols; the ability to think in mathematical symbols.

   b. The ability for rapid and broad generalization of mathematical objects, relations, and operations [here "rapid" means "from as little as a single instance"; it does not mean "fast"]

   c. The ability to curtail the process of mathematical reasoning and the system of corresponding operations; the ability to think in curtailed structures.

   d. Flexibility of mental processes in mathematical activity.

   e. Striving for clarity, simplicity, economy, and rationality of solutions.

   f. The ability for rapid and free reconstruction of the direction of a mental process, switching from a direct to a reverse train of thought (reversibility of the mental process in mathematical reasoning).

3. Retaining mathematical information

    a. Mathematical memory (generalized memory for mathematical relationships, type characteristics, schemes of arguments and proofs, methods of problem solving, and principles of approach)

4. General synthetic component

    a. Mathematical cast of mind. [By which is meant the seeing of mathematics and mathematical arguments in a wide variety of situations which on the surface might not seem mathematical]

Krutetskii specifically identifies swiftness, computational ability, memory for formulas or other details, spatial ability, and visualization of abstract relationships as "not obligatory," though useful, characteristics of mathematical giftedness.

Krutetskii's rather involved structure boils down to the following four fundamental components:

1. Flexibility (corresponding to 2d and 2f of his outline)

2. Curtailment (2c and 2e)

3. Logical thought (2a)

4. Formalization (1a and 2b)

Krutetskii's abilities 3a and 4a would seem to be byproducts of these four components, rather than distinct abilities. That is, if one thinks in terms of generalizations, then one will remember in terms of generalizations. And if one has all the other characteristics, they will create a mathematical cast of mind in the same way that devoutly religious people often see everyday events as having religious significance.

Krutetskii's components of mathematical ability agree with the qualities held by fine mathematics students and the mathematicians that I know. But they are qualities that are not usually learned in school. In fact, they are taught *against* by many teachers. Despite recommendations to the contrary in NCTM *Standards* documents (1989, 1991) and virtually all methods books, many mathematics teachers (1) stress doing problems "my way" or "the book's way" and discourage alternate solutions, (2) require students to "put in every step" in order to receive full credit for problems, and (4) purposely hold back generalizations so that they can still have specific problems on tests. In fact, the public tends to view flexibility and curtailment as noncharacteristics of mathematics. Only logical thought (3) has been a traditional goal of teaching, but even that is sometimes neglected either through the absence of any checks of problem solutions or, in some contemporary materials, through never leaving the concrete.

Because in the past decades the United States has produced more top-flight mathematicians than any other country in the world, it may be that the qualities identified by Krutetskii emerge without ever being taught. But it seems more likely many talented students do not envision themselves as future mathematicians because precisely those qualities that make for mathematical giftedness are ignored by the curriculum or negatively reinforced by teachers.

MATHEMATICAL CASTS OF MIND

The traditional view of mathematical talent as being greatly determined by genetics has been reinforced by those who believe in the validity of IQ tests. It is sustained by those who believe that there is a general intelligence factor (see, e.g., Tannenbaum [1983], pp. 96–123, but also see Gould [1981]). Even Howard Gardner, who believes that there are many "intelligences," calls one of the intelligences a general "logical-mathematical talent" (Gardner 1993).

These views do not fit with the variety of talents practicing mathematicians are known to have. Krutetskii found that some of his "very capable" subjects had an "algebraic cast of mind"; that is, they tended to interpret even the most synthetic of geometry problems algebraically. Yet, a few had a "geometric cast of mind," which caused them to recast numeric and algebraic problems in geometric terms. Ramanujan was perhaps as fine an intuitive mathematician as has ever existed, but he was not particularly competent at proof. Every mathematician can count among his or her colleagues those who are fine problem solvers and those who think that problem solving is not a particularly good indicator of mathematical intelligence; those who think geometrically and those who have extraordinary symbolic sense; those who proceed logically and those who are more intuitive; those who love generalizing from data and those who detest the idea. Mathematical ability is a multidimensional entity not able to be captured in a single number.

In perhaps the only study of its kind, Gustin (1987) interviewed twenty top-flight American mathematicians (selected by their peers) in the prime of their careers to determine how they came to be in the field. Most of Gustin's mathematicians were good enough at early mathematics to be encouraged to attend special courses for interested young students. But they did not make their first mathematical discoveries and their decisions to become mathematicians until their later college years. Once they made their decisions, for all there was a period of ten years or more during which they devoted their lives to mathematics. In that period, they had one or more individuals who guided them and became very important to them in their work.

Thus, for the most part, Gustin's conclusions belie the pictures of mathematicians portrayed at the beginning of this chapter. Most were not particularly precocious, and their talent needed to be developed over a long period of time, with considerable guidance, for them to reach the levels they ultimately attained.

WHO IS MATHEMATICALLY TALENTED?

The danger of a retrospective study like Gustin's is that we can too easily reason the converse. That is, if we ask mathematicians how they got to be where they are, then we are determining the answer to *If I am a mathematician, then I had the following early experiences*. Yet, for those who are interested in developing mathematical talent, the fundamental question is the extent to which these various mathematical abilities can be developed. *If you have certain early experiences, you will have the wherewithal to become a mathematician* (if you so wish).

Who is mathematically talented? If we consider only those who are members of the Mathematical Association of America, the American Mathematical Society, or the Society of Industrial and Applied Mathematicians, mathematicians constitute far less than 1 percent of the population. Together with all statisticians, engineers, computer scientists, and mathematics teachers at the high school level or above, those with significant mathematics beyond calculus comprise about 3 percent of the population in the United States (U.S. Bureau of the Census 1996, p. 405). Physical scientists, economists, and others in business and industry who use significant mathematics add a few percent more. These statistics present the impression that mathematical ability can be the province of only a small minority. But this line of reasoning, examining the situation from the standpoint of professionals who use significant mathematics on their jobs, is again reasoning from the wrong direction.

The danger of proceeding retrospectively can be seen if we ask how many students are "linguistically talented." If we consider only journalists and other writers, again we will produce only 1 percent of the society (U.S. Bureau of the Census 1996, p. 405). If we add lawyers, executives, and others who write or have to interpret reports, we might arrive at up to 20 percent of the population. We might also include those who know and use second languages. But however we expand this list, we do not get the number of people who might have entered these occupations or who might have had the ability to enter them.

However, it is not particularly easy to determine who is mathematically talented by examining school programs. Programs for gifted students have traditionally used selection criteria based either on percentiles (typically, allowing students who score in the top 3 percent or 5 percent or 10 percent nationally), normed tests (such as the SAT), or the number of students that can fit into one or two classrooms. Each criterion artificially limits the number of students who could be called mathematically promising. Indeed, in schools where students tend to have higher scores on tests, the criteria for selection to honors courses or special programs are typically higher than in schools where students score lower.

In some districts, enrollment in algebra in eighth grade is considered a sign of potential talent in mathematics. When the nationwide percentage of students enrolled in such courses was about 13 percent, as it was in 1980–81,[1] more people saw it as a sign of giftedness than today, when the percentage of eighth graders taking algebra has climbed to at least 20 percent.[2] This percentage is about 50 percent in the schools in the First in the World Consortium[3] (Kroeze and Johnson 1997),

1. Judging from the percentage of eighth grade classes in the Second International Study that were judged as algebra classes (29 out of 220) (Crosswhite et al. 1986).

2. According to National Assessment, 16 percent of thirteen-year-olds in 1986 and 20 percent of thirteen-year-olds in 1996 report taking algebra (Campbell et al. 1997).

3. The First in the World Consortium is a group of school districts dedicated to pursuing a "world-class education for their students." It is composed of fifteen elementary (grades K–8) school districts, and three high school districts (grades 9–12); the Illinois Mathematics and Science Academy; and the North Suburban Special Education District, which is located in the northeastern suburban area of Chicago; and includes thirty-two elementary schools, seventeen middle schools, and six high schools (Kroeze and Johnson 1997, pp. 8–9).

and in those schools no one sees eighth-grade algebra as a sign of giftedness any longer. Now it is seventh grade algebra that may be viewed that way.

Two lessons can be gleaned from this trend. When objective criteria are used, the number of those who might be considered mathematically talented can increase substantially. Yet we as a society do not consider an ability to be a talent or sign of giftedness when many people possess that ability, so we may change our objective criteria so that only a few can be considered talented. (For instance, in my local school district, the number of students in seventh grade algebra has doubled in recent years even though none of the selection criteria have changed. There are those who wish to raise the criteria to lower the numbers of students in this program even though there is no evidence that the ability of the students in it has decreased in any way.)

Sometimes we do not change the objective criteria but merely downplay the criteria as being inadequate measures. For instance, when Japanese students first scored highly on international tests (Husen 1967), some of the public viewed Japanese students as robots who could answer questions correctly but did not really understand what they were doing. This view persists in the minds of some despite evidence that Japanese students outscore American students across the board (Beaton et al. 1996; U.S. Department of Education 1997). And because *all* Japanese students (and all students in a number of other countries) study the equivalent of our first-year algebra and geometry in seventh and eighth grades, they would all be considered gifted under American criteria.

Eighth-grade students in the schools in the First in the World Consortium scored about equal to Japanese students on the TIMSS tests, second only to Singapore among participating nations (Kroeze and Johnson 1997). Some of my colleagues have dismissed their scores as being misleading indicators of U.S. education because these schools lie in affluent areas and traditionally have high-performing students. However, as recently as ten years ago, these schools did not have more than about 10–15 percent of their students in eighth-grade algebra, and reports of both SIMS (Westbury 1994) and TIMSS results (Schmidt et al. 1996) have pointed to the significance of algebra study for scoring well on the tests. Thus, there is no way these schools would have performed as well had they not strengthened their programs for grades K–7 to allow for increased participation in eighth-grade algebra.

The First in the World Consortium results demonstrate that it is possible for U.S. students to score as high as any in the world if the curricula and the expectations of the school and community will allow them the opportunity. This substantiates the major conclusion of the Second International Mathematics Study; namely, that we offer many of our students an underachieving curriculum (McKnight et al. 1987). In fact, one can only speculate how well the students in the First in the World Consortium would have performed if the curriculum for grades K–6 had been strengthened so that studying algebra and geometry in seventh and eighth grades was the norm.

THE BENEFITS OF STARTING EARLY

Through the 1970s and 1980s, many school districts invoked Piagetian theory to justify the placement of small numbers of seventh- and eighth-grade students in substantial mathematics. Thus, they ignored common practice in other countries of the world, failing to realize that the level of symbol recognition and manipulation inherent in learning and comprehending the written word is at least as "formal operational" as that found in mathematics.

Learning a second language, which is what mathematics is for many students, is easier when one is younger. Thus, in a sense, some precocity is not a special feature of those who are gifted as much as it is a necessary feature for anyone who wishes to attain high levels of competence. Therefore, if school districts wish to maximize the number of students who are mathematically promising, they must start well before students reach the sixth or seventh grade even though, in the earlier grades, they may not have teachers dedicated to mathematics.

The advantages of starting early can be seen in another sector in which talent is often thought to be native: music performance. In fact, my experiences with the learning of music (my teaching minor) have very much influenced my beliefs about the learning of mathematics, so I ask the reader to indulge me in some personal reflections.

In the early 1970s, a friend of mine was a Chicago public elementary school music teacher who introduced a new program in her school—the Suzuki method for teaching violin. Despite her zealousness for this method, I dismissed it. Through that decade and well into the next, I would hear of Suzuki performers, and on occasion I would see groups of violinists, eight-years-old and younger, on television playing—in unison—Bach's "Double Concerto for Two Violins." They were quite good, but those who disliked the method criticized it for creating children who were robots and who lacked musicality. However, my curiosity was piqued.

Then, in 1989, just before her sixth birthday, my daughter Laura began a Suzuki cello program, and I became the cello parent. I had never played a string instrument and so I could not help Laura in any way except to be with her. As is the rule in Suzuki programs, I was there; for the next six years until last year (when she began twice-a-week lessons), I attended virtually every lesson and heard virtually every practice. Thus, in a way not available in the learning of mathematics, I was able to see and hear her progress almost daily. Also, since these sessions were group classes and group workshops, I was able to see the progress of many other cello students.

Now fifteen, Laura is a good cellist, who has even won a couple of local competitions. As you might expect, those who hear her comment on her talent. But she was not always talented. She began with the same pieces and with most of the same difficulties that other cello students do. And her musical ear, the ability to discern pitches of tones, which seemed neither as good as mine or her older brother's when she began the cello, is now the best in the family. It now is clear that she had the musical *promise* even when she did not have the exhibited *talent*. The philosophy behind the Suzuki program helped to develop that promise.

Suzuki's book, *Nurtured by Love* (1969) begins with his philosophy. The first line of the preface is, "Talent is no accident of birth." The introduction, with a section titled "All Japanese Children Speak Japanese," begins,

> Oh—why, Japanese children can all speak Japanese! The thought suddenly struck me with amazement. In fact, all children throughout the world speak their native tongues with the utmost fluency. Any and every Japanese child—all speak Japanese without difficulty. Does that not show a startling talent? How, by what means does this come about? I had to control an impulse to shout my joy over this discovery.

DEVELOPING THE PROMISING

Elsewhere (Usiskin 1993), I have told the story of my son Robert, who due to a school test given at the end of first grade was placed in a special second-grade mathematics class and, thus, started on a road that led to his placement in special mathematics classes from then on. In this school district, because of curriculum changes whereby every child is given an enriched program like that once offered only to students who, like Robert, scored well early, algebra is taken in the seventh grade by about 25 percent of the students.

However, when Robert got to sixth grade, we changed school systems, and our new superintendent believed that gifted students "are made in bed" (i.e., get their smarts from their parents at conception). This belief was used to justify the school not offering anything special—either in class or out of class—for students who already knew the curriculum. As a result, only 4 of the 162 students in Robert's grade in this new school scored well enough to be eligible for algebra in the seventh grade. But were these scores a result of genes? I think not. Including Robert, three of the four had been educated in mathematics outside the district.

Evidence that giftedness is due to nurture is coming from an interesting source: the rise in IQ scores. The average IQ score in the United States has risen 24 points since 1918; the average score in the Netherlands rose 20 points in the past thirty years (Shea 1996). Furthermore, the increase is strongest on the sections of the tests that psychometricians thought most directly measured IQ, namely, the abstract reasoning involved in mazes and completing patterns. Among the explanations are improved diet, longer spans of formal education, the increasing appearance of puzzles and games in our culture, and the visual stimuli of television and computers. All but the first of these explanations implicate the environment as a major force in determining individual performance and suggest the percentage of our students who are mathematically promising is at its highest point in history.

The problem in determining how well we have done with developing the mathematically promising is that we never know who might have promise until later when the promise is developed. In fact, we may not recognize the talent even when it has been exhibited. There are a number of first-rate mathematicians (e.g., Fourier and Galois) whose work was not considered valuable at first (Kline 1972, pp. 672, 736).

The conditions that raise the probability of developing promise not only seem to be the same for mathematics as for music but are already in place for much of society when it comes to language. These conditions are a good teacher and a curriculum with high expectations, a supportive environment, and a great deal of work on the part of the student. (These conditions are neither necessary nor sufficient, for there are exceptions to both.)

Let us consider the conditions for the learning of language first. Almost all humans are born with high language capabilities, and these capabilities are developed in ways quite dependent on where one lives. The first teachers for most infants are their parents and others with whom they live. Educated parents know that they should talk to their children even before their children have the capability to respond with speech; they should read to their children to set an environment for reading; and they should encourage their children to speak, read, and write. Even this is not enough to bring the high level of performance our society expects of language skills (a level once thought to be only attainable by the aristocracy). Thousands of hours in school, over every year from pre–K to grade 12, are devoted to reading, writing, and speaking. As a result, the linguistically promising become the language proficient. We would call adults gifted or talented in language were it not that such a large percentage of our society gains this proficiency. In the United States, we reserve such appellations for those who know a few languages, even though we know that knowledge of several languages is attained by almost everyone in Europe and Africa.

The Suzuki method for learning to play a musical instrument is more formalized, both because music is less embedded in our society than language and because generally there are not high expectations for learning music. The curriculum is carefully sequenced to cover the skills and pieces that are necessary prerequisites for later high performance. The Suzuki teacher occasionally supplements this curriculum with other pieces and skill work. The expectations are high but, as the title to Suzuki's book suggests, no child is ever criticized for errors.

The Suzuki social environment is particularly special. Since first grade, Laura had a weekly session with a group of children at about the same level as she, so that she realized she was not alone and so that she heard others working on the same pieces. When a piece was finished (approximately once monthly in early years), she would perform it at a workshop where she would hear many of the pieces she would play in later years. Periodically there were concerts at which the older students played along with the younger students. And, as has been noted, parents were expected to be present at lessons, at these performances, and to monitor practice. I played a stronger role with my daughter, since for many years I was able to accompany her cello playing on the piano, and it seems that for about half of the advanced students, the parents were musicians enough to be able to play with their children.

One cannot downplay the importance of work on the part of the student. Listening to music, going to concerts, and practicing or playing continually are necessary to achieve a high level of competence.

DEVELOPING THE MATHEMATICALLY PROMISING

There is little reason to believe that the development of mathematical talent requires different general principles from the development of highly developed language skills or musical ability. There must be both good teachers and a curriculum with high expectations. Without the former, children lose interest. Without the latter, children do not progress.

All of us who are in mathematics or mathematics education are occasionally asked if we do or did anything special with our children in mathematics. This is especially true if your children have taken algebra in seventh grade. Yet, my wife and I never did anything special except to have a supportive environment for everything mathematical. We gave our children calculators from birth; we bought occasional mathematics games for the computer; and we had rulers and graph paper and good pencils—the equipment one needs for mathematics. We gave them allowances before they could add or subtract so that when we went to the toy store, they could buy things and learn about dollars and cents and percentages. We took tape measures with us to furniture stores so that our children could help us decide whether a particular piece of furniture would fit where we wanted it. Although we purposely did not do school-type activities at home, our children saw us doing mathematics when we did tax work or room or graphic layouts, and they heard us discuss sports and weather statistics and other numerical data in the newspapers. In short, we did not hide the mathematics that is in our lives from our children.

But even with all this, our children would not be at their current levels of mathematics were it not for a great deal of work on their part. From first grade on, they did all the assignments given to them by their teachers, and they called on their friends (and only occasionally their parents) for help whenever they did not understand something, because they expected to do well. In hindsight, it looks like they were very talented, but in the interim there was a great deal of work.

The development of the mathematically promising should not be confused with the development of future mathematicians. Should children wish to become mathematicians, if the research of Gustin has any meaning, they will need more than they can get from school, and we would encourage them to attend one of the numerous extracurricular and summer programs in mathematics. Having to go outside of school for this development should not come as a surprise. Computer camps, sports camps, music camps, and many other activities exist for students who are far more interested in these areas than schools can be expected to provide. In no country in the world do the best mathematics students receive all of their mathematics education from their local public schools.

CLOSING THOUGHTS AND A BRIEF SUMMARY

When it comes to the development of almost any ability, the human organism is a dynamical system. With an initial state that begins at birth, stimuli affect all succeeding states. Because evolution proceeds slowly, and there is no evidence that mathematical ability or anything like it has been needed for survival since the dawn of mathematics, it is difficult to see how mathematics could occupy a special place in anyone's brain. Indeed, studies show that geometry performance is more closely related to reading comprehension than to the sorts of spatial abilities measured on IQ tests (Friedman 1994). All this suggests that virtually any child who is able to learn to read well can learn a significant amount of mathematics, say, through calculus, and with understanding. If we call such a child "mathematically promising," then the vast majority of our populace early in their lives are mathematically promising.

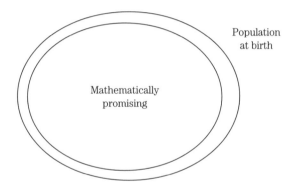

However, by analyzing the work of Krutetskii, we find that it is not uncommon for teachers to teach against many of the traits that differentiate the mathematically capable from those who are not so capable. Also, many schools do not provide curricula of sufficient quality and high enough expectations for their students. These teachers and schools are inadvertently shrinking the pool of the mathematically promising. By thinking that students can catch up later on any deficiencies they may have while young, these teachers fail to realize the similarity of mathematics to a language and the advantages to learning languages while young.

Our success in teaching our mother tongue and models from music education to the next generation suggest that three conditions could help to keep the percentage of mathematically promising in the population high as the population gets older: good teachers teaching a curriculum with high expectations; a supportive environment; and a great deal of work on the part of the student. Although we in mathematics education can most easily work on the first of these conditions, and the last of these is up to our students, our most significant work needs to be done in creating a social environment supportive of the notion that virtually all students start out as mathematically promising. We need to convince the public that to keep the potential for the mathematically talented as high as possible, we need to nurture the education of the mathematically promising every step of the way.

REFERENCES

Albers, Donald J. and Gerald. L. Alexanderson, eds. *Mathematical People: Profiles and Interviews.* Boston: Birkhäuser, 1985.

Albers, Donald J., Gerald L. Alexanderson, and Constance Reid, eds. *More Mathematical People.* Boston: Harcourt Brace Jovanovich, 1990.

Beaton, A. E., I. V. .S. Mullis, M. O. Martin, E. J. Gonzalez, D. L. Kelly, and T .A. Smith. *Mathematics Achievement in the Middle School Years: IEA's Third International Mathematics and Science Study.* Chestnut Hill, Mass.: Center for the Study of Testing, Evaluation, and Educational Policy, Boston College, 1996

Bell, E. T. *Men of Mathematics.* New York: Simon & Schuster, 1937.

Campbell, Jay R., Kristin E. Voekl, Patricia L. Donahue, et al. *NAEP 1996 Trends in Academic Progress.* Washington, D.C.: National Library of Education, Office of Educational Research and Improvement, U.S. Department of Education, 1997.

Crosswhite, F. Joe, John A. Dossey, Jane O. Swafford, Curtis C. McKnight, Thomas J. Cooney, Floyd L. Downs, Douglas A. Grouws, and A. I. Weinzweig. *Second International Mathematics Study Detailed Report for the United States.* Champaign, Ill: Stipes, December 1986.

Eves, Howard. *An Introduction to the History of Mathematics.* 5th ed. New York: Saunders College Publishing, 1983.

Friedman, Lynn. "The Space Factor in Mathematics: Gender Differences." *Review of Educational Research* 65, no. 1 (Spring 1995): 22–50.

Gardner, Howard. *Frames of Mind: The Theory of Multiple Intelligences.* 2nd ed. New York: Basic Books. 1993.

Gould, Stephen Jay. *The Mismeasure of Man.* New York: W.W. Norton, 1981.

Gustin, William. "Talented Research Mathematicians: A Retrospective Study of Exceptional Cognitive Development." Unpublished doctoral dissertation, University of Chicago, 1987.

Halmos, Paul R. *I Want To Be a Mathematician.* Washington, D.C.: Mathematical Association of America, 1985.

Hardy, G. H. *Ramanujan: Twelve Lectures Suggested by His Life and Work.* Cambridge: Cambridge University Press, 1940.

Husén, Torsten, ed. *International Study of Achievement in Mathematics.* Vols. 1 and 2. New York: Wiley, 1967.

Kanigel, Robert. *The Man Who Knew Infinity: A Life of the Genius Ramanujan.* New York: Charles Scribner's Sons, 1991.

Kline, Morris. *Mathematical Thought from Ancient to Modern Times.* New York: Oxford University Press, 1972.

Kroeze, David J., and Daniel P. Johnson. *Achieving Excellence. A Report of Initial Findings of Eighth Grade Performance from the Third International Mathematics and Science Study.* Northbrook, Ill.: First In the World Consortium, 1997.

Krutetskii, V. A. *The Psychology of Mathematical Abilities in Schoolchildren.* Translated from the Russian by Joan Teller, edited by Jeremy Kilpatrick and Izaak Wirzup. Chicago: The University of Chicago Press, 1976. (Original work published 1968.)

McKnight, Curtis C., F. Joe Crosswhite, John A. Dossey, Edward Kifer, Jane O. Swafford, Kenneth J. Travers, and Thomas J. Cooney. *The Underachieving Curriculum: Assessing U.S. School Mathematics from an International Perspective.* Champaign, Ill.: Stipes, 1987.

National Council of Teachers of Mathematics. *Curriculum and Evaluation Standards for School Mathematics*. Reston, Va.: National Council of Teachers of Mathematics, 1989.

———. *Professional Standards for Teaching Mathematics*. Reston, Va.: National Council of Teachers of Mathematics, 1991.

Newman, James R. "Srinivasa Ramanujan." In *The World of Mathematics*, edited by James R. Newman, pp. 368–376. New York: Simon & Schuster, 1956.

Reid, Constance. *Hilbert*. New York: Springer-Verlag, 1970

———. *Courant in Göttingen and New York: The Story of an Improbable Mathematician*. New York: Springer-Verlag, 1976

Schmidt, William H., Curtis C. McKnight, and Senta A. Raizen. *A Splintered Vision: An Investigation of U.S. Science and Mathematics Education*. Boston: Kluwer Academic Publishers, 1996.

Shea, Christopher. "Researchers Try to Understand Why People Are Doing Better on IQ Tests." *The Chronicle of Higher Education* 27 (September 1996): p. A18.

Suzuki, Shinichi. *Nurtured by Love*. Jericho, N.Y.: Exposition Press Inc., 1969.

Tannenbaum, Abraham J. *Gifted Children: Psychological and Educational Perspectives*. New York: Macmillan, 1983

Ulam, S. M. *Adventures of a Mathematician*. New York: Charles Scribner's Sons, 1976.

U.S. Bureau of the Census. *Statistical Abstract of the United States: 1996* (116th edition). Washington, D.C.: U.S. Government Printing Office, 1996.

U.S. Department of Education National Center for Education Statistics. *Pursuing Excellence: A Study of U.S. Fourth-Grade Mathematics and Science Achievement in International Context*. Washington, D.C.: U.S. Government Printing Office, 1997.

Usiskin, Zalman. "If Everybody Counts, Why Do So Few Survive?" In *Reaching All Students with Mathematics*, edited by Gilbert Cuevas and Mark Driscoll, Reston, Va.: National Council of Teachers of Mathematics, 1993.

Westbury, Ian. "Is the United States a Low Achiever in Math? The SIMS Findings Reexamined." In *In Search for More Effective Mathematics Education*, edited by Ian Westbury, Corrina A. Ethington, Laura A. Sosniak, and David P. Baker. Norwood, N.J.: Albex Publishing, 1994.

Part II

Chapter 6

EFFECTIVE LEARNING ENVIRONMENTS FOR PROMISING ELEMENTARY AND MIDDLE SCHOOL STUDENTS

Grayson H. Wheatley

As you enter Ms. Diaz's classroom, you see Sara and Tom engaged in a heated exchange about the interpretation of a problem they are solving while the other students are solving the same or other problems, also in pairs. Sara says there can be many possible answers, whereas Tom maintains that there is only one. Tyrone and Marta are jointly collaborating on developing a solution to the same problem, playing off each other's ideas. Ms. Diaz is moving around the room being very attentive to the interaction but not becoming too engaged with any group. After twenty-five minutes, she calls the class together and asks Sara and Tom to explain their reasoning for the problem they solved. The other students had worked on the same task, perhaps at a different time. As Sara and Tom explain their solution, some students express disagreement and others ask for clarification. Throughout their explanation, it was clear that Marcie was eager to tell about her method. It is a lively discussion, with Ms. Diaz listening and intervening to facilitate the interactions.

As described in the *Professional Teaching Standards* (National Council of Teachers of Mathematics 1991), if students are to develop mathematical power, major changes in instruction are needed. Central to the shift envisioned by the *Professional Teaching Standards* authors is a vision of social norms through which classrooms become mathematical communities with all that is implied by that characterization. In mathematical communities, individuals assume responsibility for their actions and statements, with reasoning and mathematical evidence as a test for viability rather than the teacher acting as the mathematical authority (Cobb, Wood, and Yackel 1995). This call for change is broad based. Along with selecting appropriate tasks for students constructing knowledge, negotiating a classroom culture conducive to learning is highly important (Steffe 1990).

NEGOTIATING SOCIAL NORMS

Students develop a set of expectations about each class they experience. These expectations are based on a set of social norms. The way each student acts in a class influences the microculture. A skillful teacher will negotiate rather than impose ways of interacting in the class. In some classrooms, students expect to sit quietly, not talking except to answer questions posed by the teacher and then only when recognized. In such classes, the structure imposed by the teacher dictates how students are to act, and failure to comply with the rules results in disciplinary action. The norms in other classes might include the belief that joking around and distracting class activities is a goal. Such norms are obviously counterproductive.

Social norms are defined as those ways of acting and interacting that are accepted by the group and that guide action. One example of a more positive norm would be students accepting the obligation of making sense of classmates' mathematical explanations and questioning those explanations when necessary. Other social norms that might become part of the praxis of a productive class are: (1) Students expect to be challenged and develop their own solutions rather than following a set procedure demonstrated by the teacher; (2) students expect to construct their own methods and recognize that different students will carry out an operation in different ways; (3) students expect to collaborate with other students and serve as a community of validators; and (4) students expect the process of solving a problem to take time and reflection.

In addition to the social norms just described, it is important to negotiate sociomathematics norms (Yackel and Cobb 1996). By *sociomathematics norms,* Yackel and Cobb refer to "what counts as a mathematics justification" and "why some student explanations are 'better' (we might say more elegant) than others." Both of these sociomathematics questions are part of what it means to do mathematics. It is promising students who are most likely to appreciate elegant solutions and strive toward innovative ways of thinking.

CLASSROOM CULTURES

Although the teacher plays a role in creating the learning environment, he or she alone does not establish it (Bauersfeld 1996; Varela, Thompson, and Rosch 1993). Rather, a classroom culture is coconstructed by all the participants. The learners both contribute to and are strongly influenced by the culture of the classroom. The nature of each individual's participation in this construction is a subtle and complex activity. The presence of just one person shapes the culture. The teacher may play an important role in negotiating an envisioned learning environment, but the classroom culture that results is strongly influenced by the students themselves. The reality of the classroom is continually developing and being interactively constituted (Bauersfeld 1980). Social norms for promising students should include the valuing of creativity and the joy of doing mathematics.

In some classes, students enthusiastically participate in making meaning by questioning peers, developing their own methods, and justifying their explanations in the process of constructing their mathematics. In other classes, students see their role as following directions, carrying out procedures in prescribed ways and relying on the teacher as the source of knowledge. When instruction is skill based and rule governed, many students, in self-defense, adopt a "play the game called school" stance, attempting to decide what is required to get a good grade rather than forming the intention of making sense. The classroom culture is a major determiner of which stance students take. When the culture of the classroom encourages students to inquire, question, conjecture, collaborate, and evaluate, students will learn more mathematics than if they are required to listen to teacher explanations, complete practice exercises in a prescribed way, and rely on the teacher to know if their answers are correct.

Bauersfeld (1996) contends that learning is *in* the interactions of individuals and therefore gives importance to the culture of the classroom. For him, a culture where students are encouraged to construct meaning for themselves through interactions with others is essential. If there are no student-to-student interactions, then the learning environment is impoverished. Thus, establishing a learning environment in which challenging others' mathematical reasoning is viewed as constructive and positive translates into rich learning opportunities for promising students. Student-to-student interactions can play an important role in how promising students become mathematically powerful.

PROBLEM-CENTERED LEARNING

One instructional model that has proved effective with promising students is problem-centered learning (Wheatley 1991). In problem-centered learning, the class begins with a problem posed by the teacher—or perhaps by a student. For example, the teacher might pose the following problem to a second-grade class: "I have a pocket full of just pennies, nickels, and dimes. If I reach in and pull out three coins, how much might the three coins be worth? Try to find all the possibilities." The class is then organized into small groups (two or three students of similar capabilities), and the students work collaboratively in their groups on the tasks posed.

After about twenty-five minutes, the students are assembled for class discussion. Students present their solutions to the class for consideration by the group, which then serves as a community of validators. During the class discussion the teacher is nonjudgmental and the viability of solution methods is determined by the class, not the teacher. In problem-centered learning the teacher has four main roles: selecting appropriate tasks on the basis of his or her knowledge of the students, organizing the groups, listening carefully as groups work, and finally, facilitating the class discussions. The success of this model is dependent on the classroom culture and the social norms that have been negotiated.

Tasks

Promising students thrive on intellectual challenges. Many promising students who languish in a skills-based mathematics program come alive when given the opportunity to pursue nonroutine mathematics problems. Some of our most promising students turn away from mathematics because they see it as a set of procedures to be done in a prescribed way. Investigations for promising elementary and middle school students should have the following characteristics:

- Be potentially meaningful to students;
- Be problem-based;
- Be replete with patterns;
- Encourage students to make decisions;
- Lead to rich mathematical experiences; and
- Promote discussion and communication.

Example

Inspired by Kennedy's article in the *Mathematics Teacher*, the following week-long activity was designed (Kennedy 1993). Annette Smith, a middle school teacher, used this activity with a seventh-grade class. Students were provided with one-inch dot paper and organized in groups to work on the following problem.

> Draw all possible noncongruent triangles that have their vertices on the dots on the four-by-four square grid. How many are there? How could you convince someone you have them all? (You may want to stop reading and try to draw all twenty-nine possibilities.)

$$
\begin{matrix}
\bullet & \bullet & \bullet & \bullet \\
\bullet & \bullet & \bullet & \bullet \\
\bullet & \bullet & \bullet & \bullet \\
\bullet & \bullet & \bullet & \bullet
\end{matrix}
$$

Students were asked to draw triangles on the dot paper, cut them out and post them on the bulletin board. Duplicates, if students spotted them, were removed when agreement was reached that they were indeed congruent. Examples of the triangles posted are shown in figure 6.1.

To draw all possibilities, students had to develop a system for classifying the triangles. This generated much discussion with a variety of classification plans used. The triangles on the bulletin board were often rearranged by the students to help develop patterns. Each day, Mrs. Smith would have a class discussion in which students would describe their reasoning and conjectures. This also generated much discourse. The classification of triangles by sides and angles was a topic of interest for several days. Students were surprised they could not draw an equilateral triangle on the four-by-four grid.

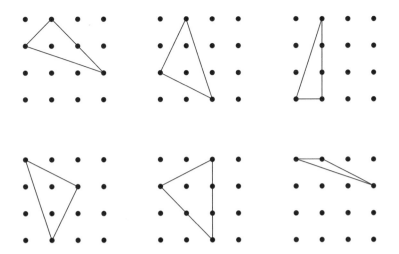

Fig. 6.1. Examples of triangles formed on a 16-point grid

Mrs. Smith had students keep portfolios of their investigations and asked them to write descriptions of their activities and what they learned. Students were encouraged to pose and investigate additional questions in this setting. Some students wondered how many triangles there would be if the grid were five-by-five. Others attempted to determine all quadrilaterals that could be formed on a four-by-four grid. (There are many!)

Extensions

Other questions that were raised included:

- What perimeters are possible? What is the largest perimeter? Smallest? (This led to a discussion of ways to find the distance between two points, the Pythagorean theorem, and square roots.)
- What areas are possible? What is the largest area possible? The smallest?
- What angle measures are possible? What is the largest angle measure? The smallest?

This activity involved seminal mathematical concepts such as systematizing, transforming, and classifying. The task seemed simple—just draw triangles—but it proved to be quite challenging. Students had to develop a way of systematically classifying the triangles to know when they had them all. They had to make many decisions. The activity promoted much discussion, and students were challenged to investigate related, deeper mathematical concepts. The investigation was replete with patterns and involved fundamental mathematical ideas.

In addition to investigating geometric concepts, it is important for promising intermediate and middle school students to learn to reason proportionally. Two proportion tasks that have proven effective follow.

1. A photograph that is 6 inches high and 4 inches across the bottom is to be enlarged so that it will be 6 inches across the bottom. How high will it be? (Many students give 8 as an answer, adding 2 because 6 is 2 more than 4.)

2. A videotape can record 2 hours on short play and 4 hours on long play. After 37 minutes have been recorded on short play, the recorder is switched to long play. How many minutes can then be recorded on long play?

Collaboration

Differing patterns of interaction evolve among students in small groups. If one of the students in a pair becomes a mathematical authority—that is to say, the other student does not question the validity of what he or she does and defers to that person for decision making—little or no learning occurs (Cobb 1995). This finding conflicts with the folk wisdom of pairing a "good" student with a weaker one. The evidence is strong that pairs should be formed of students who will challenge each other. It is the resolving of the perturbations resulting from disagreements that produces learning. Thus, we should attempt to pair individuals who will challenge each other's thinking as they attempt to give meaning to their mathematical experiences.

Class Discussion

If students interpret the environment as a recitation, then the way they act will reflect that interpretation and they will see themselves in an evaluative position. In contrast, we can negotiate a classroom environment that is interpreted by students as a sense-making place where their ideas are valued and listened to. When classrooms are seen as learning places, rather than work places, the dynamics can foster risk taking and result in lasting learning.

The belief must be fostered that a peer has something to say that is worth listening to. But this fostering is a delicate matter. For example, if student utterances are filtered through the teacher, students do not develop a sense of communicating with one another. Repeating student comments "so all can hear" will discourage true discourse and the building of community.

Students learn in many different ways, and we must be supportive of the individual differences. Some very capable students are "active" listeners in class discussions. They do not listen easily when sitting still and looking at the speaker but understand what is being said better when they are in motion. Some individuals think best while they are physically moving or doodling. Krutetskii (1976) reports that when he gave a task to a five-year-old girl, she got up, did a somersault, sat back down and wrote the answer. Although students moving around and perhaps making utterances can be distracting, we may want to explore ways of allowing certain students to be physically active during class discussion.

As another example, during class discussion Brad, a third grader, was observed playing with pencils and not looking at the speaker (Lo, Wheatley, and Smith 1994). Afterward, in a video-recorded interview, he could describe what the speaker said, whether it made sense, what her intentions were, what other students were doing, and how the teacher was reacting to the class. Brad could actually listen better when he was active. Some adults have the practice of doodling while listening to a speaker and claim they can attend more easily that way. Thus "paying attention" is not a prerequisite for meaningful participation in class discussion (Langer 1997).

CHARACTERISTICS OF PRODUCTIVE CLASSROOMS FOR PROMISING STUDENTS

According to Maker (1996, p. 31), learning environments for promising students should have the following characteristics:

- Learner-centered rather than teacher- or content-centered
- Independence rather than dependence emphasized
- Open rather than closed to new ideas, innovations, explorations
- Acceptance rather than judgment exercised
- Complexity rather than simplicity as a focus
- Varied groupings rather than one grouping as a general organization
- Flexibility rather than rigid structure or chaotic lack of structure
- High mobility rather than low mobility permitted and encouraged

To Maker's list, I would add that it is important for promising students to be in a setting where the instruction is fast paced. Such an environment encourages students to become mentally agile, to respond quickly, and thus to develop a brain that responds rapidly. One intermediate teacher, Mrs. Joyner, used time that might be lost in transition from one activity to another to present mental mathematics questions such as "What is $21 + 19$?" or "What is $100 \times 7 - 250 + 5000$?" or "How many cubes of whole numbers are there less than 100?" Note that the choice of tasks encouraged students to construct number patterns and build relationships among numbers.

The study of mathematics for promising students should be fast paced and problem centered, focusing on concepts rather than procedures. Algebra texts usually have sequential lessons where students plot points in a plane, make tables, and then sketch linear equations. Promising students respond well to lessons using graphing calculators where quadratic, cubic, and linear equations are dealt with conceptually—all in the same lesson—through the posing of problems. By considering these different types of equations together, students gain a broader perspective on functions. This has quite a different effect from a typical beginning algebra course that would have several lessons just on procedures for solving and graphing linear equations. Lessons that consider concepts and relationships encourage the construction and interrelating of powerful mathematics and appeal to promising students.

Too often mathematics instruction has emphasized computational procedures, such as borrowing in subtraction of whole numbers and long division, rather than patterns and relationships. I recently observed an eighth grade class of promising students solving equations. A procedure to be followed was demonstrated, and twenty-four problems, all of the form $ax = b$, were assigned. For example

1. $-4x = 20$ 2. $6x = -48$ 3. $-8x = -56$ 4. $-3x = 39$

These promising students were instructed to show on paper the multiplication of both sides of the equation by the multiplicative inverse of a and, of course, check their solutions. The effects were stultifying. Students were confused, frustrated, and certainly not pleased with their experience. They saw no reason to adhere to a complex written procedure when they could determine the solution by inspection. In contrast, another teacher, Mr. Santos, formed the class of thirty students into pairs and asked them to determine the values of x that satisfied each equation shown below. No procedures were demonstrated and students were not expected to use any particular method.

1. $2x - 5 = 7$ 2. $3x + 4 = 20$ 3. $21 = 7 - x$ 4. $x^2 = 6$

After students had discussed these problems in their pairs and devised their own methods, they came to the front of the room and explained their thinking to the class. Varieties of solutions were explained for each of the four different types. For example, one student explained her solution method for number four by saying, "I saw that 30 divided by 5 was 6, so $x - 3 = 30$. Then it was easy to see that $x = 33$ since $33 - 3$ is 30." Students were eager to explain the creative ways they had devised for solving the problems and showed much interest in the methods used by others. Everyone was required to justify his or her reasoning to the class. There was an intention of making sense. These problems could be followed by others that would raise their mathematical reasoning to an even higher level such as $3x^2 - 6 = 42$, $x^2 + x + 3 = 23$, or $x^2 + 1 = 0$.

"Fast-paced" should not be interpreted as short-answer, skill-based lessons. Mathematics tasks should require more than a few minutes to solve. For example, middle school students could be challenged to find how many numbers from 1 to 180 inclusive have 2, 3, or 5 as factors. In solving this problem, students might need considerable time to explore and search for patterns, consider alternative methods, try several approaches, make generalizations, and determine the validity of their answer. Thus, fast-paced lessons should feature challenging tasks.

ENCOURAGING CREATIVITY

It is vital that the teacher negotiate a set of social norms that foster curiosity, creativity, and sense making. For example, beginning a class with a challenging problem is one way of getting students involved in thinking mathematically. However, before discussing the value of such an approach, it is important to think about what is meant by a *problem*. To design an appropriate task, the teacher must have some sense of what each student knows about the topic so that a task can be designed that is within her or his zone of potential constructions— it is challenging but possible. Once students have become engaged in a task, curiosity and creativity can be encouraged by extending the problem, by asking "what if" questions and encouraging students to formulate related problems. As Brown and Walter (1983) point out, having students pose problems takes mathematics to a higher plane, a plane where they are acting mathematically in quite powerful ways.

SUMMARY

The dynamic culture of a mathematics classroom for promising elementary and middle school students is an important influence on the nature of mathematics learning. As a teacher develops a vision of mathematics classrooms compatible with the recommendations of NCTM (1991), steps can be taken to negotiate a culture of the classroom that encourages intellectual autonomy, curiosity, and sense making. A classroom culture will develop, and the teacher can play a vital role in negotiating, not legislating, a learning environment that encourages promising students to become mathematically powerful (Cobb et al. 1988). The social norms that come to be established in a class will constrain or facilitate the mathematics learning of promising students.

One model of instruction that has proven effective is problem-centered learning (Nicholls et al. 1991; Wood and Sellers 1996). Problem-centered learning is designed to encourage promising students to construct knowledge for themselves in ways that the learning will be lasting. As students work collaboratively on challenging tasks and have their ideas tested in an intellectual community, they develop confidence and knowledge. The explain-practice method of teaching has serious weaknesses and is inappropriate for promising students. New technologies allow attention in mathematics classes to be focused on concepts rather than procedures, thus freeing students to consider more challenging and meaningful tasks.

As we learn more about classroom cultures and how they form, we are in a better position to design more effective learning environments that empower promising students. For too long, schools have encouraged a transmission view of teaching. More recent theoretical and practical studies have shown that knowledge cannot be transmitted but that meaning is evoked by each individual's experiences in a learning setting. By encouraging promising elementary and middle school students to construct mathematical patterns and relationships, we can help them become powerful learners for a lifetime.

REFERENCES

Bauersfeld, Heinrich. "Hidden Dimensions in the So-called Reality of a Mathematics Classroom." *Educational Studies in Mathematics* 11 (February, 1980): 23–41.

Bauersfeld, Heinrich. "Social Constructivism, Classroom Cultures and other Concepts: What Can They Mean for Teachers?" Paper presented at the Annual Meeting of the Psychology for Mathematics Education—North American Chapter, Panama City, Fla., 1996.

Brown, Stephen, and Marion Walter. *The Art of Problem Posing.* Philadelphia: Franklin Institute Press, 1983.

Cobb, Paul. "Mathematics Learning and Small Group Interaction: Four Case Studies." In *The Emergence of Mathematical Meaning: Interaction in Classrooms' Cultures,* edited by Paul Cobb and Heinrich Bauersfeld. Hillsdale, N.J.: Erlbaum, 1995..

Cobb, Paul, Erna Yackel, Graceann Merkel, and Grayson Wheatley. "Research into Practice: Creating a Problem Solving Atmosphere." *Arithmetic Teacher* 36 (September 1988): 46–47.

Cobb, Paul, Terry Wood, and Erna Yackel. "A Constructivist Approach to Second Grade Mathematics." In *Radical Constructivism in Mathematics Education,* edited by Ernst von Glaserfeld. Dordrecht, Netherlands: Kluwer, 1995.

Kennedy, J. "Problem Solving on Geoboards." *Mathematics Teacher* 86 (January 1993): 82.

Krutetskii, V. A. *The Psychology of Mathematical Abilities in School Children.* Translated from the Russian by Joan Teller, edited by Jeremy Kilpatrick and Izaak Wirszup. Chicago: University of Chicago Press, 1976. (Original work published 1968.)

Langer, Ellen. *The Power of Mindful Learning.* Reading, Mass.: Addison-Wesley Publishing Company, 1997.

Lo, Jane, Grayson Wheatley, and Adelle Smith. "The Influence of Mathematics Class Discussion on the Beliefs and Arithmetic Meaning of a Third Grade Student." *Journal for Research in Mathematics Education* 25 (January 1994): 30–49.

Maker, June, and Arleene Nielson. *Curriculum Development and Teaching Strategies for Gifted Learners.* Austin, Tex.: Pro-Ed, 1996.

National Council of Teachers of Mathematics. *Professional Standards for Teaching Mathematics.* Reston, Va.: National Council of Teachers of Mathematics, 1991.

Nicholls, John, Paul Cobb, Erna Yackel, Terry Wood, Grayson Wheatley, Beatrice Trigatti, and Marcella Perlwitz. "Assessment of a Problem Centered Second-Grade Mathematics Project." *Journal for Research in Mathematics Education* 22 (January 1991): 3–29.

Steffe, Leslie. "Adaptive Mathematics Teaching." In *Teaching Mathematics in the 1990s,* edited by Tom Cooney and Christian Hirsch. Reston Va.: National Council of Teachers of Mathematics, 1990.

Varela, Francisco, Evan Thompson, and Eleanor Rosch. *The Embodied Mind: Cognitive Science and Human Experience.* Cambridge, Mass.: The MIT Press, 1993.

Wheatley, Grayson. "Constructivist Perspectives on Mathematics and Science Learning." *Science Education* 75 (January 1991): 9–21.

Wood, Terry, and Patricia Sellers. "Assessment of a Problem-Centered Mathematics Program: Third Grade." *Journal for Research in Mathematics Education* 27 (May 1996): 337–353.

Yackel, Erna, and Paul Cobb. "Sociomathematical Norms, Argumentation, and Autonomy in Mathematics." *Journal for Research in Mathematics Education* 27 (July 1996): 458–77.

Chapter 7

A COMMUNITY OF SCHOLARS: WORKING WITH STUDENTS OF HIGH ABILITY IN THE HIGH SCHOOL

Mark Saul

One gray August morning several years ago, I found myself in a car with five high school students, driving them to their internship sites. I was the director of their summer institute, and their usual driver hadn't shown up. No one was quite awake, so the conversation sagged.

"What's that odd-looking structure?" asked a young man from abroad. He pointed to an object on the horizon that must not have been a part of his usual surroundings.

"It's a water tower," I replied.

"I see," he said, "They pump the water up there, and then it runs down to the houses without adding any further energy."

"Exactly," I said.

It started to rain, but not to pour. I had to fuss with the windshield wipers, turning them on and off as the rain varied in intensity. "It's too bad I have to keep after these windshield wipers," I complained.

One student muttered, "It would be nice if the wipers themselves knew how much it was raining."

"Sure," said one young woman. "You could put sensors into the windshield. Then the wipers could read the sensors and adjust their speed."

"But …" started another, "The sensors might obstruct the view of the driver." A brief silence, then, "Oh, I see. You could just put them on one small part of the windshield, away from the driver's vision."

"But would this really be a convenience?" asked a third student.

"Perhaps not for a car, but it might be very useful in aircraft design," commented another.

The more I reflect on this brief incident, the more it represents, in miniature, my work with high-ability students. They respond quickly to a small hint. They engage in a problem with the most meager motivation. In a group, they quickly develop a synergism that takes them far. As their teacher, I spend much of my time keeping out of their way, except to catalyze the discussion and provide support.

IDENTIFICATION OF HIGH-ABILITY STUDENTS

Although many high-ability students are identified before they reach their high school years, the high school teacher can still find students shining in his or her class who have been overlooked or whose shine needs just a bit of polish.

The most obvious and simplest way to find students with high mathematical ability is through testing. For some students, this works well. Stanley (1979) has shown that simple multiple-choice tests, such as the SAT exams, can be very effective in identifying students with high mathematical ability. However, most practiced teachers have worked with students who reason well mathematically but who do not perform well on standardized tests. Researchers have followed these leads and documented several alternative means of identification (see, for example, Sowell [1990]). We can conclude that standardized tests may be sufficient, but not necessary, indicators of high ability.

Research can document general trends, guide discussion of policy, or direct further investigation. But it cannot make predictions for particular teachers about individual students. In specific classroom situations, the teacher must trust his or her intuition and observe students closely. The student who finishes his or her work early may have high ability—or may have learned the material last year. The student who gives an unexpected answer or who asks the unexpected question should be considered as possibly having high ability, as should the student who brings up fresh insights about a topic weeks after class discussion has moved on. Finally, the student who enjoys her work, whether or not she gets the right answer each time, probably has untapped ability in mathematics.

Errors in identification are inevitable. In probing a student's ability, an overestimate is usually easier to recover from than an underestimate. For example, it is easier to simplify a problem than to make it more challenging in midstream, and it is impossible to take back a hint that has proven unnecessary.

THE HIGH-ABILITY STUDENT IN THE CLASSROOM

How do high-ability students "do" mathematics? What is it that they are so good at? This question is not at all simple, and cognitive psychologists have just scratched its surface. The work of Polya (1954, 1957, 1962) on problem solving and the use of heuristics are seminal in this effort. More recently, Wickelgren (1974) and Schoenfeld (1985, 1987) have given more refined discussions of how Polya's work might be useful. Most of this research is in the anthropological tradition, observing individual students working on particular problems. This methodology is very close to what the classroom teacher must do to develop a sense of what constitutes high ability.

In my own practice, I have found that the patterns of thought, the pathways to the solution of a problem, are remarkably similar for students on different levels. The high-ability student who jumps to a solution often describes, when queried, the same mental processes, the same application of heuristics, the same metacognition as the student who works slowly toward a solution. Even in instances where the slower student does not achieve a solution independently, I often learn how best to guide him from working with high-ability students.

This is not a trivial statement: The gifted problem solver will sometimes make connections that seem to emerge from the void without motivation. I have found, most often, that when we can trace the connection (and sometimes this is difficult—the student himself is often unaware of it), the same connection can be found, or can be planted, in the minds of other students as well. Indeed, I do not consider that I have understood a student solution to a problem unless I can help another student to achieve it.

The working hypothesis, then, is that the minds of high-ability students don't differ all that much from those of other students—they are just more efficient. Like any other learner, students with high mathematical ability take in stimuli, react to them, adjust their reactions, and find places to rest and enjoy what they have thought about. The chief difference seems to be in the rate at which the processes occur and in the amazingly crude and meagre stimuli that can start them running.

It follows that most of the basic principles of good teaching transfer over to work with high-ability students. The teacher must start out with respect for their abilities. The students' need for growth and self-affirmation must come before the teacher's need to feel effective. The problem situations to be resolved must be more difficult than the student might be secure with—but not so difficult as to discourage his or her efforts. All these fundamentals of teaching (and many more) are as valid and important in teaching high-ability students as in work with remedial students, or adult students, or handicapped students—or average students.

Yet there are special problems that the teacher of high-ability students faces. These minds represent a precious resource to society. The process of developing and encouraging them raises issues relating to the balance of the needs of society and the needs of the students themselves.

I once overheard a colleague remark, "It's easy to be good in math. You just have to do your homework every night." Even the student to whom this comment was addressed (who was not of especially high ability) could see that it was not accurate. High-ability students who have no trouble with mathematics homework are understimulated and will soon turn their eager minds to other subjects. Or, their particular talent for mathematics will be overlooked so that their abilities will remain untapped as a source of progress for society and a source of enjoyment for the student herself.

The need to be challenged is central to high-ability students. They must be given problems whose solution they cannot readily see. The hints and stepping-stones to a solution must be spread out widely and doled out frugally. They must be free to think in many directions, including those not pursued by the teacher. However, frustration is not good for any student, and the teacher must be able to assess the student's ability to cope with frustration as the activity proceeds.

Work with high-ability students also presents the teacher with unique opportunities. Teaching is an enterprise that entails certain risks. The active teacher is always trying new ideas—but is not trying enough of them unless a certain fraction of the new ideas don't work out. Working with high-ability students minimizes this risk because these students can recover more quickly from a pedagogical misstep.

A CLASSROOM EXAMPLE

We are fortunate to be working in the field of mathematics, where we can construct meaningful and interesting problem situations for students out of very simple mathematical material. Such problems typically have numerous points of entry and several places where the discussion might rest. A stockpile of such problems is an important resource for the teacher of high-ability students.

An example follows of a set of problems that can be worked in a number of ways and on many levels, with discussion drawn from the author's own classroom experience. The order and wording of the problems may need adjustment for any particular group of students. While some students may need to work all of the problems, many will work best starting with problem 4 or 5.

Problem 1

How many subsets are there of the set $S_4 = \{a, b, c, d\}$? List them all.

For many students, this will not be a problem at all but just a simple exercise in combinatorics. However, students just beginning to explore this area of mathematics will find it interesting, and even a bit challenging, to make a list of subsets that includes each exactly once. Of course, the null set, and the set S_4 itself are usually the last to emerge.

Problem 2

How many subsets are there of a set of n elements?

The usual formula (a set of n elements has 2^n subsets) can be approached in a variety of ways. Students might make lists, then conjectures. Or, they may reason in some more abstract way. In either case, the chance to check their reasoning or conjecture with a concrete list is useful.

Problem 3

Arrange the four subsets of the set $S_2 = \{a, b\}$ in a sequence, so that each member of the sequence can be obtained from the previous one by either inserting a single new element or deleting a single element. Can this be done in more than one way?

The task is not difficult, and this problem is a good one for the teacher to solve completely before giving students problem 4. One way to visualize all the solutions to this problem is to picture the four subsets in the shape of a square.

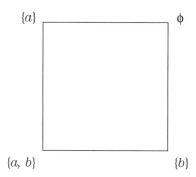

We can start at a vertex and trace around the square, recording the subset labeling of each vertex as we pass through it. Any such path will give us a sequence of subsets that is a solution to problem 3. Because we can start at any vertex and proceed in either direction, we get eight solutions to the problem. (It is a bit more difficult for students to see that this scheme gives all possible solutions.)

Problem 4

Arrange the eight subsets of the set $S_3 = \{a, b, c\}$ in a sequence, so that each member of the sequence can be obtained from the previous one by either inserting a single new element or deleting a single element. Can this be done in more than one way?

This is an excellent starting point for advanced students, with or without the preparation of previous problems. Usually, students begin by preparing a list of the eight subsets, and usually this list is ordered by the number of elements in each subset. Students quickly progress to the realization that this is the wrong ordering: In the sequence we need, no two adjacent subsets can have the same number of elements. They then begin constructing sequences, and it is not too difficult to find at least one solution. The question of finding all possible solutions is more difficult.

Problem 5

Start at any vertex on a cube and trace a path along the figure's edges, passing through ("visiting") each vertex exactly once.

In classical graph theory, such a path is known as a *Hamiltonian* path. There are, once more, numerous solutions, and counting them leads to a discussion of the symmetries of the cube. In fact, this problem can be made to look exactly like problem 4. We can think of the cube as a unit cube in a three-dimensional coordinate system. Then each vertex can be assigned three coordinates, each of which is either a 0 or a 1.

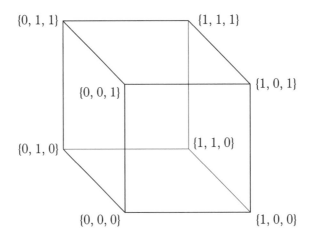

We can then introduce a function on the set of subsets of S_3 that puts these in one-to-one correspondence with the set of coordinates of the vertices. If the subset contains the letter a, then the first of its three coordinates is a 1; otherwise it is a 0. The second coordinate is 1 or 0 according to whether the subset contains or does not contain a b, and the third coordinate corresponds to the element c in the same way:

Subset	Coordinate
ϕ	{0, 0, 0}
{a}	{1, 0, 0}
{b}	{0, 1, 0}
{c}	{0, 0, 1}
{a, b}	{1, 1, 0}
{a, c}	{1, 0, 1}
{b, c}	{0, 1, 1}
{a, b, c}	{1, 1, 1}

(In more advanced work, this correspondence is related to the "characteristic function" of each subset.)

We now note that any two vertices that are connected by an edge have coordinates differing in exactly one entry. This means that the problem of finding our way around the cube is exactly the same as that of constructing a sequence of subsets as required in problem 4. This interpretation of problem 4 also lends itself to a counting of the number of possible solutions by considering the symmetries of the cube.

Problem 6

Arrange the sixteen subsets of the set $S_4 = \{a, b, c, d\}$ in a sequence so that each member of the sequence can be obtained from the previous one by either adding a single element or deleting a single element. Can this be done in more than one way?

For many groups of students, it will not be necessary to state this problem. Either they will state it themselves, or they will formulate it after a brief hint. Again, the solution can be a simple example of such a sequence, or it can be an advanced counting argument of the number of distinct solutions. A sophisticated argument might involve investigating the geometry of the four-dimensional cube. And one need not stop there. By considering S_5, S_6, and so on, a generalized problem can be formulated and discussed whose solution is not a trivial task.

There are several features of this set of problems that have proved useful in the classroom. We have already noted the multiple entry points and places to conclude discussion. At each level, there are also many useful approaches. Most of the questions asked fall to trial and error in a way that leads students to learn from their errors. Students can be supported in a transition from trial and error to more-abstract explorations. Noting patterns that can then be proved or extended using inductive techniques can solve many questions. These problems also lend themselves to cooperative work. For example, problem 5 can be worked on by several students at once, each sharing his or her discoveries—or his or her dead ends.

As it happens, these problems also connect to a piece of useful and by now classical mathematics, the construction of so-called *binary Gray codes* for computers. A Gray code (for a given value of n) is a set of symbols for the integers from 0 to $2^n - 1$. Each symbol consists of a ordered n-tuple of 0s and 1s, and each differs from the coding of the previous integer in a single coordinate (the idea is to have the computer count efficiently, resetting as few bits as possible when the count is increased or decreased). There are several good algorithms for constructing these codes, and students can continue their investigations with the help of a textbook in computer science.

CLASSROOM TECHNIQUE

The example given above illustrates some important techniques of work with high-ability students. It is open-ended but not so open-ended as to lack structure. It is conducive to cooperative learning situations. It allows for independent exploration after group discussion.

But what about the staples of classroom life, the acquisition of specific mathematical techniques and familiarity with mathematical style and terminology? Here, as in so many areas, the usual techniques of the classroom can be modified or exaggerated to accommodate the needs of high-ability students.

For example, many good lessons build on specific examples to elicit, or even derive, a formula. High-ability students can make do with fewer examples than other students can. Using another approach, high-ability students can often find a formula by tying together a series of examples. In this way, even the most routine lessons can sometimes be turned into problem-solving sessions.

Instances of this technique are not difficult to find. Students who have learned the quadratic formula may need only a few well-organized exercises to understand the role of the discriminant. The quadratic formula itself can be derived as an exercise if students have understood completely the process of completing the square. Students who have understood the formula for $\sin(a+b)$ can derive for themselves the formula for $\sin 2a$. Having learned that an inscribed angle is measured by half its intercepted arc, many students will be able to derive the corresponding relationships for angles formed by two chords or two secants independently, perhaps with a series of numerical exercises as hints. This technique also is one that can sometimes be transferred to work with students whose ability level is not particularly high.

The learning of high-ability students is deep as well as swift. For example, many students learn the "factoring pattern" $x^2 - y^2 = (x+y)(x-y)$, but the deeper meaning of this formula often eludes them. Even high-ability students may not see the relationship between this identity and the pattern:

$$2 \times 2 = 4 \qquad 1 \times 3 = 3$$
$$3 \times 3 = 9 \qquad 2 \times 4 = 8$$
$$4 \times 4 = 16 \qquad 3 \times 5 = 15$$
$$5 \times 5 = 25 \qquad 4 \times 6 = 24$$

This connection is an interesting one to explore with many different kinds of students. For the high-ability student, it can be further exploited. For example, it can be used to elicit the factorization of $x^3 - 1$, of $x^3 - y^3$, or of $x^n - 1$ for various integers n. The latter leads directly to the formula for the sum of a geometric progression.

EXAMPLES FROM CURRICULUM

High-ability students can frequently achieve results that relate to ordinary curriculum but that also probe more deeply into the underlying mathematics. Examples are not difficult to find, but because most textbooks are written for a wide range of students, no single text will have enough of these problems. The set of problems below draws from the typical precalculus syllabus and is intended to show how even highly-structured problems, with numerical answers, can offer a rich problem-solving experience to high-ability students. The only "exotic" ingredient in their solution is the "chain rule for logarithms": For all positive numbers a, b, c, $(\log_a b)(\log_b c) = \log_a c$.

1. Compute $\log_{\frac{1}{125}} \sqrt[3]{25}$.

2. If $\log_{10}(\log_{10}(\log_{10}(\log_{10} x))) = 0$, then $x = 10^k$. Find k.

3. Solve for x: $(2 + \log_{10} x)^3 + (-1 + \log_{10} x)^3 = (1 + \log_{10} x^2)^3$.

4. Compute

$$\log_{10} \frac{1}{2} + \log_{10} \frac{2}{3} + \log_{10} \frac{3}{4} + \ldots + \log_{10} \frac{n}{n+1} + \ldots + \log_{10} \frac{99}{100}$$

5. Simplify $(\log_2 3)(\log_9 4)$.

6. Solve for x: $\log_3 x + \log_9 x + \log_{81} x = 7$

7. If a and b are positive numbers, show that $\log_a b = \dfrac{1}{\log_b a}$

8. Solve for x: $\log_x 4 + \log_4 x = \dfrac{17}{4}$

9. If $\log_{10} 3 = a$ and $\log_{10} 7 = b$, express $\log_7 9$ in terms of a and b.

10. Find all ordered pairs of integers (x, y) such that
$\log_{10}(\log_{10} xy) = \log_{10}(\log_{10} x) + \log_{10}(\log_{10} y)$.

PITFALLS

The most common error made by teachers who first approach high-ability students is to give them more of the same materials. If ten factoring problems make them smart, won't twenty such problems make them smarter? One quickly learns that this is not the case, that "more of the same" is stultifying and contrary to the spirit of learning mathematics.

In working with high-ability students, particularly on the high school level, it is very important to bring them together, at least part of the time. This is a controversial point but one that has been borne out time and time again in practice. Perhaps the most valuable resource that high-ability students can be given is access to each other's minds.

Some researchers cite cooperative learning as a way to serve the needs of high-ability students at the same time as other students, but the research in this area is equivocal (see, for example, Slavin [1990, 1991] and Matthews [1992]). The classroom teacher, then, is left to evaluate this method for his or her classroom, teaching style, and students' needs. In my own experience, the success of cooperative grouping depends heavily on the personality (*not* the ability) of the students involved. It is important to recognize that teaching and learning are two different skills and that the student who learns mathematics well may or may not be proficient in transferring his or her knowledge to another student. Furthermore, it may or may not be desirable for the student to develop proficiency in teaching during a particular lesson.

WHAT ABOUT SOCIAL SKILLS?

Matt was a talented computer programmer who could not negotiate the high school social landscape. When he arrived in the summer program, he tried to impress everyone with his knowledge of computer programming. Unfortunately, numerous other participants had similar abilities, and Matt got nowhere. His stuffy and condescending attitude grew worse the less it worked for him. After two days of telling everyone his SAT scores and citing his triumphs in local science fairs, he gave up. His formal affect melted away, and he found a group of friends—of both sexes—with whom he worked and played. He developed a smile, then a giggle, and then a belly laugh that quickly became his trademark.

Sooner or later, the teacher of high-ability students will come across the student who defines himself as different and isolated because of his ability. This sort of personality has made such a strong impression on the public that a stereotype has developed of the socially maladjusted but bright student. Like most stereotypes, this one is usually but not always wrong.

In dealing with students lacking social skills, the teacher must keep in mind two important points. First, it is crucial to recognize that this attitude is not central to the student's personality but is a costly and burdensome defense. For some reason, such a student has found difficulty relating to his peers and has taken refuge in the idea that it is his ability that is rejected. The adoption of a "nerdish" pose allows him an identity in the group as well as the luxury of pursuing his intellectual strengths (at the expense of his social and emotional development). The second important point is that the reason for adopting this defense is not directly related to high ability. Despite the widespread stereotypes, many high-ability students have perfectly adequate—and sometimes highly developed—social skills.

One effective way to draw out a bright student who is lacking social skills is to place him or her with other high-ability students. In such an environment, he or she cannot keep up the pretense that it is ability that causes the isolation and is required to negotiate socially with others.

LEADERSHIP, NOT CONTROL

Perhaps the most serious error a teacher of high-ability students can make is to regard their talents with fear, rather than respect. It is easy for the teacher to regard the students' ability, which may surpass his or her own, as a threat to his or her control of the classroom. It is difficult but vital to be willing to exchange control for leadership. The teacher has more experience and more maturity than even high-achieving students do—to mediate the discussion, ask meaningful questions, or make comments for students to react to.

These are not simple tasks. It takes some adjustment, for example, for the teacher to ask a question he or she knows is significant, but to which he or she may not know the answer. And it takes some mathematical judgment, experience, and intuition to guess which lines of inquiry will be useful to pursue. But the result is perhaps the most productive of classroom surroundings: the community of scholars, all playing different roles and all pursuing their development of mathematical understanding.

Solutions to Problems on Pages 88–89

1. Let $x = \log_{\frac{1}{125}} \sqrt[3]{25}$. Then $\frac{1}{125} = \sqrt[3]{25}$. Recognizing that 125 and 25 are positive integral powers of 5, we can write this as $5^{-3x} = 5^{2/3}$. Hence $-3x = 2/3$ and $x = -2/9$.

2. If $\log_{10}(\log_{10}(\log_{10}(\log_{10}x))) = 0$, then $\log_{10}(\log_{10}(\log_{10}x)) = 1$, or $\log_{10}(\log_{10}x) = 10$, or $\log_{10}x = 100$. Thus $x = 10^{100}$, and $k = 100$

3. We could write out the expansion of each binomial and collect terms. But the solution proceeds more neatly if we set $A = (2 + \log_{10}x)$ and $B = (-1 + \log_{10}x)$, then note that $1 + \log_{10}x^2 = 1 + 2\log_{10}x = A + B$. The equation then takes the form $A^3 + B^3 = (A + B)^3$, and expanding the right hand side leads to $A^2B + AB^2 = AB\,(A + B) = 0$. This means that $A = 0$ or $B = 0$, which leads to $x = .01, 10,$ or $1/\sqrt{10}$.

4. We can write $\log_{10}(1/2) + \log_{10}(2/3) + \log_{10}(3/4) + \dots + \log_{10}(n/(n + 1)) + \dots + \log_{10}(99/100) = (\log_{10}1 - \log_{10}2) + (\log_{10}2 - \log_{10}3) + (\log_{10}3 - \log_{10}4) + \dots + (\log_{10}n - \log_{10}(n + 1)) + \dots + (\log_{10}99 - \log_{10}100)$.

   This sum "telescopes" (most of the adjacent terms cancel each other out), and we are left with $\log_{10}1 - \log_{10}100 = 0 - 2 = -2$.

5. Using the "chain rule" (or otherwise), we can write $\log_9 4 = (\log_9 3)(\log_3 4) = (1/2)(\log_3 4)$. Hence $(\log_2 3)(\log_9 4) = (\log_2 3)(\log_3 4)(1/2) = (\log_2 4)(1/2) = 1$

6. Using the "chain rule," we can write $\log_9 x = 2\log_3 x$, and $\log_{81}x = 4\log_3 x$. Hence the give equation can be written as $7\log_3 x = 7$, and $x = 3$.

7. In the "chain rule," set $a = c$. Then we find that $(\log_a b)(\log_b a) = \log_a a = 1$, so $\log_a b = (1/(\log_b a))$.

8. If we set $A = \log_4 x$, we can rewrite this equation as $A + (1/A) = 17/4$. This can be solved as a quadratic equation or by inspection by noting that $17/4 = 4 + (1/4)$, so $A = 4$ or $1/4$ (because the equation is quadratic, these are the only possible roots). Then $x = 1$ or -1.

9. We have $\log_7 9 = 2\log_7 3 = 2\,(\log_7 10)(\log_{10}3) = 2\,(1/(\log_{10}7))(\log_{10}3) = (2a)/b$.

10. If we set $A = \log_{10}x$, $B = \log_{10}y$, then $\log_{10}xy = A + B$. Then the given equation can be written as $\log_{10}(A + B) = \log_{10}A + \log_{10}B$, or $A + B = AB$. Then $B = A/(A - 1)$. For integer solutions, we need $A - 1$ to divide A, so $A = B = 2$ or $A = B = 0$. The latter leads to no solution for (x, y), while the former gives $(x, y) = (100, 100)$.

REFERENCES

Matthews, Marian. "Gifted Students Talk About Cooperative Learning." *Educational Leadership* 50, no. 2 (October 1992): 48–50.

Polya, George. *How to Solve It.* Garden City, N.Y.: Doubleday and Company, 1957,

———. *Mathematical Discovery* (2 vols.). New York: John Wiley and Sons, 1962.

———. *Mathematics and Plausible Reasoning.* Vol. 1, *Induction and Analogy in Mathematics.* Vol. 2, *Patterns of Plausible Inference.* Princeton, N.J.: Princeton University Press, 1954.

Schoenfeld, Alan. *Mathematical Problem Solving.* New York: Academic Press, 1985.

———. *Cognitive Science and Mathematics Education.* Hillsdale, N.J.: Lawrence Erlbaum Associates, 1987.

Slavin, Robert E. "Ability Grouping, Cooperative Learning and the Gifted." *Journal for the Education of the Gifted* 14, no. 3 (Fall 1990): 3–8.

———. "Are Cooperative Learning and 'Untracking' Harmful to the Gifted?" *Educational Leadership* 48, no. 6 (March 1991): 68–71.

Sowell, Evelyn J., et al. "Identification and Description of Mathematically Gifted Students: A Review of Empirical Research." *Gifted Child Quarterly* 34, no. 4 (Fall 1990): 147–54.

Stanley, Julian C. "Identifying and Nurturing the Intellectually Gifted" In *Educating the Gifted: Acceleration and Enrichment,* edited by William C. George, Sanford J. Cohn, and Julian C. Stanley. Baltimore: Johns Hopkins University Press, 1979.

Wickelgren, Wayne A. *How to Solve Problems.* San Francisco: W. H. Freeman and Company, 1974.

Chapter 8

HELPING STUDENTS SEE THE WORLD MATHEMATICALLY

Solomon Garfunkel
Gary Froelich

I am so glad to have taken this course. I feel as though I have learned more than my friends in other math courses. They have math class for an hour a day. I have math class 24 hours a day because I have learned to see math in every real life situation.

—A student in the third year of
a modeling-based curriculum

The National Council of Teachers of Mathematics Task Force on Promising Students believes that promising students are those "who have the potential to become leaders and problem solvers of the future." Moreover, among promising students there are those "who have been traditionally excluded from previous definitions of gifted and talented, and therefore excluded from rich mathematical opportunities" (NCTM 1995).

The authors of this chapter have worked for many years, particularly at the secondary and undergraduate level, to extend the appeal of mathematics to larger groups of students by portraying the subject in the light of its contemporary applications. In this chapter, we describe how applications can encourage an interest in mathematics among more students.

The authors believe that a major failing of experiences traditionally offered to talented mathematics students is that they do not engage a sufficiently large group of promising students. For example, very few students are willing to explore the problem of determining the number of 7s in 99^{21} beyond getting a right answer, if that far. Although this problem is certainly useful in identifying prospective number theorists, it and other problems of a purely mathematical nature require a level of abstraction that may turn off some students.

Good mathematical experiences must ensure that the "leaders and problem solvers of the future" appreciate the importance of mathematics in their world. Finding and nurturing promising students should not be confused with a search for the next Gauss: The leaders and problem solvers of the future will not all be professional mathematicians.

The authors believe that good mathematical experiences have one or more of the following characteristics:

1. They are engaging. They attract and challenge students.

2. They are accessible at different levels to students with varying degrees of mathematical experience, and they are amenable to several approaches.

3. They are extendible. They provide an experience that may last a few hours, a few days, or even a few months or years.

Although good experiences need not possess all three characteristics, the first is essential (although somewhat subjective). A problem that fails to engage students is not one that students are interested in solving in more than one way or extending to other situations.

Consider an example of a problem that has all three characteristics. The following is one of two problems that appeared on the 1989 Mathematical Contest in Modeling (MCM). Although the MCM is an undergraduate competition, many of its problems, including this one, have been used successfully in high school classrooms.

In 1981, two new varieties of a small biting insect called a midge were discovered in Brazil. W. L. Grogan and W. W. Wirth, the discoverers, called one an Apf midge and the other an Af midge. The latter is harmless and a valuable pollinator, but the former carries a debilitating disease that affects humans. In an effort to distinguish the two varieties, Grogan and Wirth took measurements of wing and antenna length from several individuals of each variety (table 8.1). Is it possible to use these data to distinguish between the two varieties?

Table 8.1

Af									
Wing length (cm)	1.72	1.64	1.74	1.70	1.82	1.82	1.90	1.82	2.08
Antenna length (cm)	1.24	1.38	1.36	1.40	1.38	1.48	1.38	1.54	1.56
Apf									
Wing length (cm)	1.78	1.86	1.96	2.00	2.00	1.96			
Antenna length (cm)	1.14	1.20	1.30	1.26	1.28	1.18			

The problem engages some students because it is a real-world problem whose solution has consequences for health and agriculture. Teague and Compton (1995) have found that students of differing mathematical backgrounds can produce good solutions. The problem is extendible because there isn't a single right answer—it can be revisited as students gain mathematical sophistication. Indeed, a desire to solve the problem can motivate students to learn new mathematics. Moreover, the problem can be extended to other kinds of classification questions.

Students often begin this problem by using technology to produce a scatter plot (fig. 8.1). How can the two groups of points be divided? Many students fit either a least-squares or median-median line to each set of data. Figure 8.2 shows the calculator-generated least squares lines $y = 0.479x + 0.549$ and $y = 0.588x + 0.151$. Can these two lines be used to establish a single boundary? Should the lines be weighted equally? Students produce a variety of arguments. Some, for example, argue that the boundary line should be drawn closer to the Af line because it is better to kill a harmless midge than to allow a dangerous one to escape. Others argue that the two lines should not be weighted equally because the samples are of different sizes. Students with a sufficient background in statistics can conclude that the difference in sample sizes is insufficient evidence of a difference in population sizes. They can also determine a boundary line so that a midge on the line has the same probability of coming from either group (Teague and Compton 1995).

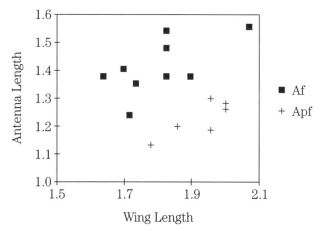

Fig. 8.1. Midge measurements

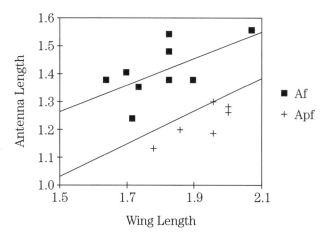

Fig. 8.2. Least square lines

The contest from which the previous problem is taken demonstrates the impact this type of problem can have. The MCM, which had 393 teams from 225 schools in 1996, receives outstanding entries from a diverse group of institutions. (Among schools recognized in the 1996 contest are Abilene Christian University, Bellarmine College, Eastern Mennonite University, Gettysburg College, Kenyon College, Lewis and Clark College, Luther College, Mount St. Mary's College, Rhodes College, Pomona College, Trinity University, University of Northern Iowa, and Youngstown State University.) Over the years the contest has not been dominated by a few institutions, and schools that enter more than one team often find that the best solution does not come from the team the school administrators feel is the most mathematically talented.

A question that naturally arises is, "How does one find problems that are engaging, accessible, and extendible?" One way is by being observant: such problems can be found in or adapted from common events.

For example, Daniels (1993), a high school mathematics teacher in Massachusetts, describes a conversation with a baseball coach that led to an excellent problem. The coach planned to put a fence around a baseball field's outfield at a distance of 325 feet from home plate down each base line and 400 feet to center field. The coach wanted to know the length of the fence. That the problem is engaging is demonstrated by the fact that it so intrigued Daniels' students that they produced a total of ten different solutions. It is accessible in part because there is no single right answer: there are quite a few ways to connect the three points. Finally, the problem is extendible because students can revisit it as their mathematical experience grows. For example, students who draw scale models and measure a fence drawn with a series of line segments can return to the problem to fit a parabola when they study data analysis or quadratic functions.

The news media are a source of situations that can produce good problems. For example, during the war in the Persian Gulf, news reports about high-tech weapons used by the United States were common. One report (Budiansky, Auster, and Cary 1991) discussed a form of radar that allowed U.S. forces to accurately return enemy artillery fire before it hit the ground. How can the source of artillery fire be determined quickly from information about a portion of an artillery shell's path? How can the location of the source be used to accurately aim return fire (Froelich 1991, 1994)?

Some publications are sources of problems suitable for promising students. Occasionally articles with such problems appear in *Mathematics Teacher*. Helen Compton and Daniel Teague, who teach at the North Carolina School of Science and Mathematics, write the column "Everybody's Problems," which appears quarterly in *Consortium*. Often their column features an engaging real-world problem and several different solutions produced by their students.

The previously mentioned Mathematical Contest in Modeling is also a source of problems, but the problems are designed with college undergraduates in mind. At this writing the Consortium for Mathematics and Its Applications (COMAP), which developed and runs the MCM, is planning a high school modeling competition.

The National Science Foundation (NSF) has funded curriculum projects at the primary, middle, and high school levels that have student engagement as a goal. (See the appendix to this chapter.) Good problems are sprinkled throughout the materials these projects are producing. They can be found in daily lessons, in assessments, and in projects. In some cases, a single problem serves as the basis for an entire unit. For example, the question "What is the best location for a fire station?" is the basis for a unit in the ARISE project. The problem is used as a springboard for the development of concepts of distance and absolute value.

Agreement on the meaning of *best* is essential to any mathematical approach to the fire station problem. For example, is the best location one that minimizes the average distance the fire truck must travel or one that minimizes the greatest distance the truck must travel? Why? The problem engages students, and it permits them to discuss and make important decisions about an issue that has consequences for everyone.

At its most basic, the fire station problem is accessible to students whose background includes nothing more than familiarity with a number line. These students can experiment with a simple community with one street and only a few houses, build tables of data, and draw conclusions. More sophisticated students can plot the data, write functions to model it, and extend their conclusions to two dimensions. One student gathered data for a one-dimensional village with three, four, five, six, seven, or eight houses, plotted the data, and modeled the data with absolute value functions.

What is the best way to package soda cans? What is the best way to handicap Special Olympics events when participants have varying kinds of disabilities? What are the best guidelines for military instructors to determine excessive exposure of trainees to severe climate conditions? What is the best way to rate mountain trails so that hikers can judge the severity of ascent or descent? How should a building's elevators be scheduled to best serve passengers? The world is replete with situations that teachers have turned into problems for which students have developed interesting, unusual, and often pleasantly surprising mathematical approaches.

Teachers who are otherwise sympathetic to the use of applications sometimes express reservations because of concerns about classroom implementation or because of other priorities. Implementation concerns can derive from a lack of confidence in one's own abilities that diminishes with experience. Devising a few simple problems is often a good first step. Look for situations in which *best* can be defined quantitatively. For example, the best way to package soft drinks might mean maximizing the percentage of package or shelf space used by the cans—or it might mean minimizing the amount of packaging used. Next, look for factors that might influence the criteria used to define *best*. For example, does the rectangular arrangement in figure 8.3 use space more efficiently than the triangular arrangement in figure 8.4? Does the number of cans in the package affect the way packaging material is used? Experiment. Gather data on, for example, the number of cans in a package and the amount of packaging material per can. What conclusions can be drawn from the data?

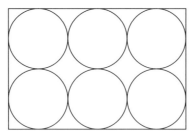

Fig. 8.3

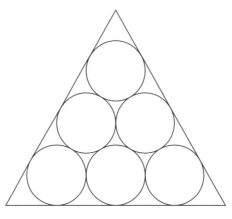

Fig. 8.4

Implementation concerns can also focus on students. The old paradigm held that students must master mathematical skills in a vacuum before they can apply mathematics to real-world problems and that, therefore, only mathematically adept students can tackle applications. The previously mentioned NSF-funded curriculum projects are showing that the truth is very different; all students can learn new mathematics in a contextual setting. Technology deserves partial credit for enabling the paradigm shift. When students have created a mathematical model, they can choose from several solution methods, such as creating tables with a spreadsheet or calculator, creating a graph on a graphing calculator, constructing a figure with a geometric drawing tool, or using symbol manipulation. No longer is there only one option.

The issue of priorities is resolved if one understands society's changing demands. Mathematical modeling of real-world situations often involves working in teams to solve unfamiliar problems and preparing written or oral reports in defense of one's solutions—skills that several studies have deemed critical. (See, for example, Murnane and Levy 1996.) Moreover, these are skills that can and should be developed in mathematics classes. As one student described her experience in a modeling-based course, "Leadership qualities I never knew I had are coming out: working with others, expressing my ideas, and developing the need to succeed."

For more than a decade, our society has documented its need for more and better problem solvers. (See for example, the Mathematical Sciences Education Board [1989].) That need cannot be met unless schools recognize and nurture mathematically promising students. Mathematical experiences that engage students and provide them with the opportunity to experience the power of mathematics in solving important problems are a significant tool for identifying promising students and helping them "see the world through math-colored glasses"—a giant step on the road to becoming the leaders and problem solvers of the future.

APPENDIX

NSF-Funded Curriculum Projects

Primary School Level

Cooperative Mathematics Project, Developmental Studies Center, 2000 Embarcadero, Suite 305, Oakland, CA 94606. Published by Addison Wesley Innovative Learning.

Investigations in Number, Data, and Space. TERC, 2067 Massachusetts Ave., Cambridge, MA 02140. Published by Dale Seymour/Cuisenaire.

TIMSS. University of Illinois at Chicago, 950 South Halsted, M/C 250, Room 2075 SEL, Chicago, IL 60607. Published by Kendall/Hunt.

University of Chicago School Mathematics Project. University of Chicago, 5835 South Kimbark Ave., Chicago, IL 60637. Published by Everyday Learning.

Middle School Level

Mathematics in Context. Wisconsin Center for Education Research. 1025 W. Johnson St., Madison, WI 53706. Published by Encyclopaedia Britannica.

Middle School Mathematics through Applications Project. Institute for Research on Learning, 66 Willow Pl., Menlo Park, CA 94025.

Seeing and Thinking Mathematically. Education Development Center, 55 Chapel St., Newton, MA 02158. Published by Creative Publications.

Connected Mathematics Project. 101 Wills House, Michigan State University, East Lansing, MI 48824. Published by Dale Seymour Publications.

Six Through Eight Mathematics (STEM). Department of Mathematical Sciences, University of Montana, Missoula, MT 59812. Published by McDougal/Littell/Houghton Mifflin.

High School Level

Application Reform in Secondary Education (ARISE). COMAP, 57 Bedford St., Suite 210, Lexington, MA 02173. Published by South-Western under the title *Mathematics: Modeling Our World.*

Connected Geometry. Education Development Center, 55 Chapel St., Newton, MA 02158-1060.

Core-Plus Mathematics Project. Department of Mathematics and Statistics, Western Michigan University, Kalamazoo, MI 49008. Published by Janson/Everyday Learning.

Interactive Mathematics Program. 6400 Hollis St., Suite 5, Emeryville, CA 94608. Published by Key Curriculum Press.

Math Connections. 370 Asylum Street, Hartford, CT 06103-2022. Published by It's About Time, Inc.

Systemic Initiative for Montana Mathematics and Science (SIMMS). Department of Mathematical Sciences, University of Montana, Missoula, MT 59812. Published by Simon and Schuster.

University of Chicago School Mathematics Project. Department of Education, University of Chicago, 5835 South Kimbark, Chicago, IL 60637. Published by Scott Foresman–Addison Wesley.

REFERENCES

Budiansky, Stephen, Bruce B. Auster, and Peter Cary. "Preparing the Ground." *U.S. News & World Report* (4 February 1991): 32–34, 39–41.

Daniels, David S. "Gary O's Fence Question." *Mathematics Teacher* 86 (March 1993): 252–54.

Froelich, Gary. "The Victory Arc." *Consortium* 38 (Summer 1991): 4–5.

———, ed. *Consortium's Technology in the Classroom.* Lexington, Mass.: COMAP, 1994.

Mathematical Contest in Modeling. Lexington, Mass.: COMAP, 1989.

Mathematical Sciences Education Board. *Everybody Counts.* Washington, D.C.: National Academy Press, 1989.

Murnane, Richard J., and Frank Levy. *Teaching the New Basic Skills.* New York: Free Press, 1996.

National Council of Teachers of Mathematics. "Report of the NCTM Task Force on the Mathematically Promising." *NCTM News Bulletin* 32 (December 1995): Special insert.

Teague, Daniel, and Helen Compton. "The Midge Problem." *Consortium* 55 (Fall 1995): 8–9, 12.

Chapter 9

THE OPEN APPROACH TO TEACHING MATHEMATICS— CREATING A CULTURE OF MATHEMATICS IN THE CLASSROOM: JAPAN

Yoshihiko Hashimoto

Jerry Becker

> What *we teach, and* how *students experience it, are the primary factors that shape students' understanding of what mathematics is about.*
>
> —NCTM *Curriculum and Evaluation Standards*

Traditionally it has been common for students in their mathematical studies to encounter problems that have only one unique answer that is determined in only one way. From these experiences, students come to hold beliefs that all problems have exactly one correct answer that is determined in exactly one way. This is especially detrimental to promising students.

In the Japanese open approach to teaching, mathematical problems are selected that exemplify a diversity of approaches to solving a problem (the process is open) or multiple correct answers (the end products are open). There is also emphasis on having students formulate new problems (ways to create problems are open). Student responses to these problems, called *students' productions,* are then used by the teacher to give students experiences in learning something new by combining their previous knowledge, skills, and mathematical ways of thinking with their new experiences. This is related to the idea of *matheracy* defined by Kawaguchi (1984).

In this article, the Japanese open approach to mathematics is explored. We first give examples of the types of problems used in this approach. We then discuss possibilities for how the teacher can develop lesson plans and classroom activities. After presenting some ideas for assessment of problems, student work, and lesson plans, we show a sample lesson.

The authors express their appreciation to Linda Sheffield and Eugene Smith for their constructive reactions to an earlier draft of this paper.

EXAMPLES OF OPEN PROBLEMS

Steen (1989) has commented that too often mathematics is judged "dull" by students, even good students, because teachers, textbooks, and tests insist that each problem must be solved by one proper method yielding a single correct answer. The Japanese open approach speaks directly to this concern. In our experience, the approach offers opportunities for especially bright students to exercise their creative abilities and devise insightful ways to deal with mathematical topics and problems. Three aspects of the approach are presented below: open process, open end product, and open problem formulation.

The Process Is Open

To create interest and stimulate creative mathematical activity in the classroom, the Japanese developed a tradition in teaching to focus on the different ways of solving a problem when the answer is unique—here we say the *process is open*. At all grade levels, it is possible to have students put their own natural mathematical thinking abilities to use in approaching a problem. In doing so, students will exhibit a variety of approaches, and these can be shared and discussed in class. Some examples of these problems are given below, with anticipated or actual responses of students.

Example 1. (Elementary)

How many chocolates are there in the box?

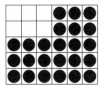

(1) Counting one by one, so 24
(2) Grouping by threes, so $8 \times 3 = 24$

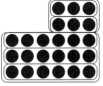

(5) $2 \times 3 + 3 \times 6 = 24$

(3) $5 \times 6 - 6 = 24$

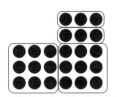

(6) $2 \times 9 + 2 \times 3 = 24$

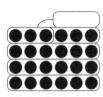

(4) $4 \times 6 = 24$

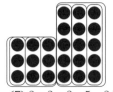

(7) $3 \times 3 + 3 \times 5 = 24$

Example 2. (Elementary)

Which is larger: 4/5 or 3/4 ?

(1)

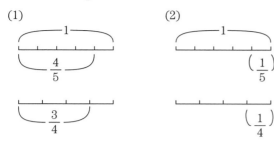

(2)

$$\left(\frac{1}{5}\right)$$

$$\left(\frac{1}{4}\right)$$

(3)
$$\left.\begin{array}{l}\dfrac{4}{5} = 4 \div 5 = 0.8 \\[2mm] \dfrac{3}{4} = 3 \div 4 = 0.75\end{array}\right\}\ 0.8 > 0.75$$

(4)
$$\left.\begin{array}{l}\dfrac{4}{5} = \dfrac{8}{10} = \dfrac{⑫}{15}\ \cdots \\[2mm] \dfrac{3}{4} = \dfrac{6}{8} = \dfrac{9}{12} = \dfrac{⑫}{16}\ \cdots\end{array}\right\}\ \dfrac{4}{5} > \dfrac{3}{4}$$

(5)
$$\left.\begin{array}{l}\dfrac{4}{5} = \dfrac{8}{10} = \dfrac{12}{15} = \dfrac{16}{⑳}\ \cdots \\[2mm] \dfrac{3}{4} = \dfrac{6}{8} = \dfrac{9}{12} = \dfrac{12}{16} = \dfrac{15}{⑳}\ \cdots\end{array}\right\}\ \dfrac{4}{5} > \dfrac{3}{4}$$

Example 3. (Junior High)

In the figure below, how many degrees are in angle *ABC*? (Horizontal lines are parallel.)

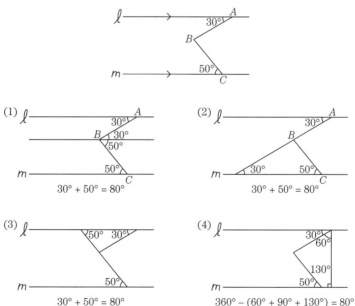

(1) $30° + 50° = 80°$

(2) $30° + 50° = 80°$

(3) $30° + 50° = 80°$

(4) $360° - (60° + 90° + 130°) = 80°$

Example 4. (Senior High)

Given a circle with no center indicated, determine the center of the circle.

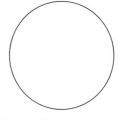

1. Fold the paper twice to get two intersecting diameters of the circle. Use a right-angle ("carpenter's") square to make two inscribed right angles (each in a semicircle)—the lines connecting the endpoints of the two pairs of legs that intersect at the center.

2. Draw a chord (not a diameter) and make perpendiculars at the endpoint; then connect the points of intersection of the perpendiculars with the circle to the opposite vertices—they intersect at the center.

3. Circumscribe an equilateral triangle about the circle; then connect the points of tangency to the opposite vertices—they intersect at the center

4. Draw two chords and construct their perpendicular bisectors—they intersect at the center.

For each problem above, several approaches to finding the answer are given. (There may be others.) The different student responses can be compared and discussed in terms of their mathematical features and their qualitative differences. Students are exposed to the variety of thinking and approaches emanating from their peers. Promising students can use peer responses as a springboard to explore each problem in even greater depth.

The End Products Are Open

Traditionally, problems are so well formulated that answers are either correct or incorrect (including incomplete ones). We regard such problems as "closed" or "complete" problems. In contrast, problems that are formulated to have multiple correct answers are "incomplete," "open end," or "open-ended" (Shimada 1977; Becker and Shimada 1997). Such problems involve students finding one, several, or many correct answers to one problem, and they may use various methods to finding those answers.

The Japanese use three types of problems when the end products are open: finding rules or relations, classifying, and measuring. Some examples follow.

Finding Rules or Relations (Middle School)

Example 5. Baseball Standings Problem (Intermediate or Middle School)

The following table shows the records of five baseball teams (A, B, C, D, and E). Among the numbers in this table, there are certain or rules or relations. Find as many of these as you can and write them down.

Team	Games	Wins	Losses	Draws	Ratio	Behind
A	25	16	7	2	0.696	—
B	21	11	8	2	0.579	3.0
C	22	9	9	4	0.500	1.5
D	22	8	13	1	0.381	2.5
E	22	6	13	3	0.316	1.0

The context of the problem above can be seen in newspapers in Japan and is familiar to students. Also, students know that baseball games can end in a draw or tie in Japan.

Many relations can be observed in the table. Some are given below.

1. The additive relation among the number of games, wins, losses, and draws: (Number of games) = (number of wins) + (number of losses) + (number of draws)

2. The multiplicative relation among the winning ratio, number of wins, and number of losses: (Winning ratio) = (number of wins) ÷ [(number of games) − (number of draws)]

3. The relation between the numbers of wins and losses of two teams determines the number of games behind (e.g., for teams C and D: difference in wins is 1; difference in losses is 4; so, (1 + 4)/2 = 2.5 and D is 2.5 games behind C).

4. The total number of games is even.

5. The total number of wins is equal to the total number of losses.

As mentioned, the purpose of this problem is to have students find as many rules or relations as possible from several points of view. The rules may range from lower to higher levels; for example, rule 1 may be easier than the others to find, whereas others may be more difficult since they involve somewhat more complicated processes.

Classifying (Middle School and Senior High)

Example 6. Classifying Problem (Space)
There are several solid figures as follows:

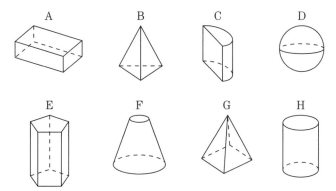

Choose the figure(s) that share(s) the same characteristic(s) with figure B and write down the characteristic(s). Next, choose the figure(s) that share(s) the same characteristic(s) with figure H and write down the characteristic(s).

An expected response with respect to figure B is G: (1) is a pyramid; (2) has triangular faces; (3) the view from the side is a triangle; (4) all faces are polygons; (5) the cross section parallel to the base is similar to, but not congruent to, the base.

Measuring (Intermediate and Middle School)

Example 7. Marble Problem

Three students, A, B, and C, throw five marbles that come to rest as in the figures above. In this game, the student with the smallest scatter of marbles is the winner. To determine the winner, we will need to have some numerical way of measuring the scatter of the marbles.

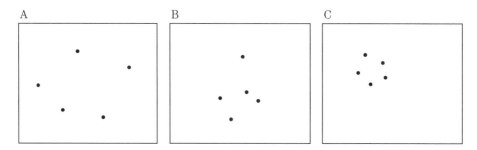

A   B   C

(a) Think about this situation from various points of view and write down different ways of indicating the degree of scattering.

(b) Which way appeals to you?

In the problem above, the students have to quantify the degree of scattering. Generally, no unique working interpretation has been devised for two-dimensional scatterings, so several ways of quantification are possible according to the variety of students' points of view. The problem can be used in both the elementary and secondary schools. Students may discover the following methods for measuring the scattering:

1. Measure the area of the polygonal figures formed by joining the points.

2. Measure the perimeter of the polygonal figures formed by joining the points.

3. Measure the length of the longest segment connecting two points.

4. Add the lengths of all segments connecting two points.

5. Add the lengths of the segments connecting one fixed point with all other points.

6. Measure the radius of the smallest circle that includes all points.

7. Calculate the standard or average deviation using a coordinate system.

Each method has advantages and disadvantages. When the problem is posed, some students may make a polygonal figure by connecting points and then trying to find its area. Other students, however, may question this approach because, for example, if all points are on a straight line, such an approach will lead to difficulty. In this case, it is important for the teacher to help students to see both the advantages and disadvantages in generalizing about the proposed method of measuring. Overall, bright students are able to devise unconventional ways to view problem situations; thus, they provide opportunities for all students to see these ways.

The Ways of Formulating Problems Are Open

Students may formulate or pose new mathematical problems from a given problem by using generalization, analogy, or the idea of converse (or other ideas), and then solve the newly formulated problems by themselves (Sawada et al. 1980; Hashimoto and Sakai 1983). When first encountered, problem formulation or posing is novel to almost all students. Below we give some examples of original problems and possible or actual problems that students may formulate from them.

Example 8. (Primary)

There are four butterflies. If three more butterflies arrive, how many are there altogether?

1. Children may only change the number of butterflies.

2. Children change the objects.

3. Children change the addition problem to a subtraction problem.

> Example: There are seven butterflies on the tulips. If four butterflies flew away, how many are left on the tulips?

Example 9. (Intermediate or Junior High) (Hashimoto 1987)

Toothpicks are placed to make squares as in the figure below. When the number of squares is five, how many toothpicks are used?

To formulate problems,

1. Change the number of squares.

2. Change the number of rows of squares.

3. Change the figure (e.g., from a square to triangles, pentagons, etc.).

4. Write the converse problem.

5. Change from two to three dimensions.

6. Change a combination of the above.

Example 10. (Senior High)

There are two points A and B on a plane. What is the locus of point P that satisfies the condition $AP = BP$?

1. Change the plane to a line or to space.

2. Change the number of points from two to three.

3. Change $AP = BP$ to $AP : BP = m : n$ or to $AP + BP =$ constant.

4. Change point P to a line.

5. Change a combination of conditions.

DEVELOPING LESSON PLANS AND CREATING CLASSROOM ACTIVITIES

Developing a Lesson Plan

In this article, we share the approach that Japanese mathematics teachers and researchers, working collaboratively, have developed since 1971. We call it the open approach—the results of the research are presented in Shimada (1977), Becker and Shimada (1997), Takeuchi and Sawada (1985), and Becker, Takeuchi, and Sawada (in preparation).

The Japanese organized lesson plans according to the following scheme:

1. *Introducing the Problem or Topic*
   The teacher presents or poses a problem (pertaining to a preselected objective) on the overhead projector, chalkboard, or poster.

2. *Understanding the Problem*
   The teacher ensures through speaking and soliciting questions that students know what is expected of them before they begin work.

3. *Problem Solving by the Students*
   Students are given a worksheet with the problem written on it and space to write their work. They work individually or in small groups. Students' natural ways of thinking are encouraged, thereby "drawing out" a variety of responses. The teacher moves among the students, purposefully scanning their work and selecting thinking approaches or answers pertaining to the objective that will be discussed with the whole class.

4. *Comparing and Discussing*
   Individual students (or groups) write their approaches or answers on the blackboard (or overhead projector) for all students to see. The teacher then guides a comparison and discussion of the responses according to their mathematical features and quality.

5. *Summary of the Lesson*
   The teacher plays an important, crucial role in pulling together the outcomes of the discussion and lesson as they relate to the lesson's objective. (Becker et al. 1990; Hashimoto 1987; Miwa 1992; Sugiyama 1989; Nohda 1984; Shimada 1977).

Typically, in Japan, the lesson is developed around one single objective. The main role of the teacher is to *guide* learning and not to "dispense knowledge." Students are expected to express their ideas, sometimes in a lengthy manner, and the teacher's wait time is crucially important (Stigler 1988). Toward the end of the lesson, the teacher pulls together students' ways of thinking, highlights their mathematical quality, and then summarizes or polishes up the lesson. Discussion (whole class or small groups) among students or between the teacher and students is extensive and is a prominent factor in achieving the objective of the lesson (Becker et al. 1989; Stigler 1988; Stigler and Stevenson 1991; Miwa 1992).

In developing a lesson plan, then, the following points are addressed:

- Students' expected responses are listed and grouped by their mathematical features.
- The purpose of the problem is made clear.
- Students are helped to understand the problem and what is expected of them.
- Students are given time to fully explore and discuss the problem.
- Students record their responses on a worksheet or in their notebooks.
- Certain students write their work on the chalkboard for all to see.
- Students' work is compared and discussed.
- The teacher summarizes the learning in the lesson.

The philosophy and reality of lesson plans in this approach are considerably different from those in the United States. For example, in Japan, as part of the lesson plan, all the anticipated responses of the students to the problem are written down in detail by teachers when they develop the lesson plan. There are several reasons for this: (1) They are used as part of the assessment approach; (2) this helps the teacher to understand the problem and its answers or solution methods; and (3) the teacher is able to understand the students' thinking and anticipate and deal with students' responses, questions, and viewpoints.

Creating Problems and Classroom Activities

It is challenging to find and select appropriate problem situations around which a lesson plan can be developed at the various grade levels. However, by trial and error and sharing, Japanese researchers and classroom teachers have worked collaboratively to derive some guidelines for creating problems. (See Shimada [1977] and Becker and Shimada [1997], for examples.)

1. Choose a physical situation that involves variable quantities in which mathematical relations can be observed.

   Example: Observe a tape recorder that is playing. Observe what is happening to see if, for example, there is a variable quantity that involves a mathematical relation (e.g., time and width or radius of the spool).

2. In geometry, instead of asking students to prove a proposition such as "If P, then Q," change the problem to "If P, then what relationships can be found?"

   Example: Given a rectangle with its diagonals drawn in, what relations can you find?

3. Show students geometric figures concerning a theorem in geometry, then have them draw other figures like the given one. Then ask them to make conjectures.

   Example: Look at the two figures below. Then draw another figure with the same relations. Can you make a conjecture about the line segments labeled ">" in each figure?

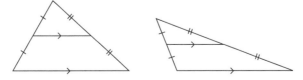

4. Show students a table of numbers and ask them to search for some mathematical patterns or rules.

Example: Find different number patterns in the table below:

1	2	3	4
2	4	6	8
3	6	9	12
4	8	12	16

5. Ask students to find a common feature(s) in different figures.

Example: Look at the figures below and identify those that appear to have right angles:

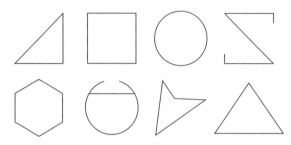

6. Show students several similar exercises or problems. Ask the students to solve them and find properties common to at least two of them.

Example: A. Graph the functions below.

B. Write down as many properties as you can that two or more functions have in common.

(a) $y = \dfrac{2}{5}x$ (b) $y = \dfrac{2}{5}x^2$ (c) $y = \dfrac{2}{5}x^3$

(d) $y = -\dfrac{2}{5}x$ (e) $y = -\dfrac{2}{5}x^2$ (f) $y = -\dfrac{2}{5}x^3$

7. Show students real applications involving variation. Ask students to create methods for interpreting the variation.

Example: Several students rank their preference for the soft drinks Coke, Pepsi, 7-Up, and Sprite. Devise a way to measure or determine the extent to which the students' rankings are in agreement or differ.

8. Show students a concrete example for which an algebraic structure exists (e.g., a group structure) and numerical data are easily collected. Then ask the students to find mathematical rules that seem to be true.

Example: Cut out two paper circles of different sizes. Call them A and B, with the radius of A larger than B. Write 0, 1, 2, 3, 4, on the edge of each circle at equal distances. Fasten the two circles together at their centers so they can be rotated.

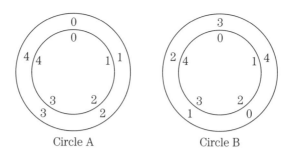

Circle A   Circle B

Now define a new addition, represented by +, such that $x + y$ means rotate the circles so that 0 on A is aligned with x on B. Then find y on A and read the answer on B. To compute 2 + 4, 0 on circle A lines up with 2 on circle B; find 4 on A; the number on B aligned with this is 1. Therefore, 2 + 4 = 1. Similarly, 3 + 2 = 0 and 3 + 4 = 2. What rules seem to be true for this new operation?

The classroom activities are structured to help students to (Shimada 1977; Becker and Shimada 1997)—

- mathematize situations appropriately;
- find mathematical rules or relations by making use of their knowledge and skills;
- solve problems; and
- check the results;

while

- seeing the discoveries and ways of thinking of other students;
- examining, comparing, and discussing the different ideas of students; and
- modifying and further developing students' own ideas accordingly.

APPROACH TO ASSESSMENT

Because an open approach encourages many student productions in the class, especially for bright or highly motivated students, assessment ideas are also numerous and flexible. In this section, we detail assessment of problems, student work, and lesson plans. Again, we outline what the Japanese have done in their development of the open approach.

Assessing Problems

In general, problems, like those above, are assessed from the following perspective before developing a lesson plan:

- Is the problem rich in mathematical content?
- Is the level of mathematics appropriate for the students?
- Are there features that lead to further mathematical development and provide opportunities for bright students to offer original and insightful observations?

Because the heart of the open approach is to appeal to students' natural or mathematical ways of thinking, the problems that are used are *tried out in the classroom* to determine whether or not they work well with students (Nagasaki and Becker 1993; Nagasaki and Hashimoto 1985; Shimada 1977). If not, then they are revised and tried again.

With practice and experience, teachers can become skilled at turning traditional problems into open-ended ones. Here is an example.

Traditional Problem
The sum of three consecutive odd numbers is 177. What are the numbers?

New Problem
When the sum of three consecutive odd numbers is 177, find the numbers in as many ways as you can.

Whereas the first problem statement very probably leads to the answer 57, 59, 61 in a straightforward manner (i.e., $x + (x + 2) + (x + 4) = 177$), the second provides for a wide latitude of approaches:

1. Let x be the first number, then $x + (x + 2) + (x + 4) = 177$.

2. Consider the first three odd numbers: 1, 3, 5. Their sum is 9. For 3, 5, 7, their sum is 15. For 5, 7, 9, their sum is 21. So, a sequence of these sums is 9, 15, 21, 27, 33, ...; this leads to $(177 - 6) \div 3 = n$, where n is the first of the three numbers. So, 57, 59, 61.

3. Choose a number less than half of 177. Then use trial and error to get 57, 59, 61.

4. Let x be the first odd number, then $x + (x + 2) + (x + 4) = 3x + 6$; so $3x + 6 = 177$, and $x = 57$, and the numbers are 57, 59, 61.

5. Find the mean of the three numbers, since one must be two less and one two more than the mean. So, $177 \div 3 = 59$ and the numbers are 57, 59, 61.

6. Let the three numbers be $x - 2, x, x + 2$. The $(x - 2) + x + (x + 2) = 177$; so $3x = 177$ and $x = 59$. So, 57, 59, 61.

7. Systematic trial and error

Guess (x)		$x + 2$		$x + 4$		Sum
41		43		45		129
51		53		55		159
55		57		59		171
So, 57	+	59	+	61	=	177

8. $3 \times 50 = 150$

   $3 \times 60 = 180$

   Therefore the middle number is between 51 and 59. By trial and error, the numbers are 57, 59, 61.

9. The sum of the three odd numbers is 177. Therefore, the sum of the two "included" even numbers must be $2/3 \times 177 = 118$. Now, $177 + 118 = 295$, and $295 \div 5 = 59$. So, the numbers are 57, 59, 61.

10. 177 rounded to the nearest 10 is 180. Now $180 \div 3 = 60$; so, the numbers must be around 60. By trial and error we get 57, 59, 61.

11. Let the three numbers represent the lengths of the sides of a triangle.

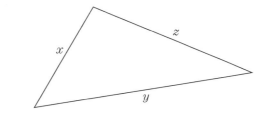

$x + y + z = 177$

$x + 2 = y$

$x + 4 = z$

Solving the equations: $x = 57$, $y = 59$, $z = 61$.

12. Because the sum of the three numbers is 177, the sum of the digits in the units' column of the three numbers is 17. Therefore, the three numbers are 57, 59, 61.

13. Round 177 to 180. Now, $180 - 177 = 3$ and $180 \div 3 = 60$. So, $60 - 3 = 57$ and the numbers are 57, 59, 61.

One way to assess students' learning in the above problem is to classify the different approaches. The richness of the thirteen approaches can then be discussed. For instance here is one categorization:

Name of Category	*Approach Number*
Systematic trial and error	3, 7, 8, 10
Dividing by 3 for finding the mean	5, 13
Patterns	2, 12
Linear equations	1, 4, 6
Simultaneous equations	11
Taking 2/3 of the included numbers	9

Through seeing other students' approaches and through discussion, students can understand the important mathematical features of the different methods; further, motivated students can build on new approaches seen in others' work to deepen their own mathematical development.

Assessing Student Work

Assessing Solutions

Teachers can collect assessment data by examining students' worksheets that are collected at the end of a lesson, by purposeful scanning of students' work while they work on the problem, and by observation during students' discussion of their productions. These observations can be recorded. Thus, during the lesson, the chief means of assessment is by teacher observation; after the lesson, the teacher can examine students' worksheets. The approach is a formative one during and after the lesson, but when the results of the assessment are accumulated over time, they become information for a summative assessment of students.

An assessment scheme that has been used by the Japanese has the following four features.

1. *Fluency.* How many different answers or approaches to finding the answers did the student produce?

   The number of a student's (or group's) correct responses (from a certain point of view) is the measure of fluency of the student's (or group's) mathematical thinking.

2. *Flexibility.* How many different mathematical ideas were discovered by the student?

   After responses are partitioned into several categories according to their mathematical features (as in the previous example), then the number of categories in which a student (or group) has at least one response is a measure of flexibility of the student's mathematical thinking—the larger the number, the greater the flexibility.

3. *Originality.* To what extent are the student's ideas insightful, original, or innovative?

   A student or group that discovers or develops a unique idea is demonstrating originality.

4. *Elegance.* To what extent is the student's (or group's) thinking expressed clearly and succinctly in mathematical notation?

   Elegance is a measure of simplicity and insight in a student's solution. Assessing elegance is a challenge, yet it has potential as part of the assessment of students' learning.

Assessing Problem Formulation

Because formulating problems may at first be difficult for students to learn, assessing students' problem formulations can be challenging for teachers to learn. Before teaching a lesson, teachers often prepare a list of problems that students might formulate. This list is part of the analysis of the problem and helps to organize a discussion of the formulated problems. The student work can be evaluated from considering the following three factors (Nagasaki et al. 1983): the number of problems formulated, how the students formulated their problems, and the different mathematical concepts embedded in the new problems.

For instance, students may formulate new problems by changing a number, changing an object, changing an object and a number, making an analogy, using the converse of the given problem, combining several problems, or even creating problems that don't work. Different types of problem formation demonstrate different types of thinking.

Assessing Lesson Plans

With the open approach, a teacher may not—at least at first—anticipate all that will happen in the classroom. Besides the lesson-plan scheme discussed earlier in the article, other related schemes have been developed. For instance, the following lesson plan outline shows a developmental treatment of problems (also called "from problem to problem") where, instead of a single problem, a sequence of problems is employed to fill an objective (Hashimoto and Sawada 1984; Takeuchi and Sawada 1985):

- Solve the given problem.
- Compare and discuss the methods of, and the solution(s) to, the problem.
- Formulate new problems by changing parts (conditions) of the given problem.
- Propose new problems to the whole class.
- Discuss the new problems and classify them.
- Solve problems selected by the students and teacher.
- Solve problems formulated by the students.

At earlier stages of helping students learn to formulate their own problems, teachers may employ different teaching strategies. However, in the Japanese approach (Takeuchi and Sawada 1985), students solve a stated problem and then compare and discuss their findings (stage 1). Then the teacher can lead the students to change a part (condition) of the problem and thereby formulate a new problem. After this stage, the teacher can then ask students to similarly formulate or pose problems, assisting when necessary by asking students "Which part(s) of the given problem can be changed?" or "Let's change the parts of the given problem that can be changed." Thus, a process unfolds from the original problem P_0 whose solution yields knowledge K_0; then starting from P_0 and K_0, new problems P_1 and P_2 are proposed, and solving them yields new knowledge K_1 and K_2; the process continues. This activity may lead to a deepening of students' understanding of the original problem, to placing the same mathematical theme into a broader problem solution, or to discovering a new mathematical theme (Becker and Selter 1996). It is important to share students' formulated problems with other students, and promising students, especially, can formulate excellent problems for all students to solve.

A SAMPLE LESSON

In the following lesson, credited to Sugiyama (1989), the open approach is demonstrated through an entire lesson plan.

Objective: To teach the strategy that when a problem situation involves two variables, fix the value of one and compare the other.

1. Posing the problem

   Parks Problem

   There are three parks, A, B, and C, in which many boys and girls are playing. The areas of the parks A, B, C are, respectively, 500 m^2, 500 m^2, and 300 m^2. The number of children playing in these parks is, respectively, 40, 30, and 30. Which park is the most crowded?

2. Understanding the problem

Students may think in the following way initially: Park A has an area of 500 m^2 and 40 children; Park B has 500 m^2 and 30 children; Park C has 300 m^2 and 30 children.

Discussion leads to:

A is more crowded than B (equal areas, but A has more children).

C is more crowded than B (same number of children, but C has a smaller area).

Now, which is more crowded, A or C?

3. Problem solving by students

Let students work on the question of which park is most crowded (A or C) using their own mathematical thinking abilities. The teacher selects students' responses (ways of thinking) and asks them to put their solutions on the blackboard. Anticipated responses by students follow:

Solution 1. Park C was more crowded than Park A

Because in Park A (40 ÷ 5 =) 8 children are found in 100 m^2; whereas in Park C (30 ÷ 3 =) 10 children are in the same area.

Solution 2. Park C was more crowded than Park A

Because in 1500 m^2 (40 × 3 =) 120 children are found in Park A; whereas in Park C (30 × 5 =) 150 children are in the same area.

Solution 3. Park C was more crowded than Park A

Because 10 children would have (500 ÷ 4 =) 125 m^2 in Park A; whereas in Park C (300 ÷ 3 =) 100 m^2.

Solution 4. Park C was more crowded than Park A

Because 120 children would have (500 × 3 =) 1500 m^2 in Park A; whereas in Park C (300 × 4 =) 1200 m^2.

Solution 5. Park C was more crowded than Park A

Because a child would have (500 ÷ 40 =) 12.5 m^2 in Park A; whereas in Park C (300 ÷ 30 =) 10 m^2.

4. Comparing and discussing students' solutions

After students have written their solutions on the chalkboard and explained them to the class, ask the students: "Now, what is the common idea that runs through all these solutions?" A student may reply: "In solution 1 and solution 2, the areas are made the same and the numbers of children in the same area are compared; in solutions 3, 4, and 5, the number of children is made the same and the areas are compared." All these solutions make one of the variables have the same value. Therefore, if you have two variables in a problem situation, it is important to fix one of them, and in doing so, you can compare them.

5. Summary of the lesson

The teacher should review and summarize the lesson at the end, with a focus on the main objective.

6. Homework

   Suppose, now, that there is a Park D with area 520 m² and there are forty-seven children in it. Is Park D more crowded than C or A?

   It is expected that students will work on the homework problem on their own. At the beginning of the next class, the teacher will ask for students' results and ways of thinking. Suppose the following homework responses were produced.

   Solution 6:

Park A	Park B	Park C	Park D	[m² for a child]
12.5	16.7	10.0	11.1	

   Solution 7:

Park A	Park B	Park C	Park D	[child in 1 m²]
0.08	0.06	0.10	0.09	

Possible discussion questions could include the following:

• Are decimal fractions appropriate to express the number of children?

• What can be noticed about the numbers in solutions 6 and 7—are both OK?

• Which solution do you think is best? Why?

According to Sugiyama, the president of the Japan Society of Mathematical Education, "When you find the answer to a problem, then mathematics begins. Also, teaching mathematics is a big job!"

CONCLUSION

To foster students' mathematical thinking, it is crucially important to allow them to think freely—that is, to use their own mathematical ways of thinking. This is at the heart of the open approach. Although Japanese mathematics lessons involve whole-class instruction, it can be seen that mathematics teachers indeed address individual students' activities or needs. In particular, opportunities are provided for students with great mathematical potential to exercise their creative abilities and share their insights with other students.

Even if a problem has only one solution, there may be several ways to find the solution. Indeed, this is often the starting point to developing students' different ways of thinking. In addition to using several ways to solve a problem with a unique answer, the open approach employs problems that have different correct solutions and allows students to formulate or pose problems of their own. Lesson plans are geared toward exploring these open problems, and the observation of students during lessons and analyses of students' worksheets after the lessons are important vehicles for carrying out the assessment of students' learning.

The open approach to teaching mathematics is clearly related to the priorities given in The National Research Council's *Everybody Counts* (1989), NCTM's *Curriculum and Evaluation Standards for School Mathematics* (1989), and

NCTM's *Professional Standards for Teaching Mathematics* (1991). The open approach places students at the heart of the problem-solving process and has them *doing* mathematics and thinking mathematically. Using the open approach to teaching both standard curriculum content and other more nonroutine problems has potential for both significantly developing students' mathematical thinking abilities and changing both students' and teachers' beliefs about mathematics. It also fosters reasoning, communication, and making connections in mathematics. As such, we believe that it helps to engender many aspects of mathematical culture in the classroom and to challenge the creative thinking of bright, highly motivated students at all grade levels.

REFERENCES

Becker, Jerry P., and Shigeru Shimada, eds. *The Open-Ended Approach: A New Proposal for Teaching Mathematics.* Translated from the 1977 Japanese version by Shigeru Shimada and Shigeo Yoshikawa. Reston, Va.: National Council of Teachers of Mathematics, 1997.

Becker, Jerry P., and Christoph Selter. "Elementary School Practices". In *International Handbook of Mathematics Education,* edited by Alan J. Bishop, Ken Clements, Christine Keitel, Jeremy Kilpatrick and Colette Laborde, pp. 511–564. Dordrecht: Kluwer Academic Publishers, 1996.

Becker, Jerry P., and others. *Mathematics Teaching in Japanese Elementary and Secondary Schools—A Report of the ICTM Japan Mathematics Delegation.* Columbus, Ohio: ERIC/SMEAC Clearinghouse (ED 308 070), 1989. (Also available from the author)

Becker, Jerry P., Edward A. Silver, Mary Grace Kantowski, Kenneth J. Travers, and James W. Wilson. "Some Observations of Mathematics Teaching in Japanese Elementary and Junior High Schools." *Arithmetic Teacher* 38, no. 2 (October 1990): 12–22.

Becker, Jerry P., Y. Takeuchi, and T. Sawada, eds. *From Problem to Problem—Developmental Treatment of Problems.* Translated by Ms. Hiromi Nagata (in preparation).

Hashimoto, Yoshihiko. "Classroom Practice of Problem Solving in Japanese Schools." In *Proceedings of the U.S.–Japan Seminar on Mathematical Problem Solving,* edited by Jerry P. Becker and Tatsuro Miwa, pp. 94–112. Columbus, OH: ERIC/SMEAC Clearinghouse (ED 304 315), 1987.

Hashimoto, Yoshihiko, and Toshio Sawada. "Research on the Mathematics Teaching by the Developmental Treatment of Mathematical Problems." In *Proceedings of the ICMI-JSME Regional Conference on Mathematical Education,* edited by Tadasu Kawaguchi, pp. 309–13. Tokyo: Japan Society of Mathematical Education, 1984.

Hashimoto, Yoshihiko, and Yutaka Sakai. "A Study of the Developmental Approach to Mathematics Problems." *Journal of Japan Society of Mathematical Education* 65, no. 11 (1983): 265–72. (In Japanese)

Kawaguchi, Tadasu. "Evidence for a Pattern of Problem Solving of a 'Matheracy' Type—The Decisive Usefulness of a Programmable Calculator." In *Proceedings of the Problem Solving Group,* edited by Hugh Burkhardt, Susie Groves, Alan Schoenfeld, and Kaye Stacey, pp. 207–14. Nottingham, U.K.: The Shell Centre for Mathematical Education, Nottingham, 1988.

———. "Fundamental Philosophy on Curriculum Making of Mathematical Education." In *Proceedings of ICMI–JSME Regional Conference on Mathematical Education,* edited by Tadasu Kawaguchi, pp. 3–9. Tokyo: Japan Society of Mathematical Education, 1984.

Miwa, Tatsuro. "A Comparative Study on Classroom Practices with a Common Topic between Japan and the U.S." In *Teaching of Mathematical Problem Solving in Japan and U.S.,* edited by Tatsuro Miwa, pp. 135–71. Tokyo: Toyokan Shyuppanshya, 1992. (In Japanese)

Nagasaki, Eizo, and Jerry P. Becker. "Classroom Assessment in Japanese Mathematics Education." In *Assessment in the Mathematics Classroom,* edited by Norman Webb, pp. 40–53. Reston, Va.: National Council of Teachers of Mathematics, 1993.

Nagasaki, Eizo, Kohzo Tsubota, Yohziroh Nakano, and Tatsuichi Tohara. "Research on the Instruction of Developmental Treatment of Mathematical Problems in Grades 3–4." In *Proceedings of the ICMI-JSME Regional Conference on Mathematical Education,* edited by Tadasu Kawaguchi, pp. 166–72. Tokyo: Japan Society of Mathematical Education, 1983.

Nagasaki, Eizo, and Yoshihiko Hashimoto. "Various Problems about Research in Teaching of Developmental Treatment of Mathematical Problems in Grades 1–12." In *Using Research in the Professional Life of Mathematics Teachers—ICME 5,* edited by Thomas Romberg, pp. 172–85. Madison, Wis.: Wisconsin Center For Educational Research, 1985.

National Council of Teachers of Mathematics. *Curriculum and Evaluation Standards for School Mathematics.* Reston, Va.: National Council of Teachers of Mathematics, 1989.

———. *Professional Standards for Teaching Mathematics.* Reston, Va.: National Council of Teachers of Mathematics, 1991.

National Research Council. *Everybody Counts: A Report of the Nation on the Future of Mathematics Education.* Washington, D.C.: National Academy Press, 1989.

Nohda, Nobuhiko. "The Heart of 'Open Approach' in Mathematics Teaching. In *Proceedings of the ICMI-JSME Conference on Mathematical Education,* edited by Tadasu Kawaguchi, pp. 314–18. Tokyo: Japan Society of Mathematical Education, 1984.

Sawada, Toshio, Yoshihiko Hashimoto, Kohzo Tsubota, Yohziroh Nakano, and Tatsuichi Tohara. "On a Teaching Procedure of Arithmetic Problems." *Journal of Japan Society of Mathematics Education* 62, no. 10 (1980): 8–14. (In Japanese)

Shimada, Shigeru, ed. *The Open-Ended Approach in Arithmetic and Mathematics—A New Proposal toward Teaching Mathematics.* Tokyo: Mizuumishobo, 1977. (In Japanese)

Steen, Lynn A. (1989) "Teaching Mathematics for Tomorrow's World." *Educational Leadership* 47, no. 1 (1989): 18–22.

Stigler, James W. "Research into Practice: The Use of Verbal Explanation in Japanese and American Classrooms." *Arithmetic Teacher* 36 (October 1988): 27–29.

Stigler, James W., and Harold W. Stevenson. "How Asian Teachers Polish Each Lesson to Perfection." *American Educator* (Spring 1991): 12–20, 43–47.

Sugiyama, Y. *Some Features of Mathematics Teaching in Japan.* Paper presented to the U.S.–Japan Collaborative Research Meeting on Problem Solving, Tsukuba University, Tsukuba, Japan, 24–28 October 1989.

Takeuchi, Yoshio, and Toshio Sawada, eds. *From Problem to Problem-Developmental Treatment of Problems.* Tokyo: Toyokan Shyuppanshya, 1985. (In Japanese)

Chapter 10

EMPOWERING TEACHERS TO DISCOVER, CHALLENGE, AND SUPPORT STUDENTS WITH MATHEMATICAL PROMISE

Carole Greenes
Maggie Mode

The second-grade class was exploring families of numbers. The teacher wrote the numbers, 3, 2, and 5, on the chalkboard and then demonstrated how, with those three numbers, four number sentences could be formed: $3 + 2 = 5$, $2 + 3 = 5$, $5 - 2 = 3$, and $5 - 3 = 2$. She did the same for 4, 6, and 10, this time calling on students to identify the four related number sentences, two addition and two subtraction. After replicating this process with other sets of three numbers, she announced, "There are some sets of numbers for which you can only write two number sentences. With two different numbers, 2 and 4, I can write only one addition sentence, $2 + 2 = 4$, and one subtraction sentence, $4 - 2 = 2$. With 3 and 6, there are only two sentences, $3 + 3 = 6$ and $6 - 3 = 3$."

Until this moment, Derek was sitting sideways in his chair with his feet on the floor on one side of his desk and his body arched over so that his head was almost touching the floor on the other side of the desk. After the teacher had identified several pairs of numbers with exactly two related sentences, Derek sat up, raised his hand, and when called on, said, "With two numbers, I can make four (number sentences); 0 and 7 makes $0 + 7 = 7$, $7 + 0 = 7$, $7 - 0 = 7$, and $7 - 7 = 0$." The teacher responded to Derek's contribution by pointing out that he had not been listening. As she continued by exploring 6 and 12, and 7 and 14, Derek reclined in his seat. He remained in this position until the teacher had completed her explanation. At that moment, Derek jumped up out of his seat, waved his arm furiously, and blurted out, "Well, that works for all the numbers and zero. You can always make four!" Then, with only a short pause, enough time to catch his breath, Derek exclaimed, "Wait. It doesn't work for 0 and 0. That's only two sentences."

What Derek had done was to find a situation in which two numbers could be used to write four number sentences—an exception to the teacher's examples of two number sentences for two numbers. He had generalized his discovery to zero and any number; and then he had found a counterexample to his generalization, the case in which both numbers are zeros. Derek had made a mathematical discovery! But Derek's discovery was not recognized by the teacher. As a consequence, the opportunity was lost for the teacher to capitalize on Derek's insights and move him into new, more-complex explorations.

Are there other Dereks in our classes? Have their talents been discovered? Once discovered, are these students being challenged, supported, and guided to achieve greater academic success?

The primary responsibility for identifying the strengths of students and for designing and implementing enriching educational programs for them lies with the classroom teacher. Students often exhibit their insights and strengths at unexpected times, as Derek did during a regular mathematics lesson. Teachers need to be prepared to recognize greatness. They need to be able to seize the moment and modify the curriculum to capitalize on students' talents. "There is too much raw ability going through the cracks" (Ryan 1983, as cited in Gubbins et al. [1995, p. 19]).

Requirements for the teaching of talented students give rise to a number of questions. Are all classroom teachers well suited to identifying and working with mathematically promising youth? What are the responsibilities of the teacher in the classroom? Should teachers be specially prepared to work with these students? If so, what is the nature of that preparation?

In the first section of this paper, the personality traits, skills, and competencies of teachers who have been identified as particularly capable of working with mathematically promising students are described. The second section deals with the role of the teacher in regular classrooms where there are students with unusual mathematical talents—students who may not have yet been discovered. The third section describes features of preservice and in-service programs designed to prepare teachers to teach the mathematically promising. The final section deals with myths that must be dispelled and policy issues that are related to the assignment of teachers to teach the gifted and talented.

CHARACTERISTICS OF GOOD TEACHERS OF PROMISING STUDENTS

Many studies have documented the characteristics of good teachers for the gifted and talented. Although the majority of these studies did not focus specifically on mathematics, the characteristics they identify are applicable to teachers of all subject areas.

In studies of practices with gifted and talented students in regular classrooms, good teachers were found to appreciate creativity and to enjoy the unpredictability of working with divergent thinkers. They were flexible in their thinking, willing to admit to mistakes or change their positions or opinions when evidence warranted. They often participated eagerly as coinvestigators with their students on various projects. They were willing to be flexible in terms of time on task during the school day, and they devoted extra time after school to working with their gifted students. In general, these teachers were well organized and flourished in classrooms where there were multiple activities running concurrently (Nelson and Prindle 1992; Westburg, Archambault, Dobyns, and Salvin 1993).

In studies on the reversal of academic underachievement among gifted students in regular education classrooms, Emerick (1992) and Hansen and Feldhusen (1994) found that teachers of those students exhibited many of the same characteristics as gifted students. The teachers demonstrated a love of learning, task commitment, swiftness in reasoning, an appreciation for hard problems, a desire for finding more elegant solutions, and confidence in their own abilities. Furthermore, the teachers had expectations for high levels of student performance.

In studies focusing on mathematics classrooms, expert teachers were identified as having strong backgrounds in mathematics, demonstrating expertise with and enjoyment of problem solving and being able to engage in deep mathematical thinking. Teachers also had good general knowledge, interest in nonmathematical ideas, and concern for problems facing their communities (Nelson and Prindle 1992; Sheffield 1994).

THE ROLE OF THE TEACHER

The previously cited studies, describing characteristics of teachers of the gifted, suggest a number of responsibilities for the teacher. The teacher must be a talent scout, searching for, identifying, and assessing the strengths of the mathematically promising. The teacher must deal with curriculum issues and, in particular, choose the appropriate content and tasks for each student. The teacher must recognize, reinforce, and reward greatness. As a member of the classroom's mathematical community, the teacher must model the same mathematical investigative processes that she wishes to cultivate in her students.

Identifying Students with Mathematical Promise

We do know that gifted students are of above-average intellectual ability, that they are persistent in their solution of problems, and that they are creative (Renzulli 1978). What we don't know is when these characteristics will manifest themselves. Thus, it is up to the teacher to provide a range of opportunities where students can demonstrate their mathematical talents. Unfortunately, there is no single method for identifying gifted and talented students nor for assessing their performance.

One mechanism for identifying the strengths of students is the use of stimulating problems or projects. The stimulation comes from the complexity of the tasks. In some cases, the problem statements are open to multiple interpretations. When this ambiguity occurs, students have to make one or more assumptions in order to pursue the problem. In other cases, the problem or project may be well described but multiple solutions are possible. The latter type of problem or project often evolves as a result of considering a community problem as, for example, determining where to place crosswalks in the area surrounding the school or designing a ramp for handicap access to a building. Other problems derive their complexity from the fact that they require students to bring to bear knowledge from several of the subdisciplines of mathematics (e.g., arithmetic, statistics, geometry, and algebra); apply knowledge from other content areas (e.g., history and physics); and use various reasoning methods (e.g., inductive, deductive, proportional, and analogical). The teacher must seek out these types of complex challenges and use them regularly to provide an environment in which talents can be revealed.

During and after the problem-solving process, teachers can use a variety of strategies for identifying strengths and assessing performance. One strategy involves interviewing students, one-to-one, about the solution method to a particular problem. Through the use of probing questions, teachers can get information about how the student viewed the problem and made decisions during the solution process to determine the approach taken.

Another strategy is to observe students as they work in groups tackling hard problems or complex projects. Through this type of eavesdropping, the teacher can get a sense of the creative approaches, insights, and other contributions of the students. Teachers can also have students maintain scientific notebooks during the conduct of projects. In these notebooks, students record their project plans; difficulties or needs encountered; research completed; solutions or services rendered; names of collaborators and their contributions; reflections or evaluations of experiences; and, in the case of community projects, evidence of service experiences, including letters, speeches, models, and recordings. (For example, after developing a solution to the crosswalk problem, students wrote to the city's traffic safety division with their recommendation and included their supporting background information.) Scientific notebooks are useful as windows into students' reasoning and depths of understanding (Greenes 1995; Lewis 1996).

Teachers should also establish opportunities for students to present their projects and solutions orally to live audiences composed of people with expertise in the content areas of the projects. Experts may be members of the community in which the students of the school reside, or they could be other teachers or students. Experts can question students about their understanding of the mathematics and other aspects of the problem and its solution, and they can analyze the students' responses, thereby providing another mechanism by which talent can be discovered.

What is evident from the preceding discussion is that to get a handle on what students know and how they reason and to prompt advanced thinking, teachers need to use a variety of types of questions. Several types of questions with examples follow:

1. *Questions that call for reasons or support of ideas:* How do you know that? Why does that work? How do you know that it is true? ... that the solution is correct? ... that it is the most elegant solution method?

2. *Questions that call for clarification and extension:* What do you mean by that statement? What else do you know about that idea?

3. *Questions that call for focus on mathematical structure and anagogical reasoning:* Does this problem remind you of other problems you have solved? Do these data look like data you have seen before?

4. *Questions that call for variety:* What else might happen? Is there another way to interpret the problem?

5. *Questions that call for focus on concepts:* What have been some of the consequences? What would happen if there was a change in (some parameter)?

ESTABLISHING CURRICULUM OPTIONS

The early educational experiences of potentially gifted students help to shape their learning habits; therefore, it is essential that young students with high abilities have access to appropriately stimulating and challenging education to help ensure that their potential is developed. When given appropriate education opportunities, children who are gifted will become increasingly knowledgeable; therefore, their need for differentiation increases as well, as compared to others of their age, experience, and environment (Rivera, Kuehne, and Banbury 1995, p. 30).

Once students who are mathematically promising have been identified—and this identification might occur at any time during their educational programs—their talents must be further developed. Often the only attempt at differentiated curriculum in classrooms is in the number of problems assigned, with talented students getting greater numbers of the same types of problems. There is a big difference between "more" and "different" problems. Different problems build on the identified strengths of the students. More problems provide practice and are not designed to respond to individual strengths and interests. When gifted students are assigned to practice mathematical skills and processes with which they have already developed expertise, they often become bored and develop a dislike for the subject (Greenes, Garfunkel, and DeBussey 1994).

Teachers must adopt the philosophy that there can be no ceiling on learning for talented students in their classes. Therefore, teachers must make modifications to their curriculum by offering opportunities for students to explore advanced content topics, either independently or by means of group study, and to engage in research projects in the classroom. Topics for exploration may be mathematical as, for example, investigating patterns and relationships on Pascal's triangle or reading and interpreting Euclid's treatise on generating perfect numbers by examining the relationship between sums of powers of two and prime numbers. Or, the topics may come from other content areas or from real life. According to Lewis (1996), the best service or community problems for eliciting the creativity and talents of students are real, have concrete products, have no predetermined answers, and require students to bring to bear knowledge from a variety of fields. Examples of such community research projects, in addition to the crosswalk and ramp projects cited earlier, include (1) determination of the best site for the location of an airport to service three cities and (2) the evaluation of the efficiency of express versus regular checkout lines in a supermarket during peak shopping hours. Recognizing that not all mathematically promising students have the same talents and interests, the teacher must always furnish choices of topics, problems, and projects.

Whether they are exploring advanced content or conducting research projects, teachers should facilitate student access to experts in the field. Experts may be mathematicians or users of mathematics who could mentor students in their explorations as well as expose them to various career options and the academic requirements for those careers.

CREATING ENVIRONMENTS CONDUCIVE TO DEVELOPING TALENTS

In addition to identifying talent, assessing strengths, and establishing curriculum options, the teacher must also create an environment safe for exploration—an environment that encourages students to think divergently and to experiment (Mann 1994). In a safe environment, student-posed questions are encouraged and attended to. In some cases, the questions will lead students in directions that are different from those intended by the teacher. For example, in a ninth-grade algebra course, all students were working on the Tower of Hanoi puzzle, in which a pile of seven disks, graduated in size from small to large, must be transferred, one disk at a time, from one peg of a three-peg holder to another peg. Only one rule applies to the movement of the disks: a larger disk may never be placed on top of a smaller disk. Students were directed to practice transferring the disks and, when they were successful, to then generate a function that given the number of disks in the stack, identifies the least number of disk moves necessary to transfer the stack from one peg to another. As the students worked on this problem, Suzanne asked, "Does the number of pegs make a difference in the number of disk moves? What will happen if there are four pegs instead of three?" The teacher encouraged Suzanne to take on this problem as a group study project and to select two other students to work with her. While the teacher worked with the rest of the class on the three-peg problem, Suzanne and her group attacked the more complex four-peg problem.

Obviously this type of question would not arise in classrooms in which questioning was not prized, nor would it occur in classrooms in which little time is provided for thinking. In problem-solving situations, teachers must give students ample preresponse and postresponse time. Preresponse refers to the time after a problem or question has been posed. This is the time for students to ponder the problem, identify ambiguities, make assumptions, create a solution path, and generate a solution. Postresponse refers to the time immediately after the problem is solved or question is answered. This is the time for students to elaborate on or support their solutions or methods and to formulate next questions (Gubbins, St. Jean, Berube, and Renzulli 1995).

An environment should be established that fosters scientific inquiry. In such an environment, the teacher not only helps students develop expertise with the investigative processes but also models them in instruction. According to Greenes (1995), such processes include—

- making observations and then formulating conjectures about relationships observed;
- gathering information through survey and experimentation or from information sources and then organizing and displaying the information to identify other relationships or inconsistencies;
- analyzing the information, either hypothetically through "thought" experiments or by mathematical means, and drawing conclusions from the results;
- evaluating conclusions in light of the problem's context and in terms of what makes sense mathematically;
- communicating results, conclusions, persuasive arguments to justify the solution, and other information about the problem.

REWARDING GREATNESS

I always had the same dream when I was a kid. There I was, standing on the pitcher's mound, solving a very difficult algebraic equation. When I finished, everyone in the grandstands, the box seats, and the bleachers stood up and applauded and applauded. Unfortunately, it was only a dream.

—Richard, now a high school
teacher of mathematics

Unlike students involved in sports, music programs, and theater arts, students with strength in mathematics do not have opportunities to receive the kinds of applause afforded by games, concerts, and productions. The classroom teacher must either provide the recognition herself or set up situations in which students can perform and receive recognition from others. Two successful methods are: (1) issuing award certificates to students for expert solutions to difficult problems; and (2) publishing the solutions in school newspapers, magazines, or in journals such as *Mathematics Teaching in The Middle School, The Mathematics Teacher,* or *Quantum.* Recognition also can come from participation in mathematics competitions such as MATHCOUNTS for Grade 7 and 8 students and the Mathematical Olympiad for high school students. Bringing experts to the school in person or on the Internet to mentor students or to interview them on their problem and project solutions is another vehicle for providing recognition. Bringing parents, siblings, and members of the community to the schools for minicourses conducted by students is yet another way of promoting talented students.

PREPARING TEACHERS TO WORK WITH MATHEMATICALLY PROMISING STUDENTS

The need for well-trained teachers to work with mathematically promising students is well documented. In studies of regular classrooms with mathematically promising students, Hansen and Feldhusen (1994) found that teachers without specialized training—in contrast to teachers with training—often used whole-group instruction and typically spent more time with students slower in learning than with students who quickly acquired concepts and skills. In these classrooms, talented students were given less time to respond to questions; were assigned nonchallenging tasks as, for example, extra practice of skills already mastered; and were often directed to mentor their less-able peers.

As a nation concerned with individuals, we know that the future of the world is related to the education of our children and recognize that as a society we need highly educated and intelligent leaders. Therefore, we cannot allow our mathematically promising students to go undetected and undeveloped. We must prepare teachers to identify and nourish the talents of these youngsters. This specialized education, ideally, should take place at both the preservice and in-service levels.

Although a number of colleges and universities offer gifted and talented education programs, most of them are generic and do not focus on a specific academic area. Thus, in describing ideal programs for teachers of the mathematically promising, we cannot draw fully on the content of those programs but must also include ideas that evolve from consideration of the role of the teacher, as described in the previous section.

PRESERVICE PREPARATION

Recognizing that most teacher preparation programs have to meet a great many state certification requirements, the recommendations for the preservice education of teachers—specifically for the mathematically promising—are fewer in number and less comprehensive than are those for the in-service program. The components of the preservice program identified below can be met with perhaps a three- to four-course specialization or minor.

As with any preparation program for mathematics teaching, there must be extensive coursework in mathematics in the areas of analysis, algebra, geometry, probability, statistics, and the history of mathematics. In addition, the preservice program for teachers of the mathematically promising should include research apprentice opportunities with mathematicians and other users of mathematics; training in the use of advanced technologies; experiences in complex problem solving; instruction on strategies for identifying and assessing the needs and talents of mathematically promising students; practica experiences with gifted students, serving as their mentors; and development of an individualized learning plan for a mathematically promising student.

To come to understand the knowledge needed and appreciate the effort required to attack and solve complex problems, teacher preparation programs should include opportunities for future teachers to deal with problem-solving situations similar to those that they will use with their gifted students. They should have experience working on these problems and projects on their own as well as collaboratively, in pairs and in small groups. As they wrestle with the problems and projects, they will gain insight into the attributes of appropriately complex problems and will know what it feels like to deal with ambiguities in problem statements, multiple variables, and alternative solution paths. They will gain greater understanding of the environmental requirements for problem solving and the need for access to multiple resources; opportunities for regular conferencing with peers, with the teacher, and with experts; and increased time for explorations.

Among the course requirements, there must be one dealing with the identification of gifted students. In such a course, the characteristics and needs of the gifted in mathematics should be delineated, and strategies for their identification and assessment should be discussed. As a requirement of this course, each prospective teacher should carry out an assessment of a child thought to be mathematically promising. Subsequently, with supervision, prospective teachers should have opportunities to mentor talented students. This mentoring may be in a face-to-face situation or may be done through electronic mail. The face-to-face experience may occur during the in-school conduct of a project or may be part of an after-school or summer program. Throughout the mentoring, future teachers should maintain logs of daily experiences and questions they have about their observations and interactions with the talented students (Ballard 1993; Felshusen and Huffman 1988).

As part of the mentoring experience, each future teacher should develop a Mathematics Individualized Learning Plan for one gifted student. Similar to an Individualized Education Plan, the MILP is a comprehensive plan for instruction and assessment (Greenes, Garfunkel, and DeBussey 1994). The MILP identifies mathematical talents, other strengths, and specific interests and needs of the student; the mathematics goals to be achieved; strategies, materials, and other resources for accomplishing those goals; and methods for assessing achievement of the goals. As they develop MILPs, prospective teachers learn the relationship between assessment and instruction and how assessment can be used to strengthen instruction. Prospective teachers will need to examine various instructional materials and resources to match the materials to the strengths and interests of the students.

Although the courses and experiences described in this section are targeted at future teachers of mathematically promising students, this curriculum would no doubt be a valuable part of all preservice mathematics teacher preparation programs. With so many undiscovered mathematically promising students, all teachers must search for and nurture talent in all classrooms.

IN-SERVICE PROFESSIONAL DEVELOPMENT

With the staff cutbacks and the aging population of mathematics teachers, rather than seeking university preparation for the teaching of talented students, teachers are more likely to turn to school systems and participate in their in-service professional development programs. Assuming that teachers already possess the personal characteristics cited earlier and have strong backgrounds in mathematics, an in-service program should include examination of, and experience with, techniques for assessing students' strengths and identifying appropriate curricula; exploration of new instructional materials and resources and the formulation of instructional plans; study of methods for designing and implementing programs in regular classrooms; and investigation of strategies for providing academic, career, and family counseling.

To enhance understanding of student strengths while concurrently developing their own talent-scout observation skills, teachers might experiment with various tools designed to help them document traits, aptitudes, and behaviors of gifted and talented students. One such observation tool is Panning for Gold, which produces a profile of the talented student and includes—in addition to traits and aptitudes—information about the student's communication, inquiry, and problem-solving abilities (Frasier et al. 1995). Teachers might visit regular classrooms and use this instrument with students identified as showing mathematical promise. They might also collect information about the out-of-school interests and activities of the same students. The latter information has been particularly useful in identifying underachievers with mathematical promise. In her study of academically underachieving gifted students, Emerick (1992) found that these children often sought their own enrichment and that it was their out-of-school success that kept them going to school. These same children began to prosper in school when given hard problems related to their interests, choices of tasks to complete, opportunities to work on their own, and regular feedback on their contributions.

To gain experience with other assessment-identification techniques and with strategies for working with talented students in regular classrooms, teachers might observe demonstration classes taught by specially trained expert teachers. As the expert works with the students on projects and challenging problems designed to elicit mathematical strengths and creativity, teachers in the in-service program focus on individual children, noting behaviors and recording discourse for later analysis. In some demonstration lessons, the focus might be on the expert teachers, documenting their instructional methods and, in particular, the nature of their questions and responses to students' questions.

To become familiar with problems, projects, and other resources for challenging students and identifying their talents, teachers in in-service programs should collaboratively tackle some of the student challenges. In this way, they will gain greater understanding of the multiple methods for approaching problems or projects, the kinds of questions and related problems that may arise, and the types of resources that may be needed. Time should be spent on evaluating projects, problems, and other curricular materials to determine their suitability in evoking the talents and creativity of students.

Teachers should also devote some time to analyzing the products of mathematically promising students, to gain experience in detecting strengths and interests from logs and other written productions. It may be useful to maintain a file of outstanding student work, not only for teachers to study but also for students to see, so that they will have models against which to compare their own productions.

Because talented students often have interest in extracurricular activities, teachers should have regularly updated lists of after-school and summer programs through which students can hone their skills, including mathematics clubs and competitions. For older students, after-school and summer job opportunities related to their mathematical interests should be identified.

Finally, in in-service programs, teachers should learn strategies for academic and career counseling. For younger students and their families, counseling may focus on selecting the appropriate courses and out-of-school activities, and on ways in which the family can support their children's interests. For older students and their families, the focus may be on preparing for higher education, identifying the educational requirements of various vocations, finding after-school and summer work, and selecting the colleges that best match the students' talents and interests.

WHO SHOULD TEACH STUDENTS SHOWING MATHEMATICAL PROMISE?

A number of long-standing myths interfere with the offering of specialized educational services for the gifted. Among those are the following:

- Gifted students, because of their strengths, can learn on their own and need no guidance.
- If students are not achieving academically, they cannot possibly be in possession of any mathematical talents.
- Equal opportunity in education means the same curriculum at the same pace and employing the same pedagogy for all students.

These beliefs must be dispelled. We know that gifted students who are not challenged and guided may lose interest, perform poorly, and even discontinue their study of mathematics. We know that academic underachievement can be reversed and talented students identified among former underachievers. Finally, equal opportunity is not synonymous with having the same experiences. Every child should be given maximum challenge, support, and guidance in the learning process, but the nature of these may be quite different from child to child.

From the studies that have been done, it is clear that teachers with specialized training in the teaching of the gifted, who also have extensive backgrounds in mathematics and who possess the personality characteristics described earlier, are the best suited to identifying and teaching our mathematically promising students. Although it is possible that all teachers could receive the preparation described in the previous sections—and might greatly prosper from such training—not all teachers possess the personality traits or interest in working with the mathematically promising. School districts have obligations to their students to fully develop their potential. To meet these obligations in the case of the mathematically talented students, districts must hire well-prepared teachers, identify gifted teachers in their schools, assign them to work with students with strength in mathematics, and give them ongoing support and continuing education. In this way, these teachers can identify, challenge, and support students with a flair for mathematics.

REFERENCES

Ballard, Leslie. "Finding the Right Button." *Gifted Child Today* (January/February 1993): 26–29.

Emerick, Linda J. "Academic Underachievement among the Gifted: Students' Perceptions of Factors that Reverse the Pattern." *Gifted Child Quarterly* 36 (Summer 1992): 140–46.

Feldhusen, John F., and Lois E. Huffman. "Practicum Experiences in an Educational Program for Teachers of the Gifted." *Journal for the Education of the Gifted* 12, no. 1 (1988): 34–45.

Frasier, Mary M., Scott L. Hunsaker, Jongyeun Lee, Vernon S. Finley, Jaime H. Garcia, Darlene Martin, and Elaine Frank. *An Exploratory Study of the Effectiveness of the Staff Development Model and the Research-Based Assessment Plan in Improving the Identification of Gifted Economically Disadvantaged Students.* Athens, Ga.: The National Research Center on the Gifted and Talented, University of Georgia, 1995 (No. RM95224).

Greenes, Carole. "Mathematics Learning and Knowing: A Cognitive Process." *Journal of Education* (Boston University) 177, no. 1 (1995): 85–106.

Greenes, Carole, Frank Garfunkel, and Melissa DeBussey. "Planning for Instruction: The Individualized Education Plan and the Mathematics Individualized Learning Plan." In *Windows of Opportunity,* edited by Carol A. Thornton and Nancy S. Bley, pp. 115–35. Reston, Va.: National Council of Teachers of Mathematics, 1994.

Gubbins, E. Jean, David St. Jean, Bruce N. Berube, and Joseph S. Renzulli. *Developing the Gifts and Talents of All America's Students.* (NRC/GT—1990–95). Storrs, Conn.: The National Research Center on the Gifted and Talented, University of Connecticut, 1995 (No. RM95218).

Hansen, Jan B., and John F. Feldhusen. "Comparison of Trained and Untrained Teachers of Gifted Students." *Gifted Child Quarterly* 38 (Summer 1994): 115–21.

Lewis, Barbara. "Serving Others Hooks Gifted Students on Learning." *Educational Leadership* 53, no. 5 (February 1996): 70–74.

Mann, Christine. "New Technologies and Gifted Education." *Roeper Review* 16 (February 1994): 172–76.

Nelson, Karen C., and Nancy Prindle. "Gifted Teacher Competencies: Ratings by Rural Principals and Teachers Compared." *Journal for the Education of the Gifted* 15, no. 40 (1992): 357–69.

Renzulli, Joseph. "What Makes Giftedness? Reexamining a Definition." *Phi Delta Kappan* 60 (November 1978): 180–84, 261.

Rivera, Deborah B., Carolyn C. Kuehne, and Mary M. Banbury. "Performance-Based Assessment." *Gifted Child Today* (September/October 1995): 34–41.

Ryan, Judith. "Identifying Intellectually Superior Black Children." *Journal of Educational Research* 76, no. 3 (1983): 153–56. (Cited in Gubbins, E. Jean, David St. Jean, Bruce N. Berube, Joseph S. Renzulli. *Developing the Gifts and Talents of All America's Students.* [NRC/GT—1990–95]. Storrs, Conn.: The National Research Center on the Gifted and Talented, University of Connecticut, 1995. [No. RM95218], p. 19.)

Sheffield, Linda Jensen. *The Development of Gifted and Talented Mathematics Students and the National Council of Teachers of Mathematics Standards.* Storrs, Conn.: National Research Center on the Gifted and Talented, University of Connecticut, 1994 (No. RBDM 9404).

Westberg, Karen L., Francis X. Archambault, Jr., Sally M. Dobyns, and Thomas J. Salvin. *An Observational Study of Instructional and Curricular Practices Used with Gifted and Talented Students in Regular Classrooms.* Storrs, Conn.: National Research Center on the Gifted and Talented, University of Connecticut, 1993 (No. RM 93104).

Chapter 11

WHY JANE DOESN'T THINK SHE CAN DO MATH: HOW TEACHERS CAN ENCOURAGE TALENTED GIRLS IN MATHEMATICS

Sally M. Reis
M. Katherine Gavin

Eva loved science and mathematics as a child and her parents were delighted by her excitement and aptitude. When she was four, she asked her mother how long it was until her birthday and her mother replied, "Two months." She immediately asked, "How much is eight times seven?" Her mother answered, "Fifty-six. Why do you want to know?" Eva replied, "I want to know how many days until my birthday." Eva's favorite activities included taking apart radios, clocks, and old appliances and then trying to put them back together. She loved to build with many different kinds of materials—everything from blocks and Lego toys to materials she found in the kitchen, such as marshmallows, uncooked pasta, and cans and boxes of food. She also loved computer work, especially mathematics programs, and routinely requested these types of gifts while most of her friends were asking for Barbie dolls.

Unfortunately, Eva's interests and talents in mathematics began to fade in elementary school. By the third grade, she had stopped wanting to do mathematics at home and repeatedly told her parents that "school" mathematics was boring. Because of her attitude and her lack of interest in doing mathematics homework at home, she had fallen behind in memorizing her multiplication tables and was not even considered mathematically talented by her third-grade teacher. It is doubtful that she will either be interested in, or qualify for, the prealgebra class when she reaches middle school in two years. How could such a promising child lose her motivation to learn and achieve in mathematics? And—just as important—what can educators do to restore that motivation or, better yet, to avoid the loss of motivation in the first place?

Eva isn't alone. Gifted young females may not receive necessary encouragement to achieve in mathematics. An American Association of University Women report (Wellesley College Center for Research on Women 1992) concluded that "all differences in math performance between girls and boys at ages eleven and fifteen could be accounted for by differences among those scoring in the top 10 to 20 percent" (p. 25). This means that many of our brightest female mathematics students are not keeping up with their male counterparts. It is clear from this and other research studies discussed in this chapter that many mathematically talented females perform at levels that are not commensurate with their abilities (Reis 1987; Reis and Callahan 1989). This unfortunate situation can be improved: teachers and parents can help talented girls succeed in mathematics.

STEREOTYPING ABOUT FEMALES AND MATHEMATICS

Before we can alleviate the problems experienced by girls like Eva, it is important to try to understand the factors underlying those problems. One of the main reasons that girls do not succeed in mathematics is not any lack of ability or effort—it is simply that they are not expected to. Stereotypes influence perceptions and performance in school and in life, and they are often cited as contributing heavily to girls' shortcomings in school. A great deal of stereotyping and prejudice affects girls in mathematics classes. Unfortunately, mathematics is often thought of as a field for men, and our society's traditional images of scientists, engineers, and mathematicians are almost always male. Most university mathematics professors are male, and evidence exists that girls are regarded as less capable in mathematics by some of their teachers and parents.

As early as 1973, Good and Brophy learned that when teachers treated boys and girls differently in class, these differences were the most pronounced for gifted females. In a more recent study by Cooley, Chauvin, and Karnes (1984), similar findings emerged. Both male and female teachers regarded gifted boys as more competent than gifted girls in critical- and logical-thinking skills and in creative problem-solving abilities, whereas they believed gifted girls were more competent in creative writing. Fennema (1990), in her analysis of the role of teacher beliefs on mathematics performance, reported in a study she conducted with Peterson, Carpenter, and Lubinski that "teachers selected ability as the cause of their most capable males' success 58 percent of the time, and the cause of their best females' success only 33 percent of the time. Most capable females' successes were due to effort 37 percent of the time, whereas best males' successes were due to effort only 12 percent of the time" (p. 178). They also concluded that even though teachers did not tend to engage in sex-role stereotyping in general, they did stereotype their best students in the area of mathematics—attributing to males characteristics such as volunteering answers, enjoyment of mathematics, and independence.

CURRENT RESEARCH ABOUT GENDER DIFFERENCES IN MATHEMATICS TESTS

One source of stereotypes about females' ability in mathematics is probably the fact that they often perform poorly compared to males on standardized mathematics tests. This performance reinforces beliefs that males are superior in mathematics and gives females lower self-esteem and less confidence in their abilities. Evidence exists that current differences in standardized tests favor males at the highest levels. For example, Halpern (1989) pointed out that "large and consistent differences favoring male students are still found among the upper levels of mathematics aptitude on the PSAT and the SAT" (p. 1156). In 1996, the population of girls taking the SAT averaged 46 points lower than boys on the mathematics section. The number of top-scoring males on the quantitative section of the SAT far exceeded the number of top-scoring females. Eight percent of males (39 369) but only 3 percent of females (19 005) scored 700 or greater (Educational Testing Service 1996). When one examines the numbers of males and females scoring 750 or higher, sex differences are even more pronounced. Girls also score lower on the PSAT/NMSQT, which is used by the National Merit Scholarship Corporation for awarding scholarships to promising college students (Rosser 1989).

Only a few researchers have investigated why these differences occur, but time constraints may have some effect. For example, Dreyden and Gallagher (1989) tested the effects of changing time limits and directions on the performance of academically talented males and females on the SAT. Students took either the SAT-Mathematics subtest or the SAT-Verbal subtest under timed or untimed conditions. Female students' scores on the SAT-M dramatically increased when the test was untimed, suggesting that the difference in the scores of males and females on the SAT-M "may be due more to speed of performance than to ability" (p. 196).

Potentially damaging implications directly relate to the different scores obtained by boys and girls on these tests. Not only do lower scores on the traditional college admissions exams have potential for denying opportunity for scholarships and admission to selective colleges, they may also deny access to certain programs for gifted and talented students—particularly at the secondary level. (In some states, for example, PSAT scores are used as part of the selection process for attendance in Governor's School programs. In Washington, D.C., students who earn high scores on the SAT-Q have the opportunity to attend college courses in mathematics during the summer.) Lower scores may also have an impact on girls' selection of careers.

CLASSROOM CONDITIONS TO ENCOURAGE GIRLS

What type of classroom environment avoids and helps nullify these harmful stereotypes and discrepancies? Eccles (1987) draws several conclusions from the existing literature on mathematics and science teachers who have been successful in reversing stereotypes and keeping females interested in mathematics and science. She notes a pattern of conditions in these classrooms, including:

- Frequent use of cooperative learning opportunities
- Frequent individualized learning opportunities
- Use of practical problems in assignments
- Frequent use of hands-on opportunities

- Active career and educational guidance
- Infrequent use of competitive motivational strategies
- Frequent activities oriented toward broadening views of mathematics and physical sciences
- The presenting of mathematics as a tool in solving problems
- Frequent use of strategies to ensure full class participation

Furthermore, Eccles (1987) suggests an examination of other stereotyped aspects of our society that seem to influence the differential achievement of males and females, supporting the need to find ways to counteract the effects. For example, research has been conducted on strong stereotypes existing in our society about the possession of "natural talent." Mathematics achievement, more than achievement in any other discipline, is often linked to innate abilities. Further, our culture subscribes to an assumption that males have more of those innate abilities.

THE ROLE OF THE TEACHER

Other recent research addresses the critical role of the teacher in encouraging girls in mathematics. For example, Leroux and Ho (1994, p. 45), in a qualitative study of fifteen gifted female high school students, concluded:

> Female math teachers who act as role models are significant influences. Teachers who treat both genders equally, provide a warm, uninhibiting environment, and are approachable seem to provide the most "psychologically safe" environment that is conducive to girls learning.

Demonstrating the kinds of effects that teachers can have on students, Rogers (1990), in a study of high-ability students, found that significant success in attracting females to higher-level mathematics courses was achieved by teachers, either male or female, who created a classroom environment that was open and supportive of all students—one in which the teacher's style was conducive to the nature of mathematical inquiry. In a qualitative study of female mathematics majors at a very competitive college, Gavin (1996) found that almost half attributed their decision to major in mathematics to the influence of a high school teacher. In fact, one-third of the students developed and maintained a personal relationship with these high school teachers throughout their college years. Confirming this at the graduate level, Rossi Becker (1994) conducted in-depth interviews with thirty-one graduate students and found that a successful teacher was frequently described as one who piqued students' interests by providing an enriched curriculum. She concluded that teachers and instruction can make a difference in all students' career choices.

GENDER DIFFERENCES IN MATHEMATICS GRADES IN SCHOOL

Kimball (1989), in her review of literature on women's mathematics achievement, found that although standardized test scores favor boys, grade differences favor girls. The pattern of performance on standardized aptitude assessment measures is very different from the pattern of grades. For example, while males' mean scores on both the verbal and mathematics sections of the 1996 SAT were higher than females', the females who took the test had a higher mean high school grade point average: 3.27 overall, versus 3.11 for males (Educational Testing Service 1996).

How does this affect gifted females in particular? Rosser (1989) reported that the higher the grades, the greater the gender gap. "Girls with an A+ grade point average averaged 23 points lower on the SAT-Verbal section (9 points lower than the overall verbal male-female gap) and 60 points lower on the SAT-Mathematics section than boys with the same GPA" (p. iv). The information that girls are actually not at a disadvantage and in fact have a grade advantage in many courses may be useful in increasing girls' confidence in their mathematics ability.

CAREER CHOICE

Many gifted females continue to reject mathematics and science as courses of study (Grandy 1987). Using data from the federal National Education Study of 1988, a ten-year data collection project, Gavin (1997) examined a cohort of approximately 1400 high-mathematics-ability students. As seniors in 1992, these students were surveyed to determine their intended fields of study in college. Although all students had been identified as having high mathematics ability, only 27 percent expressed interest in a mathematics or science major, with only 1.8 percent intending to major in mathematics. The numbers for females were quite revealing: Only nine (0.7 percent) selected computer science, forty-six (3.3 percent) engineering, nineteen (1.4 percent) mathematics, and twenty-seven (2 percent) physical science. Examining data on intended majors for females who took the SAT in 1996, of those intending to major in engineering, only 19 percent were female, in computer or information sciences, 25 percent (Educational Testing Service 1996). These remarkably low percentages of career interest in mathematics and science occur despite data cited earlier suggesting that females receive consistently higher grades in elementary school, in secondary school, and in mathematics- or science-related subjects in college.

Much attention has been given to research studies that have reported equal numbers of males and females who declare mathematics as their major field of study. However, it is important to examine which students actually graduate with a mathematics major and pursue a mathematics career. Even though equal numbers of males and females start with a mathematics major, females comprise 43 percent of those completing the undergraduate major and only 20 percent of those completing the doctorate (Linn and Kessel 1995). In terms of related fields, an examination of the distribution of the Ph.D. degrees awarded in 1992 reveals that women were awarded 16 percent of the degrees in computer science, 11 percent of the degrees in physics, and a mere 8 percent of the engineering degrees (National Science Foundation 1992). And although the number of women in the life sciences fields has grown steadily since the early 1970s, the participation of women in physics and engineering reached a plateau at about 15 percent and has remained at this level for the past decade (Campbell 1996).

PARENTAL INFLUENCE ON THE MATHEMATICAL TALENTS OF FEMALES

Recent research has established the importance of parents' attitudes and beliefs on the academic self-perceptions and achievement of their children (e.g., Hess, Holloway, Dickson, and Price [1984]; McGillicuddy-De Lisi [1985]; Parsons, Adler, and Kaczala [1982]; Stevenson and Newman [1986]). Phillips (1987) confirmed this finding in her study of high-ability students, and a recent study of parental influence on mathematics self-concept with gifted female adolescents as subjects found consistently significant correlations between parental expectations and student mathematics self-concept (Dickens 1990).

The area of mathematics achievement appears to be particularly susceptible to the influence of parental beliefs, and it is also characterized by greater gender differences in attitudes about performance (Chipman, Brush, and Wilson 1985). Compared to parents of boys, parents of girls are more likely to report that mathematics is less important than other subjects (Parsons, Adler, and Kaczala 1982) and are more likely to attribute good performance to training and effort rather than ability (Parsons, Adler, and Kaczala 1982).

SPECIFIC STRATEGIES TO HELP EDUCATORS ENCOURAGE GIRLS IN MATHEMATICS

According to the National Research Council's 1989 national report on mathematics, by the year 2000 the need for workers in fields requiring mathematics and science backgrounds will have increased by 36 percent from the 1986 level. We must encourage more females to enter mathematics-related fields. We have failed in our efforts to do this in the past. Research has consistently demonstrated that teachers can affect how girls perceive and relate to mathematics. In fact, many female mathematicians cite teachers as the primary persons who encouraged them as children, and some even attribute their career choice or research interests to one teacher who introduced them to the topic and encouraged them to become more involved in the area. Based on these findings, the following strategies can be implemented fairly easily and quickly and have been suggested by experts or proved to be effective in encouraging young girls in mathematics (Sanders 1986, 1994; Hanson 1992; Campbell 1992). Bear in mind that although these suggestions were written with specific reference to females, most of them can apply to improving and equalizing the classroom environment for students of either gender.

1. Provide a Safe and Supportive Environment

All girls, especially adolescent ones, need a mathematics classroom in which they will be heard and understood and where they can discuss ideas before coming to conclusions. Teachers should not allow students to call out answers randomly or rush to provide closure to a lesson, for time to think and reflect is often essential for talented girls studying advanced topics. One effective strategy is the Think-Pair-Share technique in which, after time for private thought, students share their answers with a neighbor and then with the entire class. The paired discussion lends credibility to their thinking, fosters mathematical communication, and develops a sense of confidence.

Teachers should also become personally aware of the additional attention they sometimes give to boys. It is hard to deny a waving hand or someone calling out, but increased attention, even negative attention, can reinforce behaviors. Girls need equal attention, and to ensure that teachers provide it, peer observations can be established with colleagues. Using this technique, a teacher observes a peer's class and tallies the number of times girls and boys are called on. One way that some teachers address the issue of classroom equality is simply to alternate between calling on males and females in class.

Opportunities for students to reflect in writing about their ideas and fears about mathematics can also be provided in a safe and supportive mathematics class. A "comment box" enables students to drop a note about their feelings or their under-standing of the content of the daily mathematics lesson, including questions they have and related topics they would like to pursue. Feelings can also be addressed in creative journal assignments, including mathematics metaphors, as suggested by Buerk and Gibson (1994). A sample assignment might be the following: If mathe-matics were a food (color, animal, etc.), what would it be … and why? The results can quickly foster communication and provide information about personal feelings. Consider the following entries written by mathematically talented adolescent girls:

> If math were a food it would be a pineapple. On the outside it appears to be all rough, tough, and prickly. But on the inside, it's soft—sometimes sweet, some-times sour.

> If math were a food, it would be a lobster. It takes a while to get to learn how to eat it, but once you learn, it can be kind of fun.

> If math were a food, it would be jelly. It's fun to have, to play with, but it also can be a mess and can taste bad.

Journals can also be used to encourage communication about mathematical concepts and offer talented students a way to bring deeper understanding and new insight to areas they wish to pursue. Journals can stimulate creative writing assignments focusing on feelings about math. The following poem, written by a fifth-grade student, expressed the feelings of uncertainty that may accompany the risk taken by a student who answers a question aloud in math class. The need for a supportive environment that welcomes risk and conjecture is evident:

> Death by Math

> A million people to pick
> You had to call on me.
> Everyone else had their hand up
> You had to call on me.

The chalk sounds like a thousand knives, slicing
through the air.
I can't think, everyone's watching, a scream for every stare.
I want to say, "Can't it wait?"
But it's too late.
She's made the date.
"You're right, the answer is forty-eight!"
You're lucky you called on me.

Girls often enjoy the intimate student-teacher dialogue created by the journal writing process. An outgrowth of this experience could be the creation of discussion groups at lunch or in after-school clubs in which girls can discuss their feelings and explore interesting mathematics topics.

2. Assume Personal Responsibility to Encourage Talented Females

Adolescent girls who are talented in mathematics may receive mixed messages from their parents, their peer group, and society in general. They may need specific encouragement from parents, teachers, and peers to help them believe that they are truly talented in mathematics and to encourage them to continue to pursue mathematics in high school, college, and beyond.

In the mathematics classroom, teachers who try to encourage talented girls may believe that they should help their students solve problems. However, *merely* giving them extra help may be detrimental to females' sense of self-confidence. Teachers must establish an environment in which students are encouraged to persist in seeking solutions for themselves, and they should answer questions with a question, giving hints but not solutions. They must have high expectations for girls, let them know it, and praise them for being able to solve challenging problems.

Teachers must also be aware that females who are talented in mathematics are often talented in other academic areas as well. Without encouragement to pursue their talent in mathematics, they often choose other more traditionally female oriented fields. Teachers must make parents aware of the need to support their daughters' talents in mathematics. In school, older girls taking advanced placement courses can be asked to come and talk to younger students to encourage increased participation in these courses. And at every stage, all opportunities should remain available to talented female students to encourage them to take and remain in advanced mathematics classes.

3. Employ Instructional Strategies That Address the Characteristics of Females

During middle school and usually continuing through their adolescent years, mathematically talented females exhibit great attention to detail in their work, strong organizational skills, and for some, a sophisticated level of maturity. These skills can be used to motivate girls' interest in mathematics. One way to do this is by encouraging them to organize a family mathematics night (Stenmark, Thompson, and Cossey 1986) at the elementary school for parents and children to engage in fun mathematics activities. A book published by EQUALS has a variety of activities specifically designed for such an event. Girls may choose activities for the evening, issue invitations, set up, and actually run the entire event (under the auspices of a teacher-mentor). (See the Family Math Web site: equals.lhs.berkeley.edu.)

Tutoring younger children and organizing mathematics clubs or Saturday enrichment mathematics programs also may encourage and empower talented adolescent females. Some current research indicates that some girls tend to thrive in small-group work, especially all-female groups. In coed groups, boys may dominate, becoming the leaders in the group and monopolizing the discussion, while girls become the recorders of the discussions. This is especially true in computer work. If students work in pairs or small groups, boys often demand and get to use the keyboard far more often than girls, and encouraging girls to work together usually resolves this problem. Because some girls have been socialized to play more often with dolls rather than blocks, for example, they may need more time to work with manipulatives. They may also need in-class time to build models, to see how things work, and to develop their sense of spatial relationships. The activity Cooperative Geometry (EQUALS 1986) is another excellent example of group work with manipulatives that develops spatial thinking as well as encourages a true cooperative problem-solving spirit. The extensions are especially challenging for talented elementary and middle school students.

4. Use Language, Problems, and Activities That Are Relevant to Girls

Suzanne Damarin (1990) examined our traditional mathematics vocabulary and found that it reflects a strong male influence. The language contains goals of *mastery* and mathematical *power*. We teach students to *attack* problems, and our instructional strategies include *drill* and *competitions*. She believes that instead of talking about working toward mastery, teachers should talk about *internalization* of concepts. Instead of attacking problems, students should be encouraged to *interact* with them, *sharing* problems and working *cooperatively* toward solutions.

Rather than focusing on activities relating to football yardage, baseball statistics, and housing construction, teachers should also consciously incorporate problems and activities that more girls enjoy. Problems dealing with endangered species, recycling, the spread of disease, population growth, and quilting have proven to be excellent suggestions. Activities involving patterns including tangrams, paper folding, and tessellations appeal to many girls, as well as those activities involving art, such as making mobiles, computer graphics, and scale drawings.

Some favorite teacher resource materials with activities to encourage girls in mathematics are listed in the appendix to this chapter.

5. Create a Challenging Curriculum That Promotes Deep Mathematical Thinking

Teachers must encourage talented females to feel comfortable with, and even seek, a state of challenge when studying mathematics. Challenging the familiar with ideas that stretch the mind should be a major goal of a program for talented mathematics students. By providing the safe and supportive environment discussed earlier, teachers can nurture this spirit of risk taking in girls. From elementary school exposure to such topics as different numeration systems, the Fibonacci numbers, Lego-Logo, and nonroutine problem solving to secondary school study of non-Euclidean geometry, fractals, chaos theory, and combinatorics, students need to struggle with a change of mindset and relish this struggle, for it fosters a deep, intimate, and broadened understanding of mathematics. NCTM has published a series of addenda books to the NCTM *Standards* that are an excellent source of ideas for topics.

In designing a curriculum for talented females, teachers should include a variety of alternative assessments. Research indicates that females may not do their best thinking during timed tests. Independent and small-group projects provide an ideal medium for these students to showcase their talent. These projects should go beyond a typical term paper and should focus on investigative activities in which students assume the role of firsthand inquirers—thinking, feeling, and acting like a practicing professional. In an enrichment program model called the "Enrichment Triad" model, Renzulli (1977) advocates creating student products to develop research skills and afford an opportunity to use authentic methodology. These projects are most effective when directed toward bringing about a desired impact on an audience, whether it be fellow students, administrators, town officials, mathematicians, or senior citizens. The teacher functions as a facilitator, pointing the student in the direction of resource persons and materials as needed or offering direction in learning methodology to conduct the investigation. Some examples of these projects might include contacting local community officials for needed surveying or design projects, such as a population survey or a statistical analysis on the use of current library facilities, or an energy audit of town hall using mathematical analysis with recommendations to the town council for improved efficiency. The NCTM Addenda series book, *Data Analysis and Statistics across the Curriculum: Grades 9–12* (1992), another resource for such projects, outlines guidelines for both long- and short-term projects with time lines and evaluation criteria.

Another means for offering challenging and interesting mathematics to students is the use of enrichment clusters. *Enrichment clusters* are groups of students who share common interests and who come together during designated time blocks to pursue these interests (Renzulli 1994). The increased use of block scheduling in middle school and high school might make the enrichment clusters easier to schedule. Single-sex enrichment groups, if feasible, might provide an increased sense of confidence for females. During these extended time periods, students can pursue mutual mathematical interests. For example, they might study fractals using computer models and decide to create programs that generate original fractal pieces. Or, they might gather to start a young architects' guild focused on learning about architectural design and using this knowledge to create a play space for children at a local preschool or redesigning a veterinarian's office space. Again, the teacher acts as a guide and the students are empowered to discover the mathematics and see its relevance in the real world. They learn to value mathematics and, one hopes, become inspired to continue study and pursue a mathematically related career.

6. Provide Female Role Models and Mentors for Girls

Many girls have a unique connectedness to people they view as role models. Teachers should capitalize on this and include an historical perspective in their mathematics curriculum to help students become aware of both the people and the creative processes behind mathematics. The lives of mathematicians, their interest in the subject, and how they made their mathematical discoveries will help young female students to appreciate the creative process as well as the difficulties faced in getting new theories accepted. Concepts as basic as the notion of zero, irrational numbers, and negative numbers were quite controversial when first presented and were adopted only with great difficulty.

The names of the following female mathematicians are usually not recognized by boys or girls: Hypatia, Marie Agnesi, Sophie Germain, Evelyn Boyd Granville, Sonya Kovalevskaya, and Mary Somerville. These female mathematicians made distinguished contributions, and teachers can make these women come alive by celebrating their birthdays, hanging their portraits in bulletin board displays, and encouraging females to perform autobiographical skits dressed in their period costumes. Videotaped interviews conducted between student reporters and a remarkable woman who has suddenly come back to life in the twenty-first century can also be effective. This provides a creative twist to the historical perspective that appeals to some talented females. Role models need not all be historical; examples of women currently working in the fields of mathematics and science—astronauts, engineers, physicists, astronomers, etc.—can be presented as well. Some modern women who have made important contributions to their fields include Rita Levi-Montelcini, a Nobel laureate biologist; Reatha Clark King, chemist administrator; Shirley Jackson, theoretical physicist; Edna Paisano, statistician; Gertrude Elion, a Nobel laureate pharmacologist; Maya Lin, architect; Grace Hopper, computer scientist; and Judith Ressnick, astronaut. Some excellent resources on the lives of female mathematicians and scientists, including interesting family and personal stories, are included in the appendix to this chapter.

A rewarding experience for teachers as well as girls is organizing and participating in a career day in mathematics, science, and technology for girls. At these conferences, which are generally held for girls in middle school or high school, female professionals conduct hands-on workshop sessions with girls, interacting with them and exposing them to actual on-the-job activities that spark career interest in girls. It is exciting and rewarding to visit these sessions and observe girls listening to a dog's heartbeat with a veterinarian, performing a chemical test on local river water with an environmental engineer; or trying, with an actuary, to determine car insurance rates for teenage girls. Some associations that can assist teachers in planning these days are these:

- Multiply Your Options, PIMMS, Wesleyan University, Middletown, CT 06457
- Expanding Your Horizons, Math-Science Network, 2727 College Ave., Berkeley, CA 94705
- Girls + Math + Science = Choices, Rose Arbanas, Calhoun ISD, 17111 G Dr. North, Marshall, MI 49068.

We have conducted several of these career days and found that, in addition to the hands-on workshops, panels of professional women are also effective and allow a greater variety of careers to be represented. To enliven these panels and encourage interaction between the women and the often shy female students, we highly recommend the Tool Clues activity (EQUALS 1989). In this activity, female professionals provide bags of "tools" used in their careers, and students working in groups try to guess their profession using a twenty-question format.

One of the greatest benefits from these interactions with professional women is the opportunity to establish mentorship and internship programs. Participating in these programs gives mathematically talented females the opportunity to work directly with a female role model in a high-level mathematics-related career position. As Sheffield (1994) points out, "We especially need to encourage girls and other traditionally underrepresented groups to consider careers in highly technical fields that involve strong mathematical backgrounds, and mentorships are an effective means of doing this" (p. 25).

CONCLUSION

Our society is just beginning to address many crucial issues involving gender equity. Far fewer females than males pursue careers in mathematics and related fields. It is our duty to try to make high-tech, high-paying professional careers equally available to all students. As pointed out in this chapter, few talented students of either sex indicate an interest in majoring in mathematics. The majority of the strategies we have suggested above are of the type recommended not only for girls but for all students by the NCTM *Curriculum and Evaluation Standards for School Mathematics* (1989). These strategies and activities focus on constructivist, discovery-oriented learning as the key to building mathematical confidence and understanding in all students. So, in reality, promoting equality in the classroom is also promoting good teaching techniques, developing student problem-solving abilities, and instilling a genuine appreciation for mathematics. Only the wider use of these strategies will provide answers to questions about how we can continue to recruit the number of talented persons we need in mathematics in the future. What should be clear to all of us is that few women see a career involving mathematics as an attainable goal, and so it is important to encourage and support more females to pursue mathematics and science in the future.

REFERENCES

American College Testing Program. *State and National Trend Data for Students Who Take the ACT Assessment.* Iowa City: American College Testing Program, 1989.

Buerk, Dorothy, and Helen Gibson. "Students' Metaphors for Mathematics: Gathering, Interpreting, Implications." *WME Newsletter* 16, no. 2 (1994): 2–8.

Burrill, Gail, John C. Burrill, Pamela Coffield, Gretchen Davis, Jan de Lange, Diann Resnick, and Murray Siegel. *Data Analysis and Statistics across the Curriculum.* Reston, Va.: National Council of Teachers of Mathematics, 1992.

Campbell, George, Jr. *Research Letter of the National Action Council for Minorities in Engineering.* New York: National Action Council for Minorities in Engineering, 1996.

Campbell, Patricia B. *Nothing Can Stop Us Now: Designing Effective Programs for Girls in Math, Science, and Engineering.* Newton, Mass.: Women's Educational Equity Act, 1992.

Chipman, Susan F., Lorelei R. Brush, and Donna M. Wilson, eds. *Women and Mathematics: Balancing the Equation.* New York: Erlbaum Associates, 1985.

Cooley, Denice, Jane C. Chauvin, and Frances A. Karnes. "Gifted Females: A Comparison of Attitudes by Male and Female Teachers." *Roeper Review* 6 (1984): 164–67.

Damarin, Suzanne K. "Teaching Mathematics: A Feminist Perspective." In *Teaching and Learning Mathematics in the 1990s,* 1990 Yearbook of the National Council of Teachers of Mathematics, edited by Thomas J. Cooney, pp. 144–58. Reston, Va: National Council of Teachers of Mathematics, 1990.

Dickens, Margie N. "Parental Influences on the Mathematics Self-Concept of High Achieving Adolescent Girls." Doctoral dissertation, University of Virginia, 1990.

Dreyden, Julia I., and Shelagh A. Gallagher. "The Effects of Time and Direction Changes on the SAT Performance of Academically Talented Adolescents." *Journal for the Education of the Gifted* 12, no. 3 (1989): 187–204.

Eccles, Jacquelynne S. "Gender Roles and Women's Achievement-Related Decisions." *Psychology of Women Quarterly* 11, no. 2 (1987): 135–71.

Educational Testing Service. *1996 College-Bound Seniors: A Profile of SAT Program Test Takers.* Princeton, N.J.: Educational Testing Service, 1996.

EQUALS. *Cooperative Geometry.* Berkeley, Calif.: Lawrence Hall of Science, University of California, 1986.

———. *Family Science.* Portland, Oreg.: Northwest Equals, 1989.

Fennema, Elizabeth. "Teachers' Beliefs and Gender Differences in Mathematics." In *Mathematics and Gender,* edited by Elizabeth Fennema and Gilah C. Leder, pp. 1–9. New York: Teachers College Press, 1990.

Gavin, M. Katherine. "The Development of Math Talent: Influences on Students at a Women's College." *Journal of Secondary Gifted Education* 7, no. 4 (1996): 476–85.

———. "A Gender Study of Students with High Mathematics Ability: Personological, Educational, and Parental Variables Related to the Intent to Pursue Quantitative Fields of Study." Doctoral dissertation, University of Connecticut, 1997.

Good, Thomas L., and Jere E. Brophy. *Looking in Classrooms.* New York: Harper & Row, 1973.

Grandy, Jerilee. *Trends in the Selection of Science, Mathematics, or Engineering as Major Fields of Study among Top Scoring SAT Takers.* Princeton, N.J.: Educational Testing Service, 1987.

Halpern, Diane F. "The Disappearance of Cognitive Gender Differences: What You See Depends on Where You Look." *American Psychologist* 44 (1989): 1156–58.

Hanson, Katherine. *Teaching Mathematics Effectively and Equitably to Females.* Newton, Mass.: WEEA Publishing Center/Center for Equity and Cultural Diversity, 1992.

Hess, Robert D., Susan D. Holloway, W. Patrick Dickson, and G. Price. "Maternal Variables as Predictors of Children's School Readiness and Later Achievement in Vocabulary and Mathematics in Sixth Grade." *Child Development* 55 (1984): 1902–12.

Kimball, Meredith M. "A New Perspective on Women's Math Achievement." *Psychological Bulletin* 105 (1989): 198–214.

Leroux, Janice A., and Cheeying Ho. "Success and Mathematically Gifted Female Students: The Challenge Continues." *Feminist Teacher* 7, no. 2 (1994): 42–48.

Linn, Marcia C., and Cathy Kessel. "Participation in Mathematics Courses and Careers: Climate, Grades, and Entrance Examination Scores." Paper presented at the annual meeting of the American Educational Research Association, San Francisco, 1995.

McGillicuddy-De Lisi, Ann V. "The Relationship between Parental Beliefs and Children's Cognitive Level." In *Parental Belief Systems,* edited by Irving E. Sigel, pp. 7–24. Hillsdale, N.J.: Lawrence Erlbaum Associates, 1985.

National Council of Teachers of Mathematics. *Curriculum and Evaluation Standards for School Mathematics.* Reston, Va.: National Council of Teachers of Mathematics, 1989.

National Research Council. *Everybody Counts: A Report to the Nation on the Future of Mathematics Education.* Washington, D.C.: National Academy Press, 1989.

National Science Foundation. *Undergraduate Origins of Recent Science and Engineering Doctorate Recipients.* Washington, D.C.: National Science Foundation, 1992.

Parsons, Jacquelynne E., T. F. Adler, and Caroline M. Kaczala. "Socialization of Achievement Attitudes and Beliefs: Parental Influences." *Child Development* 53 (1982): 310–21.

Phillips, Deborah A. "Socialization of Perceived Academic Competence among Highly Competent Children." *Child Development* 58 (1987): 1308–20.

Reis, Sally M. "We Can't Change What We Don't Recognize: Understanding the Special Needs of Gifted Females." *Gifted Child Quarterly* 31, no. 2 (1987): 83–88.

Reis, Sally M., and Carolyn M. Callahan. "Gifted Females: They've Come a Long Way—or Have They?" *Journal for the Education of the Gifted* 12, no. 2 (1989): 99–117.

Renzulli, Joseph S. *The Enrichment Triad Model.* Mansfield Center, Conn.: Creative Learning Press, 1977.

———. *Schools for Talent Development: A Practical Plan for Total School Improvement.* Mansfield, Conn.: Creative Learning Press, 1994.

Rogers, Patricia. "Thoughts on Power and Pedagogy." In *Gender and Mathematics: An International Perspective,* edited by Leone Burton, pp. 38–46. London: Cassell, 1990.

Rosser, Phyllis F. *Sex Bias in College Admissions Tests: Why Women Lose Out.* Cambridge, Mass.: National Center for Fair and Open Testing, 1989.

Rossi Becker, Joanne. "Research on Gender and Mathematics Perspectives and New Directions." Paper presented at the annual meeting of the American Educational Research Association, New Orleans, 1994.

Sanders, Jo Shuchat. *Bibliography on Gender Equity in Mathematics, Science, and Technology: Resources for Classroom Teachers.* New York: Gender Equity Program, Center for Advanced Study in Education, CUNY Graduate Center, 1994.

———. *The Neuter Computer: Computers for Girls and Boys.* New York: Neal-Schuman Publishers, 1986.

Sheffield, Linda Jensen. *The Development of Gifted and Talented Mathematics Students and the National Council of Teachers of Mathematics Standards.* Storrs, Conn.: National Research Center on the Gifted and Talented, 1994.

Stenmark, Jean K., Virginia H. Thompson, and Ruth Cossey. *Family Math.* Berkeley, Calif.: University of California, 1986.

Stevenson, Harold William, and Richard S. Newman. "Long-Term Prediction of Achievement in Mathematics and Reading." *Child Development* 57 (1986): 646–59.

Wellesley College Center for Research on Women. *The AAUW Report: How Schools Shortchange Girls.* Washington, D.C.: American Association of University Women, 1992.

APPENDIX

Annotated List of Teaching Resources

1. Cook, Marcy. *Team Estimation and Analysis.* Balboa Island, Calif.: Marcy Cook, 1990.

   This workbook is a series of group estimation activities integrating social studies and mathematical computation and concepts. Using a series of mathematical clues, teams work together to predict numerical information on historical or geographical topics. The final clues guarantee success—a positive cooperative learning experience for the entire class in grades 4–8. (312 Diamond, Balboa Island, CA 92662)

2. Downie, Diane, Twila Slesnick, and Jean Kerr Stenmark. *Math for Girls and Other Problem Solvers.* Berkeley, Calif.: EQUALS, Lawrence Hall of Science, 1981.

   This book presents a variety of activities that make mathematics fun and challenging. Topics explored include logic strategies and patterns, creative thinking, estimation, observation, spatial visualization, and careers.

3. Erickson, Tim. *Get It Together.* Palo Alto, Calif.: Dale Seymour, 1989.
   Erickson, Tim. *United We Solve.* Oakland, Calif.: eeps media, 1996.

   These books outline activities for groups using manipulatives ranging from pattern blocks to M&M's and toothpicks. Problems have a wide range of topics and difficulty but all have the same format—six clue cards that together provide the information needed to solve the problem. Everyone in a group must work together because each member has different information needed for the solution.

4. Fraser, Sherry. *Spaces: Solving Problems of Access to Careers in Engineering and Science.* Palo Alto, Calif.: Dale Seymour Publishing Co., 1982.

   The activities in *Spaces* were designed to stimulate students' curiosity and interest in doing mathematics. The classroom-tested lessons develop problem-solving skills and logical reasoning, build familiarity with mechanical tools, strengthen spatial visualization skills, and teach the importance of mathematics for opening occupational doors. (Resources 2–4 listed above are available from Dale Seymour Publishing Co., P.O. Box 10888, Palo Alto, CA 94303-0879.)

5. Research and Planning Center, University of Nevada. *Add-Ventures for Girls: Building Math Confidence.* Newton, Mass.: WEEA Publishing Center, n.d.

   This book combines teacher development with strategies that work in teaching mathematics to girls. It includes a chapter on computer equity issues, which gives a list of questions for schools and teachers to assess the computer learning climate for girls. Strategies are also discussed for making computer education more accessible and appealing to girls. (Women's Educational Equity Act Publishing Center, 55 Chapel Street, Newton, MA 02160.)

6. Skolnick, Joan, Carol Langbort, and Lucille Day. *How to Encourage Girls in Math and Science.* Palo Alto, Calif.: Dale Seymour, 1982.

   This book focuses on ways to help girls acquire the skills and confidence they need to pursue a full range of interests in mathematics and science. It includes strategies and activities for developing spatial visualization, working with numbers, logical reasoning, and scientific investigation.

Other Teaching Resources

Gruver, Nancy and Joe Kelly, eds. *New Moon: The Magazine for Girls and Their Dreams.* Duluth, Minn.: New Moon Publishing.

National Council of Teachers of Mathematics. *Curriculum and Evaluation Standards for School Mathematics.* Reston, Va.: National Council of Teachers of Mathematics, 1989.

———. *Data Analysis and Statistics across the Curriculum.* Reston, Va.: National Council of Teachers of Mathematics, 1992.

———. *Professional Standards for Teaching Mathematics.* Reston, Va.: National Council of Teachers of Mathematics, 1991.

Perl, Teri. *Math Equals*. Menlo Park, Calif.: Addison-Wesley Publishing Co., 1978.

Sanders, Jo Shuchat. *Lifting the Barriers: 600 Strategies That Really Work to Increase Girls' Participation in Science, Mathematics, and Computers*. Port Washington, N.Y.: Jo Sanders Publications, 1994.

Resources on Notable Women

1. Cooney, Miriam. *Celebrating Women in Mathematics and Science.* Reston, Va.: National Council of Teachers of Mathematics, 1996.

   This book features twenty-two biographies of notable female mathematicians and scientists and shows how their determination, creativity, and intellectual passion helped them excel in their fields. Appropriate for use at the middle and high school levels, the text supplies many references that can be used for history of mathematics courses and is filled with excellent illustrations similar to wood-cuts. (National Council of Teachers of Mathematics, 1906 Association Drive, Reston, VA 20191-1593)

2. Edeen, Susan, John Edeen, and Virginia Slachman. *Portraits for Classroom Bulletin Boards: Women Mathematicians.* Palo Alto, Calif.: Dale Seymour Publishing Co., 1990.

   This kit is a set of black-line drawings (8 inches by 11 inches) of fifteen pioneering mathematicians with accompanying one-page biographies for quick bulletin boards or student handouts. It is also available with Hypercard program for student exploration or classroom presentation. (National Women's History Project, 7738 Bell Road, Windsor, CA 95492-8518)

3. Perl, Teri. *Women and Numbers: Lives of Women Mathematicians plus Discovery Activities.* San Carlos, Calif.: World Wide Publishing/Tetra, 1993.

   This multicultural book relates the biographies of thirteen outstanding mathematicians from the nineteenth and twentieth centuries, examining where and how these women's interests in mathematics originated and their accomplishments in their chosen fields. It also includes enjoyable activities based on each woman's contributions to mathematics.

4. National Women's History Project. *Telling Our Stories: Women in Science* (CD-ROM). Windsor, Calif.: National Women's History Project, 1996.

   The compelling stories of eight women scientists and their work are told through interviews, personal photos, interactive experiments, multimedia field trips, and more. A text and photo database highlights an additional 130 women scientists. (For PC Windows or Macintosh)

5. Veglahn, Nancy. *Women Scientists.* Windsor, Calif: National Women's History Project, 1991.

   This book features biographical sketches of eleven women whose accomplishments have won them recognition in their field. Included are Annie Jump Cannon, Margaret Mead, Alice Hamilton, Barbara McClintock, Rachel Carson, Rosalyn Yalow, and Gerty Cori.

6. Warren, Rebecca L., and Mary H. Thompson. *The Scientist within You* (Vol. 1) and *Women Scientists from Seven Continents—the Scientist within You* (Vol. 2). Windsor, Calif.: National Women's History Project, 1994 and 1995.

   In these two volumes, international female scientists take the stage. Each chapter features the work and biography of a scientist, along with a lesson plan including a related experiment, worksheets, and bibliography to make the subject area come alive for students.

Chapter 12

BUILDING PROGRAMS FOR PROMISING STUDENTS BEYOND THE CLASSROOM

Harvey Keynes
Andrea Olson
Doug Shaw
Karen Singer

The focus of this article is building mathematics enrichment programs for promising students beyond the classroom. What might enrichment mean in this context? Standard dictionaries define the verb *to enrich* as "to make fuller, more meaningful, or more rewarding." The authors believe that a successful enrichment experience for promising students presents an intense, mathematically challenging, and imaginative activity in a highly supportive and success-oriented environment. This nurturing environment gives promising students a sense of participation in the culture of mathematics and a sense of how this culture can help them in their careers and throughout their lives. These out-of-school enrichment activities include elements that (1) broaden promising students' understanding of mathematics by introducing innovative topics that go beyond the standard curriculum, (2) encourage meaningful insights, and (3) offer opportunities for promising students to become a part of the mathematics community.

Enrichment events may be used as stand-alone activities that do not rely on prior student knowledge, group involvement, or connections to the larger community of mathematicians and scientists. One way, however, to maximize the effectiveness of enrichment activities is to develop them as a series of events that focus on a central theme and that take place on a regular basis or are part of a larger, ongoing program. These thematically based sessions enable promising students to develop new relationships with the following:

- Peers who have similar talent and motivation for mathematics
- Potential mentors, students who are on more advanced levels, teaching assistants, and instructors
- Professionals who can initiate interest in specific college and career opportunities
- Theorists and researchers (from the past and present) who are introduced while exploring topics on a deeper level

A variety of enrichment activities or programs can be developed that meet the goals of promoting insightful thinking and broader linkages to the mathematics community. One effective gauge for measuring the quality of enrichment activities is by examining how they measure up to the "sixteen essential components of programs for the gifted" (House 1987, pp. 47–49). Of the sixteen guidelines presented, these six criteria—good mathematics, sound pedagogy, higher-order thinking skills, use of applications and problem solving, communication skills, and the encouragement of creativity—are primarily emphasized in this chapter.

Many of the examples reviewed in this chapter are based on activities used in various enrichment programs at the University of Minnesota (Keynes 1997). Several other distinguished programs offer excellent models, including summer programs at the University of Chicago, Ohio State University (Shapiro 1997), Boston University (Osserman 1997), and Southwest Texas University (Chen, Sorola, and Zhang 1997). A variety of opportunities also exist through the Johns Hopkins Institute for Academic Advancement and its related programs. The Mathematical Association of America has networked many fine academic year and summer programs through its SUMMA Project (Fasanelli 1996). Finally, the Committee on American Mathematics Competitions has well-developed program models.

MATHEMATICS ENRICHMENT COMPONENTS

A series of enrichment activities and programs that help build a community for mathematically promising students beyond the classroom will usually include several of the following components: workshops, speakers, field trips, newsletters, summer institutes, and leagues and competitions.

Workshops

Interactive events that offer several hours of hands-on exploration of a mathematics topic deliver an effective enrichment program, especially with topics that have visual and modeling aspects. A series of workshops can be linked together to form an academic year program involving a directed group activity, a demonstration or tour, and time for socialization. Successful workshops have been held, within the University of Minnesota Young Emerging Scholars projects and the University of Minnesota Talented Youth Mathematics Program (UMTYMP) for middle school students, that focused on topics such as symmetry, polyhedra, statistical sampling, the fourth dimension, and graph theory. Visualizing fractals or graphs of parametric equations have worked well as topics for more advanced students. These topics are easily related to other areas of mathematics; they also have conceptual frameworks that engender wonder at the beauty of mathematics while being accessible enough to be understood and appreciated without much prior knowledge. Each workshop in the Minnesota programs includes some mixture of instructor-led demonstration or discussion, cut/paste/color/construction, joint problem solving, and computer lab experiences. Producing models, diagrams, or charts to bring home from the activity encourages the students to share their excitement with friends and parents.

One of the most successful events has been the graphing calculator workshop, which consists of the following components:

1. Interactive demonstrations to small groups (fifteen to twenty students) on the basic use and functions of the graphing calculator, led by an instructor and teaching assistant

2. Rotation of teams through three stations using the graphing calculators with calculator-based laboratory systems (CBLs) to graph data from experiments that explore motion, sound, and temperature (CBLs are handheld data collection devices with sensor probes for collecting "real world" data that can be retrieved by graphing calculators for analysis.)

3. Reconvening of the groups to discuss their experiences and the implications of their findings

Between the rotations, there is a refreshment break for socialization. The workshop concludes with the participants answering a short (four or five question) evaluation. Student comments endorse the positive effects of this workshop—understanding the relevance of using graphs when solving problems in the classroom and real world.

In table 12.1 the details of another successful three-and-one-half hour workshop on symmetry given for mathematically promising fifth- and sixth-grade students indicate the high content level and mathematical depth of this workshop.

Table 12.1
Symmetry Enrichment Workshop Curriculum

Introductory lecture/slide show on the basic types of mathematical symmetry and the seven possible band patterns	20 min.
Using Kali software (freeware) to see how student initials look in the seven band patterns	45 min.
Making a chart of symmetries for regular polygons	15 min.
Constructing paper snowflakes that exhibit 4-, 5-, and 6-fold rotational symmetry	20 min.
Snack break	10 min.
Choreographing movements to show transformations between symmetry types	30 min.
Reflecting and translating in xy-coordinate systems	25 min.
Cutting pictures out of magazines that exhibit symmetry and identifying the types of symmetry	25 min.
Discussing and summarizing "Why is this mathematics?"	10 min.
Viewing video about reflection in 2 and 3 dimensions	15 min.

Students who attended the symmetry workshop brought home their snowflakes and all of the worksheets that were distributed. Most of the motivation for these activities came from two sources: (1) a book for the general public on symmetry, and (2) curricular materials developed by the NSF-Geometry Center, University of Minnesota, to go with the Kali software.

Sources for curricula include books, the Internet, NCTM journals, conferences, and local faculty and scientists who use mathematics. The World Wide Web has many sites with ideas and projects to be shared that have been contributed by a diverse group of mathematics educators, mathematicians, researchers, and historians. Some Internet sites have software that can be downloaded and distributed for free. The NSF-Geometry Center at the University of Minnesota (McGehee 1997), the Mathematics Forum, Swarthmore College (Weimar 1997), and MEGA-MATH (Casey 1997b) are three particularly rich sites. An excellent enrichment activity is guiding students through a mathematical site exploring topics such as mathematical games, fractals, or predator-prey relationships.

Speakers

Industrial and educational professionals provide another rich source of enrichment opportunities. Topics for presentations might include the mathematics behind games such as nim or tick-tack-toe, a short engineering-design project, or a description of how mathematics is used in a particular individual's workplace.

Speakers can come from several sources. A professor or student in mathematics, engineering, or a laboratory science at a nearby college or university might be interested in giving a talk or a laboratory tour. Chairs of departments or deans may have suggestions for speakers. Local corporations frequently have lists of employees willing to speak. Talks given on campuses or at companies are likely to make a greater impression on students and enable them to understand the influence of mathematics on the sciences and other disciplines. Another source of potential speakers is the parents of the promising students who use mathematics in their careers, and who may be especially well attuned to the attention span and interests of the group.

A key component of an activity involving speakers is the interaction between students and presenters. Students should be prepared and encouraged to ask relevant questions to find out any hidden details that interest them. Briefing speakers and hosts about what ages, grade levels, and mathematical backgrounds to expect in their student audience helps them understand how their activity fits into the program. In addition, some speakers alert promising students to educational and professional opportunities that may affect their future collegiate and career decisions. Interactions between students and presenters can transform a good explanatory session into one that is also energetic, lively, and relevant. At a career panel for middle school students, for instance, the initial introductory panel could be followed by breakout sessions, in which students rotate in small groups to meet with each of the speakers for a question and answer period.

An effective college night meeting might include information about how to choose a college, what colleges look for in an applicant, how to request letters of recommendation, and financial aid programs. Alumni, professors, or admissions representatives from colleges that have honors programs or special residential programs might describe their opportunities, including academic and research opportunities geared to talented students. Parents are usually interested in attending these events because they often begin thinking about college opportunities before the students do.

Field Trips

Activities that include a visit to a new location can build a stronger sense of community, help students to recognize the diversity within the field of mathematics, and reinforce the relevance of mathematics in a variety of industries. In addition to the more obvious field trips to museum exhibits about mathematics or to high-tech companies, students might visit a local public service company or a hospital radiology lab with someone who can explain how mathematics is used on a daily basis.

Prior to the field trip, teachers might share industry-specific or background information with the students. Students who see something in print or on the World Wide Web related to the speaker or institution may appreciate that these professionals and their skills are important in the real world. Some large companies have speaker bureaus that arrange for employees to assist during school and program visits, often with prepared workshop materials. Contact their human resources office to find out whether they offer such programs. Some companies may recruit employees as program speakers using an in-house bulletin board or newsletter.

The organization of the field trip is important, so consider having students meet with hosts in small groups and creating many opportunities to ask questions. Developing a previsit activity or self-guided tour sheet for the visit is also useful. Finally, choosing a topic or investigation that provides challenging mathematics or science for promising students is a very important factor.

Newsletters

A newsletter is an excellent way to connect the curriculum of individual activities to other program events and help the students continue to explore a topic or unit independently. The articles can remind students of what they have learned so far, mention related topics, and prepare students for the next meeting. A newsletter can also inform parents about the activities in which their child is involved and refer to related books, materials, and Web sites.

Newsletters can also serve as a forum for promising students to show their interest and ideas in mathematics. If each issue invites students to submit solutions to a problem or puzzle and publishes the names of those students who send in correct solutions, this can encourage students to spend more time on mathematics. For female or minority students, in particular, seeing solutions from other promising students in their evolving cohort of mathematics friends may make them feel less isolated and motivate them to join the larger mathematics community. Sending the newsletter to local newspapers and businesses or placing a newsletter on the Web helps to publicize the program to a wider audience so that student recognition extends beyond the program.

Some magazines with articles on mathematics topics are geared toward talented high school students. *Quantum* (National Science Teachers Association 1997) is a magazine inspired by the Russian publication, *Kvant.* COMAP, in Lexington, Massachusetts, offers publications for students and teachers that are oriented toward explaining applications. Mu Alpha Theta, a national mathematics honors fraternity, publishes a newsletter and a series of monographs on mathematical topics that are appropriate for promising middle school students and more-advanced high school students.

Summer Institutes

One particularly valuable type of enrichment opportunity for promising students is a multiday summer institute. Topics can be foreshadowed, introduced, developed, and applied—a process best done in multiple days. It is frequently easier for promising students to form friendships in a setting where they share deep learning, recreation, and meals. A summer institute can serve either as an excellent conclusion to an academic year enrichment program or as the inaugural event to an academic year program.

An effective summer institute for promising students should provide a diverse range of activities that thematically hinge on several mathematical and scientific topics. Table 12.2 summarizes the content that has been developed for three summer institutes within University of Minnesota Talented Youth Mathematics Program intervention projects.

Table 12.2
Curriculum Summaries for Three Summer Institutes for Promising Students

Exploring Perfection	Mathematics Enrichment Institute	The Mathematics of Music and Art
During the one-week institute, students explore a variety of mathematical objects that are in some way "perfect." What properties do these perfect objects exhibit? Is there a limit to how many different objects can share the same properties of perfection? Students also investigate concepts like numbers and ratios. Is there such a thing as a perfect number? A perfect ratio?	The three-and-one-half week institute enables students to learn how to appreciate mathematics on a deeper level. It engages the students in challenging mathematical enrichment activities on several topics including units on chaos and computing, physics of motion, and architecture/civil engineering, along with forays into applications of math in other areas.	During the two-week institute, several topics surrounding the mathematics of music and art—music of the spheres, how do computers make music?, computer art, the mathematics of Escher, art in mathematics, and perspective geometry and art—are investigated using mathematical induction, hyperbolic geometry, and other mathematics.
Grade level: Students entering the 6th or 7th grade.	Grade level: Students entering the 7th or 8th grade.	Grade level: Students entering the 8th grade.

A well-conceived summer institute needs a rich set of classroom activities, while ensuring that the institute as a whole has some content coherence. Even a broad subject like physics, combinatorics, or problem solving can be used to connect a set of activities to form study units.

Assuming that the components will relate to one or two themes, it is important to choose the right topics to cover. The main trade-off is breadth versus depth. One or two topics, covered in depth using a variety of approaches, are more likely to be retained by students than a brief introduction to a breadth of topics. Given that talented students can learn most subjects on a rudimentary level from a book, a good summer institute is an opportunity for them to do something different, within an educational experience that may not be duplicated until they go to college.

One challenge that arises for teachers is to develop activities that give each student something of interest in every topic covered, in contrast to designing activities that are too narrowly based or overly repetitive. For example, a variety of rich activities were developed for the five-day unit on chaos and computing at the Mathematics Enrichment Institute (table 12.2). The concept of the unit was based on materials developed by Robert Devaney at Boston University (Devaney 1995) and built on the topics of chaos, fractals, and algorithms. Algorithms, such as those used in computer programming, naturally tied together the seemingly diverse topics that comprised the unit. Iterative algorithms define dynamical systems, such as those generating the Mandlebrot set fractals. The winning strategy for the Chaos Game (Devaney 1995) was an algorithm that the students could discover and execute for themselves using the geometry of the Sierpinski triangle. Using simple graph theory representations for sets of points, the students were able to discuss algorithms for finding the shortest path between two points and for choosing a set of points to solve the "ice-cream shop location" problem (Casey 1997a), which required mapping out where ice-cream shops can be most efficiently located in a specific area. More than twenty activities, ranging from investigating computer-generated images to playing outdoor games on graphs, were developed to help promising students learn these contemporary mathematically challenging topics.

When possible, each topic should offer opportunities for interactive classroom activities, field trips, speakers, study groups, physical recreation breaks, and informal time for socialization. For motivational excitement it is hard to top a well-chosen field trip that is integrated into the curriculum. Like any classroom activity, a good field trip requires an introduction, foreshadowing the ideas that the students are expected to gain from the trip, and a conclusion.

Guest speakers can also be a valuable resource in summer institutes. In addition to preparing the students for the speakers, it is also a good idea to prepare the speakers for the students. Tell the speakers about what the students know, what they've done the previous days, and what their attention span is—even talented middle school students have a different attention span from the average college student or professional. Following up the visit with an interesting activity pertaining to the talk is a good way of ensuring that the students will value the visit. For example, during the 1996 UMTYMP Summer Enrichment Institute, an entire unit on building bridges began with a class activity in the morning and continued with an activity led by a civil engineer from the Center for Interfacial Engineering. By the end of the day, the students were excited about the concept of making their own wooden bridges and were eager to learn the mathematics needed to structurally strengthen their bridges. The unit concluded with the students entering their bridges in a competition held during the open house for families and friends.

Although students attending a summer institute may not all be from the same neighborhood, school, or district, it is extremely useful to create peer study groups that promote cooperative learning. Schedule time for informal student groups to meet as independent teams to work on projects or presentations outside of the formal structure of the institute. Allowing the students to blur the distinction between "learning" and "relaxing" is useful for all students, but especially so in helping promising students to develop a sense of community with their peers. Initially, these groups may need guidance from the instructional staff, but they should become independent as soon as possible.

Physical recreation and refreshment breaks are two other aspects of a summer program that enable students to form relationships with their peers and instructors. The release of energy during the physical recreation breaks also provides a release from the formal nature of interaction in the classroom. Over informal or family-style meals, students can discover peers and mentors who have similar interests in mathematics and perhaps other academic areas. The relationships that are established when promising students form friendships within the mathematics community might continue through their college years and beyond.

One of the primary influences on the development and implementation of a successful summer institute is staffing. Because talented students place large intellectual demands on the instructional staff, developing an instructional team makes it possible to divide up the work according to expertise, which ultimately affects both learning and community building. Instructional team members include an appropriate combination of the following personnel:

- Experienced middle school and high school instructors and some college professors, who will be responsible for developing the curriculum and leading several activities

- Outstanding high school seniors and undergraduate and graduate students, who will work as teaching assistants, lead cooperative workshop activities, and be responsible for monitoring recreational and refreshment breaks

- Parents or other community volunteers, who help monitor recreational and refreshment breaks and field trips as well as help construct classroom materials and manipulatives

Investing in preparation and organization time to coordinate an instructional team can strongly influence the success of the learning experience.

Leagues and Competitions

Mathematics competitions afford opportunities for talented students to work together on solving math problems. They offer promising students recognition of their talents by their classmates, instructors, families, and the public. For many students, even competitions involving individual participation on written tests can be social occasions as well as valuable educational opportunities.

Competitions may be appropriate for both middle school and high school students. However, if the problems are too easy or too hard or if they contain errors, the positive energy of the participants can be lost. Competitions work best when used to motivate a student to further mathematical involvement, such as coaching sessions or individual projects. The formation of a league, with teams of competitors, creates a stimulating environment for promising students. These leagues and competitions may be organized locally, with groups of students from the same school competing. Another option is to affiliate with state or national programs, such as MATHCOUNTS (junior high school) and the High School Mathematics Leagues (Minnesota State High School Mathematics League 1996). The Committee on American Mathematics Competitions also organizes several national contests.

One issue surrounding competitions is that, without some encouragement or intervention, female students tend to be underrepresented on the teams. The experiences of leagues that have successfully recruited female team members indicate that some familiarization with the concept of competitions and practice sessions prior to the events may increase female participation. Changes in the structure of the competitions to include more cooperative teamwork also positively influence the interest level of the female members.

BUILDING RELATIONSHIPS WITHIN THE PROGRAMS

Socialization with Peers

For most promising students, the usual pursuit of mathematical knowledge is essentially a solitary activity. Many students interested in mathematics find themselves wishing they had someone else with whom to discuss their ideas. Enrichment programs show promising students that there are others who are similar to them—and how diverse other talented students can be. Social interaction needs to be built into all enrichment activities. The overall length of the event may restrict the amount of time that can be scheduled for socialization, but even conversations among peers during a ten-minute refreshment break can facilitate new relationships.

Student interaction is inherent in many of the previously suggested activities. There are many other ways to foster a group spirit and communication among enrichment program participants, including study groups in homes, group work in the classroom, recreation during events, and the distribution of a student directory. Directory information of interest in addition to the participants' names, addresses (including e-mail addresses where available), and phone numbers may include a car pool list, a school listing, and a brief list of students' other interests.

Another growing area of opportunity has emerged from the increased popularity of computers and the Internet. Several program events could be built around using the Internet, creating a program home page, and investigating other applications. To ensure that this approach does not alienate students who do not have a home computer, their first should be a survey of the computer equipment and accessibility at local schools and resource and community centers.

Interaction with Instructors and Teaching Assistants

One effective way to encourage student-instructor interaction is by holding an after-class study session. Showing new perspectives on the material, providing more challenging problems based on it, and even foreshadowing future events in a more intimate setting can enhance an after-class session building on the subject matter. Whereas the students' primary impetus for attending will be the joy of learning, a great way to overcome inertia is to ensure they will have an enjoyable time and a snack.

Another way of helping an existing program build community is to allow the students to contact a teacher, a teaching assistant, or an adult as a resource. Telephone, e-mail, and computer conferencing allow students to have virtual dialogues with the instructional staff.

Peer Mentoring and Leadership Opportunities

Offering leadership opportunities is another way of encouraging promising students to consider themselves members of the mathematics community. Peer mentoring is an excellent activity for the advanced student, and enrichment activities involving students working on problems in groups usually need peer mentors. Student mentors typically need training in how to effectively elicit answers. Program alumni or advanced students can assist with teaching and become part of the instructional team. They can serve on planning committees, prepare activities, design manipulatives, and serve as teaching assistants. Not only do they learn from their experience, but they often are closer to the students agewise and culturally.

Parental Involvement

Given the time pressures on students and their families and limited resources, it is essential to create and support family involvement with programs for promising students. It is critical for parents, as well as the education and business communities, to be aware of mathematics enrichment programs and willing to support their continuation. Many of the strongest, most committed advocates for promising students are the students' parents. Because they are the primary facilitators and advocates for enriching their student's education, parents are vital resources for enrichment programs.

Parental involvement must precede the program. It is usually the parent, not the student, who ultimately decides whether a student will enroll in or attend the program. Conducting a family orientation or information session helps to establish a welcoming environment for parental involvement. A sample activity, an introduction to the staff, and a program outline should be part of this event, as well as information on dates, times, and cost. The overall objective of the orientation is communication: The students and parents learn what they can expect from the program, and the program staff hears what the students and parents anticipate they will learn by participating.

It is important in the program to have ways of sharing the students' progress with the parents, such as giving the students something to take home—a worksheet, model, or reading. One effective venue is to have an open house at the end of the last event at which students make presentations or otherwise demonstrate what they've learned to an audience of their families. This open house can include a graduation ceremony, where students receive certificates of accomplishment and recognition of extra effort.

Parents can also assist during the events, as judges for presentations, chaperones, photographers, or newsletter editors. An often overlooked communications resource is to have parents write letters on the program's behalf to funders, community leaders, politicians, and local newspapers.

Even though parental involvement requires additional organization for the program staff, this preparation strongly influences the quality and level of participation. Ideally, parents who have been involved with a program for an extended time can serve as family participation coordinators and work with the staff to organize this essential component of a successful program.

Community Involvement

One area of community involvement that can strengthen an enrichment program is the interaction with local educational institutions at both the precollege and college level, because of the resources they can offer for speakers, leaders, and ideas for curriculum and events. For example, students majoring in education may design a workshop for credit in one of their courses. Teachers who have led enrichment programs in their own schools have ideas and expertise to share. In addition, local school personnel and systems may be among the best mechanisms for the program recruitment of promising students. Teachers and district gifted-and-talented program coordinators can help identify appropriate students and distribute information. Local math team organizers may allow programs besides their own to be promoted to their participants.

Members of the community may become involved in a program for promising students by serving on an advisory board or attending presentations or exhibits made by the students. Representatives from local industry, government, and education may be able to offer some perspectives and suggestions at advisory board meetings that complement those of parent, student, and alumni advisors. When it is time to locate speakers or to lobby for local support, these board members may have additional contacts to offer.

To encourage community support of the program, the public must know about its successes. Newspapers and television stations often will announce events and names of student participants if they receive a press release. Some of the media also can use submitted photographs and letters to the editor. Finally, a home page on the World Wide Web can be another vehicle for promoting a promising students program.

Opening certain events such as a project or exhibit fair to the public is another strong way to make the community aware of the talents of the promising students and the quality of the program. High-profile guests such as the mayor or the CEO of a local company should also be encouraged to attend student exhibitions, competitions, and graduation ceremonies. Community guests can be invited to share their own experiences and expertise with students by giving graduation speeches, career presentations, or demonstrations as a part of mathematics fairs that include exhibits from both students and professionals.

CONCLUSION

A well-designed out-of-school enrichment program should afford promising students a supportive environment in which to (1) learn challenging mathematics, (2) build friendships with like-minded peers, (3) establish relationships with mentors, and (4) begin to identify with the global community of mathematicians and scientists. This paper has offered specific suggestions and examples for developing, organizing, and implementing enrichment activities or programs for promising students that meet these objectives.

The enrichment events featured in this essay—workshops, speakers, field trips, newsletters, summer institutes, and leagues and competitions—reflect the criteria of the "sixteen essential components of programs for the gifted" (House 1987). The thematic focus of the units and programs created from these events exemplify how this approach encourages meaningful insights about mathematically challenging topics. The importance of parental involvement and the relationships developed with peers, instructional staff, industry professionals, and researchers within a nurturing program environment are central elements toward building a community for mathematically promising students. In summary, effective enrichment programs provide motivation and support for promising students to recognize their opportunities as mathematicians and scientists beyond the classroom.

REFERENCES

Casey, Nancy. "Algorithms and Ice Cream for All." <www.c3.lanl.gov/workbk/dom/dom.html> (1997a).

———. "Introducing Megamath." <www.c3.lanl.gov/mega-> (1997b).

Chen, Janet, Gus Sorola, and Mengmeng Zhang. "SWT Honors Summer Math Camp Home Page." <www.math.swt.edu/mathcamp/camp.html> (1997).

Devaney, Robert. "Chaos in the Classroom." <math.bu.edu./DYSYS/chaos-game/chaos-game.html> (1995).

Fasanelli, Florence, ed. *Directory of Mathematics-Based Intervention Projects.* Washington, D.C.: The Mathematical Association of America, 1996.

House, Peggy A., ed. *Providing Opportunities for the Mathematically Gifted, K–12.* Reston, Va.: National Council of Teachers of Mathematics, 1987.

Keynes, Harvey. "University of Minnesota Talented Youth Mathematics Program." <www.math.umn.edu/itcep/> (1997).

McGehee, Richard. "The Geometry Center." <www.geom.umn.edu> (1997).

Minnesota State High School Mathematics League. "A High School Mathematics League for Minnesota." Report. Minnesota High School Mathematics League, 1996.

National Science Teachers Association, ed. *Quantum.* New York: Springer-Verlag, 1997.

Osserman, Brian. "The Program in Mathematics for Young Scientists." <math.bu.edu/INDIVIDUAL/promys> (1997).

Shapiro, Daniel. "The Ross Young Scholars Program." <www.math.ohio-state.edu/ross/index.html> (1997).

Weimar, Steve. "The Math Forum." <www.forum.swarthmore.edu/math/welcome.html> (1997).

Chapter 13

THE MISSING LINK: CONNECTING PARENTS OF MATHEMATICALLY PROMISING STUDENTS TO SCHOOLS

Jennie Bennett

A recent report from The National Council of Teachers of Mathematics (NCTM) Task Force on Mathematically Promising Students sought to broaden the opportunity for talented mathematics students. (See the appendix at the end of this book.) This report identifies the policies, practices, and outcomes that affect students who are mathematically talented. Students with mathematical promise from all cultures and across all economic strata have the potential to become leaders and problem solvers of the future. Thus, it is important for mathematics educators, schools, and the broader community to open the doors of opportunity to all students.

The Third International Mathematics and Science Study (TIMSS) reported that the home environment is strongly related to mathematics achievement (TIMSS International Study Center 1996, p. 4). Students enter school possessing the knowledge, values, and beliefs directly or indirectly shaped by their parents and communities. Although heredity sets the stage for development (Sanborn 1979), parents play a significant role in the development of their children because they are usually a child's first and primary teacher during his or her formative years. Because parents play powerful roles in the development of their children, schools should work to involve them and the community in the life of the school. Everyone benefits when parents are involved in the education of their children.

Many research studies emphasize that student achievement improves when parents participate in and support their child's academic environment. Parents should be linked to the schools at all levels of their children's education—their involvement should not cease at the bus stop or the door of the schoolhouse. Many schools have programs that concentrate the involvement of parents at the early childhood and elementary school levels. However, students progress to the upper grades, particularly high school, parent participation decreases (Jackson and Cooper 1992) and these pivotal partners—parents—often feel disenfranchised and disconnected from the school environment. This is particularly true for parents of culturally diverse, language minority, and economically deprived students. In spite of the research on the benefits of parental involvement, traditional practices often fail to address the needs of many children in poverty (Edwards and Jones-Young 1992).

There are several reasons why parents may not be involved in schools. Parents may view schools as unsupportive and unhelpful because they themselves have experienced failure in the mathematics classroom. Moreover, parents often see their children's unsuccessful experiences as their own. Parents who dropped out of mathematics or school may not feel comfortable in school environments. These parents lack the confidence in their ability to help their children with mathematics. They also may not believe that they have the capacity to understand the mathematics curriculum and the programs for their mathematically talented children. Language minority and culturally diverse parents may not be as comfortable in a school setting when teachers of their mathematically promising children are different from them. When parents are confused about feedback on their children's performance, some withdraw from participating in their children's education. Others may display anger and frustration (Swap 1993). When parents are unclear about their role with schools and the education of their mathematically gifted youths, it is the school's job to embrace them and change parents' negative perceptions to positive ones.

Parents serve as a crucial link to their children's movement through the mathematics "pipeline." Parents of mathematically promising students should ensure that their children are immersed in rich and stimulating mathematical and technological environments. Schools must find a vehicle to support this partnership regardless of parents' past experiences in mathematics.

SOCIETAL ATTITUDE ABOUT MATHEMATICS

The weight of myths and tradition about mathematics resonates from household to household and generation to generation. Even though a child may be talented in the mathematics classroom, many parents who did not excel in mathematics find it difficult to believe their child's successes. One of the myths in *Moving Beyond Myths,* (National Research Council [NRC] 1991, p. 10) is, "Success in mathematics depends more on innate ability than on hard work." This dangerous and pervasive myth has the propensity for excluding mathematically talented minorities, women, and physically challenged students from the mathematics pipeline.

Everybody Counts stated, "Since mathematics is the foundation of science and technology, it serves as a key to opportunity and careers" (NRC 1989, p. 3). This statement lends support for studying mathematics. Yet, some traditions in our society can narrow the pathway of success for mathematically promising students. Society accepts an environment in the mathematics classroom in which participants in advanced mathematics courses are mainly white, upper- or middle-class, and male (NRC 1989). The research also documents the underparticipation of children of color, especially those who are mathematically promising, in upper-level mathematics courses. *Everybody Counts* (NRC 1989) states that girls and boys show little difference in mathematical ability, effort, or interest until adolescence. However, as social pressure increases and career choices are made, tradition shows that males outnumber females in mathematics-based careers. Many girls become dropouts in high school and college mathematics courses. Public statements such as "girls can't really do math" and "girls don't need much math" have been documented and perpetuate stereotypes (NRC 1989). Parents should work to counteract these stereotypes that reduce the participation of many mathematically talented students.

U.S. schools long ago adopted the "in loco parentis" model, delegating the role of education to the school and thereby signaling that parents do not need to be involved. (Even so, programs such as Family Math enable parents to encourage their children's participation in mathematics through hands-on activities.) As children progress through school, parental involvement decreases, especially by the time children reach high school (Jackson and Cooper 1992). One reason for the decline may be that these adolescents want independence from their parents. Another reason may be that a parent's comfort level with mathematics decreases as a child progresses through school. Yet, parents' involvement in the mathematics education of their children is critical at all levels, especially in middle school and high school.

Society frequently regards mathematically talented students as different (Colangelo and Zaffrann 1979). These unique students may be viewed by their peers as strange and different—as "nerds." This stereotype is reflected in movies and television shows that portray mathematically gifted students as social outcasts and in shows that depict other children experiencing problems in mathematics class, rather than in reading or social studies. As parents and educators, it is our job to systematically promote more positive attitudes and accurate perceptions about mathematics and mathematically talented students inside and outside school.

EXPECTATIONS

The need for changes in attitudes, expectations, myths, and practices in mathematics education is clearly evident when we examine the poor performance of U.S. students in international comparisons (Hawkins 1995), such as the Third International Mathematics and Science Study (TIMSS). TIMSS was designed to focus on educational policies, practices, and outcomes, to gain insight into those practices that promote educational achievement. TIMSS reported that in every country, strong positive relationships were found between mathematics achievement and having study aids in the home. The study aids cited include a dictionary, computer, and study table or desk for the student (TIMSS International Study Center 1996, p. 4). The study encouraged parents to give children as many of these study aids as possible and to support them in their study of mathematics at home.

Colleges and universities are fundamentally important to the teaching and learning of mathematics. They must work with schools to prepare qualified mathematics teachers today for tomorrow's students. The challenge for universities is to institutionalize parent involvement in preservice programs. Additionally, professional development opportunities should be designed to remove barriers to parent-school relationships.

Even though each family is unique in its goals and values, history, cultural practices, and language, a staff development framework coupled with multicultural awareness is essential to lower the barriers for accepting all mathematics learners, especially the mathematically talented and their parents. The *Professional Standards for Teaching Mathematics* (NCTM 1991) recommends that institutions of higher learning "collaborate with schools and teachers in the design of preservice and continuing education programs" (p. 184). To maximize the intent of this standard, mathematics faculty must integrate it into their courses and develop teachers' understanding of the influences of students' linguistic, ethnic, racial, socioeconomic, and gender backgrounds on learning mathematics. The challenge for higher education faculty is to show prospective teachers consistently how to communicate with students and their parents in a manner that is sensitive to the child's and parents' language, cultural, and racial backgrounds. The education of well-prepared mathematics teachers is crucial to what happens to students in school. "Teacher expectations are founded on knowledge and beliefs about who their students are and what they can do" (p. 145).

Attention to such changes in preservice and continuing in inservice programs, will result in improved communication with parents and, ultimately, in improved student achievement in mathematics.

CONNECTING PARENTS TO SCHOOLS

Connecting parents to schools and the mathematics classroom is one ingredient for successful efforts that will promote students' achievement in mathematics. "Parent involvement helps parents and teachers become more aware of their need to support student learning" (Banks and Banks 1993); thus teachers should first actively engage in open dialogue with parents to determine attitudes about and expectations for students' mathematics performance. The following suggestions may serve as an operative plan for active parental involvement and systemic change:

1. *Teachers might suggest to parents and other interested adults ways in which they can help their children in mathematics.* Oftentimes, community stakeholders, such as religious and community-based organizations, actively participate in helping students with mathematics when parents are not able to. They can also provide facilities for mathematics tutoring and serve as an advocate for schools.

   Adults other than the child's parents can play a parental role. For example, when one local middle school sponsored a family math night, one student who was not able to bring her parent brought her church minister and an older sister.

2. *Parents need to understand and learn to nurture the abilities of their mathematically talented children.* Counselors and teachers should work together and plan for parent education classes. These classes should support and teach the value of mathematically talented children's creativity. (Colangelo and Dettmann, 1983)

Schools across the United States have implemented Family Math, a program that originated at the Lawrence Hall of Science, University of California at Berkeley, as one method of involving parents in schools. At a Family Math session, I once suggested to Jan that her young preschooler could participate in the activities. Jan's son approached an activity for students in grades 3 through 5 with enthusiasm and interest. The poster asked participants to write "everything you know about 100." His response was "90 + 10 = 100." Jan quickly quieted this preschooler's interest in mathematics by stating, "Your older brother is supposed to answer the questions." My role as a mathematics supervisor was to encourage this mathematically promising child to participate in this activity and all mathematics activities that evening and in future events.

3. *Parents should be contacted by the mathematics teacher regarding access to programs for mathematically promising children.* Parents need to know the guidelines both for acceptance into and for participation in these programs. Applications should be in the language of the parent if the parent is non-English speaking. It is the school's responsibility to help parents understand the parameters of programs for mathematically promising students, so that parents will not place unrealistic expectations on their children to excel beyond their capabilities (NCTM 1987).

4. *Parents should be made aware of the identification process for talented students.* They need to learn how to be advocates within the school for programs that broaden the definition of who the mathematically promising are. Moreover, parents can significantly affect political issues as they relate to mathematics and the mathematically promising, serving as advisors, decision makers, or advocates in their parent-teacher organization or association. Parents may also serve on advisory committees or school improvement councils. Banding together, they can positively affect school board policy, decisions, and program planning—often more effectively than teachers and other school district personnel (Clark 1988). Parents with mathematically promising children may also choose to monitor the school's programs for mathematically promising students and work toward improving these programs for all students.

5. *Mathematics teachers should have conferences with parents to communicate their children's mathematical performance and encourage the child's continued participation in mathematics.* If a parent does not speak English, it is the teacher's responsibility to invite the parent to attend the conference with a translator present. The mathematics teacher should not use educational jargon or acronyms that are unfamiliar to the typical parent. Conferences are frequently a good time to explain to parents' resources that are available to mathematically promising students and ways in which parents might encourage these same students to continue their mathematical development.

6. *Teachers and administrators should understand the culture of the parents and the community where the students reside—to be immersed*

in community surroundings and events. Teachers today may not live in the communities where they teach; students and their parents do not run into the child's teachers in the grocery store as they might have at one time. Nonetheless, teachers should be familiar with their students' environment. In professional development sessions, as I integrate cultural diversity into the mathematics session, I suggest that teachers tour their students' neighborhoods.

7. *Teachers may establish special parental invitational events.* If parents are reluctant to attend these sessions at school, teachers might begin to build trust by hosting sessions at churches, synagogues, community centers, or other places that parents frequent. It may be helpful to get the local grocery stores to post these events on the door of the store. These events can help teachers who drive a distance to teach students and may not understand the student's environment, which may be significant to the development of their mathematical promise.

8. *Teachers should find ways to use parents' expertise in the mathematics classroom* (Finders and Lewis 1994). Parents should be empowered to work with other children as well as their own in the mathematics classroom, serving as mentors and talking to students about their careers in relation to mathematics.

Additionally, parents can participate as assistant coaches for programs and competitions such as MATHCOUNTS. MATHCOUNTS is a mathematics program for middle school students, particularly for seventh- and eighth-grade students. The purpose of MATHCOUNTS is to advance students' problem-solving skills through individual and group work. The MATHCOUNTS handbook suggests that parents can furnish refreshments or drive "mathletes" to competition events (MATHCOUNTS 1994). However, parents can play a more meaningful role by speaking to mathletes about careers in mathematics and working as assistant coaches.

9. *Bilingual volunteers can help with the two-way communication with parents.* If the parents do not speak English, notes and newsletters should be written in the language of the parents, school meetings should have a translator available to communicate with language minority parents. Clearly, this shows cultural sensitivity to the parents' native tongue if the parents do not speak English, and it enhances the possibilities for recognizing and encouraging mathematically talented students from all cultural backgrounds.

10. *Parents should be allowed to bring younger children to meetings or to the classroom, if necessary.* Some parents may not have regular babysitting or may not be able to afford a babysitter, so schools may want to offer babysitting. For example, when Family Math sessions are held, schools could hire high school students or seek parent volunteers—parents with children in different grade levels from the family math session being presented.

11. *The parents of mathematically talented students, regardless of their ethnicity, primary language, or socioeconomic status, are interested in their children's education.* Therefore, we must involve parents in the planning of mathematics programs for mathematically talented students. By interviewing or surveying them about these programs, we empower them to develop their children's mathematical abilities and to become involved in improving and expanding these programs.

12. *If parents cannot be involved in school events due to work obligations, allow a surrogate parent (older brother, aunt, grandparent, or other family member) or friend to participate in their place.* Also, have a flexible schedule so that working parents have an equal chance to visit mathematics classrooms or other activities. This means that schools may have to repeat evening activities and meetings during the day for parents who work at night and vice versa.

13. *Communication is a two-way street, important for the involvement of parents in the education of their children.* Teachers should try to answer parents' questions about mathematics curriculum, instruction, and assessment in layperson's terms without using educational jargon or acronyms. Teachers should be active listeners when in conference with parents; parents and teachers should work together to find ways to encourage and develop students' mathematical abilities.

THE ROLE OF COMPUTERS

Computers have had a phenomenal impact on our lives, and the information superhighway offers almost unlimited information to all that have access to it. Parents of mathematically promising children may use the Internet to locate information to enhance their children's mathematical knowledge. One such Web site is "More Than Just Smart," established by the Children's Television Workshop's Sesame Street Parents, which assists parents with defining giftedness and evaluating giftedness in their own children (www.ctw.org/parents).

Parents, teachers, and students can browse and use the Scholastic Web site, "The Magic School Bus Riddle of the Week" (www.scholastic.com/magicschoolbus /games/). This entertaining site presents a mathematical problem for children to solve. Another Web site where critical thinking and problem-solving opportunities can be explored by the parents and teachers of the mathematically promising is "Totally Kids Magazine!" (www.foxkids.com/fuddle.htm).

The Internet offers other options for parents to locate mathematics activities for their promising children. "Helping Your Child Learn Math—Math in the Home" and "The Grocery Store" feature activities at varying levels of difficulty (www.ed.gov/pubs/parents/Math/Mathland.html). The grocery store activities are suitable when children shop with their parents. Both activities use geometric symbols to indicate the level of difficulty.

Parents will not run out of activities when they browse the site, "365 TV-Free Activities You Can Do with Your Child" (www.family.disney.com). The activities do not require parents to purchase special materials. (There are also "365 outdoor activities".) These mathematics activities offer challenging experiences for mathematically promising students.

After parents attend Family Math Sessions, they may locate and print out variations on Family Math activities and read more about Family Math in the online Family Math Newsletter (www.lhs.berkeley.edu).

The largest and most frequently used education-related database in the world, the Educational Resources Information Center (ERIC), also has a Web site (www.ericse.org/eric/digests/digest-m04.html). Parents can locate information that will serve as a resource for helping their mathematically promising children. In "Doing Mathematics With Your Child", Hartog and Brosnan (1994) discuss ways parents can nurture their children's development in mathematics and encourage parents to find ways to work with their children's teacher. Parents also might refer to NCTM's journal *Teaching Children Mathematics* to familiarize themselves with mathematics content and teaching strategies. Moreover, parents may be interested in ERIC's annotated bibliography, *PRIME: Parent Resources in Mathematics Education.*

School administrators can access the Internet for information on involving parents. "Principals' Best Ten Tips To Increase Parental Involvement in Schools" recommends various approaches principals can employ to increase parent participation in schools. These tips can be located at the Urban/Minority Families, a part of National Parent Information Network, at www.eric-web.tc.columbia.edu /guides/tentipsl.html.

Finally, parents and children can join in seeking out and supporting educational mathematical programs as they become available. For example, some public television shows help support parents in learning about mathematics and mathematically talented children. The show "Count On Me," first aired in 1993, focuses on the importance of mathematics in an increasingly technical world. This program uses real-life vignettes to reinforce that parents must become actively involved in the education of their children. (Parents can also purchase videocassettes of this program by calling 1-800-328-PBS1.) "Newton's Apple," another PBS program, now integrates science and mathematics and to inform both parents and students. Favorite PBS characters for preschoolers, such as the Sesame Street character "the Count," and Barney and his friends, present songs and games to learn mathematics. Preschoolers may learn number recognition, number matching, and counting from programs such as Barney and Friends "Carnival of Numbers."

SUMMARY

The partnership between parents and schools is vital to education. Research shows that parent and family involvement is one of the important factors in successful schools or schools that report improved student achievement (Finders and Lewis 1994). All parents deserve the opportunity to learn as much as they can to become active participants in their children's education. The investment is great and the benefits are well worth the time and effort for the ultimate goal— mathematically talented students and citizens.

REFERENCES

Banks, James A., and Cherry A. McGee Banks. *Multicultural Education: Issues and Perspectives,* 2nd ed., p. 336. Needham Heights, Mass.: Allyn & Bacon, 1993.

Clark, Barbara. *Growing up Gifted: Developing the Potential of Children at Home and at School,* 3rd ed, pp. 566–74. Columbus, Ohio: Merrill, 1988.

Colangelo, Nicholas, and David Dettmann. "A Review of Research on Parents and Families of Gifted Children." *Exceptional Children* 50, no. 1 (1983), 20–27.

Colangelo, Nicholas, and Ronald Zaffrann. *New Voices in Counseling the Gifted.* Dubuque, Iowa: Kendall/Hunt, 1979.

Edwards, Patricia, and Lauren Jones-Young. "Beyond Parents: Family, Community, and School Involvement." *Phi Delta Kappan* 74, no. 3 (1992): 72–80.

Finders, Margaret, and Cynthia Lewis. "Why Some Parents Don't Come to School." *Educational Leadership* 51, no. 8 (1994): 50–54.

Hartog, Martin, and Patricia Brosnan. "Doing Mathematics with Your Child." ERIC Digest EDO SE 94-3. Columbus, Ohio: ERIC Clearinghouse for Science, Mathematics, and Environmental Education, 1994.

Hawkins, William. *Constructing a Secure Mathematics Pipeline for Minority Students.* Office of Educational Research and Improvement, Washington, D.C., 1995.

Jackson, Barbara, and Bruce Cooper. "Involving Parents in Improving Urban Schools." *National Association of Secondary School Principals* 76, no. 54 (1992): 31–38.

MATHCOUNTS Foundation. *1994–95 MATHCOUNTS School Handbook,* pp. 5–6. Alexandria, Va.: MATHCOUNTS Foundation, 1994.

National Council of Teachers of Mathematics. *Professional Standards for Teaching Mathematics.* Reston, Va.: National Council of Teachers of Mathematics, 1991.

———. *Providing Opportunities for the Mathematically Gifted, K–12.* Reston, Va.: National Council of Teachers of Mathematics, 1987.

———. "Report of the NCTM Task Force on the Mathematically Promising." *NCTM News Bulletin* 32 (December 1995): Special insert.

National Research Council. *Everybody Counts: A Report to the Nation on the Future of Mathematics Education.* Washington, D.C.: National Academy Press, 1989.

———. *Moving Beyond Myths: Revitalizing Undergraduate Mathematics.* Washington, D.C.: National Academy Press, 1991.

Sanborn, Marshall P. *New Voices in Counseling the Gifted,* edited by Nicholas Colangelo and Ronald Zaffrann, p. 396. Dubuque, Iowa: Kendall-Hunt, 1979.

Swap, Susan. *Developing Home-School Partnerships: From Concepts to Practice,* pp. 13–26. New York: Teachers College Press, 1993.

TIMSS International Study Center. *Mathematics Achievement in the Middle School Years: IEA's Third International Mathematics and Science Study.* Chestnut Hill, Mass.: Boston College, 1996.

Chapter 14

ORGANIZATIONAL ALTERNATIVES FOR THE MATHEMATICALLY PROMISING

Betty J. Krist

There is a peculiar sentiment in how U.S. and Canadian schools view our most able students. As cultures, we value equality. We are uncomfortable with social and intellectual distinctions and with hierarchies that stand in the way of success for industrious individuals. Thus, many of our schools have traditionally had a move toward a "middling standard" that favors conformity over deviation from the norm.

Competing with this egalitarian spirit is a conflicting assumption—that individuals should be allowed to "be all that they can be." Freedom and liberty are valued as tools for unleashing potential in citizens so that they can go as far as their talent and ambition will allow. The assumption is that people vary in interests and abilities, and those who can excel ought to be supported in their efforts to do so.

These two beliefs—a commitment to "equality" and an assumption that people should be allowed to develop to their full potential—have clashed throughout our histories and have muddled efforts to provide a quality education for our most promising students. In addition, today we struggle with other teaching problems like the significance of "algebra for all" and the public's math phobia, which complicate our efforts to provide appropriate support for mathematically promising students.

Exceptional talent is viewed as both a valuable human resource and a troublesome expression of eccentricity. We admire and reward the brilliant, creative mind after it has invented something practical or produced tangible results (Ross 1993). Yet we are not, in general, inclined to support those who want to pursue an artistic or intellectual life; in fact, we find ways to discourage them. Negative stereotypes of high-achieving students have created an atmosphere in which students do not want to be identified as very smart. In fact, participation in many special schools or programs makes a student a certified nerd, a perception that must be addressed among family and friends when acceptance into an alternative program is considered.

Further complicating the issues are the increasingly sensitive politics of equity and inclusion. Consider the following concerns:

- In a move to full inclusion, will detracking result in the dissolution of quality, the denial of individual differences, the denial of appropriate challenges for talented students, and the placing of promising students in cooperative learning situations where they are forever in the role of tutoring less-able students? (Matthews 1992)

- Will some teachers in schools with special programs be relieved that someone else is meeting the needs of gifted children or will they (and others, e.g., parents, students) feel resentful of the kinds of support these children receive? (Sapon–Shevin 1994)
- By adopting the notion that "gifted education is just good education for everyone," are we once again looking for a one–size–fits–all solution? (Tomlinson 1994)
- Can the core curriculum specified in the NCTM *Standards* be expanded in a meaningful and productive way to meet the needs of high-ability students? (National Council of Teachers of Mathematics 1989)
- Can equity thrive in a culture of mathematical excellence? (Keynes 1996)
- If we have a special program for mathematically promising students, should we develop a special program for scientifically promising students, for musically promising students,... for mathematically *un*promising students?

Also, consider the evolution of National Council of Teachers of Mathematics's (NCTM) own view over the years. *An Agenda for Action* (NCTM 1980) urged programs for the gifted, based on sequential enrichment through ingenious problem solving rather than acceleration alone. In an NCTM position paper on vertical acceleration (NCTM 1983), acceleration was recommended for only a limited number of highly talented and mathematically creative students; for others, a strong, expanded program emphasizing enrichment was preferable. A subsequent position paper on provisions for mathematically talented students (NCTM 1986) brought the recommendation of appropriate programs for the gifted that provide a broad and enriched view of mathematics in a context of higher expectation. Later, the report of the NCTM Task Force on the Mathematically Promising (1995), instead of recommending one particular programmatic philosophy, suggested that those involved in program development understand the ramifications of their decisions. Here are some of their concerns:

- Do the opportunities provide for the wide range of abilities, beliefs, motivation, and experiences of students who have mathematical promise regardless of their socioeconomic and ethnic backgrounds, and do the opportunities meet their continuum of needs?
- Are curriculum, instruction, and assessment qualitatively different and designed to meet the differing needs of promising students?
- Are there resources, projects, problems, and means of assessment that allow for differences in the level of depth of understanding and engagement?
- Are there appropriate opportunities in mathematics that have clearly defined, comprehensive, integrated goals—that are not simply isolated activities?
- Are the opportunities available to all interested students?

Clearly, the issues associated with offering opportunities for promising students have become more sophisticated, as have other aspects of mathematics teaching and learning. Nevertheless, some general recommendations can be made.

- A mathematics program for promising students should develop and capitalize on the unique abilities of these promising children (e.g., the ability to abstract at that grade level).
- The program should be challenging so that students learn to deal with the frustrations and rewards of answering questions once viewed as unanswerable.
- Students should have high-quality instruction in the material they are learning as well as guidance and firm encouragement for good work habits and study skills.
- The program should involve a long-term commitment to excellence by students, teachers, and parents.
- When the going gets tough, as it should, the students must have appropriate support and direction.

Many very bright children have never been challenged by problems that require more than a few moments' reflection, and they withdraw when their first attempts at a solution meet with failure. Their stamina for problem solving must go beyond playfulness, and they should routinely be expected to use not only good mathematics but also correct mathematical language, as well, for these students especially must be encouraged to express their ideas articulately and precisely. Finally, their work must meet a reasonable yet rigorous standard.

To gain a good sense of the thinking styles of their classmates, epistemology must be a key component of any program. Of crucial importance is the very act of answering the same question by using different techniques or working on problems that have more than one answer (or no answer). Variety and alternative approaches to problems and organization of ideas are too rare in mathematics classrooms.

Lastly, and most important, the program must have academic integrity. Mathematics by its very nature builds on itself: its powerful ideas are embedded in many of the basic notions that are taught in school mathematics. Talented students seek to be taken seriously and want someone to listen carefully to their sometimes long, involved arguments. Bright youngsters seek opportunities for knowledge-based dialogue. Furthermore, a strong high school program will surely move students beyond the secondary-school content to university-level work, for which they should perform to university standards and earn university credit. Yet this work should still be geared to the interests of the students. Elementary, middle, and high school students should not be treated as diminutive adults (NCTM 1987).

PROVIDING FOR STUDENTS IN THE EXISTING SCHOOL

Existing programs for the promising fall quite naturally into two categories: those offered for students attending a comprehensive school and those for students in schools designed solely for high-ability students. The first of these are programs within a comprehensive school ("pullout," honors, Advanced Placement, or even Internet programs). Pullout programming for superior students is likely to be hit or miss, more often characterized by zeal than enhanced by systematic planning (Cox 1985).

"Pullout" describes an administrative arrangement that places high-ability students in a heterogeneous classroom for most of their instruction but pulls them out to study with other bright youngsters in special classes. Time spent in pullout classes varies from less than an hour a week to a significant portion of each school day. In these programs, individuals who have shown distinction in a particular subject area are given the opportunity and challenge to engage in work beyond that of their classmates.

The special classes may meet in the students' home school, or the students may be bused to another school or designated center. In many cases, the high school courses are taught in conjunction with a university (generally nearby, if not by Internet) that offers students special credit for coursework completed— "regular" university credit or otherwise.

In the elementary school, pullout may be gifted and talented classes with programmatic but not conventional academic content, such as Odyssey of the Mind. If there is a mathematics specialist available, that curriculum may be addressed, but a major problem here is the practice of allowing bright students to work from the mathematics text for subsequent grades. Too often, what results is reasonable (or even very good) facility in algorithmic manipulation, but minimal understanding of concepts and principles. Also the major grade-to-grade overlap in content—often more than 50 percent (Flanders 1987)—and the stereotypical (even repeated) presentation can make this a superficial and challenge-free activity. Indeed, the problem of minimal supervision by, and interaction with, the teacher is the most serious problem of trying to accommodate gifted students at the elementary school level.

Fortunately, an ever-increasing number of useful resources are available to the elementary school teacher. NCTM has several quality publications such as those of the *K–12 Addenda Books,* classics like *Boxes, Squares, and Other Things* (Walter 1970), and new publications like *Mission Mathematics: K–6* (NCTM 1997a), *5–8* (NCTM 1997b), and *9–12* (NCTM 1997c). Of course, the NTCM journals *Teaching Children Mathematics* and *Mathematics Teaching in the Middle School* contain useful ideas that, though usually not geared specifically to high-ability children, provide a regular source of effective ideas for the teacher. Most recently published elementary school textbook series have enrichment materials for more advanced students. Only a few publishers have ever produced extensive supplemental material like the four volumes of *Challenge: A Program for the Mathematically Talented* (Haag et. al. 1986), which present distinct activities for high-ability students with extensive teaching suggestions.

At a secondary school level, fine resources are available as well. Books include *Deductive Sustems: Finite and Non-Euclidean Geometries* [Lockwood and Runion 1978]; *Numbers: Rational and Irrational* [Niven 1961]; *Fractals for the Classroom* [Peitgen, Jurgens, and Saupe 1992]; and *Knot Theory* [Livingston 1993]. Periodicals include NCTM's *Mathematics Teacher, Mathematics Teaching in the Middle School,* and *Student Math Notes;* two publications of the Mathematical Association of America: *Math Horizons, Mathematical Magazine;* and *Quantum* from the National Science Teacher's Association.)

A few less widely used elementary school programs intended for a general grades K–6 audience have special features that make them attractive and appropriate for promising students as well. One particular long-standing program used in the award-winning Manhasset, New York, school system (Chauhan 1994) is the Comprehensive School Mathematics Program (Heidema et. al. 1978–97). The program has a problem-solving focus throughout, with regular emphasis on developing higher-level thinking skills and proceeding from real situations to abstract mathematics. The program is aligned with the NCTM *Standards* and includes such topics as taxicab geometries and network analysis. Special problems and differentiated activities offer additional challenge to high-ability students.

One reasonable procedure for elementary students, which may be practiced with several classes that are at either the same or different grade levels (or even in several schools), is to establish a home base or learning center in a single school (Khatena 1992). A good example of this, the Boise, Idaho, Four-School Enrichment Program for gifted students from kindergarten to grade 6, locates a meeting place or open house in one of the four schools on a rotating basis. This program caters to the specialized interests of talented students, with each of the four schools designated as a center of specialization in one of these areas: mathematics, sciences, modern languages, and visual and performing arts. The Columbia, South Carolina, Programs for the Academically and Creatively Talented (PACE) include classes of enriched and accelerated mathematics from grade 6 on in each of the city's Richland School District One public schools. The students take their mathematics classes each day exclusively with others in the program and use distinct materials in a special curriculum (PACE 1995).

A particularly interesting programmatic variation of the pullout model that is suitable for secondary school students is the school-within-a-school arrangement. A good example of this is the Parkville Center for Mathematics, Science, and Computer Science (Baltimore, Md.) in which talented grades 9–12 students participate in several academic subjects with those of their ability cohort. At other times, these students participate with the rest of the student body in other academic subjects or activities such as physical education, music, and social events. (Parkville 1995)

A program that has gained widespread acceptance in secondary schools is the Advanced Placement (AP) program sponsored by the College Entrance Examination Board, an independent association of schools and colleges. This is a nationwide program that allows high-ability students to complete college-level courses while still in high school. It has specific curricula and standardized final examinations that are graded by teams of high school and college teachers. Scores are on a five-point scale: (1) no recommendation (a euphemism for "failure"), (2) possibly qualified, (3) qualified, (4) well qualified, and (5) extremely well qualified. Even though grading is uniform, acceptance by colleges is not. At present there are three mathematics exams: calculus AB and calculus BC, the former corresponding to a semester, the second a full-year course; and statistics; as well as a computer science examination. Small schools may have difficulty offering these courses, but students may take the examinations without first taking the courses, and the availability of technology (i.e., distance learning and internet access) may surmount those problems in many settings.

Another curriculum that deserves special attention is the International Baccalaureate (IB). IB is a Geneva, Switzerland-based program for secondary school students with special courses taught during their junior and senior years. It is now in operation in many schools throughout the world. The IB program is a system of syllabi setting forth the objectives for each course and examinations based on the concept that general education in the upper secondary level should encompass the development of all the main powers for the mind through which man interprets, modifies, and enjoys his environment (IBO 1996). Syllabi may be followed and examinations taken at two levels: high or subsidiary. The high level requires two years of study with five hours a week of classes. The subsidiary level requires two years with two or three hours a week, or one year with five hours a week. Students may take the full program or only a portion of it. The examinations are graded in Geneva, with scores from 1 to 7 assigned. The classroom teachers are, however, also involved in the assessment process.

Certificates are awarded to students who successfully complete the program, which incorporates six areas: English; another language; the study of man (involving philosophy, psychology, social anthropology, history, geography, economics, and business); experimental science (biology, chemistry, physics, physical science, and scientific studies); mathematics (mathematics, mathematical studies, and mathematics and computing); and practical and theoretical studies (art and design, music, classical language, or an additional one of the earlier courses). Additionally, the students must complete a special IB course, Theory of Knowledge; spend one afternoon a week engaging in some creative, aesthetic, or social experience (possibly a music or athletic activity); do additional independent coursework in one area; and prepare an extended essay in that area. Because IB is so widely recognized, many foreign and domestic universities give college credit or advanced standing for it. One drawback, however, is the difference from standard curricula (this is particularly true in mathematics) that confronts colleges with placement problems.

Many universities offer special classes for talented students during the academic year or during the summer months. The State University of New York, College at Buffalo Gifted Math Program (GMP) is a cooperative program among Western New York State schools, the New York State Education Department, the university, and families. This complete grades 7–12 university-based course of study entirely replaces the students' regular mathematics coursework in their home school. GMP classes are held for two hours, twice weekly, throughout the academic year. Students not only cover standard mathematics content but also do extensive independent work. Moreover, they not only study an enriched curriculum of secondary school mathematics but can earn up to twenty-two university credits as well (Krist 1985).

The University of Minnesota Talented Youth Mathematics Program (UMTYMP) is a statewide program aimed at providing an alternative educational experience for mathematically talented students identified in grades 5–8. UMTYMP students attend one two-hour class each week throughout the academic year and do extensive homework. They complete algebra 1 and 2 the first year and geometry and mathematical analysis the second year. They then go on to study calculus, linear algebra, and differential equations in the college component (Keynes 1996).

Teachers and administrators committed to pullout classes praise their strengths, and there are many. The arrangement can be installed and become operational in short order. The special classes bring bright youngsters together for part of the time and leave them in heterogeneous classrooms most of the time.

Pullout programs are highly visible. The major weakness of this approach is that it may be a part-time solution to a full-time concern, although another serious problem for some programs is their expense.

SPECIALIZED SCHOOLS

So far, we have looked only at programs for promising students within an existing school. Now, however, we turn to the second main category of special programs: those schools that have been created solely for the education of high-ability students. All such schools have some form of identification and selection process that a student must pass through to gain admission. The schools may operate on a regional basis, like the public New York City specialized schools, the magnet schools in Buffalo, New York, the nonpublic University of Toronto Schools (UTS), and the private Oaks Academy in Houston, Texas. (Often, as in the case in Buffalo, magnet schools for talented students were created to foster integration.) They may even draw from an entire state, as do the North Carolina School of Science and Mathematics (NCSSM) and the Illinois Math and Science Academy (IMSA).

Admission to high-ability schools usually requires evidence of outstanding prior work, recommendations of teachers, an essay or interview, and high scores on a battery of standardized examinations. The curriculum of the specialized schools usually follows an advanced form of the standard school curriculum. It is as if everyone in the school were taking only honors courses. Some of the schools, though, are much more specialized than others and offer many courses that would not otherwise be available. At the Bronx High School of Science (BHSS), each student in the research honors program prepares an original research project under the guidance of a teacher or team of teachers, in cooperation with community industries. Each project is submitted to several science fairs and the Westinghouse Science Talent Search (Cox et. al. 1985). This kind of visibility, for which more programs should strive, not only highlights academic achievement and is particularly meaningful to students and parents but enhances the reputation of the school.

Because the students in these schools are all either high achievers or, at least, potential high achievers, they form a critical mass that tends to be highly motivated when placed in such a challenging intellectual environment. Class size is usually kept at the level of ten to fifteen students and the teacher-student ratio is commonly high. Contributing to this ratio is the large number of specialized electives usually offered to respond to the students' special interests.

Many teachers in these schools are thoroughly challenged both by the academic pursuits of the students and the associated pedagogical problems of these aspiring youngsters. It must be recognized that the students in these schools face many of the same problems of students in other schools, and teaching them is challenging. Theft, property destruction, cheating, and drugs are here, too (Melzer 1980). On the other hand, students do gain several advantages from their attendance at these specialized schools. Foremost among the advantages is undoubtedly the opportunity to work to nearer their full potential: Many are able to win national competitions, to qualify for university scholarships, or to gain credit or advanced standing from the colleges they later attend. Another often overlooked and undervalued advantage is the opportunity to work, struggle, and succeed with the support of intellectual peers from the student's own age group. This collegiality promotes the friendships, acceptance, and understanding children need from one another.

A CLOSER LOOK

Three of these specialized schools are so outstanding and well known as to merit a closer look at their individual programs: the University of Toronto Schools (UTS), the Bronx High School of Science (BHSS), and the North Carolina School of Science and Mathematics (NCSSM). Of these three the UTS is not only the oldest (it was founded in 1908!) but serves the widest range of students. Since its founding UTS has enjoyed a close relationship with the University of Toronto's faculty of education—a center for student teaching, curriculum development, and limited research, where the staff of the school has been active in the exploration of new directions and methodologies for the effective instruction of promising students. UTS has been an institution devoted to the liberal arts and sciences where, throughout the six-year course of studies, from grade 7 to graduation, the emphasis on breadth discourages fast-tracking and early specialization (UTS 1997).

As might be expected, BHSS offers an intensive academic program that emphasizes mathematics and science. An especially interesting feature of the program is that it uses the ninth-grade year as a screen for the following years. All incoming ninth-year students participate in a model science program, and from that group of 700, a group of 100 is selected to continue in the special research honors courses. BHSS pays special attention to teacher evaluations and the possibility of identifying an underachiever who, with the right opportunity, could develop into a truly creative individual. The primary teaching method is Socratic: Questions are raised and challenges offered to students, who then must wrestle with the issues and, if possible, resolve the problems. Two measures of the success of this school are evident in the number of National Merit Scholarship finalists and student achievement in national science and mathematics contests like the Westinghouse Talent Search and the American High School Mathematics Examination.

The NCSSM is a public residential high school for juniors and seniors. It is funded by federal, state, and private sources and has its own board of trustees. Students from across the state are nominated for admission during their sophomore year. After taking standardized and locally developed tests, selected students are those judged to have a high potential for academic success, interest in intellectual concerns, a willingness to learn, inner discipline, capacity for independent thinking, the ability to work well with others, and a desire to serve the community. The teaching-learning process includes independent study, tutorials, projects, and professional research internships. The heart of the curriculum is its emphasis on developing students' ability to write, speak, analyze, use computers, and evaluate. The mathematics courses range from the traditional sequence through multivariate and vector calculus, and differential equations to discrete mathematics and computer science. The core curriculum is supplemented each year by special seminars and symposia. Every member of the faculty holds at least a master's degree (most have doctorates) and has the integrity, compassion, and dedication necessary for a high school residential program. The school also employs invited interns temporarily reassigned from other schools in North Carolina to teach and develop new materials. The school has a broader charge to serve the entire state through outreach activities. The faculty regularly conducts workshops for teachers and the school's summer program allows additional students to benefit from the curriculum and environment. The school's success is due to a combination of factors including a singular campus; dedicated faculty and staff; outstanding students; and academic, cocurricular, and residential programs tailored to their needs (NCSSM 1995).

Specialized schools for promising students have much to recommend them, for they offer the most dramatic instance of meeting the distinctive needs of very able learners. They efficiently use both equipment and personnel resources in tight economic times, their students can gain inspiration from one another, and the specific exigencies of high-ability children can be addressed seriously. What may be problematic are admission policies, standards, and goals. Criteria for admission and retention in the school must be as clear and firm as its purposes. When students, parents, staff, and the public receive mixed messages about the school's purpose, problems will abound. Thus, goals of access and achievement must be accompanied by realistic and effective support mechanisms to ensure that students develop their full mathematical potential.

Parents and students must understand that students will be expected to work harder and to learn more than if they were in a traditional program. For this effort, students should have opportunities for exemplary grades that compare them to average students in a traditional program and that recognize their accomplishments. Finally, those who fear specialized schools foster elitism should visit with Mirian Acosta-Sing, principal of Mott Hall School in the Washington Heights neighborhood of New York City. There 450 students in grades 4 through 8 are all gifted and talented and almost all African American or Latino (Quindlen 1993).

CONCLUSIONS

Taken in context, high-ability and promising students are similar in many ways to the general population; hence, there is much about the organization of good learning programs for all students that is appropriate for these students as well.

However, this gives us the tendency to modify traditional organizational strategies for high-ability students rather than consider fresh designs that capitalize on their unique qualities.

Good programs have built-in mechanisms for change and evolution. If we really want to serve promising mathematics students, and ensure their proper development we need to understand the design process of their environment as our ever-changing responsibility.

REFERENCES

Chauhan, Jennifer. "A Winning Formula." *Teacher* (September 1994).

Cox, June, Neil Daniel, and Bruce O. Boston. *Educating Able Learners—Programs and Promising Practices.* Austin; University of Texas Press, 1985.

Flanders, James R. "How Much of the Content in Mathematics Textbooks is New?" *Arithmetic Teacher* 35, no. 1 (September 1987): 18–23.

Gifted Math Program, University at Buffalo. <wings.buffalo.edu/~insrisg/gmp> (1997).

Haag, Vincent, Burt Kaufman, Edward Martin, and Gerald Rising. *Challenge: A Program for the Mathematically Talented,* Vols. 1–4. Reading, Mass.: Addison-Wesley Publishing Co., 1986.

International Baccalaurate Program. *Bulletin.* Geneva, Switzerland: Route Des Morrillons, 1996.

Keynes, Harvey B. "Can Equity Thrive in a Culture of Mathematical Excellence?" In *New Directions for Equity in Mathematics Education,* edited by Walter G. Secada, Elizabeth Fennema, and Lisa Byrd, pp. 57–92. Cambridge: Cambridge University Press, 1996.

Khatena, Joe. *Gifted: Challenge and Response for Education.* Itasca, Ill.: F. E. Peacock Publishers, 1992.

Krist, Betty J. "The Gifted Math Program at SUNY Buffalo." In *The Secondary School Mathematics Curriculum,* edited by Christian R. Hirsch. Reston, Va.: National Council of Teachers of Mathematics, 1985.

Livingston, Charles. *Knot Theory.* Washington, D.C.: Mathematical Association of America, 1993.

Lockwood, James R., and Garth E. Runion. *Deductive Systems: Finite and Non-Euclidean Geometries.* Reston, Va.: National Council of Teachers of Mathematics, 1978.

Matthews, Marian. "Gifted Students Talk about Cooperative Learning." *Educational Leadership* 50, no. 2 (October 1992): 48–50.

Melzer, Peter. "The Real World of Physics Teaching at the Bronx HS of Science." *Physics Teacher* 18, no. 4 (April 1980): 272–7.

Midcontinent Regional Educational Laboratory. Comprehensive School Mathematics Program. Kansas City: Mo.: Midcontinent Regional Educational Laboratory, 1978–97. (Distributed by Sopris West, Inc., Longmont, Colo.)

National Council of Teachers of Mathematics. *An Agenda for Action.* Reston, Va.: National Council of Teachers of Mathematics, 1980.

———. *Curriculum and Evaluation Standards for School Mathematics.* Reston, Va.: National Council of Teachers of Mathematics, 1989.

———. *Mission Mathematics: K–6,* edited by Mary Ellen Hynes. Reston, Va.: National Council of Teachers of Mathematics, 1997a.

———. *Mission Mathematics: 5–8,* edited by Vincent O'Connor. Reston, Va.: National Council of Teachers of Mathematics, 1997b.

———. *Mission Mathematics: 9–12,* edited by Peggy A. House. Reston, Va.: National Council of Teachers of Mathematics, 1997c.

———. "A Position Statement on Provisions for Mathematically Talented and Gifted Students." Reston, Va.: National Council of Teachers of Mathematics, 1986.

———. "A Position Statement on Vertical Acceleration." Reston, Va.: National Council of Teachers of Mathematics, 1983.

———. *Providing Opportunities for the Mathematically Gifted, K–12,* edited by Peggy A. House. Reston, Va.: National Council of Teachers of Mathematics, 1987.

———. "Report of the NCTM Task Force on the Mathematically Promising." *NCTM News Bulletin* 32 (December 1995): Special insert.

———. *Windows of Opportunity: Mathematics for Students with Special Needs,* edited by Carol A. Thornton and Nancy S. Bley. Reston, Va.: National Council of Teachers of Mathematics, 1994.

Niven, Ivan. *Numbers: Rational and Irrational.* Washington, D.C.: Mathematics Association of America, 1961.

North Carolina School of Science and Mathematics. North Carolina School of Science and Mathematics, 1995. *NCSSM Information.* North Carolina School of Science and Mathematics: Durham, N.C.: 1995.

Parkville Center for Mathematics, Science, and Computer Science Brochure. Personal visit, 1995.

PACE. Programs for the Academically and Creatively Talented brochure and personal visit. Richland County School District One, Columbia, S.C.: 1995.

Peitgen, Heinz-Otto, Hartmut Jürgens, and Dietmar Saupe. *Fractals for the Classroom (Part One: Introduction to Fractals and Chaos; Part Two: Complex Systems and Mandelbrot Set).* Reston, Va.: National Council of Teachers of Mathematics, 1992.

Quindlen, Anna. "A Scam That Hurts Our Smartest Kids." *New York Teacher* (29 November 1993): 27.

Ross, Pat O'Connell. *National Excellence, A Case for Developing America's Talent.* Washington, D.C.: Office of Educational Research and Improvement, U.S. Department of Education, 1993.

Sapon–Shevin, Mara. "Why Gifted Children Belong in Inclusive Schools." *Educational Leadership* 52, no. 4 (December 1994/January 1995): 64–70.

Tomlinson, Carol Ann. "Gifted Learners, Too: A Possible Dream?" *Educational Leadership* 52, no. 4 (December 1994/January 1995): 68–9.

University of Toronto Schools. <www.uts.oise.utoronto.ca/aboututs/>

Walter, Marion. *Boxes, Squares, and Other Things.* Reston, Va.: National Council of Teachers of Mathematics, 1970.

Chapter 15

PROVIDING OPPORTUNITIES THROUGH COMPETITIONS

George Berzsenyi

Although it is generally recognized that competitions provide excellent opportunities for the discovery and development of mathematical talents, it is not the purpose of this article to promote mathematical competitions unequivocally. Instead, competitions will be examined critically in a broader setting, not only from an educational but also from a cultural and historical viewpoint. The author will also attempt to provide some guidance to the educational community for making appropriate use of the many competition-related programs available in the United States.

Competitiveness is a natural part of the human psyche, and mathematics is an ideal ground for it. Ideally, competitiveness combines with cooperativeness, but even then, cooperation is often limited to a specific group, and even within the group, the competitive spirit stays alive. Thus, while one may prefer team competitions to individual ones, it is natural that the team members will compete against one another, whereas those who are not on the team will want to prove themselves worthy for inclusion.

In addition, it is assumed that all competitors are basically competing against themselves, trying to achieve personal goals, attempting to surpass their previous best efforts. Thus, in a mathematical competition, their attention should be focused on the problems, and they should rejoice whenever they succeed in solving them. The fact that some others may have succeeded in solving more of the problems or accomplished their tasks faster should be of secondary importance.

In view of the fact that most mathematical competitions are severely time-constrained, competitions are not for everyone. Some students prefer to be contemplative and don't like to work under extreme pressure. Others tend to be easily discouraged and even devastated by less than satisfactory results. Some are not yet ready emotionally for the stress that can be caused by competitions, and the experience may even stunt their intellectual growth. It is the responsibility of teachers to find alternative outlets for the creative talents of such students and to assure them that their preferences and attitudes do not necessarily reflect negatively on them.

In spite of their various shortcomings, there is a need for competitions, primarily for the discovery and development of talents, and secondarily for monitoring the individual mathematical development of the contestants. One can learn a lot of excellent mathematics while preparing for competitions. It should also be recognized that competing is fun; a well-designed and superbly organized competition can be viewed as a wonderful celebration of mathematics. Success in competitions is also encouraging, especially if the winners are properly recognized with prizes of books and journal subscriptions that can further their development. Even the losers can often be inspired if they see that the margin by which they lost is not insurmountable. Moreover, the pride in one's school, region, state, or country can play a huge role in the inspiration of the contestants toward better results and hence to more learning.

Ideally, competitions feature problems rather than exercises—straightforward challenges whose solutions call for routine application of methods carefully explained in the classroom and thoroughly understandable by a well-prepared student. To solve a problem, one usually needs at least one bright idea or a nonroutine application of some method. In general, mathematically promising students call attention to themselves by their affinity to problem solving rather than to theory building. It should be noted that they are not necessarily the best students in one's classes; they may be less concerned with their grades and may be less likely to perform well on routine examinations. Nevertheless, they can truly surprise you if you really challenge them.

Finally, in most instances, doing well in any mathematical competition must be viewed as a means to an end rather than as the ultimate goal. The problems encountered should intrigue students to learn more about their subject, attain greater understanding of the concepts introduced in the problems, and broaden their horizons. Students should never be satisfied with their results or settle for proving once again, in the next season of competitions, that they are indeed talented. The world is full of talented individuals who have never managed to fulfill the promise shown in their youths! Success in competitions should be followed by increased mathematical learning.

THE ROLE OF COMPETITIONS

In most countries that have a tradition of discovering and developing mathematically talented students, there are annual competitions at all levels (ranging from elementary schools to senior high schools) that are administered at nearly all schools to all students who show any sign of mathematical promise. Students in the United States are fortunate to have such competitions as the American Junior High School Mathematics Examination (AJHSME) and the American High School Mathematics Examination (AHSME). The AJHSME is relatively new (it was initiated in 1985), whereas the AHSME is America's oldest mathematics competition for secondary students, having been given every year since 1950. Unfortunately, still only about 20 percent of the schools in the United States take part in these truly excellent competitions, in spite of the fact that they are sponsored by nearly all of the national organizations of teachers and practitioners of mathematics.

Ideally, the students identified as mathematically promising by the AJHSME and AHSME should be receiving immediate attention from the mathematical community, and we should be working diligently to develop their talents. Generally, that is not the case. Even those few who do well enough on the AHSME to qualify for the next nationwide competition, the American Invitational Mathematics Examination (AIME), receive little attention. In fact, there is a widespread misconception that the sole purpose of the AHSME and the AIME is to select the best students for the USA Mathematical Olympiad (USAMO), on the basis of which teams of six students who represent the United States in the International Mathematical Olympiad (IMO) are selected. In fact, on the basis of our excellent performances in the IMOs, some will even conclude that we do pay proper attention to our talented students, and hence all is well with our educational system. Nothing could be further from the truth! Although our very best students are able to hold their own in international competitions, the layer of well-prepared, truly outstanding students is extremely thin in comparison to the size of our population and the ability level of our mathematically promising students.

When the first modern nationwide mathematical competition, which became known as the Kürschák Mathematical Competition (KMC), was initiated in Hungary in 1894, Hungary's mathematical community also started a high school mathematics journal, *Középiskolai Matematikai Lapok (KöMaL)*, which featured appropriate problems for the development of the students. Thus, in spite of its well-deserved reputation, the KMC was never the focal point of Hungary's mathematical program for mathematically promising students. These students grew up and developed their talents through the year-round problem solving competition of *KöMaL*. The students were allowed several weeks for solving the proposed problems and were expected to submit complete well-written solutions. For each correct solution, they received points, which were accumulated throughout the year. They were also encouraged by seeing their own solutions appear in *KöMaL*, and learned a lot from each other's solutions, as well as from the editorial comments accompanying the problems and solutions.

Unfortunately, when Hungary's system of competitions was adapted by other countries (see Freudenthal [1969]), they limited their attention to KMC and ignored the role played by *KöMaL*. Whereas the formerly communist countries of Central and Eastern Europe developed their own programs (like Bulgaria's Winter Mathematics Camp and the Moscow Mathematical Circles) to emulate *KöMaL*'s year-round creative problem-solving competition at least partially, most of the Western countries failed to set up any mechanism for developing the talents of those students who distinguished themselves in the various competitions. In fact, even though the importance of problem solving was the first item in NCTM's *Agenda for Action* (NCTM 1980), one of its first actions in 1981 was to discontinue the publication of the *Mathematics Student* journal. The *Mathematics Student* could have, at least minimally, paralleled *KöMaL*. Since then, except for *Quantum* (since 1991) and a minor effort through the *Student Math Notes* of NCTM's *News Bulletin*, we do not have a publication in the United States for our mathematically promising students. Unfortunately, *Quantum*, which consists mostly of articles translated from the Russian *Kvant,* is at a higher level of sophistication than our present needs dictate. Similarly, the USA Mathematical Talent Search (USAMTS) can only partially fill the need for a year-round competition in creative problem solving. Although everyone may participate in the USAMTS, its emphasis is mainly on the development of the proven talents of students who have already distinguished themselves on the AHSME.

The USAMTS consists of four rounds of five problems sent to the home addresses of the participants, who receive a complete evaluation of their submissions, along with a set of instructive solutions and an informative newsletter at the end of each round. The participants accumulate at most 5 points for each successful solution, and they receive a variety of prizes at the end of the year. For more information about the USAMTS and its global extension, the IMTS, see the following Web sites: www.nsa.gov:8080/programs/mepp/usamts.html and www.camel.math .ca/CMS/competitions/IMTS/.

ALTERNATIVES TO COMPETITIONS

Mathematically promising students who prefer theory building to problem solving should be made aware of the opportunities provided by science fairs like the International Science and Engineering Fair (ISEF), sponsored by Science Service, which is also responsible for the organization of the Intel (formerly Westinghouse) Science Talent Search (ISTS) for graduating seniors. Those who are disturbed by the time pressures of competitions should find the USAMTS more to their liking, since that program allows about a month for the submission of each set of problems. The USAMTS is administered by the National Security Agency (NSA) and the Consortium for Mathematics and Its Applications (COMAP). COMAP (with the assistance of NSA) is also the organizer of the Mathematical Contest in Modeling (MCM), which is primarily for teams of university students; however, in view of the fact that we don't yet have a similar program at the high school level, more and more high schools are attracted to it. The development of a high school level mathematical modeling contest has been under consideration for several years by COMAP.

Other students may prefer to work on problems proposed in various mathematical journals like *Quantum* (available from Springer-Verlag New York) and *Mathematics and Informatics Quarterly (M&IQ),* which is an English-language, international publication. (For subscription information to *M&IQ,* please see the Web site www.restena.lu/cil/training/journals.html.) In addition to various problem sections in mathematics and computer science, *M&IQ* publishes complete solutions to the problems of the International Mathematical Talent Search (IMTS), which is an extension of the USAMTS. Other journals of comparable interest include *Math Horizons, College Mathematics Journal, Mathematics Magazine,* and the *American Mathematical Monthly,* all published by the Mathematical Association of America (MAA), and *Crux Mathematicorum with Mathematical Mayhem,* published by the Canadian Mathematical Society. Until recently, *Mathematical*

Mayhem was an independent journal created by former members of the Canadian team to the IMOs. Apart from the MAA's *Monthly* and *KöMaL, Crux* is presently the world's foremost problems journal.

RECOMMENDATIONS

The recommendations that follow stem from nearly twenty-five years of personal involvement in a variety of activities aimed at the discovery and development of mathematical talent in the United States. I served on the Committee on the American Mathematics Competitions (CAMC) panel and its USAMO and AHSME committees for thirteen years and chaired the committee in charge of the AIME during its first six years. In addition, I worked with several hundred students in a year-round talent development program through the Competition Corner column of the *Mathematics Student* and the Kürschák Corner of the also defunct *Arbelos* and with thousands of students through the first eight years (1989–1997) of the USAMTS. I have also conducted Young Scholars Summer Programs, assisted in the training of the IMO teams of the United States, Canada, and Australia, and now serve as the North American representative to the World Federation of National Mathematics Competitions.

Based on these experiences, my main recommendations are to make every possible effort to strengthen the programs already in existence and to make them even more available to all mathematically promising students. The programs discussed in this article, as well as several others, like MATHCOUNTS and the American Regional Mathematics League, which are described elsewhere in this book, have already proved that they are successful, although most of them have yet to reach their full potential. Though it may be tempting to initiate new and different programs and to explore alternative methods, we should defer them until after delivering on our earlier promises. Otherwise, we will probably break even more of them.

The mathematical community will also need to create a much stronger alliance among its various organizations than in the past and share the responsibility for the work to be performed. The size and the urgency of the task requires that NCTM, MAA, and other organizations work together for the common good. We no longer need task forces to study the situation and to set agendas and standards. We need action!

In particular, we should aim at having 90 percent of our schools registered for the AJHSME and AHSME rather than the present 20 percent. These competitions are sponsored by nearly a dozen organizations, and yet rarely can one find mention of them in their publications. To learn more about the AJHSME, AHSME, AIME, USAMO, and IMO, the reader should contact Walter E. Mientka, executive director of the MAA's Committee on the American Mathematics Competitions (CAMC). The CAMC is developing a competition for younger students (at the elementary school level) as well, which we hope will be well received by the educational community. However, it would be a shame to discover even more talented students, and at an even younger age, just so that we can continue to ignore their development also. Consequently, we should see to it that more and more of them take part in programs that will assist in their development, such as the USAMTS. We should also make better use of resources such as *Quantum* and *M&IQ* and have them available in more school libraries, along with lots of other journals and books that might assist the students in their self-development.

Most school libraries are deplorably inadequate for supporting and enhancing the development of mathematically promising students. A beginning suggestion is that, at the very least, every library should have all volumes of the MAA's *New Mathematical Library* series, as well as those of the MAA's *Dolciani Mathematical Expositions*. An initial investment of $2000 and a small annual budget of $300 should right the situation and furnish an opportunity for self-development not only for our talented students but for our teachers as well. Books and journals constitute a relatively inexpensive yet effective way for self-improvement, and we should pay more attention to them. I am convinced that if we make appropriate materials available to our students and teachers, they will use them to the fullest. One should also remember that the best way to prepare for a competition is to peruse the problems posed in earlier competitions; these, along with their solutions, are available in the books recommended. In particular, *Contest Problem Book V* (Berzsenyi and Maurer 1997) features an extensive "Guide to the Problem Literature."

If everyone works together to strengthen and expand good existing programs and to disseminate mathematical problems, research, and information more widely in our schools at all grade levels, perhaps we can begin to fulfill our obligations to our most mathematically promising students.

REFERENCES

Berzsenyi, George, and Stephen B. Maurer, eds. *Contest Problem Book V.* Washington, D.C.: Mathematical Association of America, 1997.

Freudenthal, Hans, ed. "ICMI Report on Mathematical Contests in Secondary Education (Olympiads)." *Educational Studies in Mathematics* 2 (1969): 80–114.

National Council of Teachers of Mathematics. *An Agenda for Action.* Reston, Va.: National Council of Teachers of Mathematics, 1980.

IMPORTANT ADDRESSES

Canadian Mathematical Society: 577 King Edward, Ottawa, ON K1N 6N5.

Committee on the American Mathematics Competitions (CAMC): Department of Mathematics and Statistics, University of Nebraska, Lincoln, NE 68588-0322.

Consortium for Mathematics and Its Applications (COMAP): Suite 210, 57 Bedford St., Lexington, MA 02173.

Mathematical Association of America (MAA): 1529 18th St., NW, Washington, DC 20036.

Science Service: 1719 N St., NW, Washington, DC 20036.

Springer-Verlag: P.O. Box 2485, Secaucus, NY 07096-9813.

Chapter 16

INTERNATIONAL PERSPECTIVES ON CULTIVATING TALENT IN MATHEMATICS

Frances R. Curcio

Improving the economic, social, political, and intellectual lives of all people is dependent on systems of education throughout the world. Each child has special gifts and talents that have the potential for improving the human condition. In particular, fostering the development of students gifted and talented in mathematics has been recognized by the authors in this section as making an important contribution to society. Understanding how formal systems of education cultivate, reveal, and harness such gifts and talents is crucial for developing citizens of the twenty-first century. This section contains the perspectives of mathematics educators describing opportunities for students in seven countries: New Zealand, Brunei Darussalam, Japan, the United Kingdom (specifically England and Scotland), Bulgaria, Russia (specifically Saint Petersburg), and Latvia. On the basis of their participation in Working Group 7: Mathematics for Gifted Students at the Eighth International Congress on Mathematical Education, held in Seville, Spain, in July 1996, and on the basis of their work in International Mathematical Olympiads (IMO), authors were contacted and asked to report about the state of meeting the needs of the mathematically talented in their respective countries. Of the twenty mathematics educators who were contacted, we are grateful to the eight, who with their colleagues, summitted the following reports.

It is not surprising that many similar approaches are used to motivate, challenge, and engage students who have an interest and an inclination in mathematics. All the authors report that gifted students are encouraged and prepared to participate in mathematics competitions qualifying them to represent their respective countries at IMOs. For the most part, extracurricular events and activities such as mathematics clubs, summer camps, and correspondence programs are organized by teachers' organizations and universities, and they are financially supported through donations of time, money, and other resources. Little financial support for gifted programs is provided by governments, perhaps because it may be viewed as taking money away from programs that could serve the majority of the school population.

In some countries (such as New Zealand and Japan), the mathematics curriculum has been designed to accommodate gifted students. In some cases, it is up to the teacher to supplement the work once gifted children have been identified. Rather than leaving the identification process to the results on a test, many of the authors in this section believe that the classroom teacher is in the best position to recognize and identify mathematically talented children. Velikova (in press) suggests that teachers who "have an extensive background in psychology and pedagogy" are able to recognize characteristics of "giftedness." On the other hand, Gardiner argues that methods used for identifying the mathematically talented have a tendency to be exclusive and yield "false positives." Furthermore, labeling students may impede mathematical development. Attracting and sustaining all interested students in the study of mathematics and offering opportunities to participate in programs and projects may open the door to many who may not have been identified using other methods. Similar support for Gardiner's approach to wider access to gifted programs has been expressed in New York City schools (Belluck 1997; Sengupta 1997).

At a time when "detracking" and heterogeneous grouping have become key issues for school reform in the United States (Lynn and Wheelock 1997), we must consider what is fair and equitable for all children. All children may benefit from opportunities for heterogeneous interactions, but could bringing gifted students together better contribute to reaching their maximum potential? Rukshin and Golovanov have witnessed the benefits of working exclusively with mathematically gifted students.

Although we are products of our cultures and environments, we all face the challenge of meeting the special needs of our students. How we accomplish this is a function of our beliefs, values, and culture. We cannot simply transplant ideas and approaches without taking into consideration the cultural context in which the ideas and approaches have manifested success. The ideas shared in this section are intended to contribute to developing mutual respect, understanding, and appreciation of all attempts to cultivate mathematical talent in various countries.

OPPORTUNITIES FOR TALENTED MATHEMATICS STUDENTS IN NEW ZEALAND

—Coralie Daniel and Derek Holton
University of Otago, Dunedin, New Zealand

During the last decade in New Zealand, there have been significant changes for students who are talented in mathematics. Up until the early 1980s, any extra mathematics stimulation for school students came only from local ad hoc activities organized on the initiative of enthusiastic teachers. By the mid-1990s, the needs of talented mathematics students had gained recognition in New Zealand's national mathematics and assessment units.

Three events during the 1980s created a nationwide focus that considerably heightened the profile of mathematics and mathematically talented students. Although these events were initially introduced by groups of individuals, they gained acceptance quickly. First, the Australian Mathematics Competition was introduced in New Zealand and student entry was encouraged by secondary schools. Second, a similar competition, the National Bank Junior Mathematics

Competition, was developed in New Zealand, and this, too, helped to stimulate interest in mathematics in secondary schools. Third, the New Zealand Mathematical Olympiad Committee (NZMOC) was established, and it developed a program to prepare students for participation in the annual IMO.

Each year, several hundred students have the opportunity to be involved in various stages of the IMO training program, and the twenty most successful students attend a training camp, even though only six are ultimately chosen for each New Zealand team. But other more personally interactive programs are now also offered in New Zealand. Through the University of Auckland, the NZMOC has developed a correspondence course leading to the New Zealand Mathematical Olympiad Committee certificate. Students of any age can be involved in a correspondence program at the University of Otago, in which students solve a set of problems at their own pace and receive feedback with the next set of problems.

A number of universities and some local mathematics associations conduct discussion groups called "cluster groups," bringing together people with similar interests. Students from the local schools join by personal choice. Two other mathematics camps are held during the year—one for students who did not achieve inclusion in the final stages of the IMO selection process and the other for students nominated for inclusion by their schools. In the Problem Challenge, a program for ten and eleven year olds organized by the University of Otago, sets of problems are sent to schools five times a year and prizes are awarded based on the results of the five events. A number of New Zealand schools enter the Singapore Mathematical Olympiad for Primary Schools. Besides providing students with incentives and motivation, these competitions also make additional problem-solving materials available to secondary and primary teachers.

The groups who organize the programs receive some financial support from the government, but for the most part, they rely mainly on sponsorship by private companies, entry fees, and money and time donated by professional organizations and parents. Both personal experience and research have shown there is profound relief among many parents and students that something constructive is being offered for those with mathematical talent. Most of the able students identified by the programs described are dependent on help from outside the home because they do not have parents or family members who can join them in conversations that would give them real intellectual stimulation in mathematics and help them access extension material (Curran, Daniel, and Holton 1995). In a number of cases we know that self-esteem, as well as mathematical skills, was raised significantly by the opportunities arising from talking with people with similar levels of mathematical understanding and insight (Holton and Daniel 1996).

There is no claim that these methods have resulted in every able mathematics student being found or helped, but the variety in the ways of advertising these activities has helped give students opportunities for self-selection. Even now male students seem to be identified more easily than female students, but the number of female students being selected for IMO training camps has increased over the thirteen-year period. Although most of these new mathematical activities involve competition, they also strongly endorse the attitude that the principal anticipated outcome is that of helping students enjoy mathematics at whatever level their potential allows.

In the early 1990s, the New Zealand Ministry of Education decided that, in specific subject areas including mathematics, new national curricula would be written for all years of schooling. The new mathematics curriculum emphasizes problem solving as a method of learning mathematics. It also contains a set of extra learning objectives called the development band. The development band is specifically designed for more able students. Hence, all teachers are now required to recognize the existence of able mathematics students and provide them with additional work. The development band has additional assessment units, so that the talented students who use this material are given credit at the national level. The New Zealand Association of Mathematics Teachers has developed a certificate course for development band students, to provide appropriate extension material both at the senior secondary school level and below.

There is, of course, still much to be done for talented and gifted mathematics students in New Zealand. However, as the number of available activities has increased, there has been a corresponding increase in the amount of publicity given to mathematics as a rewarding and interesting ability. News media and school announcements of successes have meant that individual and team achievement in mathematics is now more likely to be applauded by the community in ways that have been more commonly reserved for sporting ability and achievement and the like. The experiences of the last thirteen years have shown that any efforts to have mathematical ability recognized as a normal talent, rather than as an unusual one, have had positive outcomes both for talented students and for the community.

ENHANCING THE STUDY OF MATHEMATICS THROUGH QUIZ AND COMPETITION IN BRUNEI DARUSSALAM

—Khoon Yoon Wong and Pick Ching Teh
Universiti Brunei Darussalam, Brunei, Darussalam

Brunei Darussalam is a small country on the island of Borneo with an area of 5 765 square kilometers and 296 000 people (*Borneo Bulletin Brunei Yearbook* 1997). There are 171 primary schools with approximately 42 000 pupils and 47 secondary schools with approximately 28 000 students.

Mathematics is a compulsory subject in primary and secondary schools. In primary 1 to 3, mathematics is taught in Bahasa Melayu, the national language. From primary 4 onward, mathematics is taught in English. At the end of secondary school, most students will have spent about 1800 hours studying mathematics. Students are assessed in mathematics in three public examinations: Primary Certificate of Education, taken at age eleven; Brunei Junior Certificate of Education Examination, taken at age forteen; and Brunei-Cambridge O-Level Examination, taken at age sixteen. Mathematics is considered essential to the creation of a technologically oriented workforce for national development.

To promote the study of mathematics, the Minister of Education declared 1990 to be the "Year of Enchantment of Mathematics." The purpose of this declaration was to raise students' interest and public awareness about the beauty of mathematics. Several activities were organized in 1990: the Fifth Southeast Asian Conference on Mathematics Education, school-based mathematics exhibits, a national "mathematics in school" exhibition, a national mathematics quiz, and participation in the Australian Mathematics Competition. The last two activities have become annual events for secondary school students. These activities have stimulated students' interest in the study of mathematics through participation in competitions. Both activities are described below.

National Mathematics Quiz

The National Mathematics Quiz is a timed oral quiz conducted in English. It tests the mental mathematical prowess of students in an individual and team setting.

Each year the quiz is organized by a school appointed by the Ministry of Education. The convening school also produces the booklet of regulations. The quiz is voluntary, and it is open to all students in government and private secondary schools. The event receives financial support from Brunei Shell.

The quiz, occurring April through July, is conducted in four stages: preliminary, quarterfinal, semifinal, and grand final. The last three stages are televised to stimulate public interest in mathematics. Each school is represented by a team of four students, one each from forms 2, 3, 4, and 5.

At the preliminary stage, the teams are divided into eight groups of four teams per group. The winner of each group then enters the quarterfinal. A similar elimination process determines the teams for the semifinal and the grand final.

There are four rounds to the preliminary stage. First, each team answers four general mathematics questions in the team round. Each question must be answered within thirty seconds (which includes discussion time) by the team captain. Second, each team member is given four arithmetic and algebra questions to be answered individually, beginning with form 2 students and moving to form 5 students. The time limit is twenty seconds per question. Third, a speed round of ten questions is presented to everyone. The first student to sound the buzzer answers that question within twenty seconds. Finally, there is another individual round of four geometry questions.

At the quarterfinal, semifinal, and grand final stages, the quiz comprises the above four rounds together with a game round and a manipulative round. The game round and the manipulative round are novel features not found in similar quizzes conducted elsewhere. A sample of items used in the game and manipulative rounds can be found in the appendix to this chapter.

Australian Mathematics Competition

The Australian Mathematics Competition is one of the largest mathematics competitions in the world. Since 1990, the competition has been organized locally by a committee of representatives from Universiti Brunei Darussalam, the Ministry of Education, and the schools. In 1996, 4972 secondary school students in Brunei Darussalam participated in the competition, representing 18 percent of the local secondary school population and evidencing considerable interest in the competition.

The competition is a written test for three grade levels: years 7 and 8, years 9 and 10, and years 11 and 12. In 1996, for the first time, a student from Brunei Darussalam won a gold medal for outstanding achievement.

Closing Comments

In the past few years, Brunei Darussalam has conducted several activities to promote the study of mathematics. The National Mathematics Quiz provides an interesting model to challenge the more able students to develop their full potential in mathematics. Participation in the Australian Mathematics Competition is a fruitful example of regional collaboration in mathematics education. We believe that research is now needed on the impact these two activities are having on participants' mathematics achievement and on their motivation to study mathematics. We expect such commendable efforts to nurture mathematics talent among young Bruneian students to be sustained.

MATHEMATICS FOR PROMISING STUDENTS IN JAPAN

—Grayson Wheatley
Florida State University, Tallahassee, Florida

—Hideki Iwasaka
Hiroshima University, Hiroshima, Japan

—Yoshifuni Kohno
Hiroshima University High School, Hiroshima, Japan

In Japan the course of study for all subjects is prescribed by the Ministry of Education, Science, Sports, and Culture. This prescription is interpreted as a basic goal for all students at the compulsory level. The national curriculum is followed by all Japanese teachers of grades 1 through 9. All elementary and lower secondary students are expected to know the concepts and skills specified by the Ministry of Education. All classes are heterogeneous, with no provisions for students who might have special needs. Furthermore, all students progress from grade to grade with their peer group. Japan conveys high expectations for students and the results of international tests (e.g., Third International Mathematics and Science Study) suggest they are quite successful. But there is concern among some Japanese educators that the curriculum does not encourage creativity and problem solving—competencies being increasingly valued.

Japanese Educational Programs for Mathematically Promising Students

In post-World War II Japan, the reorganization of the educational system with emphasis on egalitarianism made it difficult to provide special programs for mathematically promising students. Japan, which is poorly endowed with natural resources, relies heavily on an educated workforce to be economically competitive abroad. Whereas the development of a homogenous and a highly educated people has been considered crucial, pressure to obtain high scores on university entrance examinations has resulted in the neglect of students who show promise, especially in mathematics and physics.

In general, Japan offers mathematically promising students in-class enrichment in grades 1 through 9. The nature of this erichment at the compulsory level varies greatly from teacher to teacher. It may include extensions of class topics, studying advanced mathematics, and helping students appreciate mathematical ways of thinking.

Provisions for upper secondary level promising students, however, focus on learning opportunities outside the classroom. The plan's objective is twofold: (1) to respect the individuality of each student and his or her enhancement and (2) to give students who show a special interest and ability in mathematics and physics an opportunity to develop their potential. An essential component of this plan is to improve relations between upper secondary schools and universities.

Some Japanese educators believe that students with exceptional ability in such fields as mathematics and science should be encouraged. The Japanese government has recently formulated a plan for promising high school students that emphasizes coordination between upper secondary schools and universities.

In the early 1980s, the Foundation for the Promotion of Mathematical Science was inaugurated. It conducts a seminar every summer for upper–secondary school students who show strong interest and promise in mathematics. The students study university-level theoretical mathematics and are encouraged to have active discussions among themselves. As a result of these seminars, many participants return to their schools and share their knowledge with others, often in a mathematics-club setting. Additionally, some universities offer seminars for mathematically promising students during the year, considering such topics as complex numbers and topology.

With the establishment of the Mathematics Olympiad Foundation (MOF) in Japan in 1991, new opportunities were created for promising high school students. The MOF organizes the nationwide selection of the participants for international competition and leads the delegation of selected Japanese students. Preparation for the IMO has increased since the late 1980s. Additionally, teachers from universities and upper secondary schools organize seminars related to mathematics competitions.

A report of Pilot Programs aims to implement the recommendation to encourage mathematically promising upper–secondary school students to attend summer seminars and specially designed university programs. Five initiatives specified in the Pilot Programs report will be assessed: (1) accepting secondary school students in university courses as observers and affording them opportunities to experience mathematics and science research; (2) having university lecturers tutor promising high school students; (3) offering university seminars of two types—one for the general public and others especially for secondary school students; (4) designing University of the Air programs for promising secondary school mathematics and science students; and (5) offering seminars organized by private groups and organizations.

Summary

Japan differs from the United States in both its educational system and its provisions for promising mathematics students. In Japan, all students study the same mathematics through grade 9, with some enrichment provided by teachers. Promising students in the United States have received special attention and have often been accelerated, suggesting that the two countries have opposite approaches to promising students. Whereas support for more able students may seem to be waning in the United States, Japan is developing new programs for more able high school students.

In Japan, both the constitution and the Fundamental Law of Education clearly state the right of all students to receive an equal education corresponding to their ability. This ideal was a driving force in post-World War II Japanese education and has since contributed to the tremendous development of education in Japan. Unfortunately, the concept of equal chance in education has been focused on an equal education (lacking the idea of "corresponding to their ability") and inevitably has served a superficial egalitarianism ideology. Provisions for promising students in Japan are extracurricular, such as mathematics clubs. However, there is support by the Ministry of Education for special programs for more-able students within the upper secondary school mathematics curriculum.

In Japan, implementing the "Exceptional Measures in Education" project will require attention to (1) encouraging mathematically promising students, (2) determining the mathematics topics to be studied by promising students, (3) improving the articulation between secondary schools and universities, and (4) building public support for the recommendations.

An educational system that requires all students to study the same mathematics at the same pace may not serve Japan well in the coming years. Inasmuch as Japan can be proud of the quality of its education system, consideration must be given to advancing those students who have a special aptitude for mathematics—a goal that can be achieved without weakening the currently successful educational system. Given the changing nature of the world economy, the creativity of promising mathematics students must be fostered. Japan needs persons who are creative as well as diligent and broadly educated. The Exceptional Measures in Education project developed by the Ministry of Education is a first step in this direction.

CAST THE NET WIDE IN THE UNITED KINGDOM

—Tony Gardiner
University of Birmingham, Birmingham, England

The United Kingdom consists of four separate and widely differing educational systems in England, Wales, Northern Ireland, and Scotland. Scotland, for example, has a long-standing tradition of mixed high schools with the curriculum and exams being centrally controlled. In contrast, England has no such tradition. The focus of this article will be about reaching out, without government support, to mathematically promising students throughout the United Kingdom.

Until the 1960s, official provision for the needs of able students in England was limited to selecting approximately 25 percent of each eleven-year-old cohort to attend special grammar schools, whose curriculum was determined by an array of demanding exams set by various university exam boards for students sixteen and eighteen years old. This unusual system worked reasonably well for those in the top 20 percent or so. However, during the 1960s, educational planning in England reacted quite properly against this dominant concern for the needs of the top 25 percent of the student population. Unfortunately, embarrassment about the previous neglect of the other 75 percent of the student population meant that subsequent changes were often dominated by a sense of guilt. In particular, it was difficult to engage in rational discussion about how to provide, within a new framework, for the needs of able students, and it became unthinkable for any government to develop explicit policies to help meet the needs of such students. Moreover, although schools prepared future undergraduates and universities influenced school examinations, the idea of university mathematicians becoming actively involved at the school level was viewed with suspicion by both sides.

Overcoming Obstacles

In such a setting, anyone trying to develop systematic ways of nurturing promising young mathematicians faced a major obstacle: the whole subject had become almost taboo. School principals and other senior administrators appointed in the early 1970s were precisely those who had embraced the new priorities most convincingly. Thus, in 1975, when we wrote to forty local high schools inviting each to nominate up to two eleven to thirteen year-olds to attend our Saturday morning mathematics club *without charge,* only two schools took up the offer. By drawing on selective and private schools, the club still went ahead, affording us crucial experience with interested students at that age. Examples of the kind of material developed can be found in Gardiner (1987a, 1987b).

Toward a Strategy

The shift in teachers' concerns toward serving the needs of the majority led to a lowering of expectations, so that many teachers began to imagine that challenging problems were too hard for almost all students. This view was reinforced to some extent by the then existing small senior olympiad, whose primary concern was to identify a United Kingdom team for the annual IMO and whose selective function was widely perceived as excluding most good students rather than encouraging them. The need to circumvent this nervousness about hard problems is why we avoid using the word *competition* and why we have tried to develop a style of problem that makes minimal technical demands: so that the majority of students believe they can at least get started.

In this spirit, we have, since 1980, supplied local schools with sets of take-home problems for interested students to tackle during their midterm break. The problems were deliberately worded to appear nontechnical and light-hearted but have a serious mathematical core. Most of the problems were designed to be accessible to a variety of ability levels so that teachers were willing to encourage students to take part. Because the solutions are evaluated centrally, teachers are ostensibly required only to distribute copies, and to collect and send in solutions. However, we believed that if we succeeded in setting problems that captured the interest of students, teachers would consequently become involved in discussing the underlying mathematics. (The problem sets are available in Gardiner, in press.)

The Inspiration

These local events were inspired partly by examples in Scotland and around the city of Liverpool. However, I was also aware of the remarkable development of the Australian Mathematics Competition, which drew its own inspiration from the work of the Canadian Mathematics Competitions. These organizations were all committed to encouraging large numbers of students to participate in mathematical problem solving, using problems designed to challenge and to encourage large numbers of good students rather than merely to "test the best."

Identification as "Labeling" or Anonymous Targeting

It is often assumed that in order to nurture promising young mathematicians, one must know who they are. Nothing could be further from the truth! First, one can only identify those who exhibit *easily identifiable traits:* many promising young mathematicians are thereby excluded. Second, many of those who exhibit the apparent hallmarks of mathematical talent later move off in other directions. Third, by identifying, and hence labeling individuals, one distorts their subsequent development and makes it harder for their mathematical talents to blossom. Fourth, identifying a small number of individuals concentrates resources disproportionately on them, and hence away from others. Fifth, the act of labeling particular students exerts unhelpful and unnecessary pressure on their teachers to deliver the anticipated harvest.

The usual interpretation of "identification" is a crude all-or-nothing classification. It is not only exclusive, by rejecting many promising students, but it also identifies many false-positives and many even distort their subsequent development. We wanted an *inclusive* strategy. For this we thought it was sufficient to identify a target group that was (1) small enough for us to handle with the available resources and (2) large enough to include many of those likely to benefit from additional provision. That is, we wanted an approach based on *anonymous targeting,* which would allow students to work and grow out of the spotlight.

A National Format

A successful national format cannot rely on teachers to take the initiative if and when they happen to have an exceptional student. Because everything in the United Kingdom had to be unofficial, and hence voluntary, we decided to imitate the American High School Mathematics Examination, the Australian Mathematics Competition, and the Canadian Mathematics Competitions by establishing multiple-choice items aimed at the top third of the ability range at the junior (grade 8 and below), intermediate (grades 9–11), and senior (grades 12–13) levels. These events were originally set up as an end in themselves—to stimulate interest in and enjoyment of mathematics by a large group of students and teachers. Thus, the question sets were deliberately intended to be intriguing and memorable so that students might emerge from the challenge wanting to discuss the problems further (see Gardiner 1996). The top 40 percent of participants receive certificates: 6 percent, gold; 13 percent, silver; and 21 percent, bronze. No other prizes are offered, but the top 1000 or so students at each level are invited to take a harder written paper (see Gardiner [1997a, 1997b]). The popular events are large and inevitably impersonal, but the written papers give us a chance to get to know students through their work. Wherever possible, we return the written solutions to students with hints and comments on the problems. Thus, a more personal relationship develops through problem solving. When selecting students to attend residential sessions, we can then make judgments with a degree of confidence. We also go out of our way to take risks. In particular, we try to select a certain number of promising students of whom we know nothing, others whose performance is striking given that they come from unlikely schools, and as many students as possible from underrepresented sections of the community.

The Outcomes

One of our original goals in establishing this national structure was to nurture promising young mathematicians from public high schools. Thus, one possible indication of the success of the approach can be seen from the members of the United Kingdom's IMO teams in 1994 and 1995, where five out of six team members came from public schools, as compared with a typical ratio from previous years as 0 to 2 out of six. Another interesting test is to ask how many of those who are now at the senior level or in the university were encouraged in their studies by participating at junior or intermediate levels. We plan to make a careful assessment, tracking and interviewing students whose names are on our records. Here it may suffice to observe that of the six IMO team members in 1996, five of them and the two reserves had been medalists in a prior junior olympiad. Much the same was true of the 1994 and 1995 IMO teams.

MATHEMATICAL CHALLENGES IN SCOTLAND

—Bill Richardson

Elgin Academy, Elgin, Moray, Scotland

As Gardiner, the preceding author, mentions, schools in Scotland comprise one of the four independent school systems in the United Kingdom. Scottish pupils start school when they are five years old. Children attend primary schools for the first seven years of formal education. At the end of the seventh year, pupils transfer to secondary school without having to sit for an entrance examination. There are some independent schools, but all state schools are comprehensive in that they serve the complete range of abilities on the same premises. There has been much argument and debate for many years as to whether, once in secondary school, pupils should be in any way grouped by ability. Recent policy has been for mixed-ability classes, although the winds of change may be starting to blow.

Students have to remain in full-time education until they reach the age of sixteen, which, for the majority, implies four years in secondary school. There are national examinations at the end of the fourth year; these are "standard grade" examinations. In the fifth year of secondary school, many students sit for the "higher grade" examinations, which for the most part provide qualifications for progression to further education. There is also a sixth year that allows students to specialize and develop some skill in independent learning.

The Scottish Mathematical Council and Mathematical Challenges

For the most part, cultivating mathematical ability of promising students has been accomplished through competitions organized by the Scottish Mathematical Council. It was established in 1967 as a forum for discussing the mathematics scene in Scotland from a broad perspective. This breadth was obtained by including on the council representatives from industry and commerce, the teacher preparation colleges, the inspectorate, and the tertiary education sector, as well as schools. By and large, this spread has been maintained throughout its existence. One of a number of initiatives that the council undertook was to set up a problem-solving competition for secondary school students. The competition, "Mathematical Challenge," was first held in the 1976–1977 academic year. All students in Scottish secondary schools are eligible to take part, and there are no fees. As a problem-solving competition that attempts to emulate the way in which mathematicians operate in the real world, the competition is not timed, at least not in the short term. Sets of questions are sent to schools to distribute to students, who generally have approximately six weeks to solve as many problems as they can. Problems do not require any technical knowledge of calculus, although an elementary knowledge of vectors may be assumed.

Throughout the 1980s, the competition was successful and maintained the same basic format. The problems and outline solutions for the first twelve years of the competition (i.e., 1976 to 1988) were published as *Mathematical Challenges* (Scottish

202 *Developing Mathematically Promising Students*

Mathematical Council 1989). Although the main structure of the competition had remained unchanged, beginning in 1985, provision was made for younger students in the first two years of secondary schools to participate. In 1991, a major change took place. The problems were assigned to three divisions: junior, for the first two years of secondary school; middle, for the third and fourth years; and senior, for the fifth and sixth years. Problems and outline solutions from 1991 to 1994 are available in *Mathematical Challenges II* (Scottish Mathematical Council 1995). Some problems were determined to be suitable for multiple divisions. In each division there are four problems per set and there are three sets. See the appendix to this chapter for examples of problems from the three levels of a past competition.

An analysis of the first three years of this format of the competition showed that between 65 percent and 75 percent of the entries were in the junior division, between 20 percent and 25 percent in the middle division, and between 5 percent and 10 percent in the senior division. There has been much speculation as to why the numbers in the upper age range have declined. The most likely cause is that curricular changes have resulted in students in the fifth year of secondary school having to be more involved in project work in all their school subjects, which may distract them from the competition.

Nevertheless, the competition continues to expand. Its scope is also being widened, and the first three problems in each set are now being made available to pupils in primary school. Although the competition has been successful, success brings its own problems. The organization, which depends on volunteers, has great difficulty in evaluating solutions and returning the results to schools within a short time span. Even so, the future of the competition appears healthy as it continues to encourage the development of young mathematicians.

ONE BULGARIAN EXPERIENCE IN IDENTIFYING AND DEVELOPING MATHEMATICALLY TALENTED STUDENTS

—Emilia Velikova
Rousse University, Rousse, Bulgaria

Talented mathematicians and scientists are of great value and benefit to society. The development of talented individuals is a long and difficult process that obviously should start in elementary school. This is why one of the major goals of the educational system in Bulgaria is to establish conditions for creative work with talented students in mathematics. This article addresses identifying students who have the highest potential in mathematics, educating mathematically talented students in Bulgaria, and cultivating mathematical talent.

Identifying Mathematically Talented Students

Although there have been attempts in Bulgaria to design tests to identify students who are gifted and talented in mathematics, the task of identifying the gifted and talented falls mostly to teachers because we have found them to be more precise in their evaluation of giftedness. In particular, mathematics teachers in Bulgaria have an extensive background in psychology and pedagogy, enabling them to discover talents based on the work of Krutetskii (1968) and Ridge and Renzulli (1980), among others. In addition to the regular mathematics lessons given at least four times a week, teachers assign individual work for students on the basis of their abilities.

Students' talents may be manifested by their successful presentations in olympiads and competitions in mathematics and informatics. There are many attentive teachers who constantly observe and monitor students' development—a sure way of identifying those who are gifted and talented.

Educating the Mathematically Talented in Bulgaria

In Bulgaria, the extracurricular training of the mathematically gifted and talented begins in grade 4 and is carried out primarily on two levels by participating (1) in a mathematics club known as an interest circle, at individual schools, and (2) in the Center for Students' Technical and Scientific Work (CSTSW), whose programs, lectures, and other activities are conducted primarily by mathematicians from different Bulgarian universities or from abroad.

In the first level, extracurricular work for each grade at individual schools is organized by the mathematics teachers who work with students. The students volunteer to attend the after-school interest circles. All leaders of mathematics interest circles are offered syllabi prepared by specialists from the Ministry of Education and Science or they are allowed to develop programs independently. There are two lessons a week. The goals of such interest circles are to (1) expand and deepen students' knowledge, (2) develop students' skills and habits, (3) cultivate students' interest in various fields of mathematics, (4) have students acquire skills for appropriate use of reference or scientific literature, (5) have students develop the language and style of mathematics that will enable them to write short reports about the life and work of prominent mathematicians or new scientific discoveries, and (6) prepare materials for bulletin boards and newspapers.

In the second level, if the interests and the abilities of students are above the average level of the other circle members, the teacher offers them the opportunity to attend the CSTSW. Every town with more than 30 000 citizens has a CSTSW established and financed by the state. Some of the CSTSW's goals are to (1) discover and develop young talents in the field of science and technology; (2) cultivate the creative abilities of young people; (3) offer students opportunities to create new approaches and a sense of novelty; and (4) inspire students' ambition to achieve new scientific and technical results through creative work.

Thus, the CSTSW is responsible for many activities in mathematics, such as school-level, regional, and national olympiads, winter mathematics holidays, spring mathematical competitions, autumn competitions, seminars, meetings with well-known mathematicians, evenings dedicated to mathematics, discussion on methods of teaching, teams working on essay papers or scientific discoveries, and theoretical conferences.

Special mathematics schools organized by CSTSW are available for students in grades 5 and 6, 7 and 8, and 9–12. Admission may also be determined by students' level of mathematical preparation. The mathematics topics discussed have nothing in common with the required mathematics syllabus covered in the regular schools. Solutions of difficult problems from olympiads and other competitions are examined and discussed. It must be noted that mathematically talented students in grade 5 or higher may compete to enter the specialized mathematical or business high schools, or the school of exceptionally talented children in the town of Gorna Banya. The students from the mathematics schools have been the most successful in the events and activities organized by CSTSW.

Cultivating Mathematical Talent

Solving problems is a necessary but not a sufficient condition for developing creative and talented mathematicians. The Joint and Independent Creative Work between a Talented Student and a Leading Teacher (JICWTSLT) is a project that brings together a leading teacher and gifted, talented students (Bilchev and Velikova 1995). Analogous to sportsmen who spend years in training without being able to develop their own skills because they were never actively involved in real-life games with real-life opponents or real-life spectators and supporters (Ridge and Renzulli 1980), JICWTSLT goes beyond problem solving. The JICWT-SLT is a dual creative process that consists of (1) the independent creative work of the leading teacher; (2) the joint creative work of both the leading teacher and the gifted student; and (3) the independent creative work of the student. The creative work can be carried out by one or two teachers with one student or by a small group of students in the form of the following (Bilchev and Velikova 1995):

- The exploration of a particular group of scientific and mathematical problems, new mathematical methods, or new fields of mathematics and their profound acquisition

- The development and presentation of a lecture by a gifted student with the active assistance of the leading teacher

- The solution of an appropriate scientific problem, a nonstandard problem, or a group of problems

- The preparation and participation in national and international competitions and olympiads

- The development of an essay paper with a definite research problem, and its defense in organized competitions

- The preparation and publication of ideas, problems, or articles in journals dedicated to students' achievements

As teachers work closely with mathematically talented students, the teachers delve deeper into their fields of interest, solve new problems, publish new articles, and receive public recognition. Interesting examples of award-winning essay papers are examined by Bilchev and Velikova (1993, 1996) and Velikova (in press).

In every nation the creativity and talents of teachers are of great value and benefit to the entire society as they contribute to identify and develop the mathematically talented, helping students to realize their maximum potential.

SAINT PETERSBURG CENTER OF MATHEMATICAL EDUCATION—RUSSIA

—Serge Ruksh

Russian State Pedagogical University, Saint Petersburg, Russia

—Alexander Golovanov

Saint Petersburg Center of Mathematical Education, Saint Petersburg, Russia

The system of special mathematics education in Saint Petersburg began in the early 1930s. The system, created by the most prominent Russian mathematicians of the time, has become the Saint Petersburg Center of Mathematical Education. Rich mathematical opportunities for gifted and talented students living in Saint Petersburg are offered at the Center.

The system is characterized by several unique features, some of which have been adapted by other Russian centers of mathematics education. First, the system is open, universal, free, and supplements the regular school program. Any student in Saint Petersburg may enroll in the Center, which tends to attract all students able and willing to study mathematics seriously. As a result, about 300 mathematically promising students in Saint Petersburg between eleven and seventeen years old (i.e., in grades 6–11 in Russia) study in the Center.

Second, the students begin their studies at a fairly early age—most when they are eleven years old or younger. Since students begin at an early age, the program is designed to support their development by organizing instruction accordingly.

Third, the purpose of the center is to produce active mathematicians. This does not mean that all the students become mathematicians or join mathematics faculties at universities; rather, the students build options to apply their knowledge of mathematics as they pursue further study in physics, computer science, and other related fields.

Fourth, the program offered at the Center focuses on problem solving. However, unlike the practice in other institutions, the solutions of the problems are presented by the students to their teachers and to their peers. The solutions are then verified according to standards of mathematical correctness not usually discussed in school. This feature is connected with the purpose of the Center as being a place for preparing future mathematicians. This requires the active creation of knowledge, not its passive acquisition. The approach that is used originated with the Saint Petersburg Mathematical Olympiad, which is perhaps the only oral olympiad in the world: students explain their solutions directly to the jury instead of writing them.

In the Center, students are organized in parallel groups, not according to age but according to their year of study and level of ability. Because the education system in the Center is independent of the regular school curriculum, students in the same parallel or in the same group may be from different grade levels. The teachers in all parallel groups are supervised by a master teacher, who also teaches the most advanced group. The master teacher's many responsibilities include assigning the students to groups based on their abilities, recruiting other teachers, developing the curriculum, and supervising the teaching in all of the groups in his or her parallel.

The first year of study is devoted to problem solving. Twice a week, students who are eleven years old or younger are given a set of problems to solve at home. Three days later, when they attend the next lesson, all their solutions are presented to the teacher and the teacher's assistants. For the most part, the assistants are university students who are graduates of the Center. The help is essential because every student discusses all solutions with teachers. All the errors, logical and otherwise, are revealed to the students. This early training of good mathematical style forms skills necessary to avoid the usual trouble spots (e.g., confusing necessary and sufficient conditions).

The summer after the first year of study, the students attend their first summer camp. The camp, introduced in 1981 by the first author and held each year since then, is an important part of the studies offered at the Center. The twenty-six-day camp offers the possibility to control and organize the children's studies. For six hours each day, the students solve problems, discuss solutions, and listen to lectures.

The lectures presented in the first summer camp are traditional. The topics selected depend on the year of study and the interest and specialty of the teacher. Typical subjects for the first course are elementary number theory and elementary geometry.

The master teacher for the parallel groups does not teach all the courses. Other lecturers are invited to the summer camp. Topics for the lectures include polynomials, inequalities, group theory, general topology, calculus, and so on.

In the following years of study, the number of lectures increases and the focus is on more advanced subjects. Problem solving remains the most important part of the students' activity. In such theoretical courses as classical projective geometry, students are expected to prove theorems. Although this approach is more laborious than what is typically done, it proves effective when students encounter application problems.

After two years of studying in the Center, students are organized in a class in one of the leading mathematics schools in Saint Petersburg. This arrangement allows for coordination between center studies and school studies for the following four years. Traditional mathematics lessons are enhanced beyond the usual school syllabus.

As students spend more time in the Center, the lessons become longer, the number of problems assigned increases, and more attention is paid to technical skills. The courses underline the most significant ideas common to different branches of mathematics and highlight abstract notions. The main goal is to present an approach complementary to that of the university, where connections between and among parts of mathematics are not always explicitly revealed. The effectiveness of this approach has been confirmed by former students who excel in their early university years. For example, one former center student solved Hilbert's tenth problem when he was a university student.

Students at the Center are also involved in olympiad activities, which are supervised by the staff. Center students have a reputation of being highly successful in olympiad competitions. In recent years, Center students have had the best results in all grades in the All-Russian Olympiad. Every year since 1987, at least half of the Russian team for the IMO have been from Saint Petersburg (i.e., five students out of six in 1995; four out of six in 1996). And, several former Center students have won IMO medals for the U.S. team.

Almost all the female members of the Russian IMO teams were Center students (e.g., usually one out of six team members, but two out of six in 1989, 1994, and 1996). Involving girls at a young age in mathematics activities, cultivating their interests, and building their confidence are contributing factors in their success.

The work at the Center complements the work at the university. It supports mathematically gifted students' transition from school to the university. Students who attend the Center first make a smooth transition and have the tools to fulfill university expectations and requirements.

The major challenges that face the Center are financial. The reduction of state support affects all functions of the center—participation in olympiads, the organization of summer camps, staff salaries, and so on. The success of the Center, however, cannot be measured monetarily but rather in the human mathematical resources created, cultivated, developed, and supported by caring, dedicated professionals who selflessly share their understanding and appreciation of mathematics.

CULTIVATING MATHEMATICAL TALENT IN LATVIA

—Agnis Andzans
University of Latvia, Riga, Latvia

In Latvia, when preparing activities and offering opportunities for students who are gifted and talented in mathematics, we consider two components of elementary mathematics: (1) general methods of reasoning used throughout the study of mathematics but not dependent on any specific branch of mathematics; and (2) the problems that can be solved by such methods. When examining various branches of mathematics, general methods are supplemented with specific methods.

Middle school and high school students in Latvia have several opportunities to develop their mathematical talents. They may participate in after-school interest clubs, Saturday lectures, summer camps, correspondence schools, and competitions.

As an extension of the regular school day, such extracurricular interest clubs as the High School Students' Scientific Society have special mathematics sections where students discuss projects and problem-solving strategies. Students experience mathematics beyond the expectations of the regular school curriculum.

Offered every Saturday, the Little Mathematical University is available to middle school and high school students. They may participate in a series of mathematics and informatics lectures, lasting eight hours conducted by mathematics teachers, university mathematicians, and advanced students.

Every summer there are three to five camps in mathematics and informatics throughout the country. The summer camps focus on developing interest and skill in solving nonroutine mathematics problems.

Each year approximately 300 students participate in the A. Liepa Mathematical Correspondence School of the University of Latvia. Their study includes mathematics not traditionally included in the regular curriculum. Special brochures that contain mathematical theory, examples, and problems for independent problem solving have been designed for them. The solutions to the problems are submitted to the university and checked by faculty members and advanced students.

The Latvian Mathematical Olympiad, the Latvian Open Mathematical Olympiad, and the Preparatory Olympiad encourage mathematically talented students to prepare to participate in the IMO. Mathematical olympiads and contests are an essential part of the entire educational system. Olympiad problems contain mathematical content that is not usually part of the regular mathematics curriculum. By solving algorithmic and deductive problems from various branches of mathematics, students become acquainted with and acquire general mathematical methods.

Teachers who work with mathematically talented students may enroll in sixty-hour courses that focus on the advanced teaching of mathematics. Such courses are offered in Riga and in other regions throughout the country.

An Example

Combinatorial methods are used as an example of the approach taken in designing activities and problems for mathematically gifted students. Although not the only content of advanced mathematics education in high school, combinatorial methods form the basis for developing activities and problems for the mathematically talented in the A. Liepa Mathematical Correspondence School. The study of general combinatorial methods has been selected for pedagogical reasons—we can demonstrate the unity and the aesthetics of mathematics, we can extend and connect the ideas of the methods beyond the study of mathematics, we can broaden the concept of proof, and we can motivate teachers and students to become involved in independent activities. The combinatorial methods identified as a result of analyzing research papers in mathematics and computer science include mathematical induction, mean value method (i.e., generalized pigeonhole principle), invariants, method of analyzing extreme elements, and interpretation (i.e., translating the problem into appropriate language).

An attempt has been made to introduce these methods by designing problems and activities in the high school mathematics curriculum, keeping in mind that the characteristics of a mathematician include knowledge of facts embedded in hierarchical mental structures, the ability to use the facts, the ability to form and to analyze mathematical models, and the development of logical mental structures and mathematical intuition (i.e., a feel for veracity without formal proof and a sense of the direction such a formal proof would take).

Introductory problems posed to mathematically talented students employ combinatorial methods consisting of inductive constructions, inductive algorithms, recurrent relations, the application of the Dirichlet principle in finding extreme values, the invariance of counting, the idea of parity and its uses, the convex hull, and the application and physical interpretations of geometry in algebra. As methods are introduced, the general idea of the method is not hidden in the formal manipulations connected with writing down the solution for the general case. The special cases are of greatest importance.

CLOSING COMMENTS

Mathematical knowledge and the mathematical way of thinking are not only important not only in mathematical development but also in cultivating general intelligence. Contributing both to specific mathematical development and to general intellectual development supports societal needs to create mathematicians and computer scientists and to cultivate strong problem solvers across other academic disciplines. Although attempts are made to interest and attract students at all levels of formal education—elementary, middle, and high school—the challenge continues to be in identifying and reaching all students who are talented and gifted in mathematics.

BIBLIOGRAPHY

Belluck, Pam. "Gifted Programs' Criteria Vary Widely." *The New York Times* (28 February 1997): B4.

Bilchev, Svetoslav J., and Emilia A. Velikova. "The Teaching of Transformations for Solving Competition Problems as a Route Towards Higher Mathematics." *Mathematics Competitions, Journal of the World Federation of National Mathematics Competition* 6 (1993): 45–52.

_____. "Jointly and Independently Creative Work of Talented Students and Their Tutors in the Process of Learning of Mathematics." In *Mathematics and Education in Mathematics, Proceedings of the Twenty-Fourth Spring Conference of the Union of Bulgarian Mathematics*, Vol. 24, edited by Sava Grozev, pp. 88–108. Sofia, Bulgaria: House of Bulgarian Academy of Sciences, 1995.

_____. "On Some Asymmetric Trigonometric Inequalities—Another Way Of Competitions." In *Mathematics Competitions, Journal of World Federation of National Mathematics Competitions*, in press.

Borneo Bulletin Brunei Yearbook: Key Information on Brunei. Bandar Seri Begawan, Brunei Darussalam: Brunei Press and Forward Media, 1997.

Consultative Committee for Research and Surveys Regarding Exceptional Measures in Education. *Final Report on Exceptional Measures in Education*. Tokyo: Ministry of Education, 1994.

Curran, M. John, Coralie Daniel, and Derek A. Holton. "Two Surveys of Talented Mathematics Students." In *Merga 18: Galtha*, edited by Bill Atweh and Steve Flavel, pp. 210–15. Darwin, Australia: Education Research Group of Australasia, 1995.

Gardiner, Anthony. *Discovering Mathematics: The Art of Investigation.* Oxford: Oxford University Press, 1987a.

————. *Mathematics Extra.* Cambridge: Cambridge University Press, in press.

————. *The Mathematical Olympiad Handbook: An Introduction to Problem Solving.* Oxford: Oxford University Press, 1997a.

————. *Mathematical Puzzling.* Oxford: Oxford University Press, 1987b. (Available from United Kingdom Mathematics Foundation, University of Birmingham, Birmingham B15 2TT, United Kingdom.)

Gardiner, Tony. *Mathematical Challenge.* Cambridge: Cambridge University Press, 1996.

————. *More Mathematical Challenges.* Cambridge: Cambridge University Press, 1997b.

Hirona, Tomomi. "Education for the Talented in Japan." *Sophia* 44, no. 3: 341–9.

Holton, Derek A., and Coralie Daniel. "Talented Mathematics Students." In *Gifted and Talented: New Zealand Perspectives,* edited by Don McAlpine and Roger Moltzen, pp. 201–18. Palmerston North, New Zealand: ERDC Press, 1996.

Krutetskii, V. A. *The Psychology of Mathematical Abilities in Schoolchildren.* Translated from the Russian by Joan Teller, edited by Jeremy Kilpatrick and Izaak Wirszup. Chicago: University of Chicago Press, 1976. (Original work published 1963.)

Lynn, Leon, and Anne Wheelock. "Making Detracking Work." *The Harvard Education Letter* 13 (January/February 1997): 1–5.

Ministry of Education. "Special Issues for Exceptional Measures in Education." *Monbujiho* (February 1996): 48–58. (In Japanese)

Ridge, H. Laurence, and Joseph S. Renzulli. "Teaching Mathematics to the Talented and Gifted." In *The Mathematical Education of Exceptional Children and Youth,* edited by V. J. Glennon, pp. 191–266. Reston, Va.: National Council of Teachers of Mathematics, 1980.

Scottish Mathematical Council. *Mathematical Challenges.* Glasgow: Blackie & Son, Ltd., 1989.

————. *Mathematical Challenges II.* Elgin, United Kingdom: Scottish Mathematical Council, 1995.

Sengupta, Somini. "New York's Chancellor Seeking Wider Access to Gifted Program." *The New York Times* (28 February 1997): A1, B4.

Velikova, Emilia A. "The Creative Activities with Gifted Students Based On 'The Method of Transformations.'" *Mathematics Competitions, Journal of World Federation of National Mathematics Competitions,* in press.

APPENDIX

The following are sample items from mathematics competitions in Brunei Darussalam and Scotland

1. Items from Brunei Darussalam National Mathematics Quiz

   a. The *Game Round* consists of a 4 × 4 grid of squares with numbers 1 to 16 arranged in a certain order as shown below. The game host selects a number and reads the question assigned to that number. For example, the host may begin with number 5, which has the question, "What is the identity element for multiplication?" The question is open to all teams, and the team that first answers it correctly wins the square and scores one point. That team then selects a number and the host reads the corresponding question. This is repeated until a team gets four squares in a row (i.e., horizontally, vertically, or diagonally), and becomes the winning team; it also scores a three-point bonus. If no team is able to get four squares in a row, the game continues until all sixteen squares are used.

13	7	10	2
9	1	5	12
4	11	3	14
8	6	16	15

b. *Manipulative Round.* In the envelope you will find seven pieces of geometrical shapes. Your task is to use all of them to form a square.

2. Sample Questions from Scotland's Mathematical Challenges, 1993–94

a. *Junior Division.* The squares on a chessboard are numbered as shown in figure 1. Eight chess pieces are placed on the squares so that no row or column contains more than one piece. Show that the sum of the numbers on the squares containing pieces must equal 64.

1	2	3	4	5	6	7	8
2	3	4	5	6	7	8	9
3	4	5	6	7	8	9	10
4	5	6	7	8	9	10	11
5	6	7	8	9	10	11	12
6	7	8	9	10	11	12	13
7	8	9	10	11	12	13	14
8	9	10	11	12	13	14	15

Fig. 1. Junior Division Sample Item

b. *Middle Division.* The numbers 1066, 1314, and 1815 have something in common. Of course it is that each is a 4-digit number beginning with 1 that has two identical digits. How many such numbers are there? Do not list them all, but explain how you know how many there are.

c. *Senior Division.* Suppose that a, b, c, d, e, and f are six different integers. Find the least possible value of

$$(a - b)^2 + (b - c)^2 + (c - d)^2 + (d - e)^2 + (e - f)^2 + (f - a)^2$$

Chapter 17

Part IV

MAKING CHILDREN COUNT: FOSTERING MATHEMATICAL LITERACY

Mary Anne Anthony-Smith

With the current emphasis on helping all children in the United States become proficient readers, it is widely accepted that a major factor in children's reading success is having their parents read to them, even in early infancy. It should follow logically, then, that parents who do mathematics with their children, beginning when the children are very young, will help the children to become proficient in mathematics.

However, although it is easy to find opportunities for parents to read with their children and to find opportunities all around for emerging young readers to practice their skills, most parents do not see that opportunities for doing mathematics with their children abound in everyday life as well. This article will show how the children in one family—mine—have become mathematically promising students through their natural interaction with mathematics on an everyday basis.

A MATHEMATICS FAMILY

My family, most people would say, is not a typical American family. Both my husband and I are community college mathematics professors. Mathematics, how to teach it, and the difficulties many of our adult students have mastering it are common topics at our dinner table. Number books were well represented among our children's baby books, and as our children began to talk, counting was a favorite activity; we found objects to be counted everywhere we went. As the children began speaking and gave us insights into their thinking, we rewarded them with praise, as we were genuinely proud of their emerging abilities.

Our friends and colleagues heard many stories of the early mathematical discoveries of Alex, Annie, and Jeannette and praised the children themselves when they saw them. This positive reinforcement showed our children we were proud of their accomplishments, and it encouraged them to continue to speak their thoughts. In addition, sometimes out of pure amazement at their discoveries, we often asked the children to explain how they knew something so that we could learn ourselves about the process through which they acquired mathematics. I began keeping a journal in which I recorded their discoveries and explanations.

Many of our colleagues heard the story of how Alex discovered zero before he was two years old. He called me from his crib. "Mommy, Mommy, come here!" I rushed to see what he needed and found him with outstretched hand, palm up, saying, "Look, in my hand". "There's nothing in your hand," I said, and he answered "That's right! There's *nothing* in my hand!"

A few months later, while desperately trying to coax a reluctant Alex to eat all his lunch, I introduced him to subtraction. Together we counted the seven meatballs left in his bowl of SpaghettiOs, and then I said we were going to do something new—subtract. I popped one meatball into his mouth before he knew what had happened and we counted the remaining meatballs. "Seven take away one leaves six," I said, and then repeated this experiment a few more times, stating the number facts $6 - 1 = 5$, $5 - 1 = 4$, and so on, until the bowl was empty.

Being raised in a house where mathematics was spoken daily, Alex developed an early confidence with numbers. As part of a developmental assessment at preschool when he was four years old, he was asked to count all the numbers as high as he could go. "You'd better sit down," he told his teacher. "This could take a long time." He counted to ninety-nine. Not long afterward, just as he turned five, he exhibited an intuitive understanding of the associative law of addition. I was taking the children to the library. To keep Alex quiet in the car and constructively occupied, I asked him to count the traffic lights we passed. We took a different route home, again counting the traffic lights. I was about to ask him which way had fewer lights (thinking this might be developmentally appropriate for a five-year-old), and I had just reminded him that we had passed six lights on the way to the library and five on the way home. "That makes eleven altogether," he volunteered. When I asked how he figured that out, he explained, "Well, I know that $5 + 5$ is 10, and 6 is one more than 5, so $6 + 5$ must be one more than 10." $[(1+5) + 5 = 1 + (5 + 5)]$ Our youngest child, now in the second grade, uses this same "one more than" or "one less than" idea to calculate many of her addition problems.

When the children reached school age they began attending our local Irvine, California, public schools. We have been fortunate both to have had our children placed in the classrooms of excellent teachers, including the district's elementary-level mathematics mentors, and to also have work schedules that have allowed us to volunteer time regularly to help in our children's classrooms and, thus, observe firsthand what was going on. Throughout the elementary school, we have seen caring, competent teachers using a variety of methods and materials to facilitate the learning of mathematics—Calendar Math, Everyday Counts, Daily Math, Problems of the Week, to name a few—with manipulatives widely used at every level. (However, I remember seeing Alex, in the second grade, first write down the answer to a two-digit addition problem he could do conceptually and then model the problem with his base-ten blocks to please his teacher.)

Mathematics was often applied across the curriculum, connected to what was being learned in science or social studies, so students truly saw that mathematics is everywhere. Many of the techniques and materials I observed were new to me—college teachers are supposed to be subject-matter experts and many of us have had few courses in educational theories or techniques—and I have used some of the ideas and methods I saw in the elementary school classrooms in my own college prealgebra, algebra, and statistics classrooms.

My volunteering in my children's classrooms and praising their efforts and those of their teachers has benefited and encouraged my children's mathematical development as well. They feel that their work is valued and that their teacher's lessons are worthwhile and important. They are also proud when they hear that some of the things they do in their classrooms are also being done by adults in my college classes.

A HEALTHY BALANCE

Through all the turbulent discussions of recent years at the state and national levels relating to teaching mathematics, our children's school has maintained a healthy balance of emphasizing the basics and incorporating reform elements such as writing about mathematics. In the fourth grade, Annie had to pass timed tests of basic number facts (addition, subtraction, multiplication, and division up to twelve), which progressed to prealgebraic thinking ($7 + [\ ] = 15$). She had to explain her reasoning in some rather sophisticated mathematical problems in areas such as logic and discrete mathematics. Not knowing that her class had just worked out the hand-shake problem, I asked her one Sunday in church, when there were four priests officiating, how many kisses were exchanged when each priest kissed every other priest once. She gave me the correct answer nearly instantly, and then explained it to her six-year old sister, Jeannette, counting on her knuckles. She even extended the problem to seven priests and asked her sister follow-up questions to be sure *she* understood!

Dinner table discussions usually revolve around our collective schoolwork. Often, the children challenge each other with mathematics problems. Jeannette, now in the second grade, asked her older siblings to give her "algebra" problems of the "four plus what makes twelve" variety. She clearly enjoyed being able to solve these. Eighth grader Alex thought he had her stumped when he asked her "six plus what makes five." After just a moment's thought, Jeannette answered, "Why, that would be one behind zero." Although she didn't yet know the vocabulary, she was clearly developing the concept of negative numbers. Recognizing this, I praised her insight in doing this difficult problem and then gave her a few more similar questions.

Are these children mathematically promising? In the seventh grade, Alex took the School and College Ability Test (SCAT) and scored in the 90th percentile *compared to the norm of high school seniors.* He has been asked to participate on his school team in a variety of mathematics-related interscholastic competitions in elementary and middle school. His sisters appear to be following close in his footsteps, clearly demonstrating their talents for understanding mathematics.

CONCLUSION

Is this talent hereditary? Most people who know that our children have two mathematics professors as parents expect them to do well in mathematics, as if it were genetically predetermined. After spending years on my job trying to dispel such math myths to mathematically anxious students, I would hesitate to admit that there might be some genetic basis or that the mathematics they absorbed in utero (because I taught through my pregnancies) would have such long-lasting effects.

Rather, I prefer to think that their early success in mathematics comes from being raised in a house where mathematics is literally a part of everyday life. We have spoken mathematics to them from the beginning, and they have seen that mathematics is all around them. They have become accustomed to explaining their mathematical reasoning as we, their parents, have been trying to get glimpses into their learning process. As a result they have become better reasoners. We have encouraged them to estimate, to guess and check, to organize, to take risks mathematically and we have corrected their errors gently and respectfully. They have been guided to see that they can come up with the answers themselves. They know they are mathematically powerful.

One afternoon while I was helping Annie with her fourth-grade homework, 6-year-old Jeannette articulated better than I ever could my philosophy for developing the mathematical potential in my children. "Why does Annie ask you so many questions?" she asked. "She thinks she doesn't know the answers," I carefully replied. "But you never give her any answers," Jeannette continued, "you just ask her more questions."

ADDITIONAL READINGS

Burk, Donna, Allyn Snyder, and Paula Symonds. *Calendar Math: Box It or Bag It Mathematics: Teacher Resource Guide*. Salem, Ore.: Math Learning Center, 1988

Gillespie, Janet, and Patsy Kanter. *Everyday Counts*. Lexington, Mass.: D.C. Heath, 1994

Daily Math. Evanston, Ill.: McDougal Littell, 1992.

Problems of the Week. Quest 2000. Menlo Park, Calif.: Addison-Wesley Publishing Co., 1994.

Collins S. Harold. *Straight Forward Math Series*. Eugene, Ore.: Garlic Press, 1992.

Chapter 18

THE GIFTED DOZEN AS THEY MOVE FROM GRADES 2 THROUGH 4

Gerald Elgarten

July 1994: It was my first day as the director of a 109-student, grades K–5 private school in Palo Alto, California. (The previous week I had been the chair of Secondary Education at the City College of New York.) I began my new job by meeting with the parents of a current student who would be entering second grade in September.

THE SCHOOL AND THE STORY

At the meeting, the parents indicated to me that they were pleased with the first-grade program but felt that their child was gifted in mathematics and was not being sufficiently challenged in that area. They were considering withdrawing their child from the school unless they could get some assurance that their child would be challenged in mathematics. I certainly did not want to start the year with one less child, so I told them I was a professor of mathematics education and would be happy to work with their child at least once a week. They agreed to keep their child in school and to monitor my commitment.

The second week of school, I went to the second-grade classroom during D.E.A.R. (Drop Everything And Read) time. Because teachers work with some children individually while the others read alone, I thought that this was a good opportunity to provide enrichment mathematics. I worked with the child for twenty-five minutes, and he returned to class. You may have anticipated a consequence of my political inexperience. The next day, several parents from the second grade class scheduled meetings with me to question why their children were not getting special mathematics sessions with me.

The next week, the first child was joined by eleven others from his class. After two weeks, the second-grade teacher asked why I didn't work with the other children in the class. Now I worked with the original group twice a week for thirty minutes and two other groups for thirty minutes each week. These thirty minutes a week of mathematics enrichment during reading time was expanded to the fourth and fifth grades as well.

THE STUDENTS

At the start, almost all of the twelve youngsters knew basic addition and subtraction facts. All but four of them knew multiplication facts 0–9, but not well. They did not know any multiplication algorithms. With that as a background, I decided to use a methodology based on the principle that the children would have some notions about what we would be discussing. Therefore, I would allow them to explore the problem before eliciting responses from them.

The Second Grade

The children did many investigations during the year. They were able to discover that double the sum of the length and width is equal to the perimeter. The children graphed solutions to equations such as First number + Second number = 12. By placing graphs of several similar equations on the same grid, the children discovered that the lines were parallel and that you can find other solutions to the equations by extending the lines.

After many other investigations and toward the end of the year, we measured angles and looked at the sum of the angles of various polygons. After measuring various types of angles with a protractor, the children were asked to determine the sum of the angles of a triangle. After completing this task, one of the second graders said, "I wonder what the sum of the angles of a four-sided figure would be?" Most of the children drew a quadrilateral and began measuring the angles. Two of the children noticed that if you draw a diagonal (they did not know the term), you would get two triangles. They concluded that the sum of the angles should be "two triangles, or 180° + 180°." We then looked at five-sided figures to determine the sum of the angles. A few children were measuring the angles, but most were connecting vertices to determine the number of triangles they could place in the figure. The children were then asked to determine the sum of the measures of the angles of a ten-sided figure. Now there were no children measuring angles; most were trying to determine the number of triangles that they could make without crossing line segments. However, four were having some form of the following conversation: "When we have a four-sided figure, the sum of the angles is two triangles; for a five-sided figure, we have three triangles; so a ten-sided figure must be eight triangles." Quite good reasoning!

For the next session I had planned to give them the following problem: "When we examined the sum of the angles of a quadrilateral, you said that by drawing a diagonal we make two triangles. So, the sum of the angles must be equal to 180°+ 180°, or 360°. But if I also draw the other diagonal, we would then have four triangles. How can you now tell if the sum of the angles of a quadrilateral is two triangles (360°) or four triangles (720°)?"

Normally, this problem would be assigned to the group for a thirty-minute session. However, we were in the process of hiring a third-grade teacher for the next year. An applicant for that position had been invited to teach the second graders at the time I was to present this problem to the group. When I entered the classroom, the children were ready to leave with me, but I told them that the prospective teacher would be there in ten minutes to teach a mathematics lesson to the class, so we would have to cancel our session. The children said that they were disappointed because they wanted to work with me. Of course, I gave in. However, I wanted them to solve the problem in a shorter period of time. I decided to use a different methodology and ask the children questions immediately, without preliminary discussion, so that they would solve the problem more quickly.

We stood just outside the classroom, and I asked the group to compare two diagrams: one a quadrilateral with one diagonal drawn, and the other a quadrilateral with both diagonals drawn. "How do the two diagrams compare?"

The children noticed the intersecting lines in the quadrilateral with both diagonals drawn. I then asked, "Can you describe any connections between the angles of the triangles in the quadrilateral with both diagonals drawn and the angles of the quadrilateral?" Several youngsters noticed that the angles around the intersection of the diagonals were not angles of the quadrilateral. They reasoned that since a complete rotation is 360°, then the sum of the angles of the quadrilateral would be four triangles minus 360°. Excellent!

As we reentered the classroom, the children stopped, turned to me, and one of them said, "Why didn't you let us solve the problem?" The others nodded as they continued walking into the room.

Reflections

I was a believer in the method that "good questions" encouraged good thinking. I was amazed by the comment, "Why didn't you let us solve the problem?" The children *did not want* my question when they just began to look at the problem. This was strong support for assuming children have the knowledge to "solve the problem." Give them the chance … *then* ask those good questions.

Third Grade

It became clear at the end of second grade that the children in this group needed more than a third-grade mathematics experience. We decided that these twelve children would have fifty-minute sessions with me twice a week, and study with their class the rest of the week. The children in this group were required to make up any work they missed while working with me.

Some of the topics we explored included area of quadrilaterals and triangles. The idea of slope and y-intercept was introduced in the context of verbal problems. The group then graphed two equations in two unknowns to get a common solution. They were taught how to use the TI-82 calculator to solve equations graphically.

In "Probability" the children did experiments to determine whether games were fair or unfair. They also used area models to determine the probabilities of dependent events.

Fourth Grade

As these twelve students entered fourth grade, our school had grown from 109 students to 139. Every class was filled. Unfortunately, it became increasingly more difficult for me to spend large blocks of time during the day teaching mathematics. I decided to offer the children a before-school mathematics program. Each morning of the week was devoted to children in each of the grades 1–5. I decided to teach the fourth graders algebra, and what happened was quite interesting. Several parents tried to show their children how the assigned verbal problems could be solved using two variables. This was not very helpful. In fact, youngsters who were excellent at solving sophisticated problems by various forms of trial and error and other interesting approaches seemed stuck when trying to find algebraic solutions. Also, youngsters who were trying to use one variable to solve the problem seemed to be losing their creative insight into problem-solving. I stopped the algebra approach. Instead, the children spent the remainder of the year solving problems and their extensions from the Mathematical Olympiads for Elementary Schools. This allowed the group to explore other problem-solving approaches and not be stuck looking for algebraic solutions. Toward the end of the school year the following problem was assigned to the group:

> Problem: Three apples weigh the same as a banana and three cherries. A banana weighs the same as nine cherries. How many cherries weigh the same as one apple?

Several of the youngsters solved the problem using pictures. They made an equation drawing three apples equal to a drawing of one banana and three cherries. Then, they drew a banana equal to a drawing of nine cherries. This picture enabled them to see that nine cherries could replace the banana in the first equation. They then drew three apples equal to twelve cherries (the three cherries plus the replacement of the banana by nine cherries). They were then able to deduce that since three apples equals twelve cherries, each apple must weigh the same as four cherries. Interestingly, several other youngsters solved the problem using symbols as follows:

(1) 3 apples = 1 banana + 3 cherries

(2) 1 banana = 9 cherries

Then, replacing 1 banana with 9 cherries, the first equation becomes 3 apples = 9 cherries + 3 cherries, or 12 cherries

Then, 1 apple weighs the same as 4 cherries.

There was still another group of children who solved the problem using letters instead of words as follows:

$3a = 1b + 3c$; $1b = 9c$; $3a = 9c + 3c$ or $12c$

Therefore, $1a = 4c$, or one apple weighs the same as 4 cherries.

The children listened to each group's explanation with interest. Several of the youngsters said that although all the solutions were basically the same, the last explained solution was algebra! Perhaps we moved away from the algebra too quickly. It seemed that the children needed time to internalize the algebra language, which some demonstrated they were beginning to understand.

EVALUATION

The children's performance on the Olympiads significantly improved from third to fourth grade. However, I believe that a most important outcome of this program, for this group and the others I worked with, is that the children were able to be challenged when mathematics became an object of discussion. Of course, adjustments have also been made with the teachers so that there is some follow-up in the regular classroom.

BIBLIOGRAPHY

Mathematical Olympiads for Elementary Schools, 2154 Bellmore Ave., Bellmore, NY 11710-5645.

Phillips, Elizabeth, Glenda Lappan, Mary Winter, and William Fitzgerald. *Middle School Mathematics Project: Probability.* Menlo Park, Calif.: Addison-Wesley Publishing Co., 1986.

Chapter 19

RONNIE TAUGHT US WHILE WE MENTORED HIM

Marsha Nicol
James Fitzsimmons

We mean that children do not simply learn from teachers, as is commonly assumed, but that the best teachers know how to learn from students. (Jalongo and Isenberg 1995, p. xxi)

A few years ago, when we were mathematics-education doctoral students, Patricia Brosnan of Ohio State University offered us the opportunity to mathematically mentor Ronnie after he had taken and passed the AP calculus examination at the age of nine. Being teachers, we thought we were supposed to help Ronnie extend his learning of mathematics. We didn't know how much he would teach us in the process.

Ronnie's parents first suspected that their child was gifted when, at the age of eighteen months, he pointed to the numbers on the clock, naming each one correctly. As a two-year-old, Ronnie drew a picture of his dad's computer keyboard, correctly labeling all of the keys. He began writing computer programs when he was four.

Exhausting all of the available high school mathematics by age ten, he began working with us in a mentorship program at the same time that he took some calculus classes at Ohio State University. While we help him fill in minor gaps left by his quick leap through precollege mathematics, mostly we acted as a sounding board for his own mathematical exploration as we challenged him to solve problems and explain his thinking. We worked with him primarily on creating problems, solving problems posed by him or by us, and working on whatever other mathematics was of interest at the time. Because Ronnie's main interest was number theory, throughout our work we paid special attention to his understanding of the relationships among numbers and operations on them and the way he used this understanding.

It was obvious that Ronnie's ways of doing mathematics did not come from a textbook or from a teacher's explanation. While most students would search through their bag of algorithms to compute $9\,999\,999^2$ (since it is beyond the computational ability of most calculators), Ronnie looked for patterns and quickly transformed the problem to $(10\,000\,000 - 1)^2$. Calculations such as 320×150 were trivially and instantaneously computed by Ronnie by noting that "150 is really one-and-half multiplied by 100, and one-and-half of 32 is 48. So the product is 48 000."

Ronnie opened our eyes to an entirely new way of looking at mathematics. We had been traditionally trained to use algorithms to perform computations. Searching for patterns to transform problems was unexplored territory.

One of us vividly remembers an incident from her high school teaching years as follows:

> I was selling tickets and making change at a high school basketball game. People were streaming in, buying tickets at a fast-paced clip. Students' tickets were $1.25; adults' were $1.75.
>
> A voice said, "I want seven students', five adults'. Here's a $20 bill. I need change."
>
> As a high school mathematics teacher, I had always looked at and taught concepts in mathematics. I was (and am) a "big picture" person who really didn't do well in mental mathematics. I looked at arithmetic computation as a chore.
>
> I began thinking through the problem, "OK—five adults at $1.75 each—$5 \times 5 = 25$, carry the two; $5 \times 7 = 35$ and 2 more make 37 ... so, it's $8.75. Seven students at $1.25 each, add, carry ... $8.75. Add $8.75 + $8.75 (add, carry) and subtract from $20. Whew! Did I do that right? Is this change correct?"
>
> The person broke into my thoughts. "*What* do you teach?"
>
> I cringed, wanting to say language arts, or social studies—anything except mathematics!
>
> Looking at the problem through Ronnie's eyes, I would now treat the problem as a mathematical challenge rather than an arithmetic computation.
>
> My thought process might be: "Look for patterns and ways to transform the problem. Five adults at $1.75 each—well, $2 \times $1.75 = $3.50. So, four of them would be $7.00, plus another dollar, $8.00, and $0.75—$8.75. Seven students at $1.25 each—two of them would be $2.50, four would be $5.00, six would be $7.50, another dollar gives $8.50, and 25 cents is $8.75. Eight plus 8 is 16 plus 2×75 cents ($1.50) gives $17.50. So, the change is $2.50."
>
> It seems so trivial now, but never before had I looked at the big picture of computation. Never before had I looked at the patterns that emerged and at the challenge those patterns posed to reorganize the numbers to make them manageable. Ronnie opened my eyes to the mathematical richness involved in what, for me, previously was a dull, rote, tedious task.

Ronnie loved the challenge of mental mathematics, and he often chided us for using calculators when the answer could be derived through transformations. His opinion was that, in these cases, using the calculator was cheating.

Just for the fun of it, one time we asked Ronnie to compute 6 537 times 2 545. This was one of those problems that Ronnie would never compute on a calculator— it would be cheating! He used mental calculation as he voiced some partial solutions along the way. Partway through, he was frustrated because he couldn't remember all of the numbers. Eventually, he wrote down 16 636 665 and said he didn't know if he was right—but he was. Explaining his thinking, he said that he had broken the problem down into subparts. He multiplied 6 537 by 10 and divided by 2 to get multiplication by 5. Then he multiplied that by 9 to get the multiplication by 45 (subtotal is 294 165). Next, he divided 6 537 by 4 and multiplied by 10 000 to get the multiplication by 2 500 and added the result to his subtotal of 294 165. It was truly a unique way to solve what to most people would be a tedious computation.

On one memorable occasion, Ronnie gave a presentation to Ohio State mathematicians, including mathematics faculty members and doctoral students. As part of the presentation, he made up a difficult probability problem involving playing cards and posed it to the audience. As the mathematicians invoked their formulas, Ronnie solved the problem logically. Several suggested to him that he could simplify his work by using a known formula, but he shunned the idea. It didn't take him any more time to solve the problem than it did those who used formulas; and he had the satisfaction of thinking his way through the problem and meeting the challenge. It should be noted here that, although Ronnie did not like to memorize and use known formulas, he did enjoy inventing his own. See the photograph that depicts Ronnie at age eleven with a formula he devised for generating primes. He used his formula to try to find a prime of at least 100 digits.

As we watched Ronnie sparingly use memorized formulas and algorithms and thoroughly enjoy looking for patterns and relationships, our understanding of mathematics broadened, and our pedagogy changed. We now prefer to encourage and facilitate mathematical exploration, rather than to lecture about mathematical procedures. And we also have been encouraged to put down our calculators at times and perform computations for the sheer joy of manipulating the numbers.

Preschool children enjoy the challenge of learning to crawl and to walk, to get on their hands and knees and back down stairs when confronted with steps in their early walking days, to put puzzles together and fit square shapes into square holes, to tie their shoes, and to solve countless other problems. Isn't it logical to think that they also enjoy the challenge of looking for patterns and solving mathematical problems when they enter the classroom? When we give them procedures and rules to memorize, do we actually squelch their enthusiasm for rising to a mathematical challenge?

Working with Ronnie, a gifted student, greatly enhanced our appreciation for the challenge of mathematically empowering our students. Mathematics isn't about using memorized rules and procedures; it's about looking for patterns, finding relationships, and solving problems. Ronnie did mathematics the latter way because he knew he could ignore the textbook approach. Many children don't have that option, because they are not confident enough in their own mathematical abilities to ignore the directions of teachers who show them a "better" way. Even though we had learned through books constructivist ways to teach mathematics, it all became real when we worked closely with a student who obviously constructed his own mathematics.

REFERENCE

Jalongo, Mary Renck, and Joan P. Isenberg. *Teachers' Stories: From Personal Narrative to Professional Insight.* San Francisco: Jossey-Bass, 1995.

Chapter 20

A BOY NAMED BILLY

Linda Hall

He was quiet. He was very respectful. He had big brown eyes, and his brain was racing. His name was Billy.

In the eighth grade, Billy was in Honors Algebra 1 and quietly made straight A's. He always answered when called on and never complained. Toward the end of that school year, his counselor noticed his standardized test scores and learned of his ability in his algebra class, so she called the district's mathematics curriculum specialist. After reviewing his file, visiting with Billy, and speaking with his parents, they determined that Billy was eligible to take the geometry subject placement test. There is a process in this district by which students can "test out" of a subject so that they can move on to the next level. It is a comprehensive subject test written by the teachers who teach that subject for our district and is offered on specific dates in the summer. A student must pass with a score of 90 percent or better to receive credit for the course. Billy took the geometry test that summer and made a 100 percent.

As a freshman in high school, Billy entered my Honors Algebra 2 class. I had already heard of his success but thought that this class would be a challenge because there was more theory, more brand-new topics, and extensive use of the TI-82 or TI-83 calculator. In addition to these experiences, I found some enrichment experiences for Billy. He was one of our team representatives for a mathematics competition at Oklahoma State University (OSU). (Usually we send a team of seniors.) He worked outside of class on a team mathematical application contest problem that involved three other students—all upperclassmen. In all these situations, his performance was extraordinary: his understanding was beyond that of his older team members, and he began to grow socially. Underneath that quiet exterior, there was a wonderful sense of humor, and it became obvious that all of the students liked him and respected him.

But on a certain cold day in November, something happened. I was teaching a lesson in Honors Algebra 2—one of those brand-new concepts. It seemed that everyone had a question, but as I scanned the room, Billy's big brown eyes told me something else. After class was dismissed, I called Billy over and asked him if he already knew about today's subject. He said that he did. So I asked him if he already knew about conic sections, imaginary numbers, logarithms. Each time the answer was yes. We decided then to look into some other options for his mathematical education.

After visiting with the curriculum specialist and with Billy's parents, we came up with a plan. The subject tests were available only in the summer, and Billy had already completed the first three months of Honors Algebra 2. So to receive credit for this class, he took all my chapter tests for the remainder of the year between the middle of November and the Christmas break. He never made below 100 percent! When he returned from break, he completed the first semester's tests from the Honors Precalculus course. By the beginning of second semester in mid-January, he was enrolled in Honors Precalculus, having completed more than a year's mathematical work in six school weeks. It was during this time he became involved with the school's academic team and he began to bloom.

As a sophomore, Billy enrolled in AP Physics and BC Calculus among other courses. He was successful in these classes and helped the academic team win a national title that spring. But what about next year and the year after that? In the past we have had a few students who completed BC Calculus as juniors. Most of them took differential equations by correspondence from OSU or by concurrent enrollment at the University of Central Oklahoma. But Billy's case was a little different.

At this point, Billy and his parents solved the dilemma. Billy applied to and was accepted at the Oklahoma School for Science and Mathematics. This is a school for the gifted who spend their junior and senior years in a residential-type setting. They live in dormitories and attend classes in buildings near the Oklahoma University Health Sciences Center. The school's resources and course offerings are beyond that of a regular high school. In addition to that, students can participate in research and work with a mentor. Billy is nearing the end of his junior year there, still maintains his 4.0 grade point average, and continues to earn the respect of students and teachers alike.

Having a mathematically gifted student means recognizing that talent. It means having a process in place to allow a unique individual to advance. It means using outside resources for enrichment. It means being flexible. It means working with the parents to do what is best for the student. And sometimes, it means that he leaves us.

Chapter 21

YOU'LL DO BETTER NEXT TIME—YOU CAN!

Thomasenia Lott Adams

I grew up in a very small, southern farming community. The main sources of income for the residents were and still are dairy, fruit, and vegetable farms, clothing factories, and textile mills. In my early years, I perceived the town to be the world. My parents advised me that the only way to make a difference in my life was to get an education. "Go to school" was a major theme in our home. My seven siblings and I were not allowed to miss a day of school; my parents did not acknowledge the notion of "excused absences." They strongly believed that when we were not at school, we were not learning what everyone else was learning. Being the youngest of eight children only meant that I had nine people—my parents and my sibling-parents—promoting the "go to school" theme. With no escape route, I conceded to be eager and enthusiastic about school.

In elementary school, the long walk on the dirt road to the main highway to catch the bus gave me time to think while my older siblings interacted with each other. I usually thought about drawing houses. I was intrigued by the ability of someone to transform a sketch of a building into a real-life structure. I also liked to think about books that I had read: I found that I indeed could escape to far-away and exciting places in my books, and I always enjoyed the times when I could visit a house in a book. Looking at one of my childhood books (about a family and their house) in anticipation of passing it along to my toddler son, I found that I had written in the back of the book in childlike penmanship "20 + 1 = 1 + 20." At the time, I gather that I must have been fascinated by the revelation. The book itself was not mathematical in nature, but I was close to my books. They shared with me, and I obviously shared with them. I wish I could remember if this was my beginning of understanding the commutative property of addition.

Through middle school, my enjoyment of mathematics continued as teachers of mathematics who believed in active learning challenged me. I was introduced to the notions of cooperative learning and the use of calculators for learning mathematics. One of the things that I remember about my sixth-grade teacher is that even when it was not fashionable to do so, she always presented mathematics from a problem-solving perspective. She was determined to engage us in learning experiences that were meaningful, challenging, and relevant to our lives. She was a proponent of risk-taking in the classroom. When students did attempt to conjecture or hypothesize about the unknown, she became a prowler on search for the willing learner.

By the time I reached high school, my once-positive attitudes about mathematics turned sour. In hindsight, many of my problems with mathematics were comparable to the problems that my friends were experiencing. We were faced with the newness of generalizations, proofs, abstractness, unknowns, and mathematics void of applications for and relationships to real life. It seemed as if we were only studying mathematics for mathematics' sake, and so our dispositions about mathematics suffered drastically. As for me, my negativity manifested itself by my attention to any distraction from mathematics.

MY FIRST DISTRACTION: DOUBT

My first distraction was doubt. At the onset, when I did not achieve success in ninth-grade algebra, I began to doubt that I really understood mathematics. I imagined that my elementary and middle school teachers of mathematics were pretending that I could do mathematics when indeed I could not. I imagined that I had achieved success in mathematics in the past because I was lucky. Then, I lost all self-motivation to learn mathematics. I recall being called on in geometry class to complete a proof of a theorem of which I had absolutely had no understanding. I panicked and ran out of the classroom, vowing never to return. I returned, of course, but I began to fail test after test, project after project, and finally class after class. My teachers were different now, and I was completely convinced that my elementary and middle school teachers had played a terrible joke on me.

Finally, I persuaded myself to believe that it was okay not to have success in mathematics because, after all, I could read and write. So I stopped trying; I simply gave up on being able to do mathematics ever again. Being placed in the non-college track, I was not required to take any more high-level mathematics courses. For it seemed obvious to me that I would be leaving high school to work in one of the town's textile mills. My teachers never disagreed with my conclusion, and so all the while, I knew that I was a failure. That's what I told myself; that's what I told my teachers; that's what everyone accepted—that is, everyone except my parents.

My parents are still staunch advocates for education. My mother received her high school diploma in 1977 after several years of night school. My father only experienced several years of elementary school and is illiterate. By my high school years, my oldest sister had already graduated from a four-year, predominantly African American, liberal arts college, and two brothers and a sister had graduated from a two-year technical college. All my life, my parents talked about their baby going to college. So when I began to bring home F's in mathematics and only marginal grades in the other subjects, all my parents would say was, "You'll do better next time." In the ninth grade, I heard, "You'll do better next time." In the tenth grade, I heard, "You'll do better next time." In the eleventh grade, I heard, "You'll do better next time." But then in the twelfth grade, I heard, "You'll do better when you go to college!" I really thought they were joking, but always, always, my parents relayed the message that I was capable of doing better. I never heard that message from anyone else.

Fortunately, with a marginal score on the SAT, I was admitted into a very small, predominantly African American, liberal arts institution (not the same one as my sister), just eighty miles from my home. I entered college without an intended major, and my parents did not make any suggestions for a major. They just took me to the freshman orientation program, bought me a take-out dinner, settled me in my dormitory room, and left me. I did not even have an academic advisor. After days of despair, I shared this concern with a new friend, and she informed me that there was a new faculty member in the mathematics department who was eager to advise students. So be it. I went to see him. I told him that I needed an advisor and had heard he was looking for students to advise. He didn't ask any questions. He simply said that he would be happy to advise me—but that I had to meet one condition. There I stood, quite desperate, knowing that I had barely made it out of high school, also knowing that I had barely made a high enough score on the SAT to enter college, and all he had was one condition. I quickly agreed, not even knowing what the condition was. Then he said, "You must major in mathematics." I said, "I can't." He said, "You can." Four years later, I graduated with honors (3.8 grade point average) with a bachelor of science degree in mathematics.

"YOU CAN DO BETTER"

It's the "you can do better" and the "you can" attitudes of my parents and that one teacher of mathematics that broke my fears and anxieties about being a lifelong failure at mathematics. For I internalized failing and being a failure until someone I perceived to know much more mathematics than I could ever know said, "You can." At that point, I no longer equated failing with being a failure. When I introduced myself to that teacher of mathematics, I simply described myself as someone looking for an advisor. He didn't know my personal background; he didn't know my academic history. He simply saw me as a learner—so why not a learner of mathematics? He didn't treat me like a failure at mathematics. My parents treated me like I was a promising student, and most of the evidence was contrary to this idea. He treated me like I was a mathematically promising student even before he saw one piece of evidence that this was possible.

The messages we share with parents should include a note about relaying positive and high expectations to their children. My parents didn't know much about school mathematics, but they didn't let this deter them from encouraging me to learn. I expect that they saw promise in me simply because I was their child. I think the teacher of mathematics chose to see promise in me simply because I was a student.

Several years after graduating from college and having entered a mathematics education doctoral program at a major research institution, I visited my old high school to see how things had changed. When I walked into the main building, I saw one of my teachers. She asked, "What have you been doing with yourself?" I said, "Well, I graduated from college a few years ago with a degree in mathematics, and now I'm in a Ph.D. program." Her response was, "I didn't know you had it in you." It seems like a sad response, but it's not. There's a proverb that says,

"There's nothing wrong with not knowing. There's a lot wrong with not wanting to know." Well, perhaps she didn't know that I had "it" in me. Now she knows, and I hope when she and teachers of mathematics across the nation look at students, they look for "it." I hope they look for promise. That's our challenge: to look for the mathematics promise that may be hidden in our students.

As a mathematics educator, I share this personal story because there are children in our classrooms who are waiting for someone to say, "You'll do better next time—you can." They are waiting for someone to recognize, acknowledge, stimulate, and support their promise as learners of mathematics.

Chapter 22

EVERYBODY COUNTS— INCLUDING THE MATHEMATICALLY PROMISING

Christian R. Hirsch
Marcia Weinhold

The present reform movement in school mathematics is distinguished from previous reform efforts by its call for universal mathematical literacy for all citizens. The National Research Council, in its report *Everybody Counts* (1989), spearheaded the direction of reform with its call for a shift in the focus of school mathematics "from a dualistic mission—minimal mathematics for the majority, advanced mathematics for a few—to a singular focus on a significant common core of mathematics for all students" (NRC 1989, p. 81). The *Curriculum and Evaluation Standards for School Mathematics* of the National Council of Teachers of Mathematics (1989) further elaborated a set of standards for grades 9–12 that provided a framework for a core mathematics program for all students.

The call for a core curriculum in mathematics for all students has been one of the most controversial aspects of *Standards*-based reform (cf. Noddings 1994; Berger and Keynes 1995). Underneath much of the criticism of current reform efforts, one can hear an almost elitist admonition that "a mathematics program for everybody else is not good enough for my daughter (son)." Similar (cf. Kohn 1998) comments are frequently voiced on Internet discussions (such as the Math Forum at www.forum.swarthmore.edu) and at teacher-parent meetings in school districts implementing *Standards*-based reform. This concern, albeit often based on perceptions of traditional school mathematics programs, is even more acute among parents of youngsters believed to be mathematically promising.

CURRICULUM CONSIDERATIONS

In this article we identify and briefly illustrate features of one emerging high school mathematical sciences curriculum for *all* students that appears to offer new opportunities for mathematically promising students. Examples in this article are

Work reported in this chapter was supported in part by the National Science Foundation (MDR-9255257). The views expressed are those of the authors and are not necessarily those of the National Science Foundation.

taken primarily from one of the core curriculum development projects funded by the National Science Foundation: the Core-Plus Mathematics Project (CPMP). The CPMP curriculum consists of a three-year core program for all students plus a flexible fourth-year course continuing the preparation of students for college mathematics. The curriculum has been tested in schools across the country with diverse student populations, including mathematically promising students. In some cases, these promising students are enrolled in heterogeneous classes; in some cases they are identified and accelerated into CPMP Course 1 as eighth graders; and in a few cases they are enrolled in multidistrict mathematics and science centers for highly motivated and promising students (Schoen, Hirsch, and Ziebarth 1998).

Each year the curriculum advances students' mathematical thinking along four interwoven strands: algebra and functions, geometry and trigonometry, statistics and probability, and discrete mathematics. (See tables 22.1 and 22.2 for a listing of the units composing the four-year CPMP curriculum.) The CPMP curriculum, instructional model, and approaches to assessment are described in detail elsewhere (Hirsch et al. 1995; Core-Plus Mathematics Project 1999; www.wmich.edu/cpmp/).

Table 22.1
The CPMP Core Curriculum

Units	Course 1	Units	Course 2	Units	Course 3
1	Patterns in Data	1	Matrix Models	1	Multiple-Variable Models
2	Patterns of Change	2	Patterns of Location, Shape, and Size	2	Modeling Public Opinion
3	Linear Models	3	Patterns of Association	3	Symbol Sense and Algebraic Reasoning
4	Graph Models	4	Power Models	4	Shapes and Geometric Reasoning
5	Patterns in Space and Visualization	5	Network Optimization	5	Patterns in Variation
6	Exponential Models	6	Geometric Form and Its Function	6	Families of Functions
7	Simulation Models	7	Patterns in Chance	7	Discrete Models of Change
Capstone: Planning a Benefits Carnival		Capstone: Forests, the Environment, and Mathematics		Capstone: Making the Best of It: Optimal Forms and Strategies	

Information on other high school core curriculum development projects funded by the National Science Foundation can be found at www.ithaca.edu/compass/. These projects share features similar to those discussed below. It is noteworthy that these features of a core curriculum for all students were at one time approaches specifically recommended for mathematically gifted students (NCTM 1987, pp. 64–66).

Table 22.2
CPMP Course 4 Units

	Core Units		Additional Units Leading to Mathematical and Physical Sciences		Additional Units Leading to Social, Management, and Health Sciences
1	Rates of Change	5A	Polynomial and Rational Functions	5B	Binomial Distributions
2	Modeling Motion	6A	Functions and Symbolic Reasoning	6B	Problem Solving, Algorithms, and Spreadsheets
3	Counting Models	7A	Space Geometry	7B	Informatics
4	Composite, Inverse, and Logarithmic Functions	8A	Mathematical Structures	8B	Statistical and Inference in Surveys and Experiments
			Capstone: Building Mathematical Bridges		Capstone: Analyzing Published Reports

Multiple Strands

In contrast to many traditional programs in which the choice of topics in a course is based on a linear view of mathematics and what is needed for the next course, each course in the CPMP curriculum is designed around a coherent set of important, broadly useful mathematical concepts and methods. Topics often reserved for enrichment of promising students—such as networks, Monte Carlo methods, and computer and calculator graphics—are integral parts of the curriculum. More important, the organization of each year of the curriculum around multiple strands seems to nurture the differing strengths and talents of students (Hirsch and Coxford 1997). When school mathematics is seen as much more than arithmetic, generalized arithmetic (algebra), precalculus, and calculus, students with interests and ability in the mathematics of data analysis, shape, discrete structures, or chance also have opportunities to excel. In this way, such a curriculum recognizes and supports multiple intelligences (Gardner 1993, 1995) and a broader view of mathematical promise. Teachers who have been using the curriculum in specialized mathematics and science centers report that the talented students with whom they work often have broad and diverse interests, and the breadth of the curriculum and the diversity of contexts in which the mathematics is situated tap into those interests.

Flexibility

In addition to a choice of mathematical content, the approach to that content is intended to engage mathematically promising students. The units and thematic capstone experience for each year are composed of multiday lessons in which major ideas are developed through investigations of rich, applied problems. This investigative aspect enables students to develop their understanding of mathematical ideas in ways that make sense to them, including at appropriate levels of abstraction. Mathematically promising students are not constrained by a particular approach or record of mathematics laid out neatly in a text. Rather, mathematics is an active, constructive process that is shared and discussed with other students and adults. The depth of student understanding becomes a function of ability, prior experiences, interest, and effort. An investigative approach also enables teachers to assess students by observing and listening as they work on tasks. This approach helps identify mathematically promising students more easily or earlier in heterogeneous classrooms, using a broader range of criteria, as discussed elsewhere in this volume. Extending tasks and projects included in the curriculum materials can then be used to address the additional needs of these students.

The curriculum has been used in flexible ways to meet programmatic needs of schools and pupils. Promising students whose districts program them into CPMP Course 1 as eighth-graders are in a position to complete Courses 2–4 by the end of their junior year in high school and complete AP calculus as seniors. Because of the increased attention to statistics in the curriculum, these students can complete AP Statistics (perhaps in a semester) following completion of Course 3. Where classes are more homogeneous, as in a specialized mathematics and science center, an accelerated pace has permitted students to complete Courses 1–3 in two years.

Habits of Mind

The mathematical sciences have evolved not only as fields for characterizing results but as fields with characteristic ways of thinking: mathematical habits of mind (Cuoco, Goldenberg, and Mark 1996). For all students, and particularly for mathematically promising students, the methods by which mathematics is created (the techniques used by researchers) are equally as important as the results. An investigations-based curriculum requires greater attention to mathematical habits of mind, such as visual thinking, recursive thinking, algorithmic thinking, conducting experiments, searching for and describing patterns, making and checking conjectures, reasoning with multiple representations, inventing mathematics, and providing convincing arguments. These habits of mind are pervasive and serve to unify the four strands in the CPMP curriculum.

INSTRUCTIONAL CONSIDERATIONS

For many mathematically promising students, school mathematics is often seen as a race—how far one can go in the subject and how fast. Whereas pacing is a consideration when using a core curriculum such as CPMP with promising students, a more important factor is establishing a learning environment that intellectually engages students both in creating and communicating their own mathematics and in understanding the mathematics of others (including that of peers and professional mathematicians).

Establishing a Supportive Learning Environment

Investigations-based core curricula encourage students to explore and create the mathematics needed to solve real-world problems for themselves. This process includes brainstorming ideas with peers, experimenting, trying out solutions, asking one another how they know they are right (or wrong), and finally reaching consensus on the best method of solution (or recognizing that there are several equally effective methods of solution). Given that the curriculum materials do not necessarily provide summaries or boxed-off statements of important theorems or formulas, each student creates a personal mathematics tool kit for future reference.

Depending on their previous experiences, students may initially be frustrated—especially if they are accustomed to having a technique demonstrated, practicing it, memorizing it, and successfully using it in identical situations. Their first impression is that the teacher is "not teaching us anything." When students add to their complaint, "We have to figure it out ourselves!" then you know they are beginning to understand what is going on. Anticipating these frustrations, discussing new conceptions of learning and teaching, and encouraging and assisting promising students to understand the depth of their evolving mathematical knowledge will help establish a supportive learning environment.

New Roles for Teachers

Often new roles are expected of teachers, including establishing good working relationships among students in collaborative groups, encouraging a variety of approaches to problems, probing for depth of understanding, introducing standard terminology as needed, and judging the time needed to develop methods of solution. Providing different types of questions to stimulate the thinking of different groups or individuals and recognizing when and where to lead students who are ready to go beyond the scope of the initial investigation are important components of adaptive teaching. Both the teacher and the students are learning to ask probing questions. These questions help them define problems, solve problems they have defined, and find new problems that are raised in the process.

By observing and listening to collaborative groups as they work on tasks, the teacher makes decisions about when to pull everyone into a class discussion. At such a time, groups of students share their ideas with one another and seek consensus. Each group experiences firsthand the use of mathematical argument by supporting its own methods of solution. Students also gain deeper understanding by comparing the various methods proposed. As the approaches to a problem are shared and summarized, connections are discussed among verbal, visual, symbolic, and numerical representations of mathematical ideas. An important role of the teacher at this stage is to assist students in communicating their thinking with increasing precision to others.

New Expectations of Students

To illustrate how the dual perspectives of creating their own mathematics and understanding the mathematics of others jointly play out in the classroom, a segment of an investigation and a homework task from a lesson in the Course 2 unit Network Optimization are briefly discussed.

Investigation 3: The Traveling Salesperson Problem

The Traveling Salesperson Problem is one of the most famous problems in mathematics. It can be thought of as another game, but as you will see, it also has many important applications. Here's the problem:

> A salesperson must visit customers in several different cities. She will start at some city, visit all the other cities exactly once, and return to her starting point. Among the possible routes, which one will minimize the total distance that she travels?

1. Consider the Traveling Salesperson Problem in the context of this airfare graph.

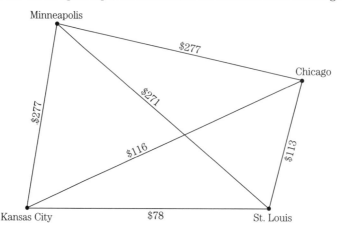

a. Individually, solve the Traveling Salesperson Problem for this weighted graph. What does "weight" represent in this case?

b. Compare your solution to those of other members of your group. Resolve any differences.

c. As a group, write a description of a method for finding the optimal circuit.

d. How do you know that there is no circuit less expensive?

e. How many different Hamiltonian circuits are there in this graph? For the purpose of finding the total cost of circuits, two circuits are different only if they have different edges. It doesn't matter where you start or which direction you go around the circuit.

f. Could you generalize your method in part c to find the optimal circuit for all 48 contiguous state capitals? Explain your reasoning.

2. Compare solving the Traveling Salesperson Problem to some of the other problems you have solved in this unit.

a. What is the relationship between a solution to the Traveling Salesperson Problem and a Hamiltonian circuit?

b. Describe how a solution to the Traveling Salesperson Problem is similar to, and yet different from, a minimal spanning tree.

c. This investigation is part of a lesson entitled "Shortest Paths and Circuits." Explain how a solution to the Traveling Salesperson Problem is a shortest path or circuit.

⋮

Fig. 22.1. Sample investigation tasks. Adapted from Contemporary Mathematics in Context: A Unified Approach, Course 2 *(Coxford et al. 1998)*

As students are deciding how to approach this problem, the teacher circulates from group to group, listening to their discussions and asking questions or facilitating group interaction. Teachers working with investigations-based curricula learn to listen more and talk less. They restrain the urge to tell students what to do to solve a problem.

In subsequent activities, students are asked to evaluate a proposed algorithm for solving the Traveling Salesperson Problem and then are asked to consider the time it would take to use a brute-force method on a computer. Because the emphasis is on creating and learning and not on finishing, students are motivated to extend their problems to include a new case or a more general case. Playing with ideas and posing problems are important habits to cultivate in mathematically promising students.

In addition to the classroom investigations, the CPMP curriculum includes sets of MORE tasks that are designed to engage students in modeling with (M), organizing (O), reflecting on (R), and extending (E) their mathematical understanding. These tasks are another way for teachers to respond to the special needs of promising students in a heterogeneous classroom. Some schools give honors designation to students who complete a specified amount of extension and project work. In homogeneous classes of talented students, teachers assign more of the extending tasks and fewer of the modeling tasks.

Extending tasks furnish opportunities for students to explore further or more abstractly the mathematics they are learning. These explorations can take students beyond the curriculum to the frontiers of mathematics, at times beyond their teacher's experiences. Such an example is the last extending task in the MORE set related to the Traveling Salesperson Problem investigation shown in figure 22.2.

Often the richest experiences for promising students are those in which a student asks a question that launches the class on another problem-solving adventure. "Is it possible to have a graph that has an Euler circuit and not a Hamiltonian circuit?" A seasoned investigative teacher does not assume the student wants her or him to answer the question and may respond, "Let's try. Who has an idea to get us started?"

CONCLUDING REMARKS

The issue of providing a mathematically rich and supportive environment for promising students is complex. In this article we have drawn on our experiences with one of several emerging *Standards*-based core curricula. At the heart of these curricula are what once were believed to be competing notions: equity and excellence. Our experiences indicate that a flexible core curriculum, accompanied with adaptive teaching that challenges each student based on what she or he can do, holds promise of increasing opportunity for, and motivation and performance of, all students—including the mathematically promising.

:

5. You have seen in this lesson that there is no known efficient method for solving the Traveling Salesperson Problem. The same is true for finding Hamiltonian circuits and paths. Most experts believe that efficient solutions for these problems will never be found, at least using traditional electronic computers. But in 1994, computer scientist Leonard M. Adleman of the University of Southern California in Los Angeles opened up the possibility of using nature as the computer to solve these problems. Adleman successfully carried out a laboratory experiment in which he used DNA to do the computations needed to solve a Hamiltonian path problem. Adleman stated, "This is the first example, I think, of an actual computation carried out at the molecular level." This method has not been shown to solve all Hamiltonian problems, and the particular problem solved was quite small, but it opens up some amazing possibilities for mathematics and computer science.

a. Below is the graph that Adleman used in his experiment. All the information in the graph was encoded using strands of DNA, and then the computations needed to find a Hamiltonian path were carried out by biochemical processes. Of course, this graph is small enough that the Hamiltonian path can also be found without gene splicing or conventional computers. Find the Hamiltonian path.

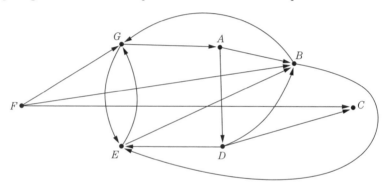

b. Find out more about this groundbreaking experiment in "molecular computation" by reading some of the articles below. Write a short report incorporating your findings.

- "Test Tube Computing with DNA." Keith Devlin, *Math Horizons,* April 1995.

- "Scientist at Work: Leonard Adleman: Hitting the High Spots of Computer Theory." Gina Kolata, *New York Times,* 15 December, 1994, late edition.

- "Molecular Computation of Solutions to Combinatorial Problems." Leonard M. Adleman, *Science,* 11 November 1994.

Fig. 22.2. An extending task. Adapted from Contemporary Mathematics in Context: A Unified Approach, Course 2 *(Coxford et al. 1998)*

REFERENCES

Berger, Thomas R., and Harvey B. Keynes. "Everybody Counts/Everybody Else." In *Changing the Culture: Mathematics Education in the Research Community,* CBMS Issues in Mathematics Education, Vol. 5, edited by Naomi D. Fisher, Harvey B. Keynes, and Philip D. Wagreich, pp. 89–110. Providence, R.I.: American Mathematical Society, 1995.

Core-Plus Mathematics Project. *Overview of the CPMP Curriculum: Contemporary Mathematics in Context.* Kalamazoo, Mich.: Western Michigan University, 1999.

Coxford, Arthur F., James T. Fey, Christian R. Hirsch, Harold L. Schoen, Gail Burrill, Eric W. Hart, Ann E. Watkins, Mary J. Messenger, and Beth Ritsema. *Contemporary Mathematics in Context: A Unified Approach, Course 2.* Chicago: Everyday Learning Corp., 1998.

Cuoco, Al, Paul E. Goldenberg, and June Mark. "Habits of Mind: An Organizing Principle for Mathematics Curriculum." *Journal of Mathematical Behavior* 15 (December 1996): 375–402.

Gardner, Howard. *Multiple Intelligences: The Theory in Practice.* New York: Basic Books, 1993.

———. "Reflections on Multiple Intelligences: Myths and Messages." *Phi Delta Kappan* 77 (November 1995): 200–209.

Hirsch, Christian R., and Arthur F. Coxford. "Mathematics for All: Perspectives and Promising Practices." *School Science and Mathematics* 97 (May 1997): 232–41

Hirsch, Christian R., Arthur F. Coxford, James T. Fey, and Harold L. Schoen. "Teaching Sensible Mathematics in Sense-Making Ways with the CPMP." *Mathematics Teacher* 88 (November 1995): 694–700.

Kohn, Alfie. "Only for My Kid: How Privileged Parents Undermine School Reform." *Phi Delta Kappan* 79 (April 1998): 568–77.

National Council of Teachers of Mathematics. *Curriculum and Evaluation Standards for School Mathematics.* Reston, Va.: National Council of Teachers of Mathematics, 1989.

———. *Providing Opportunities for the Mathematically Gifted, K–12,* edited by Peggy A. House. Reston, Va.: National Council of Teachers of Mathematics, 1987.

National Research Council. *Everybody Counts: A Report to the Nation on the Future of Mathematics Education.* Washington, D.C.: National Academy Press, 1989.

Noddings, Nel. "Does Everybody Count? Reflections on Reforms in School Mathematics." *Journal of Mathematical Behavior* 13 (1994): 89–104.

Schoen, Harold L., Christian R. Hirsch, and Steven W. Ziebarth. "An Emerging Profile of the Mathematical Achievement of Students in the Core-Plus Mathematics Project." Paper presented at the American Educational Research Association Annual Meeting, San Diego, 1998.

Chapter 23

INSTITUTING A MATHEMATICS RESEARCH PROGRAM FOR YOUR SCHOOL'S PROMISING MATHEMATICS ENTHUSIASTS

Robert Gerver

It is terrific that the mathematics education community has embraced the idea that all students should take algebra in high school. However, the intense efforts on this front must not allow us to overlook our bright, motivated mathematics leaders of tomorrow—we must provide a forum in which they can mathematically stretch. Promising students need to be empowered with the commitment to and thrill of exploration and discovery in mathematics.

One way to enrich the high school learning experience is to assign a mathematics research paper. This gives the students a chance to discover, conjecture, and play with mathematics. Mathematics research papers address many of the recommendations of the National Council of Teachers of Mathematics, especially with respect to problem solving, communication, reasoning, and connections. The skills required to do a mathematics research paper are not innate; they are rather sophisticated. They need to be taught, discussed, developed and practiced systematically. Teachers need field-tested procedures they can replicate.

A COURSE IN MATHEMATICS RESEARCH FOR HIGH SCHOOL STUDENTS

Mathematics research is a one-semester course that can be offered to high school students, with students in grades 9–12 in the same class. In this class offered since 1991 at North Shore High School, Glen Head, New York, the units included questioning, problem solving, writing mathematics, conjectures and proofs, reading and keeping a research journal, components of a research paper, and oral presentations. (An ancillary follow-up program can be offered in which students who completed the first course can write new papers or extend previously completed papers). Two textbooks, *Writing Math Research Papers—Enrichment for Math Enthusiasts* (Gerver 1997), and *Problem Solving Strategies—Crossing the River with Dogs* (Herr and Johnson 1994) provide the skeletal content. The cornerstone of the program is the use of articles from back issues of *Mathematics Teacher.* The articles are a gold mine of material essential to the program.

USING JOURNAL ARTICLES AS A SPRINGBOARD FOR RESEARCH PAPERS

As the author of a report, a student is a *reporter.* As a *researcher,* the student starts with a problem—a question that needs to be addressed. The students read related material to try to formulate an answer to the question. Throughout the research project, the central focus is the solution of a specific question or set of questions.

Focusing on one problem tends to keep research papers very specific. A student could write a mathematics *report* on the Fibonacci sequence, probability, topology, or matrices. These topics are too broad for a mathematics research paper. "The Use of Fibonacci Numbers to Create Pythagorean Triples" is a specific topic that could be the topic for a mathematics research paper. The use of journal articles can furnish students with the problems for their papers. Each article solves a specific problem and offers some information essential to the solution. The use of a journal article will allow students to pick a topic that is focused. Most of the articles are three to six pages long, and a problem or topic from the article will be built into a paper that could be twenty to 100 or more pages, depending on the depth and quality of the research—the questions, trials, testing of claims, conjectures, proofs, extensions, explanations, and so on.

Notice the primary difference between this type of research paper and the old mathematics book report—the book report condenses 1000 or more book pages, creating an expository piece. The research paper builds on just a few pages, and the added information is student-generated mathematics. Hundreds of articles are available. You can search the back issues of mathematics journals in college libraries, skim articles, and note the ones that are appropriate for high school students. You can offer these articles as a list for students or copy several and place them in a binder for students to pick from. (Be sure to follow all copyright and permission procedures.) Below are several excellent articles from the *Mathematics Teacher* that students have used:

November 1966	Geometric Solutions of a Quadratic Equation
May 1967	Five-Con Triangles
November 1967	Investigation to Discovery with a Negative Base
January 1974	All Three-Digit Integers Lead to …
November 1976	Exploring Skewsquares
April 1979	Discovery of a Property of Consecutive Integers
May 1985	Measuring the Areas of Golf Greens
November 1986	Pythagorean Triples
March 1991	The Probability That a Quadratic Equation Has Real Roots
May 1996	A Mean Solution to an Old Circle Standard

Familiarity will play a role in the choice of a research topic. In the same way students find comfort in a familiar face in unfamiliar surroundings, they should use the mathematics they are familiar with as an anchor as they pick a topic. Students should realize that interest in the topic and experience with its prerequisites are essential in choosing a topic. With this in mind, and with teacher assistance, they can look through back issues of journals to find a topic. Papers can be continued in subsequent years or combined with other articles to create original results.

If the journal articles are the cornerstone of the research program, then the periodic one-on-one consultations are the foundation of the program, for they systematically and gradually build the short article into a full, formal research paper, complete with original material. The teacher's role in the consultations is that of sounding board, questioner, editor, devil's advocate, supporter, and general mentor—the teacher is the coach.

CONSULTATIONS: THE TEACHER AS COACH

As a coach, you want steady progress from your students, and to help ensure that, you will have periodic consultation sessions with them. Students research and write their papers primarily on their own time. You must make sure the students make consistent, gradual progress on a timely basis and that they improve their reading, writing, and research skills. Students need guidance and deadlines to accomplish these goals. The consultation session is scheduled by student and teacher for a mutually agreeable time slot. The length and frequency of consultations will depend on the students' need and your own schedule, but make sure you conduct them as regularly as possible. One ten-to-fifteen-minute consultation a week per student is ideal.

The consultation procedure requires the student to engage in research between each consultation session, preparing material for the next consultation. Newly completed work must be brought to each consultation, where the student will discuss it. As a result, over the course of the entire project, the student has worked extensively on the research in many separate sittings. This is the antithesis of the infamous "paper started the weekend before it is due" syndrome. The strength of the consultation period is in the one-on-one communication—the onus is on the student because there is "nowhere to hide." This raises the students' level of responsibility, their expectations of themselves, and, resultantly, achievement. The consultation time therefore is an essential part of the research program.

What happens at each consultation? You assign readings from the article(s) the student picked. Make sure amounts of reading are appropriate; one paragraph in mathematics can get very involved. Students come to the next consultation with the material read, underlined, and annotated right on their copies of the articles. They should have notes on which they've asked questions, explained material from their articles, made conjectures, tested claims, tried proofs, or extended the reading passages. To keep track of their current assignments, each student keeps a consultation record sheet, as shown in figure 23.1, which is a shorthand journal of their tasks for the week. Each student needs one sheet per marking period.

Consultation Period Record Sheet   Marking Period __1__   Name Sebastian L.

Session	Date Time	Notes
1	7:45 Sept 20	Solve a quadratic by factoring, quadratic formula, and using TI-82 root key. Copy article. Start notes in research journal.
2	7:30 Sept 28	Read section on completing the square in textbook. Solve some quadratic by completing the square.
3	Pd. 4 Oct. 6	Use completing the square to derive quadratic formula. Sketch $y = x^2 - 7x + 12$ and $y = 2x^2 - 14x + 24$ on same axes.
4	Pd. 5 Oct. 15	Read section on the properties of secants in geometry text, p. 341. Try some problems.
5	7:30 Oct 28	Read first column of article. Review bisecting a line segment. Try construction using quadratic equation from Sept 20.
6	Pd. 4 Nov. 10	Complete chart of 20 quadratic equations by finding roots. Make conjecture about sum, product of roots. Try proof.
7	7:45 Nov. 19	Explain derivation of coordinates of points B, C and D. Find midpoint of AC. Why is AC a diameter?

Fig. 23.1. Consultation record sheet for one quarter

As the consultation session progresses, the student or teacher can fill in the consultation record sheet. It delineates what needs to be done for the next consultation. The record sheet sets up a reasonable timeline for the students— something they will need to create on their own in college. Now they have a method they can adopt and adapt for college use, and you have a way to keep them progressing in a logical and highly accountable manner. At the same time, however, you need to keep track of when students are coming for their consultations. Figure 23.2 shows a calendar that students use to sign up for their consultations.

Have your own copy of each student's article available for the consultation. At the beginning of each consultation, reacquaint yourself with the student's progress using his or her consultation sheet. Go over the work, ask questions, answer questions, discuss the material, and assign the next reading. Require students to be explicit in their explanations; this will improve their mathematical command of the material as well as their oral and written communication skills.

AN EXAMPLE OF A STUDENT'S PROJECT

Figure 23.3 shows a half-page segment of a three-page article from the November 1966 *Mathematics Teacher* that Sebastian picked for his project.

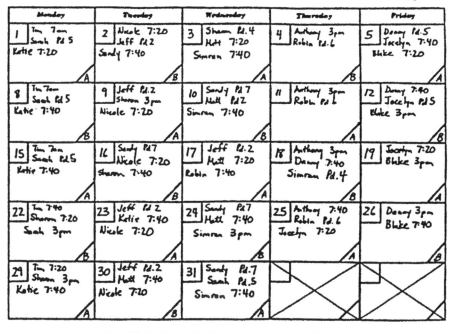

Monday	Tuesday	Wednesday	Thursday	Friday
1 Tim 7am / Sarah Pd 5 / Katie 7:20	**2** Nicole 7:20 / Jeff Pd 2 / Sandy 7:40	**3** Sharon Pd.4 / Matt 7:20 / Simran 7:40	**4** Anthony 3pm / Robin Pd.6	**5** Danny Pd.5 / Jocelyn 7:40 / Blake 7:20
8 Tim 7am / Sarah Pd 5 / Katie 7:40	**9** Jeff Pd.2 / Sharon 3pm / Nicole 7:20	**10** Sandy Pd 7 / Matt Pd 2 / Simran 7:40	**11** Anthony 3pm / Robin Pd 6	**12** Danny 7:40 / Jocelyn Pd 5 / Blake 3pm
15 Tim 7am / Sarah Pd 5 / Katie 7:40	**16** Sandy Pd 7 / Nicole 7:20 / Sharon 7:40	**17** Jeff Pd.2 / Matt 7:20 / Robin 7:40	**18** Anthony 3pm / Danny 7:40 / Simran Pd.4	**19** Jocelyn 7:20 / Blake 3pm
22 Tim 7:40 / Sharon 7:20 / Sarah 3pm	**23** Jeff Pd 2 / Katie 7:40 / Nicole 7:20	**24** Sandy Pd 7 / Matt 7:40 / Simran 3pm	**25** Anthony 7:40 / Robin Pd.6 / Jocelyn 7:20	**26** Danny 3pm / Blake 7:40
29 Tim 7:20 / Sharon 3pm / Katie 7:40	**30** Jeff Pd.2 / Matt 7:40 / Nicole 7:20	**31** Sandy Pd.7 / Sarah Pd.5 / Simran 7:40		

Fig. 23.2. Consultation appointment calendar

GEOMETRIC SOLUTION OF A QUADRATIC EQUATION

By AMOS NANNINI

Milan, Italy

MAY I remind the reader of an elegant construction, discovered by Descartes, whereby it is possible to find both solutions of a quadratic equation $ax^2 + bx + c = 0$, geometrically? [1]

Given a rectangular coordinate system, mark off on the y-axis a segment OA of length 1; on the x-axis a segment OB of length $\dfrac{-b}{a}$ (of course in the same unit chosen for the y-axis), and, on the perpendicular to the x-axis through B, lay off a segment

BC of length $\dfrac{c}{a}$. (Fig. 1.)

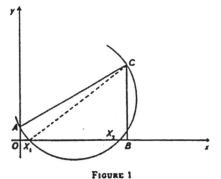

FIGURE 1

We assert that, if the circle having AC as its diameter intersects the x-axis in the points X_1, X_2, then the lengths of OX_1 OX_2 are the solutions of equation

$$ax^2 + bx + c = 0.$$

Fig. 23.3

The notes from the seven consultations shown on the record sheet in figure 23.1 show how the teacher led Sebastian through the development that was not stated in the article. Sebastian needed background in solving quadratics, the sum and product of the roots, secants, and coordinate geometry. Notice how sessions 1–3 gave the student four ways of finding roots of quadratic equations. The construction in the article is based on a property of two secants drawn to a circle from the same point; the axes are actually secants. In session 6, Sebastian discovered formulas for the sum and product of the roots, and that is what the coordinates of points B and C are based on in the article. (None of this is explained in the article, because the target audience of the article is mathematics teachers who have the prerequisite background.) The remainder of the article is dealt with in similar fashion. When completed as part of a nine-month school year, the time can be apportioned as follows:

Month	Activities
1, 2, 3, 4	Students find a topic and an article. Students begin reading and annotating their articles. Students begin research journal and consultations with coach.
5, 6, 7	Students continue research and consultations. They begin an outline for their formal papers. They start writing, submitting, and revising drafts of formal papers.
8, 9	Students stop any new research and spend time polishing the formal research paper. They submit drafts, make corrections, and discuss the formal paper at teacher consultations. Students create oral presentations.

ASSESSMENT

Consultations, actual papers, and oral presentations are assessed separately, according to the criteria listed below. Teachers can add or delete items to make these lists accurately reflect their grading criteria. They can also adjust the relative weight of the items. Students can use a copy of these criteria as a guide as they complete the activities. Students earn grades from 1 (lowest) to 5 (highest) for each of the following criteria for a consultation assessment. The raw score can be converted to a percent.

For the consultation, the following criteria are used:

- The student achieves or exceeds consultation record sheet goals.
- There is evidence of time and effort spent on the research.
- The articles are annotated and underlined.
- Notes are taken and material from the articles is reworded.
- The student asks good questions.
- Each claim is tested via a few examples.
- The student makes original conjectures.

- The student tests the original conjectures.
- Proofs are attempted or completed.
- The student makes extensions based on the readings.
- There is evidence of probing and persistence.

For the research paper grade, the following criteria can be used:

- The abstract is clear, succinct, and comprehensive.
- The problem is stated clearly.
- The paper is mathematically correct.
- The paper is well organized.
- The paper does a clearer job of explaining the material than the original article does.
- The student includes and explains original patterns or conjectures.
- There are explanations of the proofs in the article or original proofs.
- There are original extensions of some of the paper's ideas.
- Diagrams are presented in a graduated fashion where necessary.
- The physical layout of the paper is high quality.
- All edits and recommended changes are incorporated in the paper. The quality of the explanation given for not incorporating any specific recommended change is satisfactory.
- Claims made in the article are tested, and there are appropriate and sufficient examples.
- The recommendations for future research flow naturally from the completed research.
- The general depth and quality of the paper is commensurate with the student's ability.

For the oral presentation grade, the following criteria are used:

- The student writes and revises an outline for the presentation.
- The talk is logically organized.
- The introduction clearly orients a novice to the essentials of the research.
- The student creates an appropriate handout that orients the target audience.
- The student speaks in full, mathematically correct sentences.
- The student allocates time wisely and uses discretion in condensing the paper for the oral presentation.
- The student finishes on time, at an appropriate juncture.
- The student can answer questions that are asked during the presentation.
- The student knows the material and does not rely on cue cards or reading the paper.
- The boardwork is appropriate and well organized.

- The overhead transparencies and posters are effective and carefully prepared.
- The student uses color on the posters and transparencies to convey a mathematical idea.
- The audience is engaged, participates and asks questions.
- The student uses manipulatives and technology effectively and appropriately.

Certainly, a student's performance that displays the knowledge and enthusiasm manifested in a mathematics project epitomizes the academic mission of the school and deserves to be center stage. The research program gives the promising student a chance to do *mathematics* and *do* mathematics.

REFERENCES

DiDomenico, Angelo. "Discovery of a Property of Consecutive Integers." *Mathematics Teacher* 72 (April 1979): 285–86.

Gerver, Robert K. *Writing Math Research Papers—Enrichment for Math Enthusiasts.* Berkeley, Calif.: Key Curriculum Press, 1997.

Herr, Ted, and Ken Johnson. *Problem Solving Strategies—Crossing the River with Dogs.* Berkeley, Calif.: Key Curriculum Press. 1994.

Kimmins, Dovie. "The Probability That a Quadratic Equation Has Real Roots." *Mathematics Teacher* 84 (March 1991): 222–27.

Martin, Gary, and Joao Ponte. "Measuring the Areas of Golf Greens." *Mathematics Teacher* 78 (May 1985): 385–89.

Nannini, Amos. "Geometric Solutions of a Quadratic Equation." *Mathematics Teacher* 59 (November 1966): 647–49.

Nelson, Allyn. "Investigation to Discovery with a Negative Base." *Mathematics Teacher* 60 (November 1967): 723–26.

Olson, Alton. "Exploring Skewsquares." *Mathematics Teacher* 69 (November 1976): 570–73.

Pawley, Richard. "Five-Con Triangles." *Mathematics Teacher* 60 (May 1967): 438–43.

Samide, Andrew, and Amanda Warfield. "A Mean Solution to an Old Circle Standard." *Mathematics Teacher* 89 (May 1996): 411–13.

Tirnam, Alvin. "Pythagorean Triples." *Mathematics Teacher* 79 (November 1986): 652–55.

Trigg, Charles. "All Three-Digit Integers Lead to ...." *Mathematics Teacher* 67 (January 1974): 41–45.

Chapter 24

NURTURING MATHEMATICAL PROMISE DURING THE SCHOOL DAY

Paul Eenigenburg
Carol McCarthy

Sixteen years ago, several middle school students returned from a three-week summer residential program, exhilarated by the newfound joys of mathematics. In stark contrast, their school year had been punctuated by escalating apathy, discontent, and depression. Could that excitement for mathematics be recreated in their hometown, during their school year? Were there more students with extreme mathematical promise in our community—more students those without the opportunity even for summer programs?

ATYP PROGRAM MODEL

From those initial questions, the Kalamazoo, Michigan area developed a collaborative grades K–12 higher education model called Academically Talented Youth Programs (AYTP). Adapting the principles of the talent-search model (Olszewski-Kubilius 1994), ATYP identifies and offers appropriate classroom instruction—during their school day—for seventh- to ninth-graders who demonstrate mathematical promise.

In cooperation with more than fifty public and private Southwest Michigan school districts where these students have been found, ATYP's mathematics class replaces these students' school mathematics class. (Our districts' grades K–12 enrollments range from 12 500 to 1 500.) All districts recognize ATYP's students' mastery of high school mathematics curriculum and grant placement in the next course in the curricular sequence. In addition, almost all districts award high school credit based on the belief of awarding equitable credit for equitable learning—rather than for equitable seat time.

There was concern that the K–12 structures of grade level, age, and instructional time requirements would restrict the heights and depths of ATYP students' mathematical achievements. In 1987, Kalamazoo's school superintendent addressed the issue succinctly: "Kalamazoo public school students in the ATYP program will be granted credits as supported by statements documenting content completed, competencies attained, and grades assigned by the ATYP faculty. Because of the pace and depth of instruction, credits are based on competencies attained and *not time spent* to complete the course" (Rapley 1987).

STUDENT IDENTIFICATION

During sixth through eighth grade, students are notified about the identification process. Districts are asked to identify all students with scores at or above the 95th percentile on a nationally standardized achievement test. In addition, parents, teachers, and students themselves who recognize a student's mathematics ability can nominate students for this process. After receiving information, students and their families decide if they want to pursue off-level testing of the SAT. Financial support for test costs is found when necessary. To qualify for ATYP, students must meet SAT mathematics and verbal score requirements and commit to completing rigorous homework assignments every week. Their motivation to undertake our rigorous class is often a factor in their success.

Initially, most of these students believe they can master any mathematics with little effort. Over the first several months, we observe changes in their work habits, approaches to problem solving, time management, self-discipline, and self-perceptions as mathematicians. Class instruction occurs in a block-scheduled, two-and-one-half hour class meeting once each week, during the school day, from September to June. Each class is followed with homework assignments that take these students five to ten hours to complete. In this structure, they complete two years of high school algebra in one school year, with plane and solid geometry and precalculus in the second school year.

PROGRAM REPLICATION

The model's simplicity makes it easily replicable in most communities. In essence, students remain enrolled participants in their home school for all but one afternoon each week, when they converge on our centrally located campus classroom. Communities aspiring to successful programs would meet two criteria: (1) a willingness on the part of district administrators to trust that exceptional students' learning can occur beyond their district boundaries and (2) access to exceptional mathematicians and to institutions willing to provide space and an intellectual atmosphere. We are fortunate that Kalamazoo College, Western Michigan University, and all those school district superintendents all believe in nurturing mathematical talent. Parents' willingness to form carpools removes districts' transportation costs, although some districts voluntarily offer transportation. School districts, grants, and local contributions underwrite major program costs of teachers, textbooks, and program administration.

Although community coordination and cooperation is important, the students' achievement hinges on two elements: the accurate identification of student's high mathematical talent and the solid teaching of mathematics. Each year, we marvel at the accuracy of combining off-level testing and students' self-assessed motivation to identify extremely able mathematical reasoners. However, finding the right teacher is often more difficult. Our successful teachers have brought differing personalities and teaching styles to their classrooms, but they all possess an absolute, unabashed passion for mathematics, and they love transposing a student's off-the-wall question into the grand mosaic of mathematical ideas. Teachers thus combine years of advanced study of mathematics and a genuine camaraderie with young, yet-undisciplined mathematical thinkers. These teachers understand the sequence of mathematical ideas; the importance of struggling, in great depth, with certain important concepts; and the ability to shrug off preconceived notions of instructional time required for student comprehension. Fast-paced, in-depth instruction is what keeps these students challenged and hungry. Most often, these mathematical mentors have earned doctorates in mathematics; however, occasionally they are doctoral candidates in mathematics or high school mathematics teachers with that same passion, deep understanding of mathematics, and delight at processing ideas at a faster pace.

THE CLASSROOM

Because we meet only once each week, most of the real learning takes place outside our classroom. This learning comes about by working through challenging homework problem sets. Students learn to be independent and to discipline themselves to make effective use of time. If they need help, students telephone each other, the paper grader—usually a college mathematics major or ATYP alumnus, or the instructor. A help session midway between classes is also available.

To ensure that students take ownership of concepts and techniques, they solve problems from a given section in each of three consecutive weeks. Thus, their understanding in each section increases from vague after the first week to solid after the third week. To accommodate this concept-building process, and in recognition of the challenging nature of the problems, our grading scale is generous by normal standards; 75–80 percent correct on homework will equate to an A. Students who are accustomed to getting perfect scores on mathematics papers have, in the beginning, a difficult time adapting to a grading system that does not require perfection to achieve an A. But, they soon understand they can now take risks in thinking without jeopardizing their grades.

Classroom discussion centers on the major new concepts to be learned, leaving minor details for the students to work out for themselves later. The instructor leads the discussion in a Socratic style, permitting the students to discover what needs to be done to complete an idea or to solve a problem. To ensure that everyone is participating, students often work out activities in small groups and then report their results to the entire class. Almost every student has an interesting idea to share. They exhibit no reticence to express their mathematical ideas—in sharp contrast to typical college students.

Occasionally, a student will pursue an idea well beyond the level discussed in class. In our geometry class, for example, we work out the volume and surface area formulas for a sphere. In a previous class, a student came to class the week after we discussed the sphere to say that he had become curious about the surface area of the right circular cone and had worked it out. He proceeded to give a detailed presentation of his very elegant solution. Note that the problem was his own, not one assigned by the instructor.

Students who qualify for this program are capable of a deep level of abstraction and even get impatient with an excessive number of low-level exercises. Thus, we use textbooks for algebra, geometry, and precalculus that contain a large number of challenging exercises. For example, our geometry textbook presents a minimum number of theorems with proof, and it gives many other well-known theorems as exercises for the students to work out. The precalculus textbook is considered too challenging to be used at many universities, although, of course, students needing precalculus are not among the most prepared students entering college.

ATYP students tend to be particularly enamored with technology. Perhaps it is their age, combined with their innate ability. We take advantage of this enthusiasm by using graphing calculators in algebra and precalculus as well as computers in geometry. Yet, the focus is on the mathematics, with the technology playing a supporting role. This allows us to take several points of view on a given problem: symbolic, graphical, and numerical. For example, suppose the student is presented with a certain problem expressed in words—a "story" problem. It may be possible to model this problem using a *symbolic* mathematical equation or inequality. The graphing calculator or computer aids in the study of *graphical* behavior of this model. The calculator or computer also aids in the discovery of *numerical relationships* involving the model and its graph.

In geometry, the computer acts as an exploratory device that enables students to discover new theorems (new to them). We follow this discovery with deductive proof, not because we don't accept the computer evidence but because proof explains why the theorem is true.

STUDENT AND PROGRAM EVALUATION

Students' achievement and program success are evaluated in several ways. Students receive weekly informal evaluation through in-class discussion, graded homework assignments (returned with a solution key), and periodically through teacher-constructed tests. The emphasis on both independent and small group learning develops the student's self-assessment skills. Pre- and posttests of nationally standardized, content-specific mathematics tests measure achievement, normed to populations of high school students completing similar content.

At the completion of ATYP, students demonstrate significant gains on their SAT-Math scores; last year's class (predominantly eighth graders) SAT-Math score average was 724. To qualify for the program, students' SAT-Math scores must be greater than or equal to 520, and most fall in a range of 520–600. Thus, as middle school students—prior to accessing high school mathematics—they already score better on SAT-Math than the average college-bound high school senior (Burton 1988).

After ATYP, students who enroll in a high school mathematics or science half-day magnet model are consistently among the top performers in their classes; as ninth and tenth graders, they also enroll in the university's calculus-linear algebra sequence and usually set the curve. They are high scorers in state and national mathematics competitions, are national merit finalists, and dominate the list of the community's students accepted at prestigious, first-rate colleges and universities. Surveys from students and parents consistently rate the program as excellent, instruction as outstanding, and learning at just about the right pace.

Do these students like this mathematical routine, week after week? Recently, we received a serendipitous and unsolicited letter from a former student. His family had moved out of state just as he completed our two-year mathematics sequence and the eighth grade. Writing "in the back seat of the car during our family vacation," he reflected on his ATYP experience from his current ninth grade perspective. His views mirror the value we place on teachers:

> As I work through my mathematics now, I can see how ATYP has given me such an edge even among the best of the students at my private (all-boys) high school. For the first semester, I received an A in my AP calculus class and a 100 percent on my exam, although I must admit one problem was "educated guessing." I say this only to commend the ATYP program for its commitment to excellence and to show how it has helped me now. I find myself missing the very challenging yet rewarding problems of ATYP mathematics assignments, as in my class we cover only the "easier" problems. Sometimes I'll try a problem "in the 50s" just for the experience. All the ATYP teachers really stimulated my interest in mathematics and taught me a lot, to say the least. They always answered my questions, however abstract, even on their own time.
>
> In order not to appear too obnoxious now to the seniors in my class, I usually try to limit my questions, even though the class discussion falls short of the knowledge my ATYP teachers offered during their classes. Honestly, my AP classmates have accepted me quite well and often ask for help, which I'm glad to give to gain a friend. I hope to score a 5 on the AP Calculus exam; with my ATYP exam experience, I ask myself, "Can AP be any harder?" Thanks for making ATYP what it is, and for the great teachers who have helped me beyond measure." (Anonymous communication, March 1997)

SUMMARY

ATYP serves students with mathematical promise. Not unlike extraordinary athletes, experience helps them recognize the necessity of a good teacher-coach—that mentor who describes goals beyond the age or grade "glass ceiling," models the work required to reach them, and trusts the student's ability to succeed. Our community model matches the masterful coach with extraordinary young mathematicians. Together, they routinely shatter those restrictive glass ceilings.

REFERENCES

Burton, Nancy. *Young SAT-Takers: Two Surveys, Survey II: Test-Taking History for 1980–81 Young SAT-Takers.* Report No. 88–1. New York: College Entrance Examination Board, 1988.

Olszewski-Kubilius, Paula. "Talent Search: A Driving Force in Gifted Education." *Understanding Our Gifted* 6, no. 4 (1994): 1, 8–10.

Rapley, Frank. "Granting Credit for ATYP," memorandum. Kalamazoo, Mich.: Kalamazoo Public Schools, 1987.

Chapter 25

PROJECT-BASED CALCULUS 1 STUDENTS: A CASE STUDY

Cynthia Ramey

As a mathematics teacher at a suburban high school, I began an investigation with two other mathematics teachers and a physics teacher. We wanted to offer a two-hour block class of Advanced Placement physics and college-credit calculus. The course proposal included alternative styles of instruction by the teachers; a required yearlong project; use of computer technology by all students, (including access to the Internet); frequent relating of the calculus and physics topics through experimentation, using computer technology and traditional experimentation modes; and an electronic course or project journal from each student. Not only would the course permit less duplication of topic presentations but it also allowed the students to work on group projects and have the two-hour class period to extend topics and work on short-term projects and activities relating the two courses. The next fall, the physics-calculus 1 "block" class began.

OUR "STUDENT": BEN

Ben was created as a composite of a typical project-based calculus 1 student from thirty personal interviews done with students preparing to enroll in the class, those currently in the class, and graduates of the class. Because two-thirds of the project-based class students were male, Ben is male. Ben, whose parents are highly educated, participates in three extracurricular activities during his senior year. He does not work. He completes at least ten hours of community service during the school year. He probably will earn an A in the class, and he is highly motivated. When asked why he would choose to enroll in project-based calculus 1, Ben replied, "Because of college. I know that I need math and physics. I chose the block class because it is the most difficult and I will be better prepared for college." As found by Bennet (1991), students like activities that make them think, are challenging, offer something they have never done before, and have a perceived usefulness to them. When asked if his parents pushed him into the class, Ben said, "I think they would tell me that they think I should, but they haven't required me to." He appears to be looking for the challenge described by Bennet, and he will find it when he begins the school year in project-based calculus 1.

THE CLASSROOM SETUP

When Ben enters the classroom to begin the study of project-based calculus, he encounters a long rectangular room. To the right is a traditional classroom setup, complete with teacher's desk, thirty-four students' desks, and white marker boards along the front wall of the classroom. To the left of the doorway is a computer lab in a U shape and a center aisle filled with fifteen computers, a printer, and a server for the linked system, with Internet access. On the shelves above the computers are boxes of Vernier equipment for computer-aided labs and experiments.

After several class meetings and discussions regarding the yearlong projects for the class, the students divided into groups of their own choosing and settled in to an active discussion of projects, project goals, an abstract (done at the end of the year), project activities, a timetable, resources, and project extensions. The day of planning was one of only three or four days that were devoted to group project work the entire year. Ben quickly found that it required much before and after school. One of the drawbacks, according to Ben, was "It [the project] has taken a big chunk of my time … I think we have spent ten to fifteen hours per month on it. We have spent a lot of time researching, and I know that we will spend more time in the final weeks."

Not only is the class time-consuming, but Ben sometimes finds the content difficult. However, few students fail the course. Ben said, "I find it [the class] hard, but it is OK." According to the instructor, no one in the current project-based class failed. Ben views mathematics as important and useful, which was noted by Hehner (1988) as an important factor for students learning mathematics. Ben stated,

> I think what I am learning will be helpful especially in college. I feel I have a strong background in calculus and really understand it. The research will also help me with how to get information and who to talk to. This class has been more like it can be applied to the real world. Other math classes have been just how to use a formula. This class has kind of brought it all together. The projects have also taught me time management. You have to set your priorities.… We are also getting the benefit of the technology—no matter what we are going to do later, everyone needs that!

After Ben graduated, he agreed with the perceptions of the current students. He found many aspects of his college experience enhanced because of the project-based learning experience.

> The project-based learning class was probably the best class that I could have taken to prepare me for my future. The class taught me how to look at a complex problem and break it down into parts. All of the computer information, working in groups, putting together research, finding people to help us, and interviewing have all been helpful to me in college. The math and physics I learned have been helpful in college. Many of the other students are behind me in technology. I have become a computer consultant because of my background from the class.

For Ben, it is clear that basic skills are not enough. He realizes the need to explore and use the technology of today.

Project-based learning can involve a wide range of topics and activities. Specific requirements for the final projects in the project-based calculus 1 course include research with bibliography; a problem description and design; data or results, analysis of the project; project's extensions, an electronic journal, the project itself; and a World Wide Web page designed for the specific project (hobbs.leesummit .k12.mo.us/Projects). Project topics have included research on artificial intelligence, genetics, simulation of the human retina (a supercomputer simulation), cold-fusion isomers, an alcohol engine, asteroid collisions and their effect on Earth orbit, temperature and its effects on the speed of sound, drag coefficients with respect to the trajectory of a golf ball, and the nonlinear relationship of density and temperature in water (see the Web page for complete listings).

The project on the nonlinear relationship of density and temperature of water illustrates how the students research their topics and integrate mathematics and science—in this specific case, physics. The group of students planned to model a body of water as the surrounding air temperature fell below zero. The group used the equations of thermal conduction and convection, combined with the equations for the heat of fusion, to model the freezing of the body of water. After the model was set, the group experimented with what would happen if the water behaved differently.

The students began by meeting to research the project. One student and the two teachers attended a workshop for training using the Internet, FORTRAN, UNIX, and Mario. Students continued to research and struggled with writing a computer program that they felt would simulate freezing water. A university professor helped with programming, and individuals at the Army Corps of Engineers and the conservation department were consulted on freezing in local ponds. Two students in the group collaborated to figure out the graphics end of the program and the table they wanted to use. Students found an algorithm for recalculating the temperatures of water, then added the graphics part of the program. After numerous difficulties with the algorithm, the students realized that they had downplayed the interaction between conduction and convection and finally settled on a model that they perceived as real-world. Finally, the students were successful in modeling water in lakes and ponds freezing from the top down.

Because the students are responsible for developing the topics, I found they appreciate the real-life aspects of the activities. The students developed projects linking pure and applied science with issues of the day. Ben values the teaching and learning aspects of the projects compared to the traditional classroom:

> I learn a lot more from projects because it is hands-on. We got to go to the crime lab and the police department for our project and this is *not* something we would get to do in a classroom! [Projects] give you a firsthand look ... rather than having a teacher present ... we are learning how to do it. I think the projects make the class really different from other classes.

Ben's statements substantiate the beliefs of many educators that the activities viewed as worthwhile by the students produce a self-motivated student with a learn-by-doing approach. Ben said, "It [the project-based class] gave real-life applications to what we were learning, so it was easy to see why we were studying it…. It turns out that I have used every bit of knowledge that I gained in that class."

SORTING OUT RELATIONSHIPS

The teacher's relationship to the students and the project was also important to Ben. He did have some difficulty in deciding whether the teacher was a facilitator or an authority In the classroom. Ben reflected,

> It is ironic that you ask me this. Last weekend we were with the teacher and we were talking about how sometimes teachers can be debilitating to a project…. They let us experiment, but when we needed them, they were there…. They helped us when we need help, but at the same time they allowed us to roam on our own.

Ben found the class more challenging than previous mathematics classes and stated that benefits included improved problem-solving skills and finding mathematics related to other fields. As indicated by Drake (1993) the activity-oriented approach to education requires higher-order thinking skills and making connections among subject matter. Ben shared,

> Our project is science-oriented, and we get to see science used in real life. I like the calculus and physics together. We also get to see how math is used. We have been able to use the technology to enhance our learning … to see an experiment on the screen—look at velocity and acceleration, make alterations, and see the effects. So much of what we are taught in class is theoretical with very few applications—that is what projects are there for. The project will take what you have been shown and say "Here this is what you do with what you've learned."… We have had a lot of mentors so they have helped us … and we have used their expertise … we have found out about getting help. I wrote a letter to an author of a book on brain chemistry. There was an 800 number in the book, so I called the number and got the author. I asked him about his college major and his career. He said, "How old are you?" … [he] was impressed that I would call and ask for help. It was exciting!

During classroom observations, I noticed Ben hurrying into the classroom, quickly putting down books, giving a fast hello to a fellow student with a comment about the basketball game the previous evening, then, within seconds, racing to the computer to check his e-mail. Each group is required to set up a Web page explaining its project and how it was developed, and students each keep their own electronic journal. The influence of technology is evident in the response to questions regarding the most important or influential aspect of the class.

> We keep getting more technically advanced. We are going to be way ahead [of others in college]. It is one of the best things about this class. I have realized in the last two years that technology will be a part of our lives no matter what. I am glad that we are learning to do it here and not pushed into the world and not know anything.

Ben has experienced learning through classroom presentation, computer technology, research, mentors, and experimentation. Ben has experienced authentic learning as defined by Stepien and Gallagher (1993).

It appeared Ben was willing to accept a class that is difficult and challenging because he believes that colleges are interested in such a curriculum and thinks he will be better prepared for college. Once Ben is in the class, he finds it is interesting to him because it links mathematics and science through curriculum, projects, and the use of technology. Ben states that working together with a group is a benefit he perceives for both college and real life. Evidence of being a better problem solver will be clearer to Ben after he is in college, but he does realize as a high school student that the projects are giving him hands-on experience with a wide array of subjects that definitely were not available to him in previous mathematics classes. Through the use of projects, it was evident to Ben that the teacher could not possibly be an expert in everything but that technology allowed the groups to find the necessary experts. He did feel the teacher allowed the group to experiment and do the projects their own way and shepherded the group through rough spots. As a teacher, I found that high-achieving students in the project-based learning class were willing to accept the changes in the teaching of mathematics.

The link between calculus and physics was a benefit for those in the class. The students clearly expressed their realization that it is benificial to see how calculus is used in another field. However, linking calculus with physics was also the reason many students did not choose the block class. If the school could provide the project-based class without linking it to AP physics, it would appear that more students would be willing to participate due to fewer student-schedule conflicts. Educators would then need to examine whether a significant aspect is forgone without the mathematics-science link.

CONCLUSION

The students in the study were able to express clearly that the change to project-based learning has been a good one. The students are high achievers with well-educated parents, and they participate in school activities and do community service for a variety of reasons. Project-based students leave the class with a clearer sense of how mathematics can be used in the real world. They know they are better problem solvers, because they know how to research a problem and find mentors for assistance and have an arsenal of technological knowledge. When compared on a final exam with traditionally taught calculus 1 students, the project-based students exhibited equal achievement. The content was not sacrificed, as many educators fear.

It appears from the research that more high schools and mathematics teachers should explore project-based learning as an approach to instruction at various levels of classes offered in high school. Most of the upper-level students find the approach challenging; good preparation for the future and college in terms of the use of technology and the opportunity to make decisions on their own about time management; enjoyable because they learn "real-life stuff" and beneficial for building personal skills when learning to work cooperatively.

REFERENCES

Bennet, Dorothy, Elaine Debold, and Samara Solan. "Children and Mathematics: Enjoyment, Motivation, and Square One TV." Paper presented at Society for Research in Child Development, Seattle, Wash., April 1991.

Drake, Susan. *Planning an Integrated Curriculum: The Call to Adventure.* Alexandria, Va.: Association for Supervision and Curriculum Development, 1993.

Hehner, Rosemary Pataky. "The Use of the Fennema-Sherman Mathematics Anxiety and Confidence Scales as Predictors of Success among Business Calculus Students and 'Fundamental Concepts of Mathematics' at the College Level." Master's thesis, Salisbury State College, Salisbury, Md., 1988.

Lee's Summit High School. <hobbs.leesummit.k12.mo.us/Project>. Lee's Summit, Mo., 1997.

Stepien, William, and Shelagh Gallagher. "Problem Based Learning: As Authentic as It Gets." *Educational Leadership* 50 (April 1993): 25–28.

University of Missouri—Columbia. <tiger.coe.missouri.edu/~most>. Columbia, Mo., 1997.

Chapter 26

IDENTIFYING AND DEVELOPING MATHEMATICALLY PROMISING STUDENTS THROUGH HONORS CALCULUS AND THE UNIVERSITY SCHOLARS PROGRAM

John Douglas Faires
John Paul Holcomb
Nathan Paul Ritchey

The Department of Mathematics and Statistics at Youngstown State University in Ohio (YSU) has an excellent history of success in attracting and retaining undergraduate majors. This success is attributable to the conscious effort faculty make to invite undergraduates to become participating members of the mathematics profession.

A COMMON PROBLEM

A problem faced by many mathematics departments is that few students enter a college or university with a declared major in mathematics. Thus, identifying talented students and convincing them to major in mathematics are two important tasks for most departments. Typically, many mathematically promising students choose engineering as their entering major because they either know an engineer or are aware of the career opportunities available to them in engineering. However, these same students are likely to be completely unaware of the many career opportunities available to mathematics majors. It is therefore essential for mathematics professors, particularly those teaching calculus, to communicate career opportunities in mathematics subtly to each class.

The calculus sequence gives mathematics faculty a unique opportunity to offer an alternative for the students who originally chose engineering as an entering major because of their attraction to mathematics. This method has proven successful and is probably the feasible for recruiting mathematics majors for most departments of mathematics. However, the University Scholars Program, initiated five years ago, has greatly enhanced the department's ability to recruit promising mathematics students. This paper will present the various ways in which the Department of Mathematics and Statistics at YSU has benefited from this new program.

In 1992, Youngstown State University made a commitment to develop a University Scholars Program. The program is based on the premise that academic excellence deserves to be recognized at least on the same level as athletic achievement. This recognition takes the form of a financial commitment of fourty-five new, full-cost scholarships each year, for a total of 160. Successful scholar applicants generally place within the top 2 percent on nationally competitive examinations, as illustrated by their ACT or SAT composite score, and are within the top 5 percent of their high school graduating class. The university is proud that it is one of the few public universities to provide more academic full-cost scholarships than athletic scholarships.

METHODS: IDENTIFYING AND DEVELOPING PROMISING STUDENTS

Although it is possible to determine mathematically promising students by reviewing ACT and SAT scores, this approach seldom predicts interest in the subject. Moreover, it is essential to encourage the best students in beginning mathematics courses to take additional mathematics-related courses, regardless of their intended major. With this in mind, the department felt that it was critical to be in direct and early contact with the university scholars to encourage each of them to enroll in a mathematics course. University scholars must complete thirty-six hours of honors credit over the course of their studies and do a capstone senior honors thesis. For scholars majoring in engineering or science, the honors course requirement is difficult to complete because many of the courses offered for honors credit are in the areas of the humanities and social sciences. The requirements of their major leave little room for the extra courses.

The faculty in mathematics recognized this problem early on and instituted an honors calculus sequence designed for students majoring in engineering and science. After a department discussion, in which a traditional approach emphasizing the theory in the subject and a currently popular approach emphasizing applications and the use of technology were suggested, the department instead elected to cover the required material in an abbreviated schedule. The regular calculus sequence at YSU requires four quarters of course work; the honors sequence covers this material in only three. Each year, typically twenty to twenty-five students enroll in the honors calculus sequence. It has been extremely popular with the scholars, winning their "best honors course" in the first two years (with different instructors) that this award has been given.

Since the honors calculus sequence contains so many mathematically talented students, the department chooses the professor for the sequence carefully. It is important that this professor be one who enjoys getting to know the students, understands the needs of first-year students, and possesses a great deal of enthusiasm for mathematics. This instructor must also challenge the students inside and outside the classroom. Although the honors calculus sequence was designed to cover the same material as the traditional calculus sequence in a shorter time period, it also requires students to complete harder exercises, do more technology applications, give oral and written presentations, and learn more of the history of calculus. Through this experience the students become acquainted with a faculty member in mathematics who knows them well and is genuinely interested in them and their course of study. Recent experience has shown that the instructor in honors calculus informally advises many students with a variety of majors. The intention is not to convert the true engineering and physical science students to become mathematics majors but to offer alternatives to students who are not certain what area they wish to pursue. These students need and are given special attention by the department.

The department bestows this attention by encouraging students to join the mathematical community at YSU and abroad. The development of a sense of belonging to a community is of fundamental importance to our program and is accomplished in a variety of ways. First-year students are encouraged to become associate members of our chapter of Pi Mu Epsilon, the National Mathematics Honor Society, and to present talks at national and regional Pi Mu Epsilon conferences, one of which is held at our university. They are also urged to participate in the COMAP Modeling Competition and the Putnam examination seminar. In addition, the department hires some of these students to work in the Mathematics Assistance Center, to assist faculty with work on Web page development, to collect and analyze departmental assessment data, and to perform computer system administration. Taken together, these activities allow students to interact with a variety of department faculty who then act as mentors and role models. Thus these students see and experience what mathematicians do while considering mathematics as a career.

A further benefit of these activities is that new students get to know more advanced students, who are achieving success by acquiring internships and jobs or assistantships to graduate school. The talks at national conferences and Pi Mu Epsilon also help the students to get to know each other. Because the department requires all its majors to compete a capstone senior project, many students present their work at regional and national meetings. Our experience is that the entire mathematical community supports the students as they prepare each paper and oral presentation.

CONTRACT HONORS

Another way in which scholars and other honors students become immersed in the department is through a Contract Honors program. Honors students can, with the approval of the instructor and the honors program, write a contract for any university course. Once the project is approved, the student can explore, with the instructor, a special or additional project of mutual interest. These projects typically cover material in greater depth, encompass more complex concepts, and generally require at least 25 percent more effort than that required by the course itself. Contract Honors presents an important opportunity for faculty to work with students to explore a subject in greater depth, and it enables students to continue to grow in their understanding of the research process while getting to know a faulty member on a more personal level.

The final step in the development process is to assist the students in obtaining jobs or assistantships to graduate school. To facilitate placement in industry, the department has stepped up its efforts to develop internship and cooperative education programs. Faculty members have also offered appropriate classes and individual tutoring for students wishing to pursue a career in actuarial science. Students going to graduate school are urged to participate in the Putnam examination seminar, which also helps them prepare for the Graduate Record Examination in mathematics.

These are the keys to providing a vibrant mathematics community among undergraduates and faculty. The sponsoring of such organizations and projects requires faculty commitment beyond their regular teaching responsibilities. At YSU, these extra efforts are essential to a faculty member's positive review in the areas of teaching and service. Although most faculty members would participate even without this requirement, formal recognition communicates the department's commitment to undergraduate education outside the classroom.

RESULTS

The University Scholars Program is now six years old and the fifth consecutive year of honors calculus has just been completed. Approximately twenty (or 15 percent) of the university scholars currently have a major in mathematics, with a number of these pursuing a second major, which we strongly encourage. In 1996, six mathematics students gave students' research papers at the MathFest in Seattle. Of these, four won national awards, and three of the four were university scholars. In 1997, nine students attended the Math Fest, and four of them were scholars. Two YSU students won national awards, including one scholar. Our local Pi Mu Epsilon chapter recently sponsored its second regional students' paper conference. Of the twenty-eight student speakers at the conference, more than ten were university scholars. In the past three years, YSU has entered the COMAP modeling contest, and the last two years, all twelve yearly participants were university scholars. In 1997, one team received a meritorious award (top 12 percent) and two other teams received an honorable mention (top 40 percent) by the contest judges for their work. In 1998, two teams were designated meritorious.

CONCLUSIONS

The University Scholars Program has made a significant impact on Youngstown State University, and the Department of Mathematics and Statistics has particularly benefited from the large influx of superior students. Although the department always attracted a few outstanding students, having a larger number of talented and enthusiastic students enables the department to grow as a community.

Equally important, however, is that the department has not ignored its roots, the solid nonscholar students who enjoy and wish to work in some area of mathematics. The department serves both groups of students successfully by giving close personal attention to the individual needs of each student both in the classroom and in the other aspects of their lives. Given that most of our entering students have no idea what mathematicians do when they enter the university, it is our responsibility to educate them in this regard so that they can make informed career choices.

Chapter 27

SUPPORTING STUDENTS AS EMERGING SCHOLARS

James A. Mendoza Epperson

In the mid-1970s at the University of California (UC) at Berkeley, Uri Treisman designed a research study to identify the essential factors that lead to success in freshman calculus. When Treisman asked teaching assistants to identify the strongest and weakest students in their classes, he noticed that Chinese Americans were overrepresented in the high-performing group and that African Americans were overrepresented in the low-performing group. Treisman then focused his research on a group of twenty African American and twenty Chinese American students, and after an extended study, Treisman (Fullilove and Treisman 1990; Treisman 1990; Treisman 1992) identified two primary reasons for the difference in performance between the two groups. Rather than inadequate preparation, he found that the barriers to students' success in calculus were academic isolation and social isolation. Treisman designed the Mathematics Workshop at UC at Berkeley to minimize these barriers and to increase the numbers of nonmajority students who choose mathematics-based majors.

A SENSE OF COMMUNITY

The Emerging Scholars Program (ESP) at the University of Texas (UT) at Austin—an adaptation of Treisman's mathematics workshop model—is an intensive, honors freshman calculus program that targets high-achieving students who historically have been underrepresented in the mathematics-based disciplines. (ESP is a joint project of the Department of Mathematics, the Charles A. Dana Center, and the Office of the Dean, College of Natural Sciences, at the University of Texas at Austin.) The program aims to increase the number of students excelling in freshman calculus—especially women, African Americans, Latinos, and students from rural areas.

Professor Efraim Armendariz, now department chair, tailored the program at UT in response to his own observations on the importance of creating a sense of community—for high-achieving minority students, in particular—by "directly linking it to achievement in an academic discipline." (Moreno et al. in press)

ESP students are expected to uphold high academic standards, to interact with their peers, and to explore scientific career options. To support them in meeting these expectations, they are challenged in each section by working individually and in groups on worksheets of carefully crafted, demanding problems that their instructors design to deepen their understanding of calculus. Through the collaboration that occurs in the ESP sections and the social activities that take place on weekends or evenings, students begin to form a diverse community centered around a shared interest in mathematics. (African American and Hispanic students constituted almost 60 percent of the total number of ESP participants from fall 1988 through spring 1997; the rest were white, Asian American, and Native American. Forty-three percent were women.) From direct contact with faculty and graduate students, ESP students acquire both formal and informal knowledge about graduate school and other scientific career options.

The organization of ESP provides a foundation for achieving its goals. A student development specialist is on permanent assignment to direct student recruitment and to assist in non-academic issues students encounter. Because ESP is part of the structure of the regular calculus program, ESP students attend three hours of lecture a week along with other students. The distinction is the time spent in discussion sections as well as the size of the section. Non-ESP discussion sections typically include up to forty students; however, enrollment in an ESP section is limited to twenty-four. ESP discussion sections meet for a total of six hours a week, whereas non-ESP discussion sections meet for a total of two hours a week. The ESP sections also meet for two hours at a time (rather than one), allowing students to work on complex problems that require perseverance. Because of their increased time commitment, ESP students receive two pass-fail credit hours in addition to the four credit hours all calculus students receive for the lecture.

Over the course of its ten-year history at UT, more than 80 percent of the students who have participated in ESP have earned an A or B in calculus. Research (Moreno et al. in press) shows that ESP students are almost five times more likely to earn either an A or B in calculus than non-ESP students. Ostensibly, the increased time students spend on mathematics seems to explain the difference; however, the specially designed problems used in the intensive sections as well as the atmosphere of belief, community, and responsibility fostered within them are key factors explaining ESP student success.

REINFORCING POSITIVE PERCEPTIONS

Offering appropriate mathematics in the intensive sections is crucial to the effectiveness of ESP. When students see the level of work expected in them in ESP in contrast to that required in non-ESP sections, it reinforces perceptions of themselves as academically capable. This conveyed by the following comment by a Latino ESP student.

> When I saw that most us were minorities, I wondered if we were really here because of our mathematical ability … but once I saw the difference in the type of work we were doing [compared to work in the non-ESP sections], I knew that more was expected of us.

Special attention is paid to the training of the graduate student instructors in the program. Instructors attend a two-day workshop where they explore strategies in collaborative learning, topics on teaching students from diverse backgrounds, and intricacies of writing good calculus problems and worksheets. Since 1990, the ESP Instructor Workshop is an annual event sponsored by the Department of Mathematics and the Charles A. Dana center at UT at Austin that is attended by prospective ESP instructors from UT as well as prospective ESP instructors from other universities and community colleges with similar programs. The instructors meet periodically throughout the year with an experienced ESP instructor who serves as their mentor to discuss issues that arise in their sections. Comparing sections led by trained ESP instructors and sections led by ESP instructors who have had no training showed a marked difference in both student performance and experience in calculus. Consequently, Professor Armendariz created a policy requiring participation in the ESP Instructor Workshop as a prerequisite to serving as an ESP instructor.

The practice of facilitating students' ability to form friendships that integrate their social and academic lives addresses Treisman's original findings. Students' collaboration in their sections—driven by the challenging worksheet problems—initiates this process. A comment by a female ESP student conveys this.

> I've made by best friends in ESP. You know, the worksheet problems are so difficult that you learn to work with other people and you make friends ... we study together not just for calculus, but for computer science and physics. It feels good to have people I can call on if I need to.

In their sections, students receive telephone lists so that they can call their classmates if they have homework questions or want to meet in the evenings or on weekends to study. Instructors arrange study sessions over a shared meal, and ESP program staff sponsor program-wide picnics, parties, intramural sports teams, and other social events.

Affirming students' aspirations for careers in the sciences comprises another important aspect of ESP. Research suggests that access to insider information about routes to graduate school and careers in the sciences is particularly important in keeping African Americans and Latinos in quantitative majors (Asera and Treisman 1995). To this end, instructors invite mathematicians on the faculty and from the community to speak to the students about their life experiences and their work as mathematicians. Speakers that reflect the diversity of the ESP sections also serve as important role models. The power of this personal contact with practicing mathematicians emerges in this comment by a student from a rural area in East Texas.

> I didn't have any idea about what a mathematician does ... when Dr. Luecke came in to talk to us about knot theory and its impact on the study of DNA ... I just thought, wow, I want to do that.

CONCLUSION

The name Emerging Scholars appropriately describes the belief in the mathematical promise of the program's participants. Emerging scholars are regarded as future scientists, engineers, or mathematicians and are encouraged to capitalize on their academic strengths. The program empowers students in this endeavor by promoting challenge, community, and career options in the context of a supportive, stimulating learning environment. Well-established programs similar to ESP are found nationwide at many universities and community colleges. These programs represent a robust model for supporting students as emerging scholars.

REFERENCES

Asera, Rose, and Uri Treisman. "Routes to Mathematics for African American, Latino, and Native American Students in the 1990s: The Educational Trajectories of Summer Mathematics Institute Participants." *CBMS Issues in Mathematics Education* 5 (1995): 127–51.

Fullilove, Robert E., and Philip Uri Treisman. "Mathematics Achievement among African American Undergraduates at the University of California, Berkeley: An Evaluation of the Mathematics Workshop Program." *Journal of Negro Education* 59 (1990): 463–78.

Moreno, Susan E., Chandra Muller, Rose Asera, Lisa Wyatt, and James Epperson. "Supporting Minority Mathematics Achievement: The Emerging Scholars Program at the University of Texas at Austin." *Journal of Women and Minorities in Science and Engineering* (in press).

Treisman, Philip Uri. "Teaching Mathematics to a Changing Population: the Professional Development Program at the University of California, Berkeley." In *Mathematicians and Education Reform Proceedings Conference Board on Mathematical Sciences: Issues in Mathematics Education* 1 (1990): 31–46.

———. "Studying Students Studying Calculus: A Look at the Lives of Minority Mathematics Students in College." *The Colllege Mathematics Journal* 23 (1992): 362–72.

Chapter 28

THE YOUNG SCHOLARS PROGRAM AT OHIO STATE UNIVERSITY

Arnold E. Ross

T his chapter is a response from Professor Ross reprinted from the January 1998 American Mathematical Society (AMS) newsletter when he received the AMS Citation for Public Service for notable contributions to the mathematics profession. Professor Ross was "selected for a citation for public service for inspiring generations of young people through the summer mathematics programs he created and has continued to run for nearly forty years."

Dr. Ross is Professor Emeritus at Ohio State University where he directs the "Young Scholars Program" for promising high school mathematics students. This program was started in 1957 in the post-Sputnik era when there was a great concern with the need for the search and development of young mathematical talent. In more than forty years of this program, many current and future mathematicians received their first challenging, in-depth look at mathematics when they spent their summer with Dr. Ross. The program remains as important today as when it started for the development of mathematical talent.

WRITTEN RESPONSE

I do thank our colleagues of the AMS Selection Committee for the warm moral support to all of us in the program represented by the award conferred on it.

Concern with the upbringing of the new generation of scientists, although not universal, has been represented by many generations of creative members of the world scientific community. In the U.S. this tradition was kept alive by the remarkable influence of E. H. Moore at Chicago.

I have always considered the above concerns to be a vital obligation in the life of a professional. In the *Sputnik* era such concerns moved dramatically into the central position in our public life. The unexpected appearance of *Sputnik* sent up by the Soviet Union (*Fostering Scientific Talent* 1973) questioned our claims to technical superiority, and in the days of the Cold War we felt threatened. Our popular press laid the blame upon our school teachers.

Soon after, considerable material resources were available for programs designed to upgrade the scientific and mathematical background of the secondary school teachers (Ross 1996, p. 233). This was followed by material support of summer programs for able precollege youngsters.

At Notre Dame we were among the first to introduce programs for teachers and a program for able youngsters (Ross 1996, p. 234). Our program for the youngsters, which was originally closely associated with our program for teachers, was beginning to acquire a life of its own in 1960. We were confronted with the dilemma as to what purpose should be served by a program for a collection of young individuals who have in common only eagerness, curiosity, an unbounded (and hitherto undirected) supply of vitality, and possibly an ultimate destiny in science.

We settled on the objective of providing a vivid apprenticeship to a life of exploration. This has remained our guiding motivation to the present (Ross 1991, pp. 44–45).

Has our choice been relevant to the needs of our nation over the years since 1960? Is it relevant today?

The world economy, moved by the forces of the free market and shaped by science fiction technology, does not forgive weakness. The realities of weakness, however, are not presented as clearly and dramatically today as in the past, when weakness could lead to a disastrous defeat in an unequal confrontation. Appreciation of what is needed to survive and prosper in a knowledge-intensive environment grows slowly. Freedom of movement of human talent and of production prowess worldwide mitigates local economic difficulties. This is only temporary—the payment is deferred.

Education is one of the key ingredients of a healthy economy. Median performance by our young people in mathematics, in science, and in the use of language has been moving steadily downward in quality during the last few decades. Deep anxiety over what this will mean for the well-being of our nation reached upward as far as the White House. Still there is no promise of improvement.

Our problems in education are enormous and many-faceted. The component which is involved in the bringing up of practitioners in the knowledge-intensive occupations is more focused and is, I feel, the responsibility of our professions. The penalty of neglect has been heavy and promises to be even graver in the near future. The hazards of today have different faces and different names than they had in the Sputnik era, but they are equally threatening to our well-being.

Concern with the task of discovery and development of our nation's talented in all walks of life should still be one of our major preoccupations. This feeling provides for us the motive power for the effort needed to keep our program alive and on an acceptable level of excellence.

Mathematics, science, and technology look very different today than they looked forty years ago. Our program must reflect these changes.

Each group of summer participants in the Young Scholars Program has a distinct personality all its own. We must respond without losing sight of our major aims.

In selecting our summer participants, we try to ascertain that each applicant is ready to benefit by coming to us. Collaboration of master teachers is extraordinarily valuable in accomplishing this. We usually bring together for the summer a group of youngsters with reasonably happy mathematical experience and healthy curiosity not yet dampened.

We make a strong effort to achieve deep student involvement. A rapid transition from a role of very passive spectator to the role of active participant is very demanding for all of the participants, dramatically so for those in the group who are least experienced.

Young participants acquire the deeply moving experience in the use of language as they share results of their observations and of their exploration with others. In this process is born a community of young scholars (very young indeed) where a vivid exchange of ideas between newcomers and program veterans (some acting as counselors) enriches the quality of everyday life.

Happy slogans are always helpful. To indicate involvement, we used to speak of "hands on." With the advent of computer software this is no longer appropriate. Our friends in the life sciences proposed "minds on." Since this expresses our sentiments as well, we have adopted it. After we make our charges realize that "thinking deeply of simple things" is a quality of a fine, inquisitive mind, reexamining the familiar becomes for them a fulfilling experience.

In the crucible of the first summer, individual talents assert themselves. Fortunately, basic mathematical ideas have deep appeal and wide pertinence. Thus intensive participant involvement still allows us to keep many doors open. Nonetheless, deep mathematical and scientific talent also has an opportunity to flower.

Our newcomers do what we call number theory. Number theory proper reflects much of what has been happening in mathematics. On the other hand, many important mathematical ideas, such as those in abstract algebra, for example, are traced back to number theory. Number theory proper and its rich environment are a fertile ground for exploration and are a valuable source for nontrivial but accessible problems. Also, one can increase the density of encounter with new ideas without increasing unduly the computational complexity. Every so often a beginner can get a glimpse of usefulness of geometric or analytic ideas.

Those who return to us for the second summer study combinatorics very intensively. In the last forty years, combinatorics has moved into one of the central positions in mathematics. Combinatorics has many interesting and accessible ideas and provides many challenges for the exercise of ingenuity. It has many varied uses in mathematics, in science, and in technology.

Subjects studied by our advanced participants who return to us for an additional summer reflect their interests as well as their experience. Also, as often as possible, we try to provide for them an opportunity to learn some interesting mathematics that becomes important in science. This became true for knot theory soon after 1986 and for the representation theory of finite groups in the work of stereochemists about thirty years ago. Moving away from the already-established interest helps to broaden the outlook of a budding young mathematician. Failure to be concerned with this facet of education has been deplored by many influential people who oversee the careers of young scientists and mathematicians.

I am happy to say that experimentation is still alive. David Kelly at Hampshire College is much gentler than we are—he reaches out to a different audience. Glenn Stevens and David Fried at Boston University augmented their program (PROMSYS) by a symbiotic program for master teachers. The remarkable program of Manuel Berriozabal has reached deeply into the community of San Antonio, which is predominantly Hispanic. Max Warshauer at San Marcos, Texas, lays emphasis on working with underrepresented groups—students and teachers alike. The program, which began under the sponsorship of Admiral Rickover, works through faculty mentors. Paul Sally searches keenly for talent among minorities. His exploration begins through programs in the Chicago city schools at the sixth-grade level and above until college and involves teachers as well. Tom Banchoff assisted in our program while a student at Notre Dame. His deep interest in his students is still very much in evidence. George Berzsenyi of Rose-Hulman Institute of Technology revived for the United States the inspired Hungarian tradition. ARML, a society of master teachers, sponsors discussion centers throughout the nation. Julian Stanley's concern with Mathematically Precocious Youth since 1971 has enriched the lives of many youngsters (*Quo Vadis America* 1996). His imaginative exploration has been instrumental in inspiring widespread interest in the needs of able youngsters.

I am deeply grateful to Professors Daniel Shapiro, Gerald Edgar, Dijen Ray-Chaudhuri, Bogdan Baishanski, Ranko Bojanic, and Dr. Gloria Woods for their warm support and help in keeping our program alive through many trials and tribulations.

REFERENCES

Fostering Scientific Talent. Science and Technology Policies. Cambridge, Mass.: Ballinger Publishing Co., 1973.

Quo Vadis America. Intellectual Talent. Baltimore: Johns Hopkins University Press, 1996.

Ross, Arnold E. "Windmills or Steppinq Stones?" *A Century of Mathematical Meetings.* Providence, R.I.: American Mathematical Society, 1966.

———. "Creativity: Nature or Nurture?" *CBMS Issues in Mathematics Education.* Vol. 2. Providence, R.I.: American Mathematical Society, 1991.

Chapter 29

DEVELOPING MATHEMATICALLY PROMISING STUDENTS OUTSIDE OF FORMAL EDUCATION

Richard Alvarez

Community youth organizations present opportunities for identifying and developing mathematically promising students. There is a big opportunity there to motivate the students to see the value of their mathematics by providing real-world applications. This chapter describes that development process for high school students in the Boy Scouts of America who are working toward an astronomy badge and suggests several other situations and programs that are fertile ground for mathematical development.

In my role as an adult in the Boy Scouts of America, too often I see high school students who have taken two or more years of high school mathematics without seeing much real-world in-depth application for their mathematics. Some of those students consider mathematics so useless that they stop taking mathematics courses. They have only our admonition to stay with mathematics because they will need it later. For a young person, "later" is a long time.

Many of those students are bright and capable, and they can be saved mathematically by motivation. Youth and community organizations are fertile ground for motivation. In the Boy Scouts alone, here are some areas where that can happen: Explorer Posts in technical career fields like engineering and surveying; Scout camp planning, development, and maintenance; program planning; and some of the merit badge programs. Here, we look first at one particular part of the Boy Scout Astronomy Merit Badge program, and then we consider those other areas. Of course, other youth groups such as Girl Scouts offer similar opportunities.

A MOUNTAIN SCOUT CAMP

In a Scout camp in the mountains, a group of Scouts gathers to start working toward the Astronomy Merit Badge. Most of these Scouts are academically promising or they wouldn't be going for the astronomy badge. But it's summertime; September is far away, and school and mathematics don't even exist now!

One requirement for the Boy Scout astronomy badge is to find the latitude by measuring the elevation angle of the sun. From figure 29.1, we see that, to a good approximation, we can compute latitude by measuring the sun's apparent elevation angle and by knowing the sun's current declination (the angle, analogous to latitude, by which the sun is north or south of Earth's equator at that particular time of the year). The latitude computation involves an algebraic equation, and either the sun's declination or the latitude, or both, can be negative. Some Scouts feel intimidated by that equation, but for mathematically promising high school students, we turn that badge requirement into motivation.

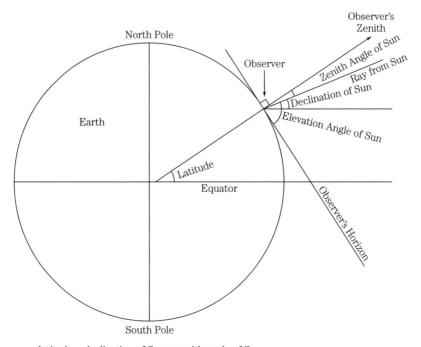

latitude = declination of Sun + zenith angle of Sun

Fig. 29.1. Approximate geometry of Earth and Sun during spring and summer

One way to measure the sun's apparent elevation angle is to measure a shadow. In this case, the shadow is cast by a large symmetrical knot in a plumb-string. (The knot must be large and symmetrical because of the considerable angle subtended by the sun.) Most Scouts know how to lash together a tripod, how to tie a suitable knot, and how to make the string adjustable in three dimensions. The Scouts mark a north-south line (meridian) on the ground, using some measurements and plane geometry. As the sun moves across the sky, when the knot's shadow is on the meridian that they marked on the ground, we drive a nail into the ground to mark that point for future use.

Now comes the clumsy part. Two Scouts hold a string with one end on the knot and the other end on the nail where the knot's shadow crossed the meridian. Thus, the string follows a sun ray. We want to measure its elevation angle. So another Scout squirms on his belly in the dirt (or maybe in mud) and tries to hold a half-round protractor level on the ground while measuring the elevation angle of the string. In a mountain camp, usually there is no such thing as level ground, or even smooth ground, so it is hard to hold the protractor level. And it is almost as hard for the other two Scouts to hold the string still. We are lucky to measure the elevation angle, hence latitude, within several degrees.

For the Scouts who have had geometry or trigonometry in high school (and that includes most of the Scouts in the astronomy badge class), I suggest that they do this measurement more accurately and more easily (and stay cleaner, too), by measuring distances and then computing the elevation angle. With a measuring tape, they measure all three sides of the triangle shown in figure 29.2. Because of the ground slope, that triangle usually is not even a right triangle, but the law of cosines doesn't mind that at all. Then, with a scientific calculator, they compute the apparent zenith-angle of the sun, which is what we really want anyway for the latitude measurement. In addition to being both easier and more accurate than direct measurement with the protractor, that method avoids the effects of ground slope and roughness. We find the sun's declination from a solar ephemeris. (An ephemeris is a numerical table or a complex algorithm that is used in predicting the position of a celestial object, in this case the sun, in the sky at any time. It is used widely by astronomers, navigators, land surveyors, and solar engineers.) Then we compare our computed latitude with the latitude scaled from a U.S. Geological Survey 7.5-minute topographic map. By this time, our Scouts want to know how accurate their answer is. Scaling is the way to find out, and it gives them still more use for their mathematics. Our latitude measurement error typically is about 0.15 degrees, which corresponds to about ten miles on the ground. That's a pretty good measurement for a Scout camp.

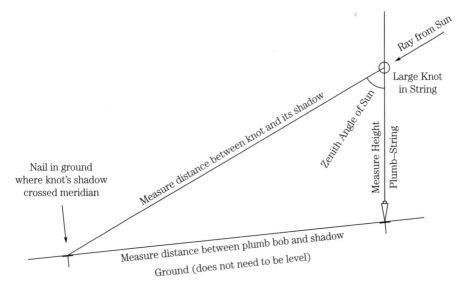

Fig. 29.2. Finding the zenith angle of the Sun (elevation view)

Developing Mathematically Promising Students Outside of Formal Education 279

By this time, some of our Scouts are on a mathematical roll. Keep it going! For a starter, I remind the Scouts that we have been speaking of apparent elevation angle. Why apparent? Isn't the sun really where it appears? Not quite, because of atmospheric refraction. The interested Scouts plug numbers into an empirical formula from the ephemeris and find that under these conditions, atmospheric refraction is negligible.

For the Scouts who have had some calculus in high school, we compute the probable error in our latitude measurement. It comes to about 0.15 degrees for the measurement equipment that we use. I point out that this accuracy agrees with our experience over the years. If the Scouts want to continue, then we compute the error bias in the azimuth of the meridian that we marked on the ground, caused by the small change in the sun's declination during the day.

One of the older Scouts explains the process and the results to the Scouts who did not go through the mathematics. The usual response to all this is, "This is the first real use that we have seen for our high school mathematics. What else can we do with it?" Around our group's campfire between the nighttime observations, I spin tales of practical uses for field astronomy. The younger Scouts get a preview of the value of what's coming in mathematics.

In other facets of the Boy Scouts, mathematically promising students have used astronomy to compute the optimum starting time for campfire programs, used probability to compute the maintenance budget for our diesel-electric generation facility, used trigonometry to design and make dipsticks for 5000-gallon diesel fuel tanks, and designed the three-phase electrical load-bank that is used for testing. Without community projects like these, which offer hands-on experience, those promising students might plod through their mathematics courses anyway. Or, if they did not see any practical value for their studies, they might drop out.

CONCLUSION

Here are two actions that you can take to develop mathematically promising students outside of the classroom: First, know what your promising students do outside of school and try to steer them into projects where they can apply their mathematics and other subjects. Second, if you are involved in an outside youth organization, watch for the mathematically promising students and find projects in which they can apply their mathematics.

Chapter 30

THE CHARLOTTE MATHEMATICS CLUB: A GREENHOUSE FOR TALENT

Ashley Reiter

Community is an important part of all people's lives, including students, teachers, administrators, and parents. A community serves as a framework in which the development of talent can be encouraged and supported. For mathematically inclined students, this community is often found within the framework of competitions. For many junior high school students, the experience of participating as a team in the MathCounts competition or local mathematics competitions is both fun and academically rewarding.

After my own very positive experiences with MathCounts in 1986–87, it was a disappointment to realize that I would no longer be able to practice and participate in mathematics competitions with my classmates. Understanding my situation, in 1987 my father, Harold Reiter (University of North Carolina—Charlotte) organized a group that came to be known as the Charlotte Mathematics Club (CMC).

Although the activities have been quite varied, the basic organization has remained unaltered over the past ten years. One Saturday morning each month, students in the eighth through twelfth grades meet to do mathematics together. Local schools provide a meeting place, Reiter or other mathematicians plan the program, and parents and teachers serve as volunteers to keep things organized. Students learn about the club from teachers, other students, or announcements in the local newspaper. Some students have commuted as far as 100 miles to join this mathematical activity.

At a typical meeting, students receive a set of problems to work on individually for a short time after they arrive. These problem sets are most often a series of open-ended problems dealing with material from outside the traditional high school mathematics curriculum, such as combinatorics, probability, or game theory. The first problems are computational and may be solved by nearly all the participants. Subsequent problems usually require proofs that challenge even the brightest students. Later, the students divide into groups to continue working on and discussing the problems. After a break and refreshments, the whole group reconvenes to discuss the problems and share solutions, or to hear a short presentation about some other mathematical topic. On occasion, another university faculty member gives a presentation—anything from a proof that there are five Platonic solids to a mathematical magic show. At other meetings, students speak about projects they are working on or summer mathematics programs that they have attended.

Given that the group has grown to as many as fifty students, Saturday mornings have become more of a three-ring circus, with students of various abilities and interests participating in any of several activities: listening to a speaker, working on problems, playing with mathematical puzzles and games (for example, using graph theory to solve the Instant Insanity puzzle), or participating in the Tournament of Towns and the Mandelbrot competitions.

The activities of the club have now expanded beyond the Saturday meetings. Home-schooled students and students from nonparticipating schools have banded together to participate as a group in area mathematics competitions. A number of students have done mathematics fair projects and received help through the club. Also, when another group formed, for fourth- through sixth-graders, members of the older club volunteered to help. The December meeting features visits from CMC alumni who return to talk about their experiences in various summer enrichment programs and in college and graduate school in mathematics. Through the club, students have been able to participate in a number of other mathematical activities around the state. For example, it has served as a sparring partner for both the North Carolina School of Science and Mathematics and the South Carolina state American Regions Mathematics League (ARML) team in weekend practice sessions.

Many factors may hinder the formation of a mathematical community for high school students. In many cases, the low density of students who are seriously interested in mathematics inhibits the formation of such a community within a single school. Local mathematics leagues enable excellent students from schools around the city to be challenged by one another, but the nature of the competition provides little chance for students from different schools to work together on mathematics. A mathematics club that is open to students from across the entire community allows students with a very high level of ability and interest to meet, in a noncompetitive situation, with other students who challenge them.

Although competitions are not a focus of the club's activity, they serve as a relatively standard measure of the success that the club has had in identifying and developing the talent located in the region. For more than thirteen years, Duke University has given full-tuition scholarships to students who excel in the North Carolina state mathematics competition. In the years before the formation of the CMC, students from Mecklenburg County (the region served by the club) made up nine of the forty Duke scholars. In the most recent eight years, when the club had been in existence for at least two years, nine of the fifteen Duke scholars have hailed from Mecklenburg County, and eight of those had participated in the CMC.

Another measure of the development of talent is participation in a training program for one of the four International Olympiads—in mathematics, chemistry, physics, and computer science (informatics). Although not limited to mathematics, each of these fields requires significant knowledge and experience in mathematics. In the years before the Charlotte Mathematics Club, no resident of Mecklenburg County participated in any of the training programs. (The computer Olympiad began only in 1992.) Since 1991, however, six alumni of the CMC have participated in these training programs—two each in physics and computing and one each in mathematics and chemistry. Furthermore, three CMC students have represented the United States in an academic Olympiad and have garnered a gold, silver, and bronze medal. One factor in this increased participation is familiarity with the process leading to the training program and Olympiad itself. This kind of personal knowledge can typically be found only in very special high schools. However, in a larger community this type of knowledge can be shared among more students and teachers.

The long-term results of this club are only beginning to appear. Of the first participants, anecdotal evidence indicates that a significant number are now pursuing a Ph.D. degree in mathematics or computer science. It is conceivable that the causation works in reverse—that the club has been so successful because of the participation of students who are already so interested in mathematics. In any case, the club has served a key role in the development of that talent and interest.

The structure of this club has also served to identify some groups of students whose mathematical promise might otherwise go unnoticed. Given the present emphasis on competition for mathematically inclined students, the club has offered a unique opportunity for students who are averse to competitions—but not to mathematics. This type of club is also an important resource for home-schooled students, who have been a particularly active component of the CMC. Finally, this type of club has provided mathematical stimulation to students who attend schools where no teacher is able to provide extracurricular mathematical activities.

Given the high workloads imposed on most high school teachers, it is significant that this type of club, run primarily by university faculty and parents, becomes a resource for teachers to offer their students rather than an additional responsibility. Furthermore, through the CMC, students, parents, and teachers have shared ideas and information that has aided teachers in their attempts to stimulate their students, and it has given the students the means by which to be aware of and take advantage of other mathematical opportunities. The CMC will not identify or meet the needs of every student who has an interest or aptitude for mathematics, but for a significant number of Charlotte students, the club has been an academic and social springboard to propel us through college and into graduate school in mathematics.

Chapter 31

ADDICTION TO MATHEMATICS: HOW CAN WE CAUSE IT?

William E. Geeslin

Several factors contribute to a successful program for mathematically promising students. This paper briefly describes some necessary beliefs and components of such a program for encouraging students to pursue mathematics and mathematics-based careers. The author is in the rather unusual position of having attended, created, and directed such programs; served as a program officer for the National Science Foundation (NSF), which has funded such programs; and had a daughter attend such programs. Participation in each of my roles was quite enjoyable—the main characteristic for most of us of a successful program. But one must remember that what one person enjoys is not necessarily to the liking of another. The creation of a successful program requires some flexibility in beliefs: (1) many students have mathematical promise and talent, (2) programs should not focus entirely on the goal of creating mathematicians (or mathematics educators), and (3) if given the opportunity, students can do far more than most of us imagine.

DEFINITIONS VARY

Definitions of *talented* and *promising* vary as well as the estimate of the proportion of the student population fitting these definitions. Certainly more than 10 or 15 percent of most schools' student population is very likely to have promise in mathematics. This promise may lead to careers in mathematics, science, engineering, statistics, and so forth. Likewise, it may be unlikely that more than 50 or 60 percent of a regular school's student body is extraordinarily talented. Wheras pursuit of a good definition and indicator of talent or promise is an intriguing and valuable educational research activity, it may be of limited use in designing and operating a program. A program should focus much more on the experiences it can offer a student than with identifying promise or talent. A program director might simply select some indicators of talent or promise and move forward. In the University of New Hampshire's (UNH) Mathematics and Marine Science program, for instance, we insisted that a student applicant completing the ninth grade had earned a B or higher in algebra 1 and asked for a mathematics or science teacher's recommendation and a guidance counselor's recommendation. Beyond that we simply noted that we were interested in students who showed talent or promise in mathematics or science and would likely benefit from participation. It is unlikely all teachers used the same definition of *talented.* More likely they simply relied on intuition and observation. Nonetheless, selecting 25 students from the 100 to 200 applications each year was always difficult, and we were never disappointed in the students who attended the program.

On completion of our program, 75 percent of our participants reported taking more mathematics and science courses than their school required. Fifty percent actually urged their schools to offer more science and mathematics-related courses. UNH is now offering four additional summer programs for talented high school students. More than half our participants attended additional special summer programs in science and mathematics and over 30 percent attended one of the new UNH programs. Ninety percent of participants went on to college, and 75 percent of those elected to study science, mathematics, engineering, or related fields.

Programs for promising mathematics students need not focus on mathematics per se, especially for students below the eleventh grade. The UNH program noted above had three components: marine science, computer applications, and probability and statistics. All data were gathered from a tidal estuary, and everything in the program was designed around low tide. Thus, the mathematics component, probability and statistics, met when the tide was high, a somewhat different time each day. The mathematics component provided tools for analyzing marine data. Public presentations and papers were about marine science. Yet, at least two of the twenty students from the first year majored in mathematics four years later in college. We had a particularly enlightening presentation by a varied group of UNH scientists, all of whom indicated that they did not settle on their particular field until graduate school and all of whom (without any prompting) indicated mathematics was one of—if not the—most important subjects they had studied.

Students can do almost anything if allowed! With training and supervision they will not damage equipment, endanger themselves, or harm the environment (natural or laboratory). Our ninth-grade group was the only group, except for a few graduate students and research scientists, allowed in certain estuary areas. We were the only noncollege group invited to certain offshore labs and allowed to use other labs without supervision. In my role at NSF, I saw students design and build lasers, reengineer computers to do things the manufacturers were unaware their computers could do, and create holograms. Some students were actually publishing scientific papers as a program requirement. They also were very creative mathematically. These were middle school and high school students in all cases. The only people that ever had to be convinced that students could do more were new program directors. Yes, the students were selected. Yes, they were talented. Nonetheless, they came from quite varied academic, ethnic, cultural, and economic backgrounds. Some programs for younger students enrolled most students who applied. Most had many more applicants than they could accommodate. (One engineering program in Texas for students entering eighth and ninth grades had more than 500 applicants for thirty-two positions during the first year that it operated.) If you build the program, students will come and will succeed.

Although mathematics and science fairs, contests, and competitions serve as an outlet for academic accomplishment, they usually are insufficient for motivating large numbers of students to pursue mathematics as either a vocation or avocation. Frequently these activities are not representative of what a mathematician actually does. In reflecting on program components that ensure success, the following characteristics appear most important:

1. The program is perceived by the student as a special opportunity.
2. Student selection for the program is perceived as being based on either talent or promise or both.
3. The program is intense.
4. The program is of sufficient length and not a one-shot effort.
5. Students have the opportunity to accomplish something significant.
6. The program introduces the student to the research experience.
7. Student participation is voluntary.
8. Some aspects of the program are held away from the school and involve nonschool mathematicians and scientists.
9. The program is difficult and challenging.
10. Students have hands-on experience in all aspects of the program.
11. Students are involved in activities that are the same or very similar to those in which a research mathematician or scientist is normally engaged.
12. The mathematical aspects of the program involve proof, derivation, and application.
13. The program director's enthusiasm for mathematics is obvious to the students.

Experience with a wide variety of programs for promising middle school and high school students has shown the following to be useful: When students receive the first notice about the program, they should know that not all applicants will be selected and that some commitment on the student's part is necessary in both the application stage and during the program. Students must realize that agreement to participate implies attendance at all sessions. They should be aware that the program is not a camp but an academic research experience that will require study, homework, and preparation. Small groups work best, but there is nothing to prevent the program director from running several similar programs to accommodate more students.

Bringing students away from the school at special times or to special places is an easy way to create this notion of special. Parents should be involved in noting both the academic nature of the program and the special selection. There is nothing like proud parents saying they never had that opportunity or were unable to understand those concepts and applications at that age to motivate a student. A beginning talk from a mathematician or scientist pitched at a high level but aimed at the program is an excellent way to set high academic expectations.

The program should be of at least three weeks' duration full time or at least a semester part time. It is extremely helpful if students can work regularly with a practicing scientist or mathematician. Show-and-tell makes a terrible program. Students must participate along with doing the showing and telling. The mathematical work must not be watered down to allow this participation. Students need to be involved in true exploration and discovery, that is, in the research process. These activities should not be "aimed at teaching mathematics." It is not necessary that a student, particularly a younger one, discover something for the first time, but it is necessary that the student be able to use current procedures and equipment and be involved in the scientific problem-solving activity for an extended time. Students should prepare, organize, and make public presentations of their research. These presentations may be to peers or parents but should be structured much like a professional presentation of research results.

The many mathematics programs that I observed while at NSF seemed to fall into two categories: (1) rediscovering high-level but mainline mathematics from areas such as number theory, algebra, and analysis, or (2) applications of mathematics to various nonmathematics fields. It is rare that a student would discover a new theorem, given that so much background knowledge is often needed to be prepared for proving a current conjecture. However, students can easily gather and analyze new data related to applied mathematics problems or other scientific areas.

In all programs, students had to read mathematics on their own, construct and understand derivations and theorems, and apply mathematics either to other mathematical problems or to other fields. Presenting, discussing, and writing about findings is a crucial program component. In both types of programs, students worked with mathematicians and other talented students. It is very important for the student to actually see that there are other students interested in and knowledgeable about mathematics. Often, in smaller schools or rural areas, students think they are the only person interested in academics and are unaware of what their peers can actually accomplish.

Program funding is difficult to obtain, especially with NSF no longer funding such programs. Charging a fee for participation to students who can afford it is helpful in ensuring student and parent commitment. These fees are ordinarily free of restrictions and can be spent on texts, calculators, T-shirts (a great way for students to identify with the program), pizza, or whatever. Local scientific and technical businesses may allow students to use labs or equipment, give funding, or furnish scientists to staff the program. Schools may have funds available for talented programs. Funds aimed at providing opportunities for minorities might be used to partially fund a program.

NO PRESCRIPTION

There is no prescription that will guarantee a successful program. Reflect on the mathematical applications in your local area (water resources; power companies; telephone, electronic, and video transmission of information; and highways are available everywhere). Determine who operates and designs these facilities and what technical problems they are encountering. Find out what mathematics is being used (everyone uses statistics and modeling). Ask if you can engage a small group of students in studying these problems. Find out which public and private bodies are studying these problems and contact them about allowing your students to assist them in their work. Involve colleagues from other disciplines in your project as appropriate. Capitalize on the interests of your students (e.g., we used marine science and a trip to the Isles of Shoals). Someone will be willing to address your group of students concerning the general problem and how they are attempting to resolve it.

Keep the application process simple, but require some student writing, such as, "What do I expect to gain from the program?" Thus students will have volunteered and expressed an interest. Have a teacher and scientist select participants from the applications. Newspapers and guidance offices are generally willing to advertise the program for free. Always calling your program a special research opportunity for "future scientists" will ensure that it's thought of as special. Do not allow prerequisite skills to dominate your thinking. Present the students with the problems to be addressed from the outset and let them proceed to gain the background knowledge as needed. Frequently, mathematics applied to other disciplines requires only simple algebra and a computer package. Program activities usually should be scheduled in two- to three-hour blocks because shorter sessions are inadequate for accomplishing much and longer ones often exceed the attention span of the participants. Also, allow students a role in deciding the direction of activities and methods for solving problems.

Finally, have fun! Mathematicians and scientists pursue research primarily because they enjoy it.

Chapter 32

NURTURING THE GROWTH OF YOUNG MATHEMATICIANS THROUGH MATHEMATICS CONTESTS

Richard Grassl
Tabitha Mingus

Young mathematicians are rarely given the opportunity to shine in front of their peers and to be praised for their mathematical abilities in the way that gifted musicians or athletes are lauded. Although these gifted mathematicians are recognized in the classroom by their teachers, all too frequently this type of recognition carries a negative connotation by their peers. Mathematics contests are a means for providing an encouraging environment in which gifted students compete, excel, and are honored for their abilities.

Historically, mathematics competitions have intrigued some gifted students as much as making the Collegiate Final Four drives thousands to practice their basketball skills for months and years. Even though not all students gifted in mathematics are positively influenced by contests, Berger and Keynes (1988) point out,

> mathematically gifted youngsters need a continuously challenging and rewarding mathematical environment. Year-round programs that support individual learning styles have more potential for long-term changes than programs that begin and end with the summer vacation.

Combined with parental, secondary school, university, and community support, properly designed competitions can influence and motivate a broad range of promising students. The University of Northern Colorado (UNC) has organized such a statewide contest for seventh- to twelfth-grade students. Throughout the year, the faculty of the mathematics department at UNC, secondary school teachers, and parents rally around these competitors in support of their efforts.

HOW IS THE CONTEST DESIGNED?

Participation in the contest at UNC has grown dramatically since its inception in 1992, from 150 students the first year to more than 1700 competitors in 1998. A November first-round examination is mailed out to all interested secondary schools throughout the state, and students who score in the top 10 percent are invited to the final round in February. The competition culminates in an awards banquet held in April. All students are welcome to compete in the first round, and no preregistration, screening or fee are required. With no preregistration, we are clearly encouraging the seemingly unmotivated student to participate; we are always pleased (and never surprised) when such a student rises to the occasion and succeeds.

Unlike other contests, each round consists of about ten essay problems, and all the students, regardless of grade, take the same examination. This allows the students to recognize growth in themselves as they take the exam from year to year. The questions are written so that several are directed at the middle school level, allowing even the youngest competitors to experience success in their efforts. The problems are carefully designed to encourage ingenuity and creativity as opposed to testing knowledge of less challenging, more structured material. Many of the problems lend themselves to multiple approaches.

All interested secondary school mathematics teachers, along with UNC mathematics faculty, are invited to grade the first round together. This cooperative effort has led to a better understanding of their respective perspectives on the state of mathematics education in Colorado, and it has promoted interesting and useful discussions that have helped to initiate joint educational efforts. We attempt to introduce basic topics such as the Pythagorean theorem, triangular numbers, and arithmetic progressions on the first round. The second round further probes many of the ideas introduced in the first round. Because the teachers are made aware of the connections between the two rounds, they are alert to their need to act as mentors and to use the intervening months to guide the first-round winners through these topics.

Care is taken to ensure that a representative number of winners in each of the grade levels are invited back to the UNC campus for the three-hour final round. While the finalists tackle the final round, teachers and parents gather for a presentation of the solutions to the same problems. These teachers are taking risks, just like their students, by being involved. For example, frequently the students will quickly devise a solution to a problem that has stumped the teacher. Thus, the dynamics of the contest and the solutions seminar constitute a learning opportunity for both the student and the teacher. Duly armed, the teachers are comfortable greeting their students in class the following Monday morning—ready to guide them with hints on the more challenging and unresolved problems. The following pair of problems is an example of the types that appear on the two rounds.

First Round

The diagonal AB passes through 6 squares of the 3×6 rectangle. Determine the number of squares that the diagonal AB passes through for a 3×4, a 4×6, and then a 12×18 rectangle.

Final Round

A 6×15 rectangle is subdivided into ninety one-by-one squares. Through how many squares does the diagonal AB pass? Repeat for an $m \times 2m$ rectangle and for an m by n rectangle.

HOW DOES THE AWARDS BANQUET CONTINUE THE NURTURING?

The top twenty winners of the final round are honored, along with their parents and teachers, at an April banquet. Also, television and newspaper coverage in their communities publicly honor their achievements. We have found that cash prizes are not necessarily the best incentive or reward for those who excel on the contest. Far more substantial and effective in motivating these students is the awarding of an expertly written mathematics text or subscriptions to appropriate level mathematics journals, along with plaques or trophies.

Awarding appropriate level books encourages these bright young mathematicians to persist with their reading; and as they gain in mathematical maturity, they "grow into" their prizes. A hardbound copy of a classic text like *What is Mathematics* by Courant and Robbins, personalized with an inscription, will remain a cherished part of the personal library of a promising student and could propel her or him toward a career embracing, rather than avoiding, mathematics. For example, a past winner remarked that reading about Mersenne primes in the text she was awarded sparked her interest in them.

HOW HAS THE CONTEST AFFECTED THE STUDENTS WHO PARTICIPATE?

Karl is a gifted mathematician, grasping new concepts quickly and holding a deep understanding of their extensions. His talent manifested itself early in the first grade, and as a fifth grader he took algebra 1. Despite skipping seventh grade entirely, Karl was still advanced mathematically compared to his now older classmates and thus took trigonometry as a ninth grader. He began participating in the UNC contest at age 13, one year after its creation. As statewide participation in the contest grew, Karl steadily climbed to the top and won the first place trophy in 1996.

When asked about his involvement in the contest, Karl said he had always wanted to do contests because they would give him the chance to exercise his "ability to formalize patterns" that he saw and the push "to explain [his] work." He said that the contest gave him an "opportunity to do math" and that he "always planned on going into mathematics; the contest confirmed my interest in combinatorics." What intrigued him most, however, was "the satisfaction of being able to find a pattern, and being honored as a winner."

As a result of his involvement in the contest, Karl has completed the calculus sequence and several other mathematics courses at UNC while attending high school. Such involvement in university courses provided Karl with quite a boost due to the association with the better-prepared, hard-working mathematics majors. His current desire is to earn a Ph.D. degree in mathematics; his quest has begun as he enters college in California.

About forty parents and teachers were asked about the influence that the competition has had on their students. Their responses were overwhelmingly favorable. The following comments are representative of their responses to the question, "How would you describe the influence that this contest has had on your students?"

- Increased her curiosity. She knew that she was capable of competing with peers statewide.

- As an extended hobby, the contest has resulted in him enjoying mathematics as a part of his life.

- This contest has greatly raised the self-esteem of my students; it has taught them to read questions carefully, be creative, be precise, how to generalize, and how to persevere.

- The excitement of coming to a university setting for the competition increased the importance to her.

FINAL COMMENTS

The senior author was involved in a similar contest for nearly twenty years at the University of New Mexico (UNM). At UNM, the awards banquet attracted such speakers as Fields medalist William Thurston from Princeton University and Senator Pete Dominici. There is hardly a more powerful influence on a young, energetic, bright sophomore than to first solve a challenging mathematics problem and then to be publicly praised by university faculty in the presence of parents and teachers—and a U.S. senator. Ross 1989–90 points out

> In the instances of the successful maturing of such young talent and of the development of high competence, one finds often the continued opportunity for contact with good mathematical and scientific ideas and with people who are capable of providing encouragement and guidance toward significant challenges. It appears that very vivid, early impressions leave their mark upon the nature of the ultimate achievement.

Over the past twenty-five years, the senior author has had the privilege of seeing many of these young mathematicians succeed both in competition and in their chosen fields. While the authors cannot show a causal link between participation in contests and subsequent career success, there is evidence to support that involvement in challenging mathematical programs (such as the contest described) results in students having many more career paths open to them, especially in the fields of mathematics and science (Berger and Keynes 1988).

One particular competitor's story stands out and demonstrates how involvement in such contests can have far-reaching influence. Joseph was a shy, gifted mathematician. A friend introduced him to some of the faculty in the UNM mathematics department and then handed over a mathematics paper he had written. After the mathematics faculty read the paper, Joseph was encouraged to compete in the UNM mathematics contest and placed first two years in a row. Completing his Ph.D. degree at Princeton, he continued on to Oxford and became chair of a university mathematics department. More than a decade after he won, in a newspaper interview, Joseph listed his participation in the UNM mathematics contest as a defining moment in his life. He stated: "Winning the contest two years in a row clinched my career choice in math. I was always interested in numbers but this proved to me that I was good." Recently the senior author ran into Joseph at a mathematics conference. Joseph informed him that he had started a mathematics contest for tenth- to twelfth-graders at his university because he wanted to replicate the contest as a means for encouraging other young students.

There are far more winners than just those who placed first. Many other winners—the hundreds who made the top 10 percent each year—have distinguished themselves in various fields. The positive influences on those who have participated in contests extend outward to impact our future generations as well.

REFERENCES

Berger, Thomas R., and Keynes, Harvey B. "The Challenge of Educating Mathematically Talented Students: The University of Minnesota Talented Youth Mathematics Program." *CBMS Issues in Mathematics Education, Vol. 1, Mathematicians and Education Reform 1988.* American Mathematical Society: 11–30.

Ross, Arnold E. "Creativity: Nature or Nurture? A View in Retrospect." *CBMS Issues in Mathematics Education, Vol. 2, Mathematicians and Education Reform 1989–90.* American Mathematical Society: 39–84.

Chapter 33

MATHCOUNTS

Madeline J. Bauer
Joseph P. Fagan

The National Society of Professional Engineers (NSPE), CNA, and the National Council of Teachers of Mathematics (NCTM) founded MATHCOUNTS in 1982. According to the 1997–98 MATHCOUNTS handbook, the mission of MATHCOUNTS is to increase interest and involvement in mathematics among all intermediate school students, to assist in developing a technically literate population essential to U.S. global competitiveness and the quality of life. Since its inception, the program, designed to stimulate interest and achievement in mathematics in seventh- and eighth-grade students, has reached more than four million students. During the 1996–97 school year alone, nearly 7 000 schools with 350 000 students participated, encompassing all 50 states plus U.S. possessions and students in the U.S. Department of State and Department of Defense school systems worldwide. Although the program is open to all students, it typically attracts those who are mathematically promising, by challenging them beyond the structured classroom.

TEAM CONCEPT

In creating the program, the decision was made to use a team concept with the individual students, termed *mathletes,* directed by a mathematics teacher or volunteer known as the *coach.* The use of the term *mathletes* refers to athletics and is meant to stir up support for the competitions just as students get excited about their school's sports teams. Having the mathletes working both individually and as a team further enforces the analogy. In preparing for the competitions, mathletes work together to solve problems and learn to evaluate each other's strengths and weaknesses, striving to attain a goal as a team. This is similar to the work environment of many technical occupations.

Coaches will generally start their MATHCOUNTS programs in September when they receive the school handbook. The handbook consists of a description of the program and thirty-four sets of practice problems covering all mathematics topics taught at the intermediate school level. Each year a special topic is chosen and many of the practice problems focus on this topic. For instance, the 1997–98 special topic was algebraic reasoning. The handbook also discusses several methods successfully used in problem solving and presents "extended activities" that can be used as group projects to illustrate the link between problem solving and real work experiences. These can be used to challenge promising mathematics students throughout the school year.

During the fall, the coach works with the mathletes using the handbook to increase their knowledge and give them confidence in their problem-solving abilities. For that purpose, the handbook practice problems appear in increasing order of difficulty. By early winter, the coach must select a team of four mathletes for the local competition, but as many students as possible are encouraged to participate in the program to enjoy mathematics and to build their problem-solving skills. Many use an in-school competition provided by MATHCOUNTS to select the teams who will represent the schools at their local competition, held in February. Other coaches use the in-school competition to supplement their selection process. At the very minimum, the top team and four top individual winners of local competitions advance to the state competition in March, with the top four individual state winners going on to the national competition in Washington, D.C., in late April or early May. National competition winners, as well as winners in some states, receive college scholarships.

The MATHCOUNTS competition begins with three written rounds. The Sprint Round, consisting of thirty problems to be completed in forty minutes, and the Target Round, consisting of eight problems presented two at a time with six minutes allocated per pair, are both individual rounds with the latter permitting the use of calculators. The final written round is the Team Round, where, guided by one mathlete designated as the captain, the four individual mathletes work as a team to solve ten problems in twenty minutes. Calculators are also permitted in this round. A winning team is chosen as a result of the team's performance in all three rounds.

On the basis of the results of the Sprint and Target Rounds, the top ten individuals then participate in the Countdown Round, a fast-paced oral competition. In this round, mathletes compete head to head, starting with the ninth- and tenth-ranked individuals, to solve problems within 45 seconds. The winner advances to challenge the next-highest-ranked individual until the top individual competes.

The Countdown Round is required only at the national level, but many state and local competitions also conduct it. This is the most visual and exciting round in the competition, both for the participants and for those in the audience. After each question is completed and the answer given, there are murmurs of "got it!" from many students in the audience. When two students tie, the tension is clearly palpable. Many of the questions are designed to be answered immediately if the student takes a creative approach. This approach may not be the typical method of solution that the student learns in class. The following is an example from the 1996–97 Chapter Countdown Round:

What is the arithmetic mean of 2, 3, 5, 7, and 8?

Clearly, one can solve this by adding up the five numbers and dividing by five. However, the true mathlete immediately notices the symmetry of the first and last two numbers to five and gives the answer without ever doing any computations at all!

THE NATIONAL COMPETITION

At the national competition, the top four finishers after the Countdown Round participate in the Masters Round. The individual competitors have thirty minutes to prepare an oral presentation regarding a specific topic and then must present and defend their solutions to a panel of judges. This round is optional at the state level.

The Pittsburgh Chapter of the Pennsylvania Society of Professional Engineers (PSPE) planned its first local program during the 1982–83 school year, conducting the first local competition in 1983–84 with twelve schools. Interest grew rapidly, and, since 1990, the competition has consistently drawn between thirty and forty schools. The local competition requires up to 100 volunteers who come from the local chapter, the Pittsburgh Chapter Auxiliary, and the University of Pittsburgh students' chapters of NSPE and Society of Women Engineers.

Volunteers are not difficult to gather because they see the value in cultivating a more mathematically educated society and enjoy observing the mathletes having fun while learning at the same time. In general, this is the first activity in which a new member of NSPE becomes involved; many find it so rewarding that they increase their commitment to the chapter.

Some chapter and state MATHCOUNTS committees hold workshops in late fall to introduce more students and coaches to the program, help them prepare for the February competition, and give them practice in solving problems similar to those encountered at the competitions. Many of these workshops do not limit the number of participants, allowing students who would not advance to the chapter competition to experience more of the program. The intent is for all participants to end the day with increased enthusiasm in addition to providing coaches with insight into properly preparing their mathletes. The underlying goal of MATH-COUNTS Day is to let students realize that not only is mathematics fun but also others share this sentiment.

It is evident that for mathematically promising students who have a natural enjoyment of mathematics and strong parental support, participating in a program like MATHCOUNTS is almost a given. However, some students may not have the motivation or support at home and would never consider joining such an activity based solely on an announcement over the school loudspeaker. Peer pressure, unfortunately, can compound the situation, especially for some girls who may be unsure of themselves or reluctant to display their mathematical talents. Consequently, a well-planned program with an enthusiastic coach is necessary to get students involved.

The MATHCOUNTS program at Sewickley Academy in Sewickley, Pennsylvania, is an example of such a program. Having participated for only seven years, Coach Carol Gambill and her teams won the Pittsburgh competition from 1994 to 1997 and the Pennsylvania competition in 1997. During a recent interview, Gambill stated that the enthusiasm for the program at Sewickley Academy equals that of the sports teams. The school's mathletes have recognition and stature equal to athletes. The first year, she had just six students. However, because the program remained challenging and fun, the number of students increased dramatically. Gambill breaks her group into several smaller subgroups of relatively equal ability so they can all feel increased confidence as they advance at their own individual pace, optimizing their personal progress. She also serves refreshments during each session to keep the mood more informal than the usual classroom.

In 1996, of the approximately 130 available students in grades seven and eight, about 70 percent showed interest in participating. Gambill attributes this increased appeal to acceptance by the student body. Sixty students were selected for MATH-COUNTS after an explanation of the program and initial problem-solving sessions after school. These sixty students continued to solve progressively more difficult problems until December, when the top twenty were chosen on the basis of weekly quiz scores and the in-school competition. Two weeks prior to the local competition, the official team and four alternates were chosen. With this system, Gambill says that many students experience the challenge and feeling of accomplishment, not just the four team members. She remarks that a few of those who don't make the team even attend the competition just to encourage their school team.

Gambill believes that the MATHCOUNTS program challenges her students, gives them confidence, and allows them to participate in a program combining academics and athletics. The students naturally form bonds after working together for the season. She also believes that this program is equally beneficial to both male and female students, giving all students the opportunity to strengthen their mathematical skills and affording the mathematically promising students topics of study beyond what they are being taught in the classroom.

LASTING EFFECTS

It is evident that the program positively affects students. Each year, after the program ends, Gambill administers a previously published SAT mathematics exam to students who have participated and reports that their scores are generally well above 700! Furthermore, many MATHCOUNTS alumni return to help her prepare the students for the upcoming competition. They do this not only to give something back to the program but also to sharpen their own mathematical skills.

During interviews with several former mathletes, each had his or her own reasons why the program was important. One stated that this was a program beyond the "plug and chug" competitions; in MATHCOUNTS, he had to use what he had learned, as well as logic and extrapolation, to solve more complex and challenging problems. Others liked the team aspect, which encouraged them to root for their team members to also perform well. One female mathlete stated that MATH-COUNTS brought her together with others with whom she may not otherwise have had contact. She considers several of them good friends four years after their team experience. She also believed she matured more rapidly because of her exposure to the program. Another mathlete stated that he competed to prove his abilities and enjoyed the pressure of solving problems in short time spans, although he fondly recalled giving two consecutive incorrect answers during the

Countdown Round because of simple mental mistakes. Whatever their personal reasons, the mathletes all agreed that two things were necessary—a desire to develop mathematical skills and a coach who could motivate and challenge them.

The National MATHCOUNTS Foundation, tracking the progress of past participants, has found that the college majors of a majority of mathletes are engineering, science, and mathematics related. According to mathletes responding to the foundation's survey, the universities most attended by mathletes are Harvard, Massachusetts Institute of Technology, Stanford, Princeton, and Yale. Records indicate that 60 percent of participants are male at the local competitions and 71 percent at the state levels; thus it is clear that more females need to be encouraged to participate in the program.

Although MATHCOUNTS is open to all students, in the end, it is the mathematically promising ones who are more often drawn to participate. Their interests are reinforced at the competitions, where they meet other students with the same enthusiasm for solving problems. Furthermore, the successful mathletes meet other peers they will likely see at many other academic competitions throughout high school and possibly college. They come in contact with coaches and adults, many of whom are in engineering and science-based professions, and may realize, for the first time, that an interest in mathematics could lead to a promising career.

FOR MORE INFORMATION

Further information about MATHCOUNTS at the national level can be found at mathcounts.org.

Chapter 34

ENRICHED STUDENTS NEED ENRICHING TEACHERS: THE AUSTRALIAN MATHEMATICS TEACHER ENRICHMENT PROJECT

Steve Thornton
Francesca Peel

In February 1997 the Australian Mathematics Trust (AMT) instituted a national professional development program designed to enhance the capacity of teachers to enrich the mathematical knowledge and understanding of students, particularly those identified as mathematically promising.

The objectives of the program are to enable teachers to

- deepen their mathematical knowledge;

- develop an effective repertoire of approaches to the identification and teaching of talented mathematics students;

- develop and implement approaches to monitor and evaluate their own teaching;

- share ideas and strategies for enriching mathematics education with other teachers.

The AMT was set up in 1992 with a vision of enriching mathematics education in schools and challenging students to realize their intellectual potential. It conducts the Australian Mathematics Competition, attracting over half a million entries annually, and organizes systematic enrichment and training programs for talented students, culminating in the selection of a team of students to represent Australia in the International Mathematical Olympiad.

With development of the Australian Mathematics Teacher Enrichment Project (AMTEP), the AMT acknowledged the central role of the classroom teacher in fostering and developing students' mathematical potential, and it attempted to equip teachers to meet the challenge of enriching mathematics for promising students.

GIFTED STUDENTS AND ENRICHING TEACHERS

There is a long history of attempts to define giftedness in students. House et al. (NCTM 1987) summarized a number of these definitions and gave several descriptions of the characteristics of gifted mathematics students. Renzulli (fig. 34.1) suggested that giftedness required a combination of content ability, task commitment, and creativity.

Despite the extensive research into students' learning and the recognition that the teacher is the key to promoting learning, the characteristics of the teacher who is able to enrich mathematics learning for talented students are less well documented.

Renzulli's model of gifted students was used to develop a vision of the characteristics of the enriching mathematics teacher (fig. 34.2). This diagram suggests that the enriching teacher has a knowledge and love of mathematics, is skilled in promoting students' learning, and views teaching as a creative art.

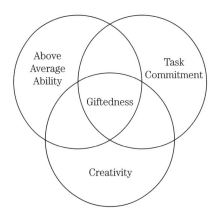

Fig. 34.1. Gifted students
(Renzulli 1978)

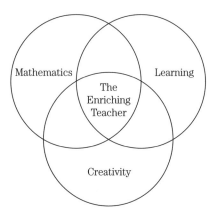

Fig. 34.2. Enriching teachers
(Thornton 1997)

ENRICHING MATHEMATICAL KNOWLEDGE: A TEACHER'S STORY

The coauthor of this article, Francesca Peel, is a teacher of seventh-grade students at Saint Peter's College in Adelaide, South Australia. She is an experienced teacher who has worked and studied extensively in the area of gifted education. Yet her own mathematics background is limited. When faced with the challenge of teaching mathematics to promising students, she was uncertain of her capacity to fully develop their potential. The following is her response to being asked to teach promising students.

My likely elevation to teaching the top two sets in mathematics in grades 6 and 7 spurred me on to doing something about my own mathematics and the way I teach it. The standard of mathematics at St. Peter's College is high, and I felt concerned that I wouldn't be able to offer our top students a challenging course that allowed them to explore many areas of advanced mathematics. Having worked in the gifted and talented area for some years, I had already initiated a hub group and it seemed to me that starting a math hub group would be a good first step.

About twenty teachers responded to my proposal, and we set up a group with the dual purposes of improving the mathematical knowledge of teachers and developing some units for gifted and talented students. Because our network is with primary people, initially it was difficult to find presenters who understood our need to work at a high level. It was not until we tapped into the secondary school network via Steve Thornton from the Australian Mathematics Trust that we found what we had been looking for—people who could teach us some mathematics.

RICH LEARNING ACTIVITIES

One of the key outcomes of AMTEP has been the development of rich learning activities that both extend students' knowledge and understanding and create an engaging, stimulating classroom environment. One such activity is the Prime Number Race (fig. 34.3).

Teachers who have used the Prime Number Race with students as young as grade 5 report that their understanding of primes and factors has been significantly enhanced through physical involvement. One of the members of the hub group is now undertaking a research project looking at the role of physical activity in the development of mathematical understanding. She has hypothesized that whole-brain activity enhances mathematical learning and is investigating other learning activities that incorporate physical involvement.

The Mathematics in Action: Francesca's Reaction

Steve was invited to lead the mathematics core for the Aurora Camp—a weeklong camp for gifted and talented students. Observing Steve teach these extremely bright students was an eye-opener in many ways, and I feel particularly privileged to have been able to see an expert modeling teaching practices that both engaged students and developed significant mathematical knowledge. It is a pity that we don't have more opportunity to observe experts at work.

Whilst Steve was in South Australia, he organized a two day workshop for upper primary/lower secondary teachers at which we were challenged to solve problems, debate issues, reflect on our own teaching beliefs and practices, and share concerns and resources with our colleagues. The pace and level was daunting but invigorating. My own limited problem-solving experience and seeing what was possible certainly accounted for a huge drop in self-confidence. I had always felt reasonably confident that I was a good, solid teacher whose students achieved remarkably good results. My world was somewhat shaken up, and I became unsure of what a good mathematics course looked like, let alone whether I could produce one. Thinking you have a grasp on a concept enough to solve a problem doesn't mean that you have enough knowledge to be able to articulate it in front of twenty-five to thirty talented students!

The Prime Number Race

Materials required

A "race track" using masking tape at approximately one pace length intervals on the ground. Ten to fifteen intervals are sufficient.

Class Activity

Select four volunteer "race horses," and line them up at the start of the race. The race horses commence counting, in turn, from 1. Each time a horse says a prime number, he or she may move forward one pace.

Suggest names for the horses. The names should describe the set of numbers called out.

Appropriate horse names are: $4n + 1$, $4n + 2$, $4n + 3$, and $4n + 4$. Writing $4n + 2$ as $2 (2n + 1)$ and $4n + 4$ as $4 (n + 1)$ shows that these numbers always have factors other than 1, and emphasizes the conceptual meaning of factorization.

Which horse wins?

It turns out that $4n + 3$ stays ahead until 26 861, when $4n + 1$ moves ahead for just one term. Above 26 862, $4n + 3$ leads all the way to 616 841, when $4n + 1$ moves back into the lead for nearly 17 000. $4n + 1$ leads again near twelve and a half billion, 1 billion, 6 billion, and 18 billion. In the last region it leads for 568 million consecutive terms, leading by 2 719 at around 18.7 billion. However, $4n + 3$ moves back in front at 19 033 524 538. The end result is unknown. (Lines 1986)

Extensions

1. *Other linear primes*

   Experiment with different numbers of horses and try to predict the "born losers."

2. *Quadratic primes*

   Some more efficient "prime thoroughbreds" can be made using quadratic expressions.
   List all the numbers of the form $n^2 - n + 41$ for $n = 1, 2, 3, \ldots$. Do you always obtain prime numbers? Can you find a value of n for which the value obtained is composite?

   Forty consecutive composite numbers are obtained for $n = 1 \ldots 40$. When $n = 41$, $n^2 - n + 41 = 41^2$ which is composite. When $n = 42$, $n^2 - n + 41 = 42^2 - 1^2 = (42 - 1) (42 + 1)$.

3. *Fermat primes*

   Calculate $F_n = 2^{2^n} + 1$ for $n = 0$ to 5

   ($F_0 = 3, F_1 = 5, F_2 = 17, F_3 = 257, F_4 = 65\,537$). Fermat conjectured that since these first five numbers were prime, all numbers of this form would be prime. It was not until the next century that Euler discovered that $F_5 = 4\,294\,967\,297$ was actually equal to $641 \times 6\,700\,417$. It is now known that all Fermat numbers from F_5 to F_{19}, as well as many others, are composite. No other primes have been found.

4. *Mersenne primes*

   Mersenne conjectured that numbers of the form $2n - 1$ were often prime.
   List the Mersenne numbers up to M_{10}, and check to see if they are prime.
   What appears to be true about n if a prime is obtained?
   Find M_{11}. Is n prime a sufficient condition for M_n to be prime?

   n must be prime for M_n to be prime. But $M_{11} = 2\,047 = 89 \times 23$ shows that this is not a sufficient condition. M_{31} held the world record for the largest prime for 120 years. Is was replaced in 1876 by M_{127}. The world record, as of January 1999, is $M_{3\,021\,377}$, containing 909 526 digits, discovered by Roland Clarkson on 27 January 1998 during the Great Internet Mersenne Primes Search (GIMPS) found by Wolfman, et al. This number, written end-to-end, would stretch for more than a mile.

Fig. 34.3. The prime number race

ENRICHMENT = MATHEMATICS, CHALLENGE, CREATIVITY

In July 1997 fourteen teachers attended a four-day course designed to enrich their teaching of students with high intellectual potential. The course was known as "$E = mc^2$" (Enrichment = Mathematics, Challenge, Creativity) to reflect the tripartite professional development model suggested in figure 34.2. Activities such as the Prime Number Race were used as a springboard for the development of teachers' rich understanding of number theory and geometry. Strategies for enhancing primary mathematical attributes such as rigor and problem solving were shared in a framework that recognized a constructivist epistemology. Each afternoon teachers worked together to solve problems, evaluate resources, and share creative teaching ideas. They were thus able to commence the task of developing creative, engaging, and mathematically rich units of work in number theory and geometry.

Francesca participated in this four-day course:

> Fortunately Steve, in his role as director of teacher enrichment for the Australian Mathematics Trust, returned to Adelaide in the holidays, this time offering a four-day workshop called $E = mc^2$ (Enrichment = Mathematics, Challenge, Creativity). Through more problem-solving activities, discussions, debates, and readings, I am beginning to add layers to my understanding of mathematics and pedagogy. I feel inspired to learn more and try out new and challenging problem-solving activities with my classes. Whilst I haven't yet figured out the all the answers, I do feel that I can offer my students more challenging and enriching experiences.

Through the workshops I have met a number of like-minded teachers who have similar problems and goals and I don't feel isolated. It is wonderful to be able to share disasters and triumphs with colleagues who are going through the same experiences and who are so nonjudgmental.

CONCLUSION

Enriching mathematics for promising students requires much more than teacher resources or a student text. Professional development that equips teachers with mathematical knowledge, teaching skills, and the desire to reflect upon and share their practice is the key to helping students to develop their potential.

Some words of advice from Francesca:

> For primary/lower secondary school teachers who, like me, do not have a mathematics degree and cannot pluck those numbers or leading questions from the air, I would like to say, "Find the person who can help you develop your thinking and expertise; find or develop a network of like-minded teachers; and have the courage to expand your comfort boundaries. Whilst it can be unbelievably threatening at times, the hive of activity, the excited interaction in the class, and the joy of being able to solve a difficult problem yourself makes it all worthwhile.

Like Francesca, teachers who enrich mathematics for students are prepared to take some risks and to learn from their own and others' successes and failures. They approach their task with a mindset that asks "What are the possibilities?" rather than "What are the problems?" Enrichment is more a teacher frame of mind than a set of student resources.

BIBLIOGRAPHY

Lines, Malcolm E. *A Number for Your Thoughts.* Bristol, England: Adam Hilger, 1986.

National Council of Teachers of Mathematics. *Providing Opportunities for the Mathematically Gifted K–12,* edited by Peggy House. Reston, Va.: National Council of Teachers of Mathematics, 1987.

Renzulli, Joseph S. "What Makes Giftedness? Reexamining a Definition." *Phi Delta Kappan* 60 (November 1978).

Thornton, Stephen J. "The Enriching Teacher." In *Mathematics—Creating the Future, Proceedings of the Sixteenth Biennial Conference of the Australian Association of Mathematics Teachers,* edited by Nick Scott and Hilary Hollingsworth. Melbourne, Australia: Australian Association of Mathematics Teachers, 1997.

WORLD WIDE WEB REFERENCES

Australian Mathematics Teacher Enrichment Project (AMTEP). <www.amt.canberra.edu.au/~sjt/amtep .htm>.

The Prime Page. <www.utm.edu/research/primes>.

REPORT OF THE
NCTM TASK FORCE ON THE MATHEMATICALLY PROMISING

TASK FORCE MEMBERS

Jennie Bennett, Manuel Berriozábal, Margaret DeArmond, Linda Sheffield (Chair), and Richard Wertheimer

The NCTM Task Force on Promising Students consists of five educators who represent a number of different constituencies including public schools, programs for promising students, parents, universities, and researchers. The task force had an initial meeting at the 1995 NCTM Annual Meeting in Boston; read relevant literature, including the NCTM publication, *Providing Opportunities for the Mathematically Gifted;* disseminated a survey on the Internet to relevant news groups and mailing lists; and met for three days to craft this report that includes issues, recommendations, and a draft of a policy statement. After the initial report was written, it was posted on the Internet for comments and revised.

OVERVIEW

In 1980, it was stated in *An Agenda for Action: Recommendations for School Mathematics of the 1980s* (National Council of Teachers of Mathematics 1980, p. 18) that, "the student most neglected, in terms of realizing full potential, is the gifted student of mathematics. Outstanding mathematical ability is a precious societal resource, sorely needed to maintain leadership in a technological world" (NCTM 1980, *An Agenda for Action: Recommendations for School Mathematics of the 1980s,* p. 18). In the fifteen years since this report, not much has changed other than an even more urgent need for technological leadership. Therefore, it is imperative that NCTM act quickly to conserve and enhance this precious resource.

DEFINITION OF PROMISING STUDENTS

In 1972, Public Law 91-230, Section 806, was passed by the federal government stating:

> Gifted and talented children are those identified by professionally qualified persons, who by virtue of outstanding abilities are capable of high performance. These are children who require differentiated educational programs or services beyond those normally provided by the regular school program in order to realize their contribution to self and society. Children capable of high performance

include those with demonstrated achievement or potential ability in any of the following areas, singly or in combination:

1. general intellectual ability
2. specific academic aptitude
3. creative or productive thinking
4. leadership ability
5. visual and performing arts
6. psychomotor ability

It can be assumed that utilization of these criteria for identification of the gifted and talented will encompass a minimum of 3 to 5 percent of the school population. [The sixth area of psychomotor ability was later dropped from the federal definition.]

Although educators have attempted to expand the definition of giftedness to become more inclusive, the 1972 definition prevailed for more than two decades. Today, many states continue to use some variation of this definition to define gifted and talented students to offer special programs. Research by Howard Gardner and other during the 1980s led to an expanded definition by the federal government. In the 1990s, with the passage of the federal Javits Gifted and Talented Education Act, the definition was broadened to the following:

Children and youth with outstanding talent perform or show the potential for performing at remarkably high levels of accomplishment when compared with others of their age, experience, or environment.

These children and youth exhibit high performance capability in intellectual, creative, and/or artistic areas, possess an unusual leadership capacity, or excel in specific academic fields. They require services or activities not ordinarily provided by the schools.

Outstanding talents are present in children and youth from all cultural groups, across all economic strata, and in all areas of human endeavor.

The Task Force on the Mathematically Promising believes that the definition of students with mathematical promise should build on this latter, broader definition. Students with mathematical promise are those who have the potential to become the leaders and problem solvers of the future. We see mathematical promise as a function of

- ability,
- motivation,
- belief, and
- experience or opportunity.

These variables are not fixed and need to be developed so that success for these promising students can be maximized. This definition includes the students who have been traditionally identified as gifted, talented, precocious, and so on, and it adds students who have been traditionally excluded from previous definitions of gifted and talented and therefore excluded from rich mathematical opportunities. This definition acknowledges that students who are mathematically promising have a large range of abilities and a continuum of needs that should be met.

IDENTIFICATION

Traditional methods of identifying gifted and talented mathematics students, such as standardized test scores, are designed to limit the pool of students identified as mathematically promising. Although these measures are commonly used to identify gifted and talented students, additional means of identification must be used.

Identification of mathematically promising students is a difficult and challenging task. Identification might be done for pedagogical, legal, or financial reasons, but in all instances it should be done to maximize the number of mathematically promising students. Programs should have clear goals that guide the identification procedures; if there are no services for these students, there is no need to identify them. To avoid bias in the selection process, identification procedures should include a wide variety of measures to identify the broadest number of both females and males from diverse cultural and socioeconomic backgrounds. Measures might include any or all of the following, depending on the goals of the program to be offered:

- self-selection
- observations of students during the problem-solving process
- teacher recommendation
- parent recommendation
- peer recommendation
- standardized tests, especially out-of-level testing
- measures of creativity
- solutions to problems
- grades in mathematics classes
- student essays
- performance in mathematics contests
- tests of abstract reasoning ability
- measures of spacial reasoning

Identification should be inclusive rather than exclusive; if a question arises about whether to include a student in the program, teachers should err on the side of inclusion.

Some opportunities for promising students may require no formal identification process. These opportunities might include such actions as investigating challenging, open-ended problems in mathematics classes, joining mathematics clubs, entering mathematics contests, using technology, or accessing mentors on the Internet. These opportunities should be readily available to any student who desires to take advantage of them.

CURRICULUM, INSTRUCTION, AND ASSESSMENT

School or district committees that are deciding on programs and materials for promising students must decide on methods of organizing instruction and assessment. There are many disagreements over the best programming for these students. Arguments over enrichment versus acceleration, homogenous versus hetergenous grouping, and theory versus application are constant. Rather than recommend one particular course of study, this task force is suggesting that those involved in program development clearly understand the ramifications of decisions made pertaining to programming. We reiterate the need to err on the side of inclusion rather than exclusion. Some of the most popular ways to empower mathematically promising students are tracking, acceleration, providing opportunities in the regular classroom, pullout and magnet programs, and extracurricular activities. To open opportunities for the greatest number of promising students, service providers must be cognizant of the dilemmas created by any particular program.

General Opportunities

Any program for mathematically promising students should consider the following questions:

- Are programs consistent with recommendations from all three sets of *Standards* documents, perhaps using recommendations from a higher grade level of the *Standards* than the student's current grade or age level?

- Is technology being used to its fullest extent to enhance the mathematical power of promising students?

- Are teachers, counselors, or other adults available and capable of challenging, supporting, and guiding these students appropriately?

- Are there means of evaluating the program and the students in it to determine success?

- Do the opportunities account for the wide range of abilities, beliefs, motivations, and experiences of students who have mathematical promise, regardless of their socioeconomic and ethnic backgrounds, and do the opportunities meet the continuum of needs?

Tracking or Acceleration

Traditionally, tracking or acceleration in many schools has had the effect of segregating students and locking out many promising mathematics students. If schools decide to track students, they should consider the following questions:

- Are students chosen for classes on the basis of a general IQ score or because of a specific mathematical aptitude?

- Are there students who have not been identified for these classes who could benefit from them?

- Are there students in the top classes who are frustrated and confused by the high level of work and who are encouraging the teacher to present problems at a lower level or are slowing the progress of the class?

- Will students who are not included in these classes have lower self-esteem and decide that they are not capable of becoming good mathematical thinkers?
- Are the methods of identifying the placement of students for tracks employing a variety of measures to identify the broadest number of both females and males from diverse cultural and socioeconomic backgrounds?
- Are students allowed to self-identify for the top classes?
- Are curriculum, instruction, and assessment qualitatively different and designed to meet the differing needs of promising students? Is the curriculum more challenging with provisions for individualization, faster pace, more higher-level thinking, and higher standards than other tracks?
- Is there flexible movement from one track to another?

Opportunities in the Regular Classroom

The "regular" classroom may take a variety of forms. It may have a heterogeneous mix of students; it may have mainstreamed promising students; it may have a cluster group of talented students; or it may be a "middle track" in a school that is tracked. All mathematics classrooms need to offer opportunities for mathematically promising students because these students exist in every classroom, even if they have somehow been tracked into lower groups. In providing for these students in the regular classroom, the following questions should be asked.

- Are there resources, projects, problems, and means of assessment that allow for differences in the level of understanding and engagement?
- Do teachers have the pedagogical techniques to work with student populations with diverse learning needs and from diverse backgrounds?
- Are there teachers who have been adequately prepared to work with mathematically promising students in the role of a facilitator?
- Does the teacher have a contingency plan to determine when students have mastered mathematical concepts and skills so that they do not unnecessarily repeat material?
- Are there opportunities for promising students to explore interesting problems with others of like interests and abilities?

Pullout and Magnet Programs for the Mathematically Promising

Pullout programs can be defined as programs that occur during the school day where students leave their regular classroom to engage in activities with other students of similar abilities or interests. Magnet programs are full-time programs or schools that have been designed for promising students or for those with special interests in mathematics. If schools or districts decide to offer these programs for mathematically promising students, the following questions should be considered:

- Are there students who have not been identified for these programs who could benefit from them?

- Will students who are not included in these programs have lower self-esteem and decide that they are not capable of becoming good mathematical thinkers?
- Are the methods of identifying the placement of students for these programs using a variety of measures to identify the broadest number of both females and males from diverse cultural and socioeconomic backgrounds?
- Are students allowed to self-identify for the program?
- Are there appropriate opportunities in mathematics that have clearly defined, comprehensive, integrated goals and are not simply isolated activities?
- In pullout programs, are activities coordinated with the regular classroom teacher so there is continual support and challenge?

Extracurricular Activities

Schools, universities, individuals, and organizations should provide meaningful experiences for mathematically promising students outside of the regular classroom. These opportunities might include summer and after-school programs, mathematics contests, correspondence programs, mentoring, resources on the Internet, and mathematics clubs and circles. In arranging for these opportunities, the following questions should be considered:

- Are there barriers to becoming involved in extracurricular activities—monetary, criteria for entry, time, parental interest and involvement, busing—that have not been addressed?
- Do extracurricular activities for mathematically promising students enhance opportunities in the regular classroom?
- Are the opportunities available to all interested students?

CULTURAL INFLUENCES

If America is to be number one in mathematics and science by the year 2000, our society must value learning, particularly in mathematics. Issues that pertain to cultural influences include the following:

- What is being done to counter the negative influence of peer and cultural pressures?
- Is diversity celebrated and encouraged rather than merely acknowledged and tolerated?
- What kinds of reinforcement and rewards are available for students who are interested in learning mathematics?
- How does the culture communicate the value of mathematical literacy to students?
- Have all stakeholders been engaged—parents, teachers, administrators and counselors, community members, religious institutions, media, business, government, and the students themselves—in the process of supporting the development of the mathematically promising?